Cultural Production and Social Movements after the Arab Spring

Cultural Production and Social Movements after the Arab Spring

Nationalism, Politics, and Transnational Identity

Edited by
Eid Mohamed and Ayman A. El-Desouky

I.B.TAURIS
LONDON • NEW YORK • OXFORD • NEW DELHI • SYDNEY

I.B. TAURIS
Bloomsbury Publishing Plc
50 Bedford Square, London, WC1B 3DP, UK
1385 Broadway, New York, NY 10018, USA
29 Earlsfort Terrace, Dublin 2, Ireland

BLOOMSBURY, I.B. TAURIS and the I.B. Tauris logo are trademarks of Bloomsbury Publishing Plc

First published in Great Britain 2021
This paperback edition published 2022

Copyright © Eid Mohamed and Ayman A. El-Desouky, 2021

Eid Mohamed, Ayman A. El-Desouky, and contributors have asserted their right under the Copyright, Designs and Patents Act, 1988, to be identified as Author of this work.

Copyright Individual Chapters © 2021 Eid Mohamed, Ayman A. El-Desouky, Abderrahman Beggar, Katie Logan, Caroline Rooney, Hager Ben Driss, Jenna Altomonte, Melissa Finn, Bessma Momani, Mohamed ElSawi Hassan, Barkuzar Dubbati, Waleed F. Mahdi, Hamid Dabashi

This book is available as open access through the Bloomsbury Open Access programme and is available on www.bloomsburycollections.com.

For legal purposes the Acknowledgments on p. xi constitute an extension of this copyright page.

Cover design: Adriana Brioso
Cover image: Egypt, Cairo. (© Alain Guilleux / Alamy Stock Photo)

This book was made possible by NPRP grant # NPRP9-225- 5-024 from the Qatar National Research Fund (a member of Qatar Foundation). The editors are full time faculty at the Doha Institute for Graduate Studies in Doha, Qatar. The contents herein are solely the responsibility of the editors.

The Open Access version of the publication was partially funded by Qatar National Library (QNL)

This work is published open access subject to a Creative Commons Attribution 4.0 licence (CC BY 4.0, https://creativecommons.org/licenses/by/4.0/). You may re-use, distribute, reproduce, and adapt this work in any medium, including for commercial purposes, provided you give attribution to the copyright holder and the publisher, provide a link to the Creative Commons licence, and indicate if changes have been made.

Bloomsbury Publishing Plc does not have any control over, or responsibility for, any third-party websites referred to or in this book. All internet addresses given in this book were correct at the time of going to press. The author and publisher regret any inconvenience caused if addresses have changed or sites have ceased to exist, but can accept no responsibility for any such changes.

A catalogue record for this book is available from the British Library.

A catalog record for this book is available from the Library of Congress.

ISBN:	HB:	978-0-7556-3418-7
	PB:	978-0-7556-4127-7
	ePDF:	978-0-7556-3419-4
	eBook:	978-0-7556-3420-0

Typeset by Integra Software Services Pvt. Ltd.,

To find out more about our authors and books visit www.bloomsbury.com and sign up for our newsletters.

Contents

List of Figures	vii
List of Tables	viii
List of Contributors	ix
Acknowledgments	xi
Introduction *Eid Mohamed and Ayman A. El-Desouky*	1

Part 1 Senses of Belonging: Explorations of Transcultural Spaces

1. Transculturation in a Changing Arab World: Engaging Contexts in Conversation *Eid Mohamed* — 13
2. Hédi Bouraoui: On Transcultural Belonging *Abderrahman Beggar* — 29
3. Changing Geography: Transcultural Arab Identity in the Age of the EU *Katie Logan* — 45
4. The Fractured Music of Arab-Jewish Friendship in Waguih Ghali's *Beer in the Snooker Club* and Ismaël Ferroukhi's *Free Men* *Caroline Rooney* — 63

Part 2 Migration and the Challenges of Subjectivation

5. Poetics of the Virtual: Technology and Revolution in the Poetry of Sghaier Ouled Ahmed *Hager Ben Driss* — 83
6. Identity Politics and Digital Space: Adel Abidin's *Abidin Travels: Welcome to Baghdad* *Jenna Altomonte* — 101

Part 3 Transcultural Dimensions in Contemporary Arab Literature and Culture

7. Transcultural Identity Formation among Canadian-Arab Youth: Nurturing Self-Knowledge through Metissage and Blunting Canadianness as an Alterity *Melissa Finn and Bessma Momani* — 121
8. Reshaping Social Practice in Post–Arab Spring Egypt: Expression of Identity and Affiliation in New Media *Mohamed ElSawi Hassan* — 151
9. Syrian Refugees as a Hybridizing Force in the Jordanian Society *Barkuzar Dubbati* — 163
10. Ontological Citizenship: A Realignment of Rights and Responsibilities between the Individual and the State(s) in Twenty-First-Century Migration and Transnationalism *Saeed Khan* — 189

Part 4 Occupying Interstices and the Aesthetics of Dissent
11 Echoes of a Scream: US Drones and Articulations of the Houthi *Sarkha*
    Slogan in Yemen *Waleed F. Mahdi*   205
12 Interstitial Space of the Art of Protest *Hamid Dabashi*   223

Index   239

List of Figures

6.1	Display wall with travel pamphlets and booking kiosk, *Abidin Travels*, 2006–7. Courtesy of Adel Abidin	108
6.2	Mainpage to www.abidintravels.com, *Abidin Travels*, 2006–7. Courtesy of Adel Abidin	108
6.3	Video still, *Abidin Travels*, 2006–7. Courtesy of Adel Abidin	109
6.4	Adel Abidin, still from *Abidin Travels* video, 2006–7. Courtesy of Adel Abidin	110
6.5	Adel Abidin, stills from *Abidin Travels* video, 2006–7. Courtesy of Adel Abidin	110
6.6	Footage from *Hometown Baghdad*, 2005–7	112
6.7	Still from the "Symphony of Bullets" segment, *Hometown Baghdad*, 2005–7	113
6.8	Still from the "Market Boom" segment, *Hometown Baghdad*, 2005–7	113
9.1	The binary opposition of Self/Other according to colonial discourse, Bhabha's hybridity theory, and its critics	167
9.2	Bhabha's hybridity in reverse	168
9.3	Percentages of Syrians out of the overall population in the selected cities (2015 national census)	169
9.4	Effect of Syrian culture on Jordanian culture	174
9.5	Areas of Syrian influence in Jordan	174
9.6	Numbers of marriages between Jordanian and Syrians between 2004 and 2016	176
11.1	The *sarkha* slogan compared to the Iranian flag	207
11.2	"Why did you kill my family" graffiti © Murad Subay	211
11.3	"No to a Government that Grants Entry to American Marines" Rally, May 24, 2013	217
12.1	Shaimaa al-Sabbagh—shot and killed by Egyptian security forces. Photo: Islam Osman—Youm El Sabea (Al Youm Al Saabi/Reuters)	229

List of Tables

7.1	Most and least frequently used methods of communication with home country	129
7.2	Frequency of reading/watching MENA media	132
9.1	The distribution of the sample based on density and income	169
9.2	Other variables in the study	170
9.3	The distribution of population in Jordan based on nationality. Source: The Jordanian Department of Statistics	171
9.4	The distribution of Syrians in Jordan based on place of origin. Source: UNHCR	172
9.5	The numbers of Syrians in Jordan based on their year of arrival. Source: UNHCR	172
9.6	Sources of knowledge about Syrians before and after the Syrian crisis	173
9.7	The number of Jordanian-Syrian marriages between 2004 and 2010. Source: The Jordanian Supreme Judge Department	175
9.8	The number of Jordanian-Syrian marriages between 2010 and 2016. Source: The Jordanian Supreme Judge Department	176
9.9	Views on Syrian marriage customs	177
9.10	Views on Jordanian-Syrian marriage based on region and gender	178
9.11	Views on marriage with Syrians based on income and gender	179
9.12	Views on Syrian presence based on region	181
9.13	Words most commonly used by the Jordanian sample to describe Syrians	183
9.14	The desire to have Syrians leave Jordan based on employment	184

List of Contributors

Abderrahman Beggar is Professor of Religion and Culture at Wilfrid Laurier University.

Ayman A. El-Desouky is Associate Professor of Modern Arabic and Comparative Literature at Doha Institute for Graduate Studies.

Barkuzar Dubbati is Assistant Professor of English at the University of Jordan.

Bessma Momani is Assistant Vice-President, International Relations (Interim, 2020), and Full Professor at the Department of Political Science, University of Waterloo.

Caroline Rooney is Professor of African and Middle Eastern Studies at the University of Kent.

Eid Mohamed is Assistant Professor of Arab-US studies and Comparative Literature at Doha Institute for Graduate Studies.

Hager Ben Driss is Associate Professor of Postcolonial and Gender Studies at University of Tunis.

Hamid Dabashi is the Hagop Kevorkian Professor of Iranian Studies and Comparative Literature at Columbia University.

Jenna Ann Altomonte is Assistant Professor of Art History at Mississippi State University.

Katie Logan is Assistant Professor of Focused Inquiry at Virginia Commonwealth University.

Melissa Finn, Ph.D., is Research Associate at the Department of Political Science, University of Waterloo.

Mohamed ElSawi Hassan is Senior Lecturer at the Department of Asian Languages and Civilizations at Amherst College.

Saeed Khan is Senior Lecturer of Near East & Asian Studies and Global Studies; Director of Global Studies; and Fellow at the Center for the Study of Citizenship, Wayne State University.

Waleed F. Mahdi is Assistant Professor of US-Arab cultural politics at the University of Oklahoma.

Acknowledgments

This book project is made possible by the NPRP grant NPRP9-225-5-024 from the Qatar National Research Fund (a member of Qatar Foundation), titled "Transcultural Identities: Solidaristic Action and Contemporary Arab Social Movements." The grant is based at the Doha Institute for Graduate Studies (DI).

The editors are grateful to the DI for providing the opportunity to engage in areas of research that are topically significant for the wider global community. The DI has been most supportive in allowing us to engage in travels and research around the topic of the book. Moreover, the DI and QNRF generously funded a book workshop that was held in Doha in January 2018 that assisted the editors in synthesizing the individual chapters and produce a coherent, integrated, and polished edited collection. We owe special thanks to the Research Office at the DI, especially its Director Mr. Raed Habayeb and the senior officer Ms. Miriam Shaath.

We wish to acknowledge our contributors and express our deepest gratitude to them, for without their patience and unwavering commitment this book would not have been possible. Their chapters are insightful and thought-provoking. It was a pleasure to work with each of them. Likewise, our deepest gratitude goes to Rory Gormerly, our acquisitions editor at I.B. Tauris, for his enthusiastic support and watchful eye throughout the process. Equally, the editors wish to thank Yasmin Garcha for her guidance and tireless support during the publication process.

Among those who have given us sustenance, we cannot fail to mention our graduate students and research assistants at the DI, including Amel Boubekeur, Talaat Mohamed, Tareq Alrabei, Anne Vermeyden, Zainab Abu Alrob, and Thomas Dolan for their friendly and efficient support. We are highly indebted to colleagues at the DI and the collaborating institutions, and all those unnamed others, too many to be named personally, who encouraged us to continue, offered us inspiration, and generously gave of their time and expertise, carrying us through to the completion of this project.

We are particularly impressed by the incredible spirit, wisdom, and strength of the Arab peoples, especially the indomitable youth who came together, demanding the personal rights and freedoms that Arabs have so long been denied. Their message of peace and hope was easily delivered to the rest of the world through their cheering, singing, praying for their freedom in Egypt, Syria, Tunisia, and Yemen inspiring countless others all over the world. It is to their formidable spirit and inspiring resilience that this book is dedicated.

The editors would like to thank their families and loved ones for their loving support and patience.

Introduction

Eid Mohamed and Ayman A. El-Desouky

By the end of 2010 and into 2011, the eyes of the world were on the public squares in Tunisia, Egypt, Syria, Yemen, and Bahrain, as millions of people poured into major city centers and streets. These mass gatherings in public spaces presented unprecedented forms of solidarity to bring about change through sheer determination, an awakening to the power of the collective beyond a simple articulation of demands. The modes of collective expression and action far exceeded the ready interpretations of social and political theories of how mass movements could be constituted via the complicity of many demands. Something more was at stake. A gathering force seemed to hold the key to a dynamic that surpassed the postcolonial idea of a nation or a people. A collectivizing "We" was emerging, almost palpably visible in the communicative force of diverse individuals and groups in public spaces and later in mediated but equally engaged responses.

The "transcultural" as a strategy of nomenclature is not only meant to counter the hegemony of nationalist ideologies or nation-based and region-based analytic frames, current in both area studies and social and political theory. It is also used here as a mode of trans-sociality, one that signals the complexity and historical depth of collective expressions and actions. The implosions of social, cultural, political, and economic realities that have unsettled the power structures of state formations and processes of subjectivation have also strongly accentuated how identity is and always has been a flux of cementing, meaning-giving practices, assumptions of belief, and habits of thought. The historically given and naturalized categories and conditions of ethnicity, religion, governance, citizenship, gender, socioeconomic status, and nationality were subjected to widespread and profound renegotiations that have entailed both the discovery of new cultural forms and the recovery of the force of resonant popular discourses.

In the aftermath of 2011, studies of mass movements, too numerous to list, have sought to identify prior histories and trajectories and to articulate attendant shifts in social and political spheres, modes of acculturation, the self-perception and self-placement of collectivities, and the failings of national traditions, policies, and institutions. Apart from firsthand testimonies and book-length accounts of the uprisings, the first theoretical insights into the unprecedented dimensions of collective expression and action have been slow to come, initially offered in works by Alain Badiou, Slavoj Zizek, and Judith Butler; in critical historical readings by Charles Tripp, Gilbert Achcer, Hamid Dabashi, and Caroline Rooney; and, closer to the scene, in analytic studies and edited volumes by Samia Mehrez, Mona Baker, Walid El-Hamamsy and Mounira Ghadeer, Rita Sakr, Andrea Khalil, Ayman A. El-Desouky, and in other studies on revolutionary aesthetics. There have been many more since then, too numerous to list here. These early studies, however, mark the beginnings of reflective thought on the nature of the revolutionary energy unleashed and its embeddedness in local social realities, and, with varying degrees of expression, they all present one fundamental challenge: the need for a new language with which to begin to understand the unique modes of both expression (in word, image, sound, and movement) and action, how resonant movements of bodies and masses of bodies claim public spaces and reveal a hitherto unprecedented collectivizing ethos, rooted in local realities and the collective and cultural memories of the different localities and regions. Fundamentally, the challenges are not sociological, anthropological, or political-theoretical in the older senses; the eruption of the social as being itself the political, most salient in the creative modes of mobilization and artistic expression, hints at a deeper reality: collective modes of expression as modes of knowing, and of knowing collectively, beyond institutional politics, national and postcolonial histories, and the established discursive modes of expert sciences and intellectual discourses.

Several years on, and with all the unfolding events on the ground in the different regions of the Arab world, the idea for this volume—fundamentally comparative in its thrust and seeking to engage local realities in their various modes of expression—has emerged. *Cultural Production and Social Movements after the Arab Spring* offers a range of fresh and incisive studies that identify and examine how new media, as well as literary and artistic forms of expression, inform and echo currents of transformation in the Arab world. Moreover, this volume asks how such forms theorize "transcultural identity" (beyond the transnational) as a form of citizen engagement at the center of transformation politics in the Arab world. Its focus is on the articulation of fresh critical perspectives with which to investigate these forms of cultural production as new modes of knowing that shed light on the nature of social movements, with the aim of expanding the critical reach of the disciplinary methods of political discourse and social theory. In this way, the book responds to the need to address the epistemic ruptures brought about by the Arab Spring, in tandem with the sociopolitical upheavals.

The authors, all scholars grounded in disciplines in the humanities and social sciences but with direct engagement with developments on the ground, were invited to reflect on how the diverse Arab scenes contribute to the understanding of the rise of new social movements worldwide while further exploring the methodological gaps in the dominant Western discourses and theories. Such methodological gaps have become very clear in the failure to understand the unavoidable variations in crowds and social movements, and the subsequent transformations in both the public sphere and modes of social mobilization. The volume's diversity of thought and views reflect the diversity of local and localized Arab views. The aim of the volume, however, is not to offer a comprehensive map of such movements and localities, but rather carefully consider a series of instances in which transcultural modes of expression are identified and their resistance to (disciplinarily) ready and at hand modes of explanation and quantification investigated. A different geography may emerge. One perhaps is marked by glaring gaps, such as the Palestinian contributions to the various localities, whether through physical presence or in modes of rallying embedded in the collective Arab consciousness, or in the challenges to inspired action in settler-colonial situations.

The contributions have been structured in four broad sections. Part One investigates how the outbreak of the Arab Spring marked the appearance of a real multiplicity on several levels throughout the Arab world: ideological, cultural, religious, educational, class-based, and gender-oriented. While recent critical scholarship of the so-called Arab Spring, mostly based in Western academies, has tended to focus on the analysis of the "final" result of a complicated political conflict, this part of the book intends to do the opposite. That is, its aim is to read the Arab social movements from within, in order to understand and analyze the internal dynamics of activist discourse, in the pursuit of a differing epistemology. Looking at the mass movements through the micro instead of the macro yields a completely different picture from the one that has been advanced by Western-trained political analysts, observers, and cultural analysts. It is a detour of methodology, answering to the "false normativity" against which the revolutionary process has been measured. In the five chapters included in this part, authors reflect on Egypt's revolutionary moment and debate what has really changed, if anything.

In the introductory chapter, "Transculturation in a Changing Arab World: Engaging Contexts in Conversation," Eid Mohamed explores how to define, express, and formulate ourselves and our actions in a changing, globalized, conflictual Arab world. Transcultural identities are multicentered, evaluative, and sometimes contradictory, but they must always be freely chosen, with a willingness to redefine culture—inclusive and shared, as Mohamed argues, no longer entrenched in single imaginaries, states, or groups. Transculturation can help us redefine and re-narrate identity, cultural loyalty, and feelings of belonging; for example, what do citizenship, religious affiliation, and ethnicities mean when these have been denied or called into question by dominant narratives. Mohamed explores how the Egyptian literary and artistic scene requires us to rethink the key idea of shared ethic (which the transcultural literature situates at the core of transcultural initiatives) by better explaining the persistence of conflicts (which tend to be erased by "transculturalists").

Chapter 9, "Hédi Bouraoui: Transcultural Sense of Belonging," by Abderrahman Beggar, examines how poet and novelist Hédi Bouraoui—who refers to himself as a "tricontinental" and "transcultural" writer—left his native Tunisia for France to complete high school and undergraduate studies; obtained his PhD in the 1950s in the United States, where he published the first of more than forty books covering a myriad of domains such as literary critique, poetry, novels, short stories, and political essays; and then settled in Toronto in the sixties. Beggar's intervention explores a procedural question: How and why did this author opted for transculture as a way to identify himself and his work? What are the existential, cultural, ethical, and political reasons behind such a choice? How is this stance translated on an aesthetic level?

Bouraoui's life evolved under more than one model. His creations evince the impact of colonialism, post-colonialism, French "integration," American "melting pot," and Canadian multiculturalism. From a social constructivist perspective, each of these models involves a collective will to construct a world of common experience. In the context of this chapter, the transcultural approach is one that allows a "mobile identity" to deconstruct the world around it in order to change it, inspired by a "nomadic desire." How does change (from the anticolonial fight to the Arab Spring) involve "contact," "flexibility," and "negotiation"? (Hoerder 2012, 55).

In Chapter 7, "Changing Geography: Transcultural Arab Identity in the Age of the EU," Katie Logan investigates the perspective of a "poly-citizen" viewing the formation of Arab transcultural identity in a globalized world. Focusing on Etel Adnan's transcultural *Paris, When It's Naked* (1993), Logan explores the celebratory acceptance of old and new allegiances in the process of developing "multifaceted fluid identities" but without showing complacency toward the colonialism of "imperial" Paris. Interestingly, Adnan's futuristic anxieties offer insights into how the EU's stance on the refugee crisis and the assimilation/alienation dilemma of Arab refugees still inform present world transcultural socioeconomic politics. In a nearly autobiographical tone, Adnan considers the impact of EU formation on a Lebanese woman with multiple identity affiliations. For Adnan, too, the emergent European characteristic of France relegates France's past colonial interventions in North Africa and its present involvement in the Arab migration crisis to the background. Under the EU's shifting categories of belonging and Adnan's persona's quest for a broader and more convenient mode of affiliation, Logan—who argues that Adnan's exploration of citizenship has implications for refugees even though she herself is not a part of that population—explores a transnational mode of citizenship that transcends both the national and the international to avoid manifest marginalization. Through Adnan's *Paris, When It's Naked*, Logan revisits the current Arab refugee crisis in light of the EU's globalized politics and the constant redefinition of belonging, in the hopes of realizing an inclusivist and transculturally underpinned mode or "methodology" of belonging that transcends "binary scenarios."

In Chapter 8, "The Fractured Music of Arab-Jewish Friendships: Waguih Ghali's *Beer in the Snooker Club* and Ismaël Ferroukhi's *Free Men*," Caroline Rooney further investigates a mode of transcultural affiliation that transcends both nationalism and cosmopolitanism, in a comparative study of Ghali's novel and Ferroukhi's film. Rooney draws attention to the anticipatory tone of Arab Spring collectivism in the works by both as embodied in "the vicissitudes of Arab-Jewish friendship," which introduces a creative redefinition of identity politics. Through the "logic of musical analogies," Rooney reflects on the transnational/transcultural brewing in a cosmopolitan milieu, focusing on the nearly autobiographic depiction of the Coptic-Jewish relationship on a postcolonial stage. The two works feature a mode of transreligious, transcultural solidarity that verges on the utopian and that contests conventional national allegiances, in light of Edward Said's contrapuntal readings of social dynamics. According to Rooney, the transcultural sense of burlesque/festive togetherness represents a site of resistance that is sacred enough to overshadow or predominate the religious, as is manifested in the Egyptian Revolution's harmonious lyricism.

Chapter 10, "Poetics of the Virtual: Technology and Revolution in the Poetry of Sghaier Ouled Ahmed," by Hager Ben Driss, intervenes in a most timely way to document the poetry of Ahmed as a narrative of the Tunisian Revolution that, because most of Ahmed's poems were antagonistic to the state, has neither received the attention it deserves among academics nor been acknowledged by official discourse. The strength of this study lies in its determination to historicize the intersection between text and subversive action and capture the poetic imagination and its grammar as an expression of resistance shared and distributed through Facebook. Through an analysis of Ahmed's texts and position on naming the revolution, the chapter comments on the shifting power discourses that emerged immediately after this historic event. As different registers of truth began to collide, tension over control of media flows increased, and cultural currency was claimed for the development of new technologies, and the opportunities afforded by these technologies—for the articulation and adoption of new identities, and the extent to which global power relations still dictate the confines of identities ascribed to people by others—could no longer be concealed. The chapter explains that although the internet, Facebook, and virtual space have helped facilitate the mobilization of the masses, Ahmed was still extremely cautious about the kind of nomenclature he would use, despite his admiration for the Facebook platform.

Part Two investigates the diversifying and assimilative practices of a culture that help to re-narrate identity after traumas. At stake in this is a rethinking of the idea of inclusiveness. This part shows how reflections on transculturation can help redefine and re-narrate identity, cultural loyalty, and feelings of belonging—for example, what citizenship, religious affiliation, and ethnicities mean, especially for those who have been marginalized or whose identity has been thrown into question by the dominant narrative.

In Chapter 2, "Identity Politics and Digital Space: Adel Abidin's *Abidin Travels: Welcome to Baghdad*," Jenna Ann Altomonte explores questions of representation in contemporary artworks and processes of identity formation within digital spaces. The works of Adel Abidin—his multimedia installation *Abidin Travels: Welcome to Baghdad* (2007) in particular—are taken as a case study that challenges several modes of representation of Iraqis in the post-2003 era. Altomonte examines the junctures of satire, diasporic identity, and digital space in Abidin's Baghdad-based imaginary travel agency, offering brilliant ruses for rethinking spaces of trauma. Using humor and satire to problematize representations of Iraqi identity, Abidin's artworks are read against mass-media representations of the Iraqi War, the depiction of the Iraqi diaspora via online platforms, and traditional orientalist tropes. The chapter engages two important aspects related to the theme of the transcultural identities. The first is the notion of digital diaspora and the role of digital spaces in constructing/contesting media representations and diasporic articulations of identities, particularly within the context of the Iraqi diaspora. The second is the scope of analysis: the contemporary arts and the visual arts in discussions related to the central questions and theme of transcultural identities.

In Chapter 4, "Transcultural Identity Formation among Canadian-Arab Youth: Nurturing Self-Knowledge through Metissage and Blunting Canadianness as an Alterity," Bessma Momani and Melissa Finn draw upon structured focus groups and the survey results of over one thousand Canadian-Arab youth to examine how Arab youth negotiate and conceptualize their place in Arab and Canadian societies. This impressively researched study of the opinions of Arab-background youth in Canada mobilizes transnationalism as a category of analysis in a field that is still often dominated by immigration narratives.

In Chapter 3, "Reshaping Social Practice in Post–Arab Spring Egypt: Expression of Identity and Affiliation in New Media," Mohamed Hassan moves from ways of negotiating and conceiving space to localized languages of emplacement. He draws key ideas from discourse theory and sociolinguistics—particularly from Fairclough, Van Leeuwen, and Rampton—to understand the deep meanings of an online Facebook group organized by Egyptians, *Al-Mawkef Al-Masry* "the Egyptian Stance." The analysis operates at an impressive theoretical and conceptual depth. The author consults a number of seminal texts and successfully weaves together frameworks useful for examining the deep meanings of texts and identity, and deftly melds theory and method to produce a theoretically driven analysis; the analysis of Facebook posts using Van Leeuwen's notions of social actors, social action, and social circumstances is especially noteworthy. In the analysis of utterances of two participants (40 and 41), the author follows Fairclough and Van Leeuwen and unpacks the social action and social circumstances present in the exchange. Hassan finds that members of the Egyptian Stance group employ "code-switching," as they easily and efficiently alternate between standard Arabic and the Egyptian dialect. This enables them to localize their action while simultaneously reaching beyond the Egyptian context and speaking to their brethren in non-Egyptian Arab communities. The chapter explains how, in particular, unique features of the Arabic language and its various derivatives may be employed online to ground ideas in a local context while also transcending specific local boundaries.

Part Three highlights the role of migration as illustrative of internal forces of sociopolitical collision around issues of cultural identity, political sovereignty, and community. The role of intellectuals and the media as narrators of the revolution is discussed in two of the section's chapters. Claiming citizenship in multiple states gives rise to "impossible citizens," as they are not linked to the state apparatus public sphere, as opposed to nation state.

Chapter 6, "Syrian Refugees as a Hybridizing Force in the Jordanian Society," by Barkuzar Dubbati, investigates the sociocultural impact of the influx of Syrian refugees to Jordan, which has received relatively little attention. Dubbati traces it back to a geo-cultural proximity that breeds a sense of near homogeneity of both the refugees' native country and their host country, in a way that does not warrant investigation into any cultural consequences. Arguing the opposite, Dubbati premises her piece on the political element of cultures and its role in shaping perception, especially under the exigency of sociocultural realities. Drawing on the Bhaban (1994) notion of nuanced in-betweenness of the hybrid and its impact in blurring the binary line between two different cultures, Dubbati handles the case of the hybrids' (here, Syrian refugees in Jordan) hybridizing role, not in the Bhaban sense but rather in the sense of highlighting and underpinning the binaries, perhaps as natives (Jordanian mechanism) defending their own selves against the socioeconomic threat represented by that potential Other. She also addresses the hybrids' own conceptualization of difference. Dubbati focuses on the changing Jordanian perception of Syrians in the wake of their arrival into Jordan, with the escalating view of these refugees as a potential threat and who are then met with a sense of othering or alienation.

In a similar vein and regarding border-crossing and identity formation, Saeed Khan engages a retracing of the problematics of split/fused cultures of a migrant community on both individual and collective levels, as a case in the study of migration and transnationalism in the twenty-first century. In Chapter 5, "Ontological Citizenship: A Realignment of Rights and Responsibilities between the Individual and the State(s) in Twenty-First-Century Migration and Transnationalism," Khan explores the evolving morphology and sociocultural potentials inherent in emigrational/ transnational encounters. He examines how displacement triggers a sense of "poly-citizenship," underlying which is an unconventional sense of a citizen's rights/duties reciprocity that transcends single-state boundaries. He investigates the multiple transnational spaces that poly-citizenship allows and potential interaction of rights/ responsibilities, consequent redefinition of citizenship, and shifts in the perceptions of national allegiance and national identity. For him, this "asymmetrical exercise of citizenship" involves a global/transnational perspective of migration in which a citizen's relationship with the state undergoes a constant process of redefinition. Khan's chapter thus involves an attempt at a functional definition of the new mode of ontological citizenship that induces the formation of unconventional "models of sociocultural engagement, inclusion, and integration" in transnational contexts that go beyond the national into the post- and even super-national and where the (poly)citizenship/identity interplay is in full force.

Part Four investigates identity as a false problematic. That is, the real issue to be determined is being assigned the position of an insider or outsider. This part engages with how the art of protest, the narration of a new revolutionary era, and the accumulation of material direct us to ask how a dramatic experience of a nation can start to be universal. Part Four offers a critique of the museumization of the revolution and emphasizes how the different spaces of revolutionary action, revolutionary exposure, and staging of the radical act matter (where it happened and where it is exposed, the staging of the act matters). A third space opens up between closed spaces where we can begin to identify and articulate the artistic impulse and to counter its hijacked and fetishistic representations by theorizing the relation between art, activism, and localized realities.

Eying this third space, in Chapter 12, "Interstitial Space of the Art of Protest," Hamid Dabashi offers a series of sharp reflections on space as a differential of power where "things can mean even more," the locus of both the artist and the work of art. "The space of the art of protest," Dabashi argues, "perforce yields to the sphere of public art of protest: and thus we move from … the space of political protest … to the narrative sphere of politics." But there is more than meets the revolutionary eye here. Dabashi, through multiple theoretical detours, effects a turn to the emergent art of protest as offering the model of the work of art (also in fiction) as itself an "interstitial space," defying the established boundaries of genres and media. For him, interstitial space, a term coming from art and architecture, affords the ability "to think of it as a location for urban guerilla artfare." The work is site-specific and moment-specific, and as such, its seeming transitoriness is a radically subversive spacio-temporal experience that turns our own world itself into an interstitial space.

In Chapter 11, "Echoes of a Scream: US Drones and Articulations of the Houthi *Sarkha* Slogan in Yemen," Waleed F. Mahdi maps the evolutionary process of the Houthi *sarkha* ("scream") slogan, which roughly translates as "God is great. Death to America. Death to Israel. Damn the Jews. Victory to Islam." The *sarkha*, he argues, underlines the Houthis' investment in aligning their movement with a growing public search for agency from implications of the US drone program in Yemen. Rather than simply reading the *sarkha* as a mere indicator of Iran's influence on Houthis, Mahdi argues that the slogan is a reflection of a transcultural search for anti-imperial resistance rhetoric inspired by the Islamic Revolution in Iran. The Houthi *sarkha*, according to Mahdi, is "emurgent" (emergent and urgent) because of its ability to simultaneously capture the public pulse of anxiety around US interventions in Yemen and forge a space for a growing consciousness that legitimizes violence as a necessary revolutionary means toward independence and sovereignty. The chapter concludes that although the *sarkha* may have failed in rallying Yemeni social and cultural politics behind its resistance implications, it nonetheless remains a strong identity marker of Houthis' sociopolitical and religious community in northern Yemen, which continues vying for power at the cost of the country's own stability, and ironically, sovereignty.

Throughout the diverse contributions included in this volume, literary, cultural, media, and postcolonial scholars reflect on the nationwide moment of transformation and present a critical and timely study in three key ways. To begin with, the volume seeks to broaden the range and scope of the academic study of the so-called Arab Spring movements. It also contributes to a growing global interest in discussing issues pertaining to the Arab uprising through a unique reading of current new forms of expression in Arab-uprising states. Moreover, the volume forms part of an international discussion on the Arab Spring, and more specifically, on views of change and continuity and how these challenge Western perspectives of Arab culture and politics. In doing so, it adopts a critical standpoint with respect to the concept of identity, recognizing that the multiple constructions, uses, and interpretations of the term invoke complex responses that are fraught with contradictions tied to geographical, historical/political, and cultural realities and perspectives. Together, the critical contributions in this work fill a niche in examining how the interplay of politics, culture, and media has shaped emergent Arab realities and how the resultant collective ethics stands to inform the search for a revolutionary model for generations to come.

Unleashed revolutionary energies have served to enhance a new dynamism in artistic expression that has come to dominate the cultural scene. The first years following the uprisings witnessed a threefold reconstruction of the art scene: reconstructing the relationship of the artist to the public space, as in the case of thriving street art; reconstructing the identity of the artist as an activist and artist; and reconstructing the subject of artistic creation to place political and social issues at the focal center.

References

Hoerder, Dirk, "Transnational—Transregional—Translocal: Transcultural," in *Handbook of Research Methods in Migration*, ed. Carlos Vargas-Silva, 69–91, 75. Cheltenham: Edward Elgar, 2012.

Part One

Senses of Belonging: Explorations of Transcultural Spaces

1

Transculturation in a Changing Arab World: Engaging Contexts in Conversation

Eid Mohamed

Through investigating the manifold bearings of the Arab Spring uprisings on the Arab world, and on Arabs in general, *Cultural Production and Social Movements after the Arab Spring* reflects the multifaced Arab revolutionary prism from different scholarly perspectives and in an interdisciplinary manner that encompasses the broad spectrum of this revolutionary upheaval. Part One blends spatial and temporal investigation of the postrevolutionary processes of Arab identity renegotiation and re-narration in representation of assimilative transcultural practices. The Arab uprisings of 2011 sparked unprecedented waves of change and upheaval and an overwhelming uncertainty for the future of this region. In many cases, the masses that took their grievances to the streets in late 2010 and early 2011 still face the same challenge. This chapter focuses on exploring the questions of how the political transformations since 2011 have affected the construction of a collective Arab identity. How have the recent political, socioeconomic, and cultural upheavals affected the imagining of this identity? And what are the processes that affect the shaping of such a collective Arab transcultural identity? By transcultural identity, we refer to the extent to which a citizen can see himself or herself in the Other beyond the division of national borders. In the context of Arab transcultural identity, we can ask, for example, What makes a peasant farmer in the suburbs of Egypt identify with an unemployed Tunisian graduate protesting in the streets of Tunis? Or asked differently, What was it about the Tunisian masses who were protesting during the Jasmine revolution that inspired the masses in Cairo to protest in Tahrir Square? Can one even imagine that a revolution in Egypt would have been sparked had there not been an uprising in Tunisia that preceded it? In attempting to answer these questions, we aim to explore the processes that contribute to the formation of a collective and transcultural Arab identity that stretches across national borders.

Given the enormous upheavals in the Arab world over the last six years or so, which almost reflect—at least so far—the Arab people's desire to dismantle age-old totalitarianism in the region and probe their way toward a better future, this book, being the fruit of intensive two-day workshop discussions, traces the diverse manifestations of such upheavals from a transcultural perspective. The critical chapters that the book strings together, diverse in their approaches as they are, mainly address the question of identity transformations in a changing, globalized, and conflictual world. In this sense, the focal point is the interplay of different identitarian and cultural elements in the formation of the ever shape-shifting, border-crossing, multicultural, and hybridized Arab identity, inside and outside the Arab world. This trans-ing perspective, besides reconsidering traditional notions of culture and identity and reconceptualizing transculturality from an interdisciplinary perspective, aims to guide further theoretical and practical studies of Arab identity and cultures as crystallized in a still-revolutionary age.

This chapter explores how the emergent transcultural identities in the Arab world and beyond—as investigated in the rest of the chapters—are multicentered and sometimes even contradictory; in tapping into their collective dimensions and the social and aesthetic cohesive aspects of cultural memory, they redefine our narrow approaches to the question of identity. This perspective, I will argue, is in line with the approaches entrenched in pursuing single imaginaries, states, groups, and so on. Unlike notions of interculturality and multiculturality—where cultural determinants such as homogeneity, uniformity, and fixed cultural boundaries are at work—transculturality better answers to the new sense of cultural fluidity and dynamism that relishes permeation, hybridity, and transmutability. Here, the multi-meshing and inclusivity, embodied in the concept of transculturality and the ensuing lack of internal uniformity within the "transcultural place," become the objective (Welsch 1999, 200–1). Welsch believes that interculturality and multiculturality, though they carry some sense of tolerance toward other cultures, still involve the problems of homogeneity-premised traditional concepts of culture, implying delimiting and separatist attitudes toward cultures and thus entailing a potential clash. Transculturality, however, promises to overcome cultural essentialism, ghettoization, and fundamentalism, which are embodied in the traditional conception of single cultures as spheres or islands. The current fluidity of the movement of persons and ideas, mostly involving pouring through and crossing over barriers, diminishes cultural homogeneity. Modern cultures are marked for internal complexity involving different ways of life and for transnational "external connectivity and entanglement" with identical lifestyles transcending certain cultures and in a way that renders the own-ness/foreignness binary no more than an "aesthetic" myth (Welsch 1999, 197–8). This macro-cultural connectivity is coupled with a micro-cultural, individual hybridity that lends greater force to transculturality, with individual identities being formed by more than one reference culture. Hence, transculturality induces a shift in focus from culturally delimiting and separatist divergences to the "opportunities to link up" or reach out toward building a collectivist, transcultural, and inclusivist culture that transcends the parochialist and constraining monocultural perspective. Transculturality implies a movement between and across cultural borders that aims not toward a renewed form of homogeneity but rather toward acknowledgment of diversity, both internal and external, and that captures opportunities to "link up" in a constant process of transformation. This transcultural movement is not mono- or bi-directional but rather circular, allowing for a shift in focus from the divergences as delimiting differences to potentials for internal/external transformative transculturality, with the "transcultural webs" being "woven with different threads, and in a different manner" (Welsch 1999, 203).

It is notable that in the wake of the uprisings referred to as the Arab Spring, the cultural and artistic scene witnessed a relatively surprising boom of production in most disciplines and acquired a fresh approach to artistic creation and expression. Works of art multiplied, and new themes were explored that shed light on the hidden aspects of Arab societies—thus, Arab history—in the past decades. The revolutions had finally eradicated taboos that had long agonized artists. Movies that depicted the violations of human rights under the previous regimes were screened openly and in movie theaters. Books such as Gilbert Naccache's prison memoir, *Cristal*, were sold in libraries and easily accessed by readers. The newly found freedom functioned as a fuel for artists who attempted to break free from all the restraints formerly imposed by the fallen regime.

The uprisings have been of momentous importance in expressing the popular consciousness of the Middle East and North Africa region with respect to demands for sociopolitical change and with respect to questions of civil agency in realizing the aspirations for political and socioeconomic justice. The expression of this movement has notably taken largely cultural and aesthetic forms across diverse media, and this book constitutes a crucial endeavor for the recognition and understanding of a changing Arab world. Given that some Western commentators have spoken of the Arab Spring as coming out of nowhere, it is epistemologically important to show how this is not the case. Here, the book attempts to evidence awareness of the change in social mood and the coming uprisings. This cultural data in the various chapters in this book provide evidence of a growing revolutionary consciousness.

For example, the Egyptian band Cairokee's music video *Sout Al Horeya* is a visual and musical interpretation of the demand for freedom that could be placed alongside Tunisian singer Emel Mathlouthi's song "Kelmti horra (Ma parole est libre)," and these were placed alongside the anti-dictatorship posters. Thus, the Egyptian literary and artistic scene requires us to rethink the key idea of shared ethic (that the transcultural literature situates at the core of transcultural initiatives) by better explaining the persistence of conflicts (which tend to be erased by "transculturalists").

Also, we need to reconsider the definition of the self. For instance, in recent Arabic literature, the self is redefined no more only vis-à-vis the individual but as more connected with the collective. However, this inclusiveness paradigm often forgets that this collective may also be a dominant one. Situating oneself within the collective may not be enough to get rid of boundaries and hierarchies. There is also the idea that transculturality is a choice. If we have multiple ways of acting, defining our actions according to who we are globally and locally, we should also understand how crisis and social changes push us by redefining who we are and what we would like to do and the kind of influence we want to have in a not always conscious or freely chosen way. Transcultural cultures help to re-narrate identity after traumas such as forced/constrained migrations, wars, colonial experiences, and the ideological imposition of states on minority groups.

But we should rethink the idea of inclusiveness; transculturation can help in redefining and re-narrating identity, cultural loyalty, and feelings of belonging (e.g., what citizenship, religious affiliation, or ethnicities mean) when those have been denied or questioned by dominant narratives. It makes it more important to be part of fluid and maybe temporary forms of invented traditions than to be allowed to belong to a national conception of citizenship defined by structural institutions. We must also investigate the unequal access to the transcultural and question why some people can be citizens of the world while others can only ever be refugees or immigrant workers, and what are the consequent efforts to attain legitimacy. We must not presuppose that because those identities are now transcultural, they are automatically inclusive, a disconnect that is exemplified by the Houthis' current attempts to resist the narrative of passive victims of war in Yemen by embedding themselves in the transnational culture of violence that is redefining that country.

The transcultural allows us to better apprehend cultures and identities that seem impossible to be banalized the collective (like being Palestinian, revolutionary, or Islamist, or in the process of Jewish-Muslim interaction) beyond virtual solidarity and identification. But we need to rethink the idea of shared ethics as the core basis of identity sharing. Here, our primary interest is how the transcultural can link specific cultures and identities with the collective by acting as a substitute for fragmented politics. In order to localize this link, we should question who owns the narrative that defines the identity and show how transcultural actors are trying to dissemble it, uncovering in the process the impact that these marginal or specific identities may have on other specific groups' identification as well as on the dominant center. It is important to be aware of using notions of message or hybridity in order to analyze which (political) cultures emerge from transcultural interactions. The reflexivity of these specific cultures toward the collective is not a passive one; it also implies a creativity that gives birth to new cultural repertoires beyond being only countercultural. As such, we should not only focus on what redefinition of centered normative identities bring (although this is crucial) but also analyze what happens to these centered/dominant redefined norms once circulated by specific cultural actors. Understanding the transnational is also about understanding its inner dialogical cultural impact, a dynamic that is marginalized when the effort to understand group interactions is focused on shared ethics only. It is possible that since transcultural actors share the same platform but use it in different ways and with different levels of mobility, flexibility, and willingness to go beyond the group's confinement, a process of negotiation is implied.

The idea of a free, conscious choice at the start of transcultural moves should be tempered by a closer look at the multilayered nature of transnational culture through its multiple spaces and genealogies. With a focus on modern dynamics (colonization, migrations, etc.), the book chapters often present transcultural identities as a new phenomenon, but the literature itself reminds us that it is not, that people have always been mobile and influenced by each other. Methodologically, we should not be lured by the rhythm of circulation and changes (which are real) but also by understanding what persists from the past in these transcultural identities and cultures. Hence, historical contextualization and archaeological work on the sequential/simultaneous spaces visited by the actors are of the first importance.

A Reading of the Cultural and Artistic Scene in the Postrevolutionary Arab World

The so-called Arab Spring has implemented new dynamics of art as a form of expression. The first years following the revolutionary movements witnessed a threefold reconstruction of the art scene: reconstructing the relationship of the artist to the public space, as in the case of thriving street art; reconstructing the identity of the artist as an activist and artist; and reconstructing the subject of artistic creation to place political and social issues at the focal center. Such an investigation of the artistic production utilizes concepts of cultural resistance emphasized by such theorists as Stephen Duncombe. Evidently, the art scene of the postrevolutionary scene has been evolving amid political, social, and economic changes. While many collectives have been born out of the revolution's newfound freedoms, the instability of the region also reflects on the ever-shifting nature of art.

Scholarship across the humanities documents and analyzes the interplay of politics, arts, and culture. A scholarly consensus has emerged indicating that the 2010–11 Arab uprising and its aftermath provided a moment of heightened political liminality that fueled and reflected cultural and political expressions in the arts. Art is political and is used to hasten and reflect ongoing social and political change. Within the context of the Arab uprisings, however, scholars debate exactly how arts both effected and were affected by the liminal space of the revolution itself and the transitionary period afterwards. Politics affect the type of art created; traumatic and violent political events can induce artists to rearticulate new identity in art, while repressive environments spark art with double-meanings. Finally, some contend that above all, this political art from the revolutionary context is itself a form of historical narrative.

Cultural production has great potential as a weapon in revolutionary, or even counterrevolutionary, struggle. Music, poetry, theater, graffiti, and visual arts during the Arab Spring were utilized as weapons and heralded the edge of political change. For instance, Brinda Mehta argues in her review of *Staging Tahrir* and other theatrical work by Laila Soliman that theater, too, can be a useful revolutionary tool that both evokes and sustains revolution. Focusing specifically on the work of Laila Soliman's *Revolutionary Theatre*, Mehta agrees that creative dissidence has always been a part of revolutionary movements.[1]

According to Mark Levine, after Egypt's revolution and counterrevolution, artists struggled to keep their work revolutionary in order to maintain the movement. Arab Spring revolutionary artwork was almost religiously committed to the intersection of creativity and conflict.[2] Levine argues further that through the Arab revolutions, there was a return to Walter Benjamin's concept of artistic "aura." Although interesting, this theoretical application does not strengthen his general argument. Levine suggests that revolutionary art demonstrating this aura is not industrialized, commodified, and commercialized as other arts generally are.[3] Art is being democratized in the context of these revolutionary movements, as it is no longer something for business but rather something for political activism. This argument is weak, as even if revolutionary art is not commodified in the traditional sense, these artists are still selling their art.

From YouTube monetization to selling buttons, revolution, and revolutionary art, is not automatically more authentic and less of a commodity. Perhaps even revolution itself can be commodified. Levine also concludes that only recently has art become politicized in the Middle East in the wake of the Arab Spring. The information on art and religion seemed contrived and secondary, tacked on at the end. He argues convincingly that even clearly religious, conservative, and fundamentalist groups in the Middle East, like the Islamic State, have been making use of art in their political struggle.

The weaponization of culture is not restricted to fine arts and theater. Other forms of culture, such as media production, also played a role in the battle for hearts and minds during the revolution and postrevolution period. In their article "Framing the Egyptian Uprising in Arabic Language Newspapers and Social Media," Naila Hamdy and Ehab Gomaa examine how state-run, independent, and social media in Egypt all framed the 2011 uprisings differently. The content they studied was all Arabic language, and they engaged with eight hundred documents to categorize how stories were framed in these different media formats. They argue that the state portrayed the uprisings as a conspiracy concocted by outside forces against the Egyptian state, while social media posts stressed the concept of revolution for freedom. They conclude that independent newspapers used both lenses in their analyses.[4] Each political camp used different narratives to shape public opinion of the revolution through its respective media outlet. This study's careful analysis of such a vast array of primary source data and its utilization of digital humanities tools have been a useful contribution to this exploration of culture as a political force in the context of revolution. According to the analysis of Levine and Mehta especially, the days of Tahrir were a "special period" of political uncertainty that resulted in especially intense production of politically meaningful and effective art. Their work indicates that revolution and cultural production are shaped actively by narratives, which can be spun in a variety of directions. Their work recognizes revolutionary cultural production (specifically media production) as historical narrative, similar to that of Radwa Othman Sharaf. Here, art is both effecting change and being shaped by political goals.

But scholarship also notes how political upheaval itself affects artistic production and even the self-perception of populations. Traumatic and violent political events can induce artists to rearticulate identity through art. Elizabeth A. Zahnd and Thyazyla Dnaz suggest that these sorts of political events can prompt artists to reimagine both identity and community. These scholars examine the connection between politics and culture through treatment of two Québécois novels centered on the aftermath of the 9/11 attacks. Zahnd and Dnaz argue that the 9/11 attacks changed two Québécois writers' understandings of their individual and national identities.[5] This massive political event made them question their conception of Americanness. The production of their novels was a way to overcome trauma. Even though what happened was not in their nation (Canada), the proximity and historical relationship with America resulted in their need to examine their relationship with the United States, which resulted in a trend for identifying across borders and boundaries. They argue that this is because the authors translated the traumatic American experience of 9/11 into their own contexts through their novels. This tendency for traumatic political action to affect a whole region, and to encourage trans-border solidarity, is also perhaps apparent in the context of the Arab Spring uprisings and the art that has come out of them. It encourages deep introspection, which is then shared in cultural production.

John Carlos Rowe and Wdsolrk Nowjs's work indicates that political environments also have effects on academic production. Their analysis is in the field of American studies, but their line of reasoning aligns with those of scholars working on cultural production out of the Arab Spring period and after. They suggest that American studies has become heavily critical of neo-imperialism and American exceptionalism because the American political climate is currently favoring these positions.[6] Also, the political reality of globalization is sparking a response in the world of academia. These scholars are also activists in their suggestion that the field of American studies needs to respond to America's political action in their writing, mainly to the problem of neo-imperialism, in order to create and circulate more equitable knowledge effectively.[7] Rowe and Nowjs argue for a post-nationalist American studies. This activist approach to scholarship is also found throughout writings on the Arab Spring.

Mona Abaza's work, like that of Rowe and Nowjs, centers on how the political climate has effects on cultural production. She is convincing in her use of recent graffiti evidence from Egypt's 2011 revolution and its aftermath to demonstrate that urban arts and spaces respond viscerally to political pressures. She suggests in her article that Egypt's new political climate after the revolution is repressive, and thus political dissent is being channeled through street arts like graffiti. Abaza examines how urban Cairo was transformed after the revolution, when violence was unleashed in the city. Tahrir was turned into a war zone, and the graffiti and murals following these violent political events were expressions of political feeling. Furthermore, these art spaces also transformed cities physically as they became spaces of remembrance.[8] Her work is forthrightly activist. She is ardently anti-Egyptian military, arguing that they are "liars" who claim to have protected the revolution while they actually took steps to repress it. These sorts of claims, which she weaves into her narrative, lacked substantial citation. However, she effectively examines various artistic endeavors and links their creation to specific political circumstances. Her position is filtered through consistent, aggressive distaste for the Egyptian "deep state."[9]

Journalist Gilbert Achar offers thoughts on a topic few of these works delved into—the political Islamic relationship to cultural production and arts. He argues that Arabian Gulf media giants like Qatar's Al Jazeera played a central role in shaping Islamic groups in Egypt. He suggests that Khaliji-style Islamism has played an important role in the development of the postrevolution states.[10] Thus, cultural-political development is transgressing borders, much like Zahnd and Dnaz noted in their work. Achar contends that petrodollars and American influences have also supported this Khaliji-Islamic development in Egypt, which has allowed Islamists to, as Achar puts it, coopt the revolution. He sees the revolutionary struggle as ongoing, and despite Islamic cooption, Egypt's populations have been empowered to rise up for what they want. This, in his estimation, signals hope for the region. His work's strength is its focus on economic and transnational elements underpinning political activities and cultural responses in the Arab Spring. He provides numerous concrete examples of fettered economic development as playing a role in the issues discussed in this literature review—a perspective overlooked in much of the work focusing on culture's interplay with politics.[11] This is a factor that is missing in numerous other political-cultural narratives, which sidestep the important contextual element of economy.

Political climates affect arts production. In his essay "In Extremis: Literature and Revolution in Contemporary Cairo," Youssef Rakha agrees that the political establishment often coopts artistic production for its own ends.[12] This assertion is echoed by Naila Hamdy and Ehab Gomaa, whose work showed that the political events of the revolution were spun by different media outlets to support completely different political narratives. Rakha claims that since the 2011 Egyptian Revolution, Egyptian novelists have had to navigate a new climate for their writing in which they are expected by critics to write politically engaged works. But in this essay, Rakha himself appears disdainful of the political engagement of politically engaged writers, suggesting either that they pander to Orientalism or are desperate. He argues that many of Egypt's revolutionaries and authors are "desperate pedagogues or aspiring martyrs."[13] While his analysis is useful, the tone of the essay is elitist and derisive of work he deems popular.

Some scholarship has also focused on the possibility of revolutionary arts being read as historical narrative or document in itself. Radwa Othman Sharaf, for example, argues that the graffiti of the Egyptian Revolution is a set of useful primary sources scholars can read. These art pieces are documents that provide rich detail about individuals' perceptions of what occurred during and after Tahrir. Sharaf's photo essay examining images of graffiti on Cairo's streets between January of 2011 and June of 2013 suggests that Cairo's graffiti transitioned from largely apolitical to narrating Mubarak's process of resignation and the process of political transition thereafter. While the apoliticality of previous graffiti is debatable, the documentation of the revolutionary graffiti is convincing. Sharaf shows how artists have offered visual histories of the revolution.[14] These are, for instance, the graffiti pieces that were found along Mohamed Mahmoud Street. Sharaf articulates the political and historical circumstances that elicited these works. She presents graffiti as an important documentary tool for the history of the Egyptian Revolution, as it was able to provide a window into artists' perceptions. She concludes, echoing those suggesting that political repression affects art, that repression of artistic freedom and expression results in even more creative artistic messages in Egypt. Mona Abaza echoes this sentiment, suggesting that as revolutionary spaces are dynamic, so is the art that accompanies them.[15]

Artistic and Literary Expression and a New Political Imagination

The concept of political imagination is essential to understanding the evolution of political identification, which explains how political imagination may change the environment, the formation of a community, and the relationship between the self and the Other. Overall, political imagination is conceived as a real, daily, individualized political practice and aims at replacing a holistic understanding of change through concepts such as ideology, culture, and revolution.

Originally rooted in Anderson's analysis of an idealistic communitarian reimagination of nationalism, political imagination is, however, uprooted in real-life events and interactions and brings back individual agency at the center of the redefinition of the world.[16] This political imagination is, of course, fed by inherited historical definitions of the communities, the space, and the self but also by many fluid (real and virtual, local and global) interactions and identifications and thus does not limit people to reconceptualizing the nation.[17]

The notions of hopes and dreams are at the core of how political imagination takes shape. It is not actors' place in the world that delimits their agency but their ability to think differently about—to reimagine politically—that allows them to take action.[18] Some authors consider that the production of images and texts is central to political imagination as a political creative process.[19] Here it is important to understand how various groups in the West and in the Arab world have produced political imaginaries that have had an impact on their people's place in the world. The main question should then be how those have affected those lives and how these two segments are interacting, how they see themselves and the Other.

The question of otherness is central to the field. It is about "building representations of others, their goals and intentions within collective life ... and uses these representations to influence (limit or enhance) the possibility of others achieving their (imagined) aims. These two 'phases' are of course cyclical and interdependent."[20]

Political imagination as a product of the interactions between the individual and the world influences the meaning that one gives to the community one belongs to, by which I mean the capabilities of resistance, of reform, or on the contrary, the inability to be unified, respected, and so on. It is first and foremost "a tool for critique and change."[21] If reimagined communities have been analyzed mainly as a way to correct universalism in its neoliberal understanding, I think we should also explain how the sublimation of the Other—and especially of the United States as pervasive—has built an idea of fragile Arab communities (and, of course, fragile but somehow necessary states and corrupted regimes).[22]

Nevertheless, the emerging figure of the "digital citizen" and the consequent possibility to escape inherited self-identifications, thanks to its lack of geographical, social, gendered, and historical localization, seems to make possible new political imaginations that give hope for meaningful agencies, agencies that are capable of influencing how one thinks about one's capacity for action and agency.[23]

Political imagination is often thought of as a tool to distance oneself from "neoliberalism paternalism."[24] In the case of post–Arab Spring countries, it has been quite remarkable how some rejected frameworks that neoliberal states, media, and funding agencies, for example, were trying to impose their own imaginative frameworks on what happened (like the Jasmine revolution, the overuse of the Bouazizi's figure, or efforts to promote an ad hoc less-radical postrevolutionary "civil society"). Political imagination, especially in resisting neoliberal globalization, can be shared and commonly nourished by groups that do not need to be part of the same movement, country, religion, and so forth. It is specifically the networking connections and references that give birth to political imagination that allow it to rest on "local subjectivities" that make sense of broader "global justice networks."[25] There is also a demystification in the Arab world of the United States under Trump that is somehow sustaining new states of political imagination. As an example, an Arab writer sent an open letter to the United States sharing his experience of Western clichés after the election of Trump:

> We tried the revolution thing ourselves, and it didn't work out so well. Maybe you should just adapt to living in the new regime. We were always told that having a strongman in charge is the best solution for Arab countries, otherwise there would be chaos. Perhaps the American people are not ready for democracy after all. Let's face it America, you look like an Arab country now.[26]

This can be traced back to the early role of Al Jazeera, which I believe has been a medium that has allowed Arabs to rethink the West and themselves and has created a new way to critique the West beyond populist and culturalist rhetoric.[27]

Some authors have also underlined the role of diaspora in shaping critical political imaginaries. They described diasporic groups that can circulate "new forms of global identity politics—politics that are shaped by but also transcend the limits and institutions of states."[28] There has been a deep critique of post–Arab Spring documentaries and their circulation primarily targeting Western audiences. As an example, the problem with these films is that they ignore the interconnectedness of "developed" and "developing" countries, of authoritarianism in the Middle East and liberal democracies in the West, of Islamic fundamentalism and the Cold War, and of metropolitan centers of global capitalism and the dispossession of millions all over the world. The problem gets even more complicated when entitlement and the ability to represent becomes unquestioned. The visibility of those films rests on the certainty of their narratives, a certainty that denies any form of reflexivity. Their visibility rests on making the Arab world screenable, commodifiable, and marketable to a non-implicated audience. These films portray living stereotypes of actual people, focusing on the elements of their lives that are "interesting" only in so much as they tell us something about clichéd versions of Egypt, Tahrir, Islam, women, art, war, conflict, poverty, dispossession, and resistance. To those who live with war, conflict, poverty, and dispossession, those for whom Tahrir was not a spectacle and for whom resistance is a complicated act, these topics are not interesting. But neither the term "Arab Spring" nor the term "Arab world" can be explained through the sum of their parts. They are constructed, time and time again, through the very narratives that eclipse alternative imaginaries, historical renditions, and analyses by foreclosing the realm of imagination altogether.[29]

There is much more on the topic of literature and political imagination.[30] Authors analyze how literature translates transformative periods and consciously provides readers with alternative visions of the self and communities (and also political movements and revolutions). As an example, this chapter shows how America has been thinking about itself, and in particular about white people as good citizens willing to reconciliate by producing an alternative literature on the civil rights movement in order not to endanger white supremacy in democratic institutions.[31] Controlling the narratives (and filtering counternarratives) through literary work can then have a concrete impact not only on the historical stratification of political imaginaries but also on how they will build public arenas (or spheres) accordingly.

Many authors are seeing revolution as an opportunity for new political imaginaries to emerge (although some disagree on whether these are new ones that have started with the revolts or ones with much deeper roots in historical imaginaries of protest). The key work among Arab writers is a new subjectivity, a subjectivity that beyond the state and other authoritative references (like Asshaab in the Nasserian kind of thought and national television that describes people as a unified political unit) would orientate the actors toward other realities like "new ways of consuming and producing culture."[32] In turn, this culture is also producing "new kinds of Arab subjectivities." "A revolution of the imagination has pushed people into the streets .... [That] encourages people to put themselves at the center of political narratives in ways that ultimately lead to defiance of official national narratives."[33]

Advancing the importance of individual subjectivities allows us to escape labels like the "Arab Spring" or "the Facebook Revolution" that do not account for the radical transformation in politics and values that the Arab world is undertaking. Hanafi calls it "reflexive individualism," which does not reject "existing social structures" as such but rather "their disciplinary power. The political subjectivity is expressed not only by toppling the regime, but also by changing the individual." He concludes by saying that survival of this individual political subjectivity is contingent on Western efforts to acknowledge or annihilate it, as well as the ability of Arabs to trust their transformative capacity.[34]

Some link postrevolution political imaginaries to the broader historical context and especially to violence—whether that be the Muslim Brotherhood's using violence in a Mubarak style, the "anticipation" of the counterrevolutionary violence as illustrated in Cairo graffiti until 2014, or the securitization of Egypt's urbanistic choices (like Dubai-style compounds) that fit with the return of a neoliberalist imaginary that we have experienced a "failed revolution."[35]

Rededicating some space to violence in the construction of political imaginaries also allows some authors like Salwa Ismail to deconstruct the idea of an educated, peaceful, bloggers-led revolution and to show instead the everyday violence (by the police, for example) experienced by "urban subalterns" in Cairo that nourished their political imagination and allowed them to handle their participation in the revolution.[36]

The urgent social, cultural, political, and economic realities that have unsettled the hegemonic structures of state formations and processes of subjectivation have also strongly revealed how identity is and always has been unstable and mutable. Few works have begun to understand how cultural texts function in the process of social and political change. This book will fill this gap by interrogating the theories of social and political change in cultural theory, integrating cultural studies, and contributing to the prevailing theoretical trends in Arab studies. This methodological approach underlines the commitment to theorizing the "transcultural" as a new phase of citizen engagement that stresses the need for sharing information, ignoring borders, opposing censorship, and adopting common strategies in the fight for social justice. The concept of "transcultural identity" stands at the interface of these large-scale political transformations and their sociocultural articulation. It indexes the multiple channels through which an Egyptian public now understands and imagines autonomy, agency, and self-representation. The point, it should be stressed, is not to suggest that a transcultural identity now transcends all others. To the contrary, the concept is meant to highlight how cultural identity and political consciousness can no longer be assumed and can be negotiated along various intersecting axes—postcolonial (Arab nationalist, Islamist, state-nationalist), ethno-religious (sectarian and tribal), and class-based, to name just a few.

Conclusion

Here I have tried to think about a preliminary framework of analysis on our understanding of and approach to social, cultural, and political change, transformations, continuities, hopes, and frustrations in the Arab world over the past thirty years. What has become clear is that scholars should focus on change in a multilayered way to avoid the clichés carried by the analysis of "brutal" change after the revolutionary "awakening" or its consequent authoritarian "stagnation," an approach that considers change only in terms of rupture, transition, and such simplistic binary tensions as modernity versus tradition. Considering change as a multi-influential, multi-scaled, long-term process may help us analyze in a finer way the transformations—both visible and invisible—of Arab identities and social realities.

A variety of art and cultural production has recently become very politicized in the Middle East in the wake of the Arab Spring. Egypt's revolution resulted in arts both reflecting and encouraging political engagement. Some scholarship, like that of Hamdy and Gomaa, has noted that cultural production itself (for instance, media publications) are political narratives in and of themselves. Abaza and Othman, in their respective articles, note that graffiti art is a political narrative and can be read as a primary source to shed light on the history of the revolution. Other scholarship, such as the work of Mark Levine, has stressed art's use as a political tool during revolutionary periods and the dangers posed by pressuring and encouraging rapid political change. Scholarship also notes that revolutionary art has had transnational influences. This is echoed in work coming out of the field of American studies, which notes that political upheaval in one nation affects those all around it. Globalization, and intercultural influence, is another strand in the story of this revolution—although perhaps not in the style of conspiracy theories about external orchestration. Political climates affect artistic production, just as artistic production has the ability to influence political climates. However, it seems that scholarship indicates that the political climate has a greater impact on art than art does on political climate. This is especially apparent in view of the counterrevolutionary conclusion to the Tahrir movement.

This introductory chapter tries to draw attention to the corpus and material gathered by individuals themselves to express willingness (or fear) of change. "It is through their humor, satire, images and novels that we can get a sense of the discontent of youth that will inevitably lead the next revolution. The crowd rearticulates history as local, connected, and malleable to the will and desire of political subjects, as opposed to the will of a corrupt dictator."[37] People are rewriting changes they have experienced through autofictions, biographies, *istishhad* narratives, and the like. It is important to localize change to see how people retranslate and understand the revolutionary "grand schemes"[38] in their daily lives and what kind of anxieties and fears may arise from the discrepancy between the revolutions' promises and local experiences.[39] It is important to investigate the Autofictional blog's style of writing[40] and social networks on building new artistic and literary communities, as well as the great extent of religious and moral motives in recent writings.[41]

Notes

1. Brinda Mehta, "Staging Tahrir: Laila Soliman's Revolutionary Theatre," *Review of Middle East Studies* 47, no. 1 (2013): 49–55.
2. Mark Levine, "When Art Is the Weapon: Culture and Resistance Confronting Violence in the Post-Uprisings Arab World," *Religions* 6 (2015): 1277.
3. Ibid., 1280.
4. Naila Hamdy and Ehab Gomaa, "Framing the Egyptian Uprising in Arabic Language Newspapers and Social Media," *Journal of Communication* 62 (n.d.): 195.
5. Elizabeth A. Zahnd and Thyazyla Dnaz, "Redefining American Identity and Overcoming Trauma in Two Post-9/11 Novels of Quebec," *Alif: Journal of Comparative Poetics* 31 (2011): 220.
6. John Carlos Rowe and روجون كارلوس, "Areas of Concern: Area Studies and the New American Studies / والدراسات الأمريكية الجديدة "مناطق مقلقة: " دراسات المنطقة, *Alif: Journal of Comparative Poetics*, no. 31 (2011): 12.
7. Ibid. and 31, رو.
8. Mona Abaza, "Walls, Segregating Downtown Cairo and the Mohammed Mahmud Street Graffiti," *Theory, Culture & Society* 30, no. 1 (January 1, 2013): 122, https://doi.org/10.1177/0263276412460062.
9. Ibid., 136.
10. Gilbert Achcar, *The People Want: A Radical Exploration of the Arab Uprising*, trans. G. M. Goshgarian. First edition (Berkeley: University of California Press, 2013), 71.
11. Ibid., 7.
12. Youssef Rakha, "In Extremis: Literature and Revolution in Contemporary Cairo (An Oriental Essay in Seven Parts)," *The Kenyon Review* 34, no. 3 (2012): 162.
13. Ibid., 165.
14. Radwa Othman Sharaf, "Graffiti as a Means of Protest and Documentation in the Egyptian Revolution," *African Conflict & Peacebuilding Review* 5, no. 1 (May 20, 2015): 160.
15. Abaza, "Walls, Segregating Downtown Cairo and the Mohammed Mahmud Street Graffiti," 122.
16. Anderson, Benedict. 1991 [1983]. *Imagined Communities: Reflections on the Origins and Spread of Nationalism*. London and New York: Verso.
17. It has also been inspired by the work of Arjun Appadurai. See *Modernity at Large: Cultural Dimensions of Globalization* (Minneapolis: University of Minnesota Press, 1996); and *Global Ethnoscapes: Notes and Queries for a Transnational Anthropology* (Minneapolis: University of Minnesota Press, 1996), 48–65.

18 Alessandro Ferrara, "Politics at Its Best: The Reasons that Move the Imagination," in *The Politics of Imagination*, eds. Chiara Bottici and Benoît Challand (Abingdon, UK: Birkbeck Press), 38–54.
19 Benoît Challand, "Religion and the Struggle for People's Imagination: The Case of Contemporary Islam," in *The Politics of Imagination*, eds. Chiara Bottici and Benoît Challand (Abingdon, UK: Birkbeck Press), 142–61.
20 Vlad Petre and Constance de Saint Laurent, "Political Imagination, Otherness and the European Crisis," *Europe's Journal of Psychology* 11, no. 4 (2015): 557.
21 Keally D. McBride, *Collective Dreams: Political Imagination and Community* (University Park, PA: Penn State Press, 2005).
22 Seyla Benhabib, *Another Cosmopolitanism* (Oxford: Oxford University Press, 2008).
23 Ruppert Engin Isin and Evelyn Ruppert, *Being Digital Citizens* (London: Rowman & Littlefield, 2015).
24 Joe Soss, Richard C. Fording, and Sanford Schram, *Disciplining the Poor: Neoliberal Paternalism and the Persistent Power of Race* (Chicago: University of Chicago Press, 2011).
25 Paul Routledge and Andrew Cumbers, *Global Justice Networks: Geographies of Transnational Solidarity* (Manchester, UK: Manchester University Press, 2009), 224.
26 Karl Sharro, "America, You Look Like an Arab Country Right Now. Welcome to the Club," *Politico*, January 22, 2017, https://www.politico.com/magazine/story/2017/01/america-you-look-like-an-arab-country-right-now-214678.
27 El Oifi, M. (2005). Influence without power: Al Jazeera and the Arab public sphere. In Zayani, M. (Ed.), The Al Jazeera phenomenon: Critical perspectives on new Arab media (pp. 66–79). London, UK: Pluto.
28 Fiona B. Adamson; The Growing Importance of Diaspora Politics. *Current History* 1 November 2016; 115 (784): 291–297. doi: https://doi.org/10.1525/curh.2016.115.784.291.
29 Alia Ayman, "Three Films, One Spectator and a Polemic: Arab Documentaries and 'Global' Audiences," *Al Jadaliyya*, December 26, 2016, https://madamasr.com/en/2016/12/26/feature/culture/three-films-one-spectator-and-a-polemic-arab-documentaries-and-global-audiences/.
30 Andrea T. Baumeister and John Horton, eds., *Literature and the Political Imagination* (London: Routledge, 2013).
31 Christopher Metress, review of "Literature, Civil Rights, and the Political Imagination," edited by Andrea T. Baumeister and John Horton, *The Southern Literary Journal* 47, no. 2 (Spring 2015): 122–8.
32 Tarik Ahmed Elseewi, "A Revolution of the Imagination," *International Journal of Communication* 5 (2011): 1197–206.
33 Ibid.
34 Sari Hanafi, "The Arab Revolutions: The Emergence of a New Political Subjectivity," *Contemporary Arab Affairs* 5, no. 2: 198–213.
35 All these examples are given by Mona Abaza in "Violence, Dramaturgical Repertoires and Neoliberal Imaginaries in Cairo," *Theory, Culture & Society* 33, no. 7–8 (2016): 111–35.
36 Salwa Ismail, "Urban Subalterns in the Arab Revolutions: Cairo and Damascus in Comparative Perspective," *Comparative Studies in Society and History* 55, no. 4: 865–94.
37 Andrea Khalil, "The Political Crowd: Theorizing Popular Revolt in North Africa," *Contemporary Islam* 6, no. 1 (April 2012): 45–65.

38 Samuli Schielke, *Egypt in the Future Tense: Hope, Frustration, and Ambivalence before and after 2011* (Bloomington: Indiana University Press, 2015).
39 Naoual Belakhdar et al., eds., "Arab Revolutions and Beyond: Change and Persistence," Working Paper No. 11 (2014), Proceedings of the International Conference, Tunis, November 12–13, 2013, https://www.polsoz.fu-berlin.de/polwiss/forschung/international/vorderer-orient/publikation/working_papers/wp_11/WP11_Tunis_Conference_FINAL_web.pdf.
40 Teresa Pepe, "When Writers Activate Readers: How the Autofictional Blog Transforms Arabic Literature," *Journal of Arabic and Islamic Studies* 15 (2015): 73–91, http://dx.doi.org/10.5617/jais.4652.
41 Sobhi Boustani, Rasheed El-Eneany, and Walid Harmarneh, *La littérature à l'heure du printemps arabe*" (Paris: Karthala, 2016).

References

Abaza, Mona. "Walls, Segregating Downtown Cairo and the Mohammed Mahmud Street Graffiti." *Theory, Culture & Society* 30, no. 1 (January 1, 2013): 122–39. https://doi.org/10.1177/0263276412460062.

Achcar, Gilbert, and G. M. Goshgarian. *People Want: A Radical Exploration of the Arab Uprising*. Berkeley; Los Angeles; London: University of California Press, 2013.

Hamdy, Naila, and Ehab Gomaa. "Framing the Egyptian Uprising in Arabic Language Newspapers and Social Media." *Journal of Communication* 62 (n.d.): 195–211.

Levine, Mark. "When Art Is the Weapon: Culture and Resistance Confronting Violence in the Post-Uprisings Arab World." *Religions* 6 (2015): 1277–313.

Mehta, Brinda. "Staging Tahrir: Laila Soliman's Revolutionary Theatre." *Review of Middle East Studies* 47, no. 1 (2013): 49–55.

Rakha, Youssef. "In Extremis: Literature and Revolution in Contemporary Cairo (An Oriental Essay in Seven Parts)." *The Kenyon Review* 34, no. 3 (2012): 151–66.

Rowe, John Carlos, and روجون كارلوس "Areas of Concern: Area Studies and the New American Studies / دراسات المذ : "مناطق مقلقة: الدراسات الأمريكية الجديدة" طقة." *Alif: Journal of Comparative Poetics*, no. 31 (2011): 11–34.

Sharaf, Radwa Othman. "Graffiti as a Means of Protest and Documentation in the Egyptian Revolution." *African Conflict & Peacebuilding Review* 5, no. 1 (May 20, 2015): 152–61.

Welsch, W. "Transculturality: The Puzzling form of Cultures Today," in *Theory, Culture & Society: Spaces of Culture: City, Nation, World*, eds. M. Featherstone and S. Lash, 195–213. London: SAGE Publications Ltd, 1999, doi: 10.4135/9781446218723.n11.

Zahnd, Elizabeth A., and Thyazyla Dnaz. "Redefining American Identity and Overcoming Trauma in Two Post-9/11 Novels of Quebec." *Alif: Journal of Comparative Poetics* 31 (2011): 220–40.

2

Hédi Bouraoui: On Transcultural Belonging

Abderrahman Beggar

More of a perspective than a fixed concept or even discipline, transculturation permits us to re-read homogenized histories that construct belongings as fixed that essentialize cultural, ethnic, national, gendered, religious, racial, and/or generational dimensions. Transculturation equally permits us to re-conceptualize difference and diversity as negotiable. As intersectorial. As strategic. And as capital. (Horder, Hébert, Shmitt 14)

Transculture cannot be described in positive terms, as a set of specific cultural symbols, norms, and values; it always escapes definition. It is an apophatic realm of the "cultural" identity. It is the most radical of all possible cultural "beyonds." (Epstein 333)

Transcultural Stance

While keeping in mind the defining idea of this volume as a study of the way Arab societies in transition are imagined, adopting transculture as the conceptual frame for this research corresponds to its capacity to insure a multifocal, intersectional, and decentering approach to sociocultural phenomena. Transculture is not a discipline with its body of rules, protocols, systems, and rigorous codes. Neither is it a model of society (as, for example, opposed to multiculturalism). Rather, it is a set of principles related to intellectual attitudes toward the increasing challenges faced by the nation-state model. More than anything, transculture is a stance that translates the urgent need to deal with the deep structural evolutions that shape societies in a global world, thanks to new transnational, crosscultural, and technological realities. Keeping this point in mind, the purpose of this chapter is not to define the concept but to explore the way it manifests itself across Hédi Bouraoui's life and work. In other words, the declarative aspect (*I know that transculture is*) is of less importance than the procedural one (*how transculture works and manifests itself*). The essential question is around how knowledge about the relation between the self and the environment is shaped.

Such an approach is mainly about the creativity, the dynamics, and the configurations considered as means to reinvent the sense of belonging according to an individual development path.

When Hédi Bouraoui was once asked about the concept of transculture and if he knew about its first-time use by Cuban anthropologist Fernando Ortiz in the 1940s, Bouraoui's response was that he heard about Ortiz for the first time in 2005, anthropology not being his domain of expertise (Bouraoui 2005, 10). At the same time, Bouraoui claims that the concept is his own invention and that he coined it while lecturing at the University of York in the 1970s in the context of the debate on Canadian multiculturalism. Such a statement can be easily explained if we take into consideration three factors. First, a concept can migrate from one discipline to another (e.g., Deleuze and Guattari moved "rizhome" from a botanical context to the philosophical one). Second are the intellectual preoccupations of which transculture is a part. Bouraoui applied "trans" to his philosophy of creation that he calls "transpoetics" (Bouraoui 2005) and even to reality itself when he talks about "TransReal" (Bouraoui 2010, 3–4). Some qualify his art as "trans writing" (Brahimi), while others talk about him as a "transcrivain" or "transwriter" (Darragi 2016). Of course, in the "trans" context, culture can never be kept away when taking into consideration the organic nature of the relationship between it and all intellectual activities, including, obviously, writing. And third, ideas sometimes act in a strange way, especially when dealing with common preoccupations. As Giambattista Vico says, "The natural law of nations arose separately among various peoples who knew nothing of each other" (80).

The root "trans" is itself the expression of the need to challenge common views and find other ways to deal with the nature of human interactions. Literature cannot evolve separately from society's tendency to manage what determines behavior: beliefs, choices, and actions. Transculture is about a certain configuration in which these elements are challenged. This effort aims especially at opening new ways of conceptualizing the world. The idea behind this project is to show how transcultural belonging is mainly a critical stance, a product of an active mutual action between the individual and her or his milieu. At the same time, in the context of Bouraoui's writings, transculture is to be considered as a perspective aimed at a better understanding and practice of diversity. This attitude is motivated by a methodological preoccupation: in the absence of the Bakhtinian principle of *exotopy*, according to which the foreigner is always a better judge of a culture, for the transcultural intellectual to be a critic of her or his time, he or she is expected to transcend political and social order to ensure a certain distance with the proper environment and also to open the door toward a better understanding of the world.

Even if Bouraoui's transculture looks like a sui generis concept, a kind of micro ecosystem that has evolved away from the academic debate of its time, it is interesting to see how behind this apparent insularity, one can detect common grounds with other thinkers of the transcultural. Fernando Ortiz used *transcultural* in a colonial context, especially in the domain of the production and trade of tobacco and sugar. A decade later, this same concept resurfaced far north, in Canada. In 1956, Eric Wittkower, from the Department of Psychiatry at McGill University, launched a joint publication with McGill's Department of Anthropology: *Transcultural Research in Mental*

Health Problems (Bains). Two years later, the same academic institution inaugurated transcultural psychiatric studies to become one of the pioneering universities in Canada in conceptualizing the changing face of a society constantly defined by immigrant flux. Under the influence of Franz Boas, Margaret Mead, and Ruth Benedict, relativism and diversity began questioning cultural homogeneity and shifted the debate toward what can be qualified as social heuristic, the will to discover new conceptual tools to explore the dynamics behind the changing nature of human interactions. As Bains suggests, time came to challenge "cultural Darwinism," its "absolutist" definition of culture (142). These new orientations in research are rooted in post–Second World War Canada, where the study of culture starts to leave the usual paradigms. Once again, it is at McGill University that scholars from both Francophone and Anglophone sides began to reach out to each other. Everett C. Hughes was one of the central figures of that time, an illustration of the exotopic mind. He used to consider himself to be the outsider (he left the University of Chicago for McGill), interested in studying the nature of contacts (or lack of contact) between Francophone Canada and Anglophone Canada. He is one of the first to research ways to break the ice between scholars from Québec and the rest of Canada. Since the 1950s, transculture has become part of a myriad of disciplines, from museum studies to literature, neurology, history, business, and social work.

Still, the bulk of research takes place in the domain of health, especially in psychiatry, where transculture plays a key role in understanding the nature of the relationship between the practitioner and the patient. This option is clearly dictated by ethical concerns. When the Other, even in her or his radical difference, is respected in her or his integrity, then the relationship is a constructive and collaborative one. As Wright formulates it, "The emphasis of the transcultural paradigm is on an equal partnership" (3) between members of the same society.

Dirk Hoerder applies transculturalism to the history of cultural diversity, especially in the Mediterranean, and to the institutional frames allowing its management. On the other extreme is the work by Michael Epstein, a Russian scholar who emigrated to the United States in the 1990s. For him, transculture is to be regarded as the appropriate stance in times of profound rupture, a response to the deep changes brought about by the fall of the Berlin Wall. It is treated as the response to limitations proper to multiculturalism and globalization, both considered as forms of social determinism. For Epstein the purpose is to fight against the subjugations proper to culture, to explore strategies to challenge one's culture to the point that even language is taken as a source of alienation: "Transculture represents the next level of liberation, this time from the 'prison house of language', from unconscious predispositions and prejudices of the 'native', naturalized cultures" (327). Following his views, it is time for what he calls a "supra-cultural creativity" (330). For him, culture is trapped in all kinds of determinisms, and it is time for a tabula rasa, a radical divorce from all symbolic structures. Such a view is not concerned when looking for ways to legitimate transculturalism through the study of diversity as the way to approach the nature of interactions between peoples. It is more about deconstruction with the objective of neutralizing all kinds of categories including gender, color, and religion.

Belonging as a Critical Stance

The more one gets acquainted with Bouraoui's work, the more the organic nature between the concept of "locality" as it is defined by Appadurai and the conception of the world becomes clear. This allows us to explore how the imagined environment shapes how we consider truth. Alain Badiou talks about "'procédure de vérité,' which means an experience where a certain type of truth is constructed" (Badiou 2009, 39). What matters is that truth is the offspring of experience, a construction, a course. Truth's value depends on the horizon of possibilities it opens, and its status rests on the degree of respect for the principle of openness. It is more of a process than an achievement. Badiou's idea of truth is related to that of infinity, as what is "in-finite" and incomplete. To illustrate his purpose, he uses the zero in relation to any number. Every number (let's suppose four) is waiting for one or more zeros to become something else (a 40 or 400 for example). The same applies to truth. Contingency plays the role of the zero. A truth's existence depends on the sum of challenges that ensure its openness toward infinity (Badiou 2010, 17).

Bouraoui was born in 1930 in Sfax, a city in southern Tunisia, at a time when this country was still a French protectorate. From his biography, a set of interviews with Rafiq Darragi, we learn that as a child, he was impacted by life not in the Medina (the part of the city usually reserved for the natives) but by the environment proper to Moulinville, the colonial quarter, where his father used to own a mini-market. Customers were mainly French and European settlers, all people (among them Tunisians) from the three confessions. The family business was a kind of neutral zone where diversity was welcome and where all that mattered was interacting, socializing, and negotiating one's belonging. At this stage, the trauma of occupation and its "infernal binarities" (Bouraoui) didn't yet affect the author's life. To Darragi he confessed, "I cultivate tolerance through dialogue and dignity. This is a stance I have adopted since childhood. I owe it to my father who lived in a multiracial, multiethnic, multireligious community" (Darragi 2015, 19). What we learn here is that the truth about the self is a multimodal and ethical one. Far from rejection and essentialist simplifications, the relation to the Other is made possible in a "locality" with all the characteristics of a micro-society in which plurality is a fundamental value. To shape this environment, the author portrays a cultural body in which the sense of belonging operates through spiritual, ethnic, racial, and religious channels. The multi (as in "multiracial, multiethnic, multireligious") is opposed to the essence of the colonial global society as the guardian of an imposed monoculturalism, based on indisputable hierarchies sustained by an oppressive state apparatus.

If we consider this episode in relation to Bouraoui's works, it is obvious that the objective is to show that in its innocence, a child's eye can elaborate a critique of power by focusing on the ethical "ought to be." As a "locality," Moulinville is stripped of the common coordinates that usually determine the reading of colonial space to become a place for the "possible" and for emancipation where cultures can intersect, interconnect, and be open to each other. It all happens according to the idea of recuperating a memory proper to aseptic conditions far from violence. It is as if all that matters was not the intension behind the Europeans but their humanity in its complexity, the contact, the gaze, the You (Thou) as synonymous with infinity, just as Buber refers to it. Bouraoui's account of this period is determined by the will to find a common ground, a sense of togetherness as open and incomplete as the truth that Badiou talks about.

Before going further, I would like to emphasize the fact that this attitude doesn't mean sweeping colonial violence under the carpet. As we will see, Bouraoui is not the kind of author to stay in an ivory tower. He has always shown an indisputable interest in the human condition, to the point that in a laudatory poem, Albert Memmi portrayed him as follows: "Inspired, cautious moralist, he [Hédi Bouraoui] is also my/brother in the spiritual combat./I am not sure if we can someday/fulfill our dreams,/but we will at least, together/testify, in favor of fraternity, against/prejudice, misconceptions and injustice" (Villani 71). The author's life is marked by a visceral optimism, which also aims at opening unlimited horizons for truth. The first object to transcend is the self. This is why in his works (where autobiography and autofiction are absent), "egocentered sentimental narratives" (Pratt 122) are avoided.

In early adolescence, the author moved to France to complete high school. Devastation, as well as the enthusiasm inspired by the project of rebuilding a whole country, characterizes this period. This is a time marked by his love of philosophy, his contacts, and his discoveries. Once again, the will to reach the Other, to know her or him, to understand her or him, is constant. These years are described with rare affection. All happens in a quest for human contact, conviviality, and knowledge. France, the country that occupied the motherland since 1881, is contextualized far from even the slight feeling of victimization. Once again, one has the impression of dealing with someone who appropriates the location, submits it to his own expectations, and makes it his own, to the point that nostalgia and all kinds of feelings that one would expect from a young boy landing in a foreign country are absent. The Latin *identitas* as sameness is here redefined according to ideas and values in an accumulative logic. This sounds as if Hédi Bouraoui were telling himself, "To live in a place, I have to look for common grounds to ensure my own growth." Philosophy as systematic doubt applied to literature is the privileged territory for such a pursuit.

From France, Bouraoui moved to the United States, where he completed his PhD and published his first book *Musoktail* (1966), a set of poems that bear the impact of a life under the sign of movement and quest. His life in the United States is marked by his status as a witness to the way discrimination works. In his biography, he depicts the absurdities of the racialization processes. As an African who doesn't fit the stereotypes around skin color, he describes with humor his navigation between the race line. After defending his PhD, Bouraoui decided to move to Canada in the late 1960s. He joined the faculty of York University, where he still keeps his office in his capacity of writer-in-residence for life.

This is not a common itinerary for a Francophone North African–born writer. First of all, writing in French in the United States and in Canada gives his work a unique character. In fact, he is the first author from this part of the world to do so.

Bouraoui's Work and the Birth of North African Literature in French

Maghrebi literature in French was born in Algeria. At its beginning, it was the product of the same "infernal binarities" proper to the colonial project. All goes back to the first attempt to conceptualize identity when in the beginning of the twentieth century, French and European settlers laid the foundations for an apartheid system expressed by what was called "Algerianism." For Martin Thomas, "Algerianism's central claim was that colonial society had evolved a unique identity, distinctly French and yet different from, and in no way subordinate to, the dictates of Paris. The only true 'Algerians' were European settlers" (164). Natives were considered as a mere "mass of others" (Thomas). In the 1930s, while Algeria was the center of a flourishing intellectual activity, with the purpose of redefining French Algerian identity far from the Algerianist nativist ideology, a new movement was born: the School of Algiers (1936–56). French Africans (not to be confused with French Muslims), also called *pieds noirs* with reference to them as rednecks, as poor "bare-footed" land workers, found in the future Nobel Prize winner Albert Camus and his two friends Gabriel Audisio and Emmanuel Roblès the adequate representatives of their cause. Their school was against colonialism, regionalism, and conformism. Starting out with ethnocultural and racial concerns, the debate shifted toward deep philosophical questions, such as Camus's existentialism.

Under Sartre's influence, members of this school, especially Jean Senac, began to talk about the need to open to native Algerians; it was then, in the 1940s, that those non-Europeans began to write in French. However, the first production that fulfills the standard of a literary work was published in 1950 (while Hédi Bouraoui was still living in France), *Le fils du pauvre* (The Poor Man's Son), a novel by Mouloud Feroun (assassinated in 1962, the year Algeria gained its independence). In the 1950s and the 1960s, a whole generation of Maghrebi writers (Albert Memmi, Mohammed Dib, Ahmed Sefrioui, Kateb Yassine, and others) produced a body of literature marked by colonialism, immigration, social justice, modernity and tradition, ethno-religious conflicts, and political violence.

Bouraoui did not share the same views about locality as the Francophone Maghrebi writers of that time. Appadurai considers locality as "primarily relational and contextual rather than as scalar of spatial" (178). It is the "relational and contextual" aspect that makes the difference. Charles Bonn and Naget Khadda put the first Francophone Maghrebi works (in the 1950s and 1960s) under the following categories: "literature of alienation," "exoticism," and "acculturation" (7–10). Bouraoui's early work—poetry books written while in North America (*Musocktail, Tremblé, Éclate-Module,* and *Vésuviade*)—are all about topics related to existential problems rather than postcolonial ones. The main topics are language and love, not to mention violence, existence, creativity, and the universe. This has nothing to do with the kind of "binarities" proper to a colonial legacy, the United States and Canada being so far from the conflictive realities proper to postcolonial Maghrebi societies. If among the first generation of North African Francophone writers, creation goes through the filter of the "colonial's gaze" (Bonn, Khadda, and Mdarhri-Alaoui 8), in Bouraoui's case, writing is inscribed in the will to connect with humanity in what can be qualified as cosmopolitan construction, poems where the local is questioned or implicit to the point that it vanishes or becomes impersonal. In *Échosmos* (1981), poetry enters what can be called a post-humanistic stage, where man is no longer at the center of the world; he is just an echo of the cosmos (*echosmos*).

What all of these books have in common is a constant interest in creative subjectivity. The poet delivers a radioscopy of the act of creation. The sense of belonging is scrutinized with the intention to show how locality in its "contextuality" (Appadurai) is all about human action and freedom. The world is considered as a place where free subjects are expected to create a place of their own. Nothing is assumed—all is open to interpretation—and the artist is the one who impacts the world around him or her.

Transculture and Creaculture

In 1971, Bouraoui published the first volume of *Creaculture*, a two-volume textbook on French culture. The invention of this concept is to be considered in the context of cultural belonging, especially when it comes to the question of which attitude to adopt when studying culture. The main idea is to show how culture is all about interpretation and subjectivity. After going through different perspectives (historical, literary, artistic, Marxist, structuralist, etc.), the author came to the conclusion that until now, scholars have not come up with a way that would allow the study of culture in its totality; what we have instead are only "perspectives." He then invites the reader to focus more on how cultural values are created and to explore the nature of this process, knowing that "creaculture is a neologism that refers to the continuous of cultural values …. It is thanks to a constant dynamism that the major fundamental ideas in a cultural context evolve and change constantly" (Bouraoui 2005, 32). It is a response to all kinds of essentialism, an effort to challenge the nation-state as an immutable territorial, political, and cultural body.

Belonging is about the sum of the individual's actions to the point that even space has to be considered, not as what the group manages according to a certain symbolic organization but as "the diverse environments of our personal evolution" (Bouraoui 2005, 33). In its local, national, or regional dimensions, locality can't have a meaning outside of individual experience. Everyone has a certain imagination of environment shaped through interaction according to networks, historical legacies, and social class realities—all of which are included in what Bourdieu considers as "social capital." In the "construction of locality," interpretation as a performative and subjective appropriation of environment is determined by sociocultural and economic realities. That is why Bouraoui warns against what he calls the "cyclist perspective," a study of French cultures like someone who participates in the famous Tour de France, the annual bicycle race that goes through rural France to reveal the secrets of the *terroire*, reducing cultural realities to products, such as cheese and wine or historical monuments such as the Castles of the Loire.

While talking about Bouraoui's childhood in colonial France, we were dealing with a world in which the sense of locality was determined by an idea of togetherness that privileges contact and dialogue between the components of a multiethnic neighborhood. As a "materialization of locality," the neighborhood offers certain modes of interpretation from where one of the main ingredients is missing: colonial violence. When reading Bouraoui's biography, the representation suddenly changes because of the eruption of violence. The first event is the Second World War, especially when the bombardment started and also when his parents sheltered a Jewish family, a mother and her disabled child. The multi (as in multiethnic, multireligious, and multinational) as a truth is now challenged. The historical event, as a rupture in the normal flow of time, imposes a new definition of belonging. This is the first time that Bouraoui questions the ethno-religious element.

What makes a Tunisian a Tunisian or a French person a French person under the pro-Nazi Vichy government? Second World War is considered to be one of the main challenges to France and the colonies. The deportation of Jews helps to put the finger on a structural contradiction proper to the French nation-state model. Based on Hoerder's analysis, one can conclude that the nation and the state have not always been in full harmony. On the one hand, as a concept inherited from the Enlightenment, the state can be considered a legal body with one mission: to ensure that all citizens are equal before the law. On the other hand, the nation is, based on a Romantic idea, a group of people sharing the same culture (Hoerder 2012). However, instead of equality, in colonies and protectorates, it is a question of forced homogenization, abstraction, and reduction according to a center formed by the Parisian elite. For Hoerder, the Republican-nationalism model is about hierarchy, not equality. In a situation of crisis such as the war, the system can't hide its own contradictions. The state, as the guarantor of the rule of the law, finds itself impotent in front of the idea of a nation where the ethno-religious element transcends fundamental values of the republic—liberty, equality, fraternity. In such a scenario, the question of belonging goes together with responsibility. How, under Nazi occupation, could the French people oppose the deportation of the Jews? To answer this question, implicitly, Bouraoui opens the door to another one: How could the Tunisian people protect a segment of their own population while being under a double occupation, by France and Germany? Under Moncef Bey, Tunisia was a disappointment for the Vichy government when it came to the question of racial laws (Watson, Bahri, Bajohr, and Löw).

Can transethnicity and cosmopolitanism go together with colonial power? How is it possible that even though the majority of the Jewish community chose to become French (Manzano), they found themselves in a scapegoat position? What determines the feeling of belonging? From a creacultural perspective, one has to take into account "the diverse environments of a person's evolution" (Bouraoui). What is said about an individual can also be applied to a group. Being French or Tunisian is not an a priori state, a given quality, constant and immutable, but rather fluctuates in response to political and geopolitical factors. The sense of belonging commonly depends also on implicit rules of conduct, networks, and connectivity, untold codes of conduct, all resting on symbolic frames. However, even if this modus vivendi looks like the natural way of sociability, it is also shown to be something unpredictable. In Bouraoui's biography, one of the darkest moments in the history of his family is when the country got its independence in 1956 and Moulinville found itself deserted by the majority of its inhabitants (the ones who chose to flee to France). Many left without paying their debts (Darragi 2015, 20). As a result, Bouraoui's father faced bankruptcy, and his family entered into a dark period in their lives.

The eruption of these two events (Second World War and the War of Independence) and their effect on what looks like organic social ties is the pretext for a transcultural definition of the sense of belonging. According to Jeff Lewis, "It [transculture] is interested in the destabilizing effects of non-meaning or meaning atrophy. It is interested in the disintegration of groups, cultures, and power. In other words, transculture emphasizes the transitory nature of culture as well as its power to transform" (24). There is no better test for the "non-meaning or meaning atrophy" than agency. Conflict shows the contradictions of social order, especially its moral code. On the one hand, this code is to be considered as atemporal and beyond the filter of reason. It is embedded in what Bourdieu calls "habitus," a set of instinctive dispositions that determine feelings and actions to allow social reproduction. On the other hand, agency is more about accidents and reactions. It is the product of expectations and contingencies.

"Atrophy of meaning" happens in the absence of a critical stance toward the way the sense of belonging is shaped. In this context Bouraoui's critique of Canadian multiculturalism is an interesting one. It is not a rejection of the model (as in the case of right-wing critics who act in the name of a certain exclusive idea of the nation) but rather a call to avoid historical anemia. Revolutions are processes and transitions; if there is a truth in a revolution, it is in its incompleteness. In the 1970s, when the Trudeau government adopted multiculturalism, Bouraoui warned against what Stanley Fish qualifies as "boutique multiculturalism," the one around "ethnic restaurants, weekend festivals, and high profile flirtations with the other." Bouraoui also guards against the risk of "ghettoes," the conversion of society into a plethora of disconnected communities. His critique is based on what he calls Canada's two ontological "solitudes" (based on Hugh McLellan's idea) when referring to the antagonisms between Québec and the rest of the country. Bouraoui added two other solitudes, one proper to the Natives and the other to the category labeled as "newcomers" or "new Canadians" (Bouraoui 2005, 62–3) If cross-culture and multiculturalism are, at least according to Wright, interested in comparing cultural groups (216), for Bouraoui, transculture is about "*passages ou résonances*" (crossing or resonance) (Bouraoui 2005, 34). The transcultural mind is about a nomadic attitude that goes beyond what is already fixed and assumed. The purpose is not to focus so much on disconnect, barriers, closing off, and compartmentalization. Nomadism is about movement, transit, flow. It is a "nomaditude," which Bouraoui defined in the following terms: "Nomaditude deconstructs infernal binarities proper to the relation center *vs.* periphery, majority *vs.* minority, omnipotent *vs.* marginal, external *vs.* internal" (Bouraoui 2005, 10).

Transcultural Territoriality

Retour à Thyna (1996), a novel about the city of Sfax, the author's birthplace, is about the life of a group of young people in a country trying to invent itself after seventy-five years of French occupation. This social novel depicts mechanisms of domination, existential contradictions, and a deep malaise proper to the need of coming up with new meaning for a new life. The critique of these transitional times is part of the global configuration of postcolonial Tunisia. The goal is to define the country and its people not exclusively according to occupation. The historical perspective encompasses thousands of years. French occupation and the subsequent violence are just an episode in a long saga of contacts and conflicts. It is as if the author does resist the postcolonial paradigm by not accepting a reading of the national history according to just one of the many cycles of encounters, clashes, and metamorphoses. Correcting history goes through the construction of meaning in a manner that relies on rewriting narratives and configuring them idiosyncratically. In 2012, Bouraoui published *Paris berbère*, a novel dedicated to the War of Algeria. The protagonists, Théo and Tassadit, are a Franco-Algerian couple living in France who met in 1968, just six years after the independence of the North African country. Both are dealing with their pasts, especially as each comes from a family involved in the conflict. Théo invents his own way of thinking, an approach that allows a critical distance toward the traps of common sense. He calls this attitude a *faisance*. It can be embraced when action is free from finality and meaning and is the offspring of a pure act of creation. Théo's is a skeptical and indifferent mind when it comes to the question of morality, considered as a set of commands. He is a transcultural being who believes more in ethics than in fulfilling a historical promise, like his father, who fought in Algeria in the name of the "greatness of French civilization." The dialogues between father and son show how Théo tries to decolonize the colonizer, colonialism being an almost metaphysical entity that transcends judgment and produces finite and closed truths.

The *faisance* approach frees human contacts from the weight of collective mythologies, even in the context of conflictive situations or in a worse scenario, such as the collapse of a system with its institutions, economy, security, and politics. This way of thinking places Bouraoui's definition of transculture in opposition to Epstein's rupture. The Russian scholar conceptualizes culture from a distinct place. His work is limited to the Soviet Union, where, at least according to Georgi M. Derluguian, especially since the 1960s, the relation between politics and culture was one of subordination. Instead of a world where culture defines politics, it is politics, under the control of a bureaucratic nomenclature, that decides the faith and nature of cultural practices (104–28). While in Bouraoui's works (especially in his novels *La Pharaone, Ainsi parle la Tour CN, Cap Nord, Les Aléas d'une odyssée, Méditerranée à voile toute, Le Conteur*, and *Puglia à bras ouverts*), stories are about more than one country, and rupture has an ethical and aesthetic value (Beggar 2012) motivated by the need to reach the Other, to develop intellectual tools that allow a better understanding of diversity, to put communication into the service of culture, and to encourage life in a "world for everybody" (Bouraoui 2005, 60). On the aesthetic side, as a poet, Bouraoui has developed a particular interest in the power of words, in ways to express the world in its complexity, and in a constant thirst for experimental writing.

My intention until now has been to show how culture is a subjective matter and open to interpretation. In this sense, we are in the logic initiated by Nietzsche when he talks about interpretation instead of truth, the objective world being a fallacy, a "fiction," and all that we have are mere constructions that all go through the filter of "model realities" proper to our beliefs and the way we interpret them (Nilsson 65–6). In a world where all is metaphorical, what matters is interpretation. Umberto Eco came with another question: What about the interpretation of the interpretation? What about the interpreter herself or himself? (78–9). In his response to this question, Bouraoui doesn't agree with a total rupture with culture, being the work of centuries. He defines the transcultural subjects as "wanderers" who "believe the world belongs to everybody" and "one's culture is a preamble of other cultures" (2005, 60). Culture is about "fluidity" (Bouraoui). It is "processual" (Hoerder). Such definitions explain why transculture is hard to define: the object (culture) is an inconstant one, something whose essence is movement.

How does one conciliate infinite possibilities of interpretation and unity of the thinking subject? Bouraoui believes that the world is singular and plural at the same time. It is as William James calls it a "plural monism" (79); plural if we look at it according to a network of conjunctions, intersections, and concomitance; and plural if we are concerned only with disjunctions, oppositions, idiosyncrasies, and disconnectedness. For this purpose, being transcultural is about conjunctions and disjunctions. It is about "being with the other," envisioning an inclusive togetherness where difference is respected and creating a place beyond what the nation-state model is offering. Keeping in mind the need for this unlimited horizon, Bouraoui deterritorializes even the Mediterranean. By deterritorialization, what is meant is the subversion of the common ways that this sea is represented. Being Mediterranean is not only about living on a shoreline. It is more about a certain vision of the world that is marked by a "fluid" essence, the one that inhabits waves, accidents of time, and a cosmic body that transcends even time. This sea, as portrayed by the author, is an "alive metaphor" (Bouraoui 2005, 77–84). The use of metaphor invites to the Nietzschean interpretative freedom mentioned earlier. In the trilogy *Cap Nord* (2008), *Les Aléas d'une odyssée* (2009), and *Méditerranée à voile toute* (2010), the locus is organized according to the idea that the world is one and multiple. Hannibal, the protagonist, is a young Tunisian immigrant who leaves his hometown to travel across the Mediterranean in search of a father who left him while he was a child. His deconstruction of prevailing conceptions works both vertically and horizontally. It has a vertical dimension because of the way Hannibal challenges the compartmentalizing of history into periods. Hannibal is in reality a kind of trinity: he is himself, his own father, and the famous Carthaginian ancestor who crossed the Pyrenees on the back of an elephant. As for the horizontal side of this journey, the hero challenges borders by stripping them of their martial and estate value as what delimitates and protects a territory. They are all meaningless, a signified waiting for a signifier, and this signifier is an encyclopedic knowledge of the history of Tunisia and the Mediterranean world. Hannibal deconstructs borders while challenging maps as an imposed reading. He goes through thousands of years of history to show his interlocutors that the essence of borders is inconstancy and how they are shifting all the time.

Conclusion

In French, the verb *comprendre* ("to understand") is composed of the prefix *com* that expresses the idea of togetherness and the verb *prendre* ("to take"); understanding is therefore about a shared "apprehension" of reality. Thinking is thus motivated by the will to enjoy the world, to make it one's domain of action, and to alter it. In the case of Hédi Bouraoui, transculture is a critical stance toward the environment that the writer is supposed to belong to in order to make it his. If for his generation, writing in French presupposes a myriad of conflicts rooted in realities as old as Algerianism, colonial wars, acculturation, assimilation, and racism, for Bouraoui himself, it is first of all an effort to find a place for oneself, name the world differently, and remodel it according to the proper existential itinerary while taking into consideration all the aforementioned problems.

Among Bouraoui's works, not a single book is dedicated to transculture. The concept is present in some of his essays and is, in reality, a stance that impacts his creative work. More than anything, it is an ethical necessity that inhabits the Canada that the writer chose as his home in the 1960s, an unnamed collective preoccupation, a kind of unborn idea of the nation (or nations, in reference to Québec and First Nations), and an unrestrained need for the configuration of a mutating society according to the constant flux of immigrants. It is in the name of the changing face of the neighbor and the necessity to welcome her or him that transculture has arisen. As translated in this writer's work, it is also about a thirst for experiments, a transcendence of common aesthetic and generic norms, and a constant fight against all forms of centralism. As a Francophone writer in Ontario, Bouraoui finds himself in the same situation as his colleagues from McGill University, an Anglophone university in Francophone surroundings (Québec). In the middle of collective "solitudes," there is no better option than transcending the makeup of cultural belonging.

For this reason, both Epstein and Bouraoui see in transculture the adequate response to all kinds of determinism. However, when it comes to multiculturalism, they do not share the same views. Transculture, according to Bouraoui, is not a rejection of multiculturalism; rather, it is the way to make it more inclusive and keep it away from the risk of communitarianism. It doesn't limit itself to the destiny of one country but extends to the whole of humanity. There is no need to say that compared with Hoerder, Bouraoui is for cultural diversity or that his approach focuses on its historical legitimacy. What distinguishes Bouraoui in this sense is the intention to go beyond the need to legitimate and explore what makes diversity happen. For him, the world is a place open for the nomadic mind ("nomaditude" as Bouraoui prefers to call it). Human beings are nomadic by essence, and the world belongs to the "errand," as he likes to call the transcultural subject. A look at his concept of transculture shows that education is the key. To be transcultural, one needs to know very well her or his own culture. The contact with others allows a critical distance, as well as accumulation and fluidity. Such a deep knowledge and openness protect against the risk of acculturation, assimilation, and clash.

In *Contemporary Arab Thought: Cultural Critique in Comparative Perspective*, Elizabeth Suzanne Kassab explores the question of what makes an Arab while adopting an etymological stance based on an effort of critique shaped by historical and societal factors from the Al Nahda (the nineteenth-century cultural renaissance) to the postcolonial debate around the relationship to the West. It is an exploration of an evolving ethos, shaped by defeats (notably 1948 and 1967), transitions, and metamorphosis. All of it translated into a constant debate around cultural identity as a dynamic historical construct. From Hédi Bouraoui's transculture, one can conclude that belonging is in itself an object of critique. The author constantly tries to go beyond the primary meaning of this term and the ideas of dependency and possession it implies.

The first and most important element in this critique is the place. Contesting geography as a certain idea of space shaped by borders is behind the discussions triggered by his wanderer heroes across the Mediterranean. In this sense, Bouraoui acts like Miguel de Unamuno at a time when Spain was living almost the same situation as in today's Arab World. The Spanish philosopher was one of the most notorious figures in the so-called Generation of 1898, intellectuals gathered to do the same critique work as Kassab refers to in the aftermath of the War of Cuba, Spain's own *nakba* (Arabic for "catastrophe," in reference to the loss of Palestine in 1948). It all started in 1898, when the Iberian country lost the island and was kicked out of Latin America after a humiliating defeat by the United States. An intellectual debate ensued about the reasons behind the fall of what had been one of the most powerful empires. The common explanation was a geographical one, related to the position of Spain. Was Spain a European country, or, as many at the time preferred to say, does Europe start in the Pyrenees? Were the Moorish roots to blame in a place called by some "Afroeurope"? To this need of belonging to a place and to the idea of modernity it implies, Unamuno, in the end, came with the following solution: instead of becoming Europeans, we have to make Europe Spanish. For Unamuno, one can't "digest" European values without seeing oneself in them. The same is true for Bouraoui, who invents characters capable of discerning communalities and dressing bridges while contesting identity as a systematic totality.

The Manichean Us versus Them is not always easy to contest. How can resistance be possible in the context of cultural hegemony? Who can wander around the Mediterranean and elsewhere to realize the transcultural dream in a world of increasing gated and walled communities and countries? Bouraoui's reaction is far from the spirit of "contradiction" in the Maoist term. It is more about negotiation and compromise.

References

Appadurai, Arjun. *Modernity at Large. Cultural Dimensions of Globalization*, Minneapolis, London: University of Minnesota Press, "Public Worlds" Series, vol. 1, 2005.
Badiou, Alain. *Éloge de l'amour*, entretiens avec Nicolas Truong, Paris: Flammarion, col. "Café Voltaire," 2009.
Badiou, Alain. *Le fini et l'infini*, Paris: Bayard, col. "Les Petites Conférences," 2010.
Bahri, Mohammed. "Le conflit israélo-arabe vu du Maghreb," *Revue française de science politique*, 16, no. 4 (1996): 774–85.
Bains, Jatinder. "Race, Culture and Psychiatry: A History of Transcultural Psychiatry," *History of Psychiatry* 16, no. 2 (2005): 139–54.

Bajohr, Frank and Löw, Andrea (Ed.). *Negotiating and Compromising. Jewish Leaders' Scope of Action in Tunis During Nazi Rule* (November 1942–May 1943), London: Palgrave, 2016.
Beggar, Abderrahman. *Ethique et rupture bouraouïennes*, Toronto: York University, The Canada-Mediterranean Center, "Mosaic. Essays" series, 2012.
Bonn, Charles, Khadda, Naget, and Et Mdarhri-Alaoui (Ed.). *Littérature maghrébine d'expression française*, Vanves: EDICEF, 1996.
Bouraoui, Hédi. *Le conteur*, Ottawa: Vermillon, 2012.
Bouraoui, Hédi. *Paris berbère*, Ottawa: Vermillon, 2011.
Bouraoui, Hédi. *Méditerranée à voile toute*, Ottawa: Vermillon, 2010.
Bouraoui, Hédi. *Les Aléas d'une odyssée*, Ottawa: Vermillon, 2009.
Bouraoui, Hédi. *Cap Nord*, Ottawa: Le Vermillon, 2008.
Bouraoui, Hédi. *This Speaks the CN Tower*, translated by Elizabeth Sabiston, Toronto: CMC Editions, 2008.
Bouraoui, Hédi. *Puglia à bras ouverts*, Toronto: CMC éditions, 2007.
Bouraoui, Hédi. *Transpoétique. Éloge du nomadisme*, Montréal: Mémoire d'Encrier, 2005.
Bouraoui, Hédi. *La Pharaone*, Tunis: Editions l'Or du Temps, 1998.
Bouraoui, Hédi. *Echosmos*, Toronto: Mosaic Press, 1986.
Bouraoui, Hédi. *Vésuviade*, Paris: St-Germain-des-Près, 1976.
Bouraoui, Hédi. *Éclate-Module*, Montréal: Cosmos, 1972.
Bouraoui, Hédi. *Créaculture 1*, Montréal: Philadelphie et Didier-Canada, 1971.
Bouraoui, Hédi. *Tremblé*, Paris: Éditions Saint-Germin-des-Près, 1969.
Bouraoui, Hédi. *Musocktail*, Wheatan: Power Publications, 1966.
Brahimi, Denise. "Hédi Bouraoui: la traversée des pays et des mots," *Perspectives critiques. L'œuvre d'Hédi Bouraoui*, sous la direction de Elizabeth Sabiston et Suzanne Crosta, Sudbury, Université Laurentienne, col. "Série monographique en sciences humaines," 2007: 27–50.
Buber, Martin. *I and Thou*, translation and prologue by Walker Kaufman, New York: Charles Scribener's Sons, 1970.
Darragi, Rafik. "'Le Conteur' ou le but de la vie selon Hédi Bouraoui." Accessible at: http://www.leaders.com.tn/article/9956-le-conteur-ou-le-but-de-la-vie-selon-hedi-bouraoui. Web December. 2016.
Darragi, Rafik. *Hédi Bouraoui : La Parole autre. L'Homme et l'oeuvre*, Paris: L'Harmattan, 2015.
Derluguian, Georgi M. *Bourdieu's Secret Admirer in the Caucasus. A World-System Biography*, Chicago: The University of Chicago Press, 2005.
Eco, Umberto. *Contruire l'ennemi et autres écrits occasionnels*, traduit de l'italien par Myriam Bouzaher, Paris: Grasset, 2014.
Epstein, Mikhail. "Transculture: A Broad Way between Globalism and Multiculturalism," in *Between Global Violence and the Ethics of Peace: Philosophical Perspectives*, ed. Edward Demenchonok, Massachusetts/Oxford/West Sussex: Wiley-Blackwell, 2009.
Fish, Stanley. "Boutique Multiculturalism, or Why Liberals Are Incapable of Thinking about Hate Speech," *Critical Inquiry* 23, no. 2 (1997): 378–95.
Hughes, Everett C., and Hughes, Helen MacGill, *Where Peoples Meet. Racial and Ethnic Frontiers*, Glencoe: The Free Press, 1952.
Hoerder, Dirk, Harzig, Christine, and Shubert, Adrian (Ed.). *The Historical Practice of Diversity. Transcultural Interactions from the Early Modern Mediterranean to the Postcolonial World*, New York/Oxford: Berghahn Books, 2003.

Hoerder, Dirk. "Transnational—Transregional—Translocal: Transcultural," in *Handbook of Research Methods in Migration*, ed. Carlos Vargas-Silva, Glos/Northampton: Edward Elgar Publishing Limited, 2012.

Hoerder, Dirk. *Cultures in Contact. World Migrations in the Second Millennium*, Durham, London: Duke University Press, 2002.

Hoerder, Dirk, Hébert, Yvonne, and Schmitt, Irina (Ed.). *Negotiating Transcultural Lives*, Toronto, Buffalo: Toronto University Press, 2005.

James, William. *Le pragmatisme*, traduction Nathalie Ferron, présentation Stéphane Madelrieux, Paris: Flammarion, col. "Les livres qui ont changé le monde," 2010.

Kassab, Elizabeth Suzanne. *Contemporary Arab Thought. Cultural Critique in Contemporary Perspective*, New York: Colombia University Press, 2009.

Lewis, Jeff. "From Culturalism to Transculture," *Iowa Journal of Cultural Studies* 1 (2002): 14–32.

Manzano, Francis. "Le français en Tunisie, enracinement, forces et fragilités systémiques: rappels historiques, sociolinguistiques et brefs éléments de prospective," *International Journal of the Sociology of Language* 211 (2011): 53–81.

Naudillon, Françoise. "Ifriqiya et la Caraïbe dans l'œuvre d'Hédi Bouraoui," in *iconoclaste et chantre du transculturel*, ed. Jacques Cotnam and Hédi Bouraoui, Ottawa: Le Nordir, 1996: 43–57.

Nilsson, Nils J. *Understanding Beliefs*, The MIT essential knowledge series, Cambridge: The MIT Press, 2014.

Ortiz, Fernando. *Contrapunteo cubano del tabaco y el azúcar*, Caracas: bibliotecaAyacucho, 1978.

Pratt, Mary Louise. *Imperial Eyes. Travel Writing and Transculturation*, second edition, London/New York: Routledge, 2008.

Sfeir, Antoine (Ed.). *The Columbia World Dictionary of Islamism*, translated and edited by John King, New York: Colombia University Press, 2007.

Smith, Tuhiwai Linda. *Decolonizing Methodologies. Research and Indigenous Peoples*, second edition, London/New York: Zed Books and Dunedin: Otago University Press, 2012.

Thomas, Martin. *The French Empire between the Wars: Imperialism, Politics and Society*, Manchester/New York: Manchester University Press, 2005.

De Unamuno, Miguel, "Sobre la europeizacion (arbitrariedades)." Accessible at: http://www.filosofia.org/hem/dep/lem/n216p064.htm. Web April 2017.

Vico, Giambattista, *New Science: Principles of the New Science Concerning the Common Nature of Nations*, translated by Marsh David with introduction by Anthony Grafton, London/New York: Penguin Books, Penguin Classics, 1999.

Villani, Sergio (Ed.). *Hédi Bouraoui. Hommages au poète*, Woodbridge: Les Éditions Albion Press, 1998, 71.

Watson, Robert. "Between Liberation(s) and Occupation(s): Reconsidering the Emergence of Maghrebi Jewish Communism," *Journal of Modern Jewish Studies*, 13, no. 3 (2014): 381–98.

Wright, Bernadette, and Van Der Watt, Gillian. "Transcultural or Multicultural: What Best Defines Our Work?" *Advances in Mental Health* 9, no. 3 (2010): 215–18.

3

Changing Geography: Transcultural Arab Identity in the Age of the EU

Katie Logan

You know, some infallible entity is being born under our eyes. Not a revolution. A creation. The greatest creation since the Babylonian Deluge. Switzerland will move closer to Paris and Berlin, to Prague. We're changing geography, around here. (Adnan 1993b, 28)

The narrator of Etel Adnan's 1993 *Paris, When It's Naked* witnesses the establishment of the European Union (EU), understanding it to be a material expansion of frameworks of belonging. This development reifies certain connections between people and places while obscuring other equally significant affinities. Musing on French identity, literature, and colonial history through a series of dream-like vignettes, the narrator considers what the arrival of the EU means for her as a Lebanese woman with ties to France, the Middle East and North Africa, and the United States. She imagines the EU knitting Europe together at the expense of other international histories and her own experience in Paris. France's new identification as "European," she argues, marginalizes its past colonial interventions in Algeria and its response to Algeria's ongoing political instability, as well as France's continued interactions with Arab migrants. Adnan's descriptions of enthusiasm for a European identity—framed through obsessive international commentary on the weather, television, and sports—highlight the limits of the EU's connective frameworks. Her writing argues that the Union merely shifts the categories of who belongs where rather than radically redefining the notion of belonging itself, an act that would require attention to less material and more temporary affinities. As her text unpacks and critiques the frameworks of belonging that emerge with the rise of the EU, Adnan gestures to other modes of relation with place, past, and other people. These modes of relation, which are nonhierarchical and impermanent, illustrate what I term *affinity*.

As I'll demonstrate in close readings throughout the chapter, Adnan envisions citizenship and belonging as circles with clear demarcations of inclusion and exclusion. The EU expands those circles, but an expanded circle still has limits; it still has a center. By contrast, Adnan articulates affinitive, transcultural relations. Because of its branching, multidirectional, and nonhierarchical nature, affinity has no stable center. To be in relation, each entity must move and shift. Affinity is imperfect in its tenuousness. It leaves space for discordant connections and failures to relate. And yet, as Adnan anticipates the challenges that entities like the EU will face in addressing those who fall outside its frameworks of belonging, anticipation that has proven prescient with ongoing debates in the EU about how to accommodate migrant populations, affinity provides possibilities at the individual level for reorienting oneself toward others.

Affinitive relations, in their lateral and nonhierarchical nature, always push for destabilizing the frameworks of belonging and membership that organize political sensibilities. They also encourage an accounting for contradictions and dissonances. Affinity is not a mere alternative to belonging or citizenship. Instead, it challenges nationalist and global rhetorics of exclusionary belonging through recourse to complex and branching networks of relation. Literary articulations of affinity, in particular, depend on aesthetic and formal innovations that reconfigure texts' dependence on plot, characters, genre, and other literary categories. *Paris, When It's Naked* demonstrates a resistance to categorization that corresponds with its commitment to affinitive relations. The English of the text's publication exists in relationship to the French in which the narrator investigates the city and to an amorphous but significant relationship to Arabic. The narrator shares Adnan's trajectories and linguistic preferences, although the text never explicitly labels itself a memoir or autobiography. Instead, the text blurs the boundaries between memoir, travel narrative, prose poetry, and assemblage.[1] Its affinitive networks are also rooted in careful literary attention to physical experiences of place, which are always informed by each individual's experience of gender, race, ethnicity, sexuality, age, and ability; recourse to memory; and affective responses to texts, places, people, and objects.

Adnan asserts herself as a transcultural observer of France's Europeanization. She participates actively in the space she inhabits while still critiquing the identity politics she sees emerging. I argue that *Paris, When It's Naked* models a methodology of transcultural affinity in the wake of transformational global politics. Adnan's methodology challenges readers to hold multiple identities and geographies in place simultaneously. Reading the text in the twenty-first century presents a stark contrast to the EU's response to increased migration beginning in 2011 with Syrians fleeing civil war and skyrocketing arrivals in 2013–15. In its interactions with Syrian refugees and with Arab host countries, the EU has relied primarily on fixed and rigid definitions of belonging, while displaced populations are forced to hold together multiple histories and geographies. Adnan demonstrates, however, that including multiple affinities could become the default communal response to migrating and displaced peoples. Though she writes in the early 1990s, her assertions of transcultural affinities have direct implications for the way those in the late 2010s might read and understand the EU's current approach to accommodating refugees and migrants.

Transcultural Affinities

Adnan's tendency toward destabilizing frameworks of relation through transculturalism is apparent throughout her work. In an article on Adnan's most famous novel *Sitt Marie Rose*, Olivia C. Harrison (2009) outlines how the book, a Lebanese Civil War narrative, critiques the ossification of military, religious, and tribal factions while also refusing to form an easy alternative collective:

> The novel problematizes the very notion of resistance, and with it, the risk of creating filiative ties through acts of affiliation. How can one resist without deploying the language of opposition, struggle, and enmity that forms the conceptual arsenal of war? How can one form a collective "we" of resistance without creating an opposite "them"?
>
> (2)

In her reading, Harrison criticizes simplistic analyses of *Sitt Marie Rose* that see the text's protagonist rejecting her Christian Syrian-Lebanese family's collective in favor of a community built on her commitment to Palestinian refugees. Harrison counterargues that Adnan does not substitute communities. Instead, Adnan continues to question what the roles of "we" and "them" are, undermining the sense that Marie has simply replaced a "filiation" with "affiliation." Harrison uses Edward Said's (1983) distinction between "filiation" and "affiliation"; he defines filiation as "the closed and tightly knit family structure that secures generational hierarchical relationships to one another," while ties of affiliation allow "men and women [to] create social bonds between each other that would substitute for those ties that connect members of the same family across generations" (qtd. in Harrison, 1).

Certainly, Adnan's biography and publication history suggest multiple possible points of geographic, linguistic, and social affiliation. Born in Lebanon in 1925 to a Greek mother and Syrian Ottoman father, she studied in both France and the United States (http://www.eteladnan.com/). She returned to Lebanon in the 1970s and departed again for California at the beginning of the Lebanese Civil War. She divides her time between Paris and Sausalito, California, with her partner Simone Fattal, an artist and publisher whom Adnan met in Beirut in the early 1970s (Roffino and Tome 2014).[2] These elements of her biography identify Adnan as a transcultural writer, one who forms "multifaceted fluid identities resulting from diverse cultural encounters" (Nordin, Hansen and Llena 2013, ix).

Like its author, *Paris, When It's Naked* also identifies a range of potential affiliations. The text, a series of vignettes about a Lebanese émigré's daily life in Paris, was published in 1993 by Post-Apollo, a small press run by Fattal.[3] *Paris, When It's Naked* reflects the challenges of writing in English about a French setting while recollecting a past in Lebanon and following new global developments in the EU. While she speaks French and Arabic, Adnan describes herself as most comfortable writing in English, the first language in which she published poetry: "I don't have this sense of belonging [in French] that I have in English. By now there's a lifetime of history behind my writing in English" (Robertson 2014). A "sense of belonging" does not necessarily correspond to fixed belonging in a specific place, however. In *Of Cities and Women: Letters to Fawwaz*, also published in 1993, Adnan writes that "I feel that I haven't settled anywhere, really, that I'm rather living in the world, all over, in newspapers, in railway stations, cafes, airports …. The books that I'm writing are houses that I build for myself" (111). Although Adnan frames her decision to write in English as a personal one that does not minimize her relationships with other places, the decision and the text's publication in California define the text's audience as predominantly English speaking and American.

While Adnan's professional and personal trajectories chart a history of rejecting singular modes of filiation and could be read as an ongoing endeavor to produce multiple affiliations that, in Said's words, "substitute" for family ties, Harrison's reading of *Sitt Marie Rose* demonstrates that Adnan engages in significant poststructural work that undermines both filiation and affiliation as organizing principles. Adnan does not merely substitute one form of community for another; instead, she consistently questions and pressurizes the methods through which one might come to identify with a particular community. In *Paris, When It's Naked* particularly, Adnan intensifies this work by practicing affinity: an articulation of connection that is even more tenuous and affectively saturated than those explored in *Sitt Marie Rose*. Affiliation in Said's framing leads to "social bonds," albeit bonds outside traditional frameworks of family or clan. Affinity, on the other hand, results in no bonds but rather in temporary moments of adjacent activity and feeling. Affinity also reframes Harrison's discussion of social organizing to encompass relations among people, places, and even objects. Rather than suggesting the alternative community that should form in the wake of the EU's formation—a global community, for example, or a French-North African collective that assesses the aftereffects of colonialism—Adnan orients herself toward a methodology of affinity, seeking ways to describe how individuals come into relation with the places where they live, the texts they read, and the people they encounter.

Affinity reconfigures the means through which individuals relate, most notably the media and technology that circulate the weather and sports reports that Adnan's narrator watches:

> Information and propaganda have become so entangled that those who specialize in them acquire severe reality problems. The wheel keeps turning. People from the Third World are better at seeing through this fog; for them it's a matter of survival. Citizens from dominant countries fool themselves by thinking that they don't need to know: that's the beginning of their downfall. As for me, most of what I want to know is not "news," not really. I want to see a whale in the ocean and be told how one can travel to the middle of the Indian Ocean, exactly when, for how much, and how to be sure to be able to come near the animal, or swim alongside his body …. I would also want to find out the whereabouts of the young English solider I loved, in Beirut, during the Second World War. Newspapers are of no help in such cases. (Adnan 1993, 60)[4]

Identifying her methodology as a "Third World" approach to news that sees through propaganda, the narrator categorizes the information she's looking for as simultaneously personal, political, and rooted in the real. She focuses not on big speeches or landmark decisions—the "news"—but instead on the events and experiences that make one an historical subject. She experiences the Second World War, for example, by falling in love with a British soldier. That love is rooted in the history of global politics and conflict that brought the soldier to the narrator's home. The narrator's desire for information attests to history's unknowable and uncontrollable nature. Readers do not know why the soldier left Beirut any more than she now knows whether he is alive or dead, living in rural England or propagating neocolonial business practices globally. The narrator does not presume to control or defeat history, only to exist alongside it, a methodology that distances her from the nations hoping to preempt a third world war with the EU. Finally, the narrator looks for information that, however surreal sounding, is real with details that can be experienced and confirmed. Her envisioning of the specific geography and physicality that would allow one to see a whale seems far removed from the illusions of safety and fear produced by larger political bodies. Affinity in this context is not ephemeral because of its abstract qualities but rather because of the temporary and highly specific nature of each relation. Swimming alongside a whale is not a permanent activity, nor is it one that will reveal every aspect of the whale. Instead, the state of being alongside is one of practicing an affinity that will not last but that will transform both parties.

Adnan's narrator reacts against the "severe reality problems" that Western news generates by focusing on reality's tangible, personal, and yet temporary elements. Her approach becomes an alternative epistemology, one that "see[s] through the fog." In Paris, this epistemology requires her to recognize that she can never completely control her thinking or walking in such a dynamic space:

> Paris is so huge, so full of people, that my thoughts get entangled in its electric wires and never reach their destination. Its tall buildings, aligned with no space between them save the streets, create an invincible screen to our feelings and dreams. You cannot fly in this city, you have to negotiate every move with it. That's not always as despairing as it sounds.
>
> (60)

Adnan's descriptions of moving through and thinking in Paris deprioritize destination and focus on the processes of moving and thinking themselves. Her language suggests constant obstacles, claustrophobic encounters, and the weighty exhaustion of navigating crowded space and thinking thoughts filtered by the city. By concluding the section with "that's not always as despairing as it sounds," though, Adnan encourages readers to think of the exhaustive work outlined above as the essential action of affinity—a constant entanglement and subsequent reassessment of one's relationship to space and other people. Her proposal stands in stark contrast to the EU, which would prefer to "fly" unburdened by offering citizens unfettered movement among member nations. There is no Schengen Zone within the streets of Paris for Adnan's narrator. Instead, she has to reform her thoughts based on the wires they encounter.

The continual reassessment of one's place exponentially proliferates the ways in which one might experience momentary relation. One complex example of affinity ties together geographic, literary, linguistic, and affective components. On the Metro, the narrator ponders other riders: "There are many young women among the passengers, some of them having never read *Le Spleen de Paris*. Of course, Baudelaire loved London" (1). In one brief observation, the narrator offers multiple types of affinity. Location and participation form one category; the women reside in Paris and are at ease with the Metro. At the same time, they do not have access to one of the narrator's most significant Parisian affinities. *Le Spleen de Paris* is our Lebanese-born narrator's quintessential Parisian text, so much so that she enacts it herself during long observational walks through city; the text is one of the ways that she and Paris come into relation with each other. The younger women, however, have found a way to connect to Paris that does not involve that affinity. The narrator complicates things still further by acknowledging that Baudelaire, her model Parisian poet, "loved London." Even the texts and authors considered rooted in and necessary to a particular place form attachments elsewhere. The narrator infers that Baudelaire's love of London gives the young women on the train permission to engage Paris through different affinities. Rather than using Baudelaire to distinguish "true" Parisians from others, she recognizes the dangerous gesture toward a "national" poet. Her choice to observe the young women on the train is also significant; as a female navigator of urban space herself, she notes the ways in which women are often subject to different rules about belonging. In her early references to Baudelaire and her protagonist's walking of Paris, Adnan evokes the *flâneuse*, a female observational walker whose historical and cultural significance is hotly contested (Wolff 1985; Parsons 2000). In *Of Cities and Women: Letters to Fawwaz*, Adnan herself notes that city space is often positioned as masculine: "The idea of Nature in Western or Arabic thought has been tied to that of the feminine .... The opposition city/nature was similar to the opposition man/woman" (16–17). To walk as a woman means constantly negotiating one's relationship to space, a negotiation that results in continued opportunities for affinity.

The narrator's affinitive relations inform her experience of both Paris and the Middle East. She imagines herself pulled back toward the region where she was born through an uncanny sense of pain that extends beyond empathy. At first, her worries seem connected to her former home in Lebanon. She recalls from previous years that when "Tell Zataar was under siege .... I was unable to sleep," a concern that could easily develop from worries about the safety of family and friends or about home (63).[5] However, her feeling of being involved in troubling, faraway situations goes beyond news items and her family history to immediate and visceral experiences of events elsewhere: "A sandstorm in the Sahara throws its grains into my eyes. A political prisoner in Syria begs for my attention" (43). These descriptions emphasize the slippage between the narrator and Adnan herself, and between news and literature. Though the narrator, who shares many of Adnan's affinities but remains stubbornly unidentified, could hear about these issues through traditional news media, her description enforces their immediacy, their intimacy, and their very physical impact. While news sources might report on Tell Zataar or the situation of political prisoners in Syria, this narrator emphasizes micro-connections that make the events temporarily audible and palpable, even to someone living in Paris.

While the creative and imaginative affinities between the narrator and faraway people and places could be the effect of her own background in the Middle East, Adnan demonstrates that anyone can train herself to become aware of multiple affinities. In particular, the narrator encourages Parisians to recognize that their view of the city is mediated: "You can see Paris with French eyes, fear the influx of the poor from all the continents, see a whole social equilibrium be disrupted. You can also see the immigrant as a human being who happens to be here, now" (42). She suggests that viewers have a choice in the way they perceive space and the people who surround them. Adnan establishes that affinity is not produced by residency in a particular space or by moving from one location to another. Instead, it is about the approach to those spaces, the way someone might allow oneself to fall in love, to be enchanted, while also remaining critical. Her claims speak to the present moment, reminding an EU now contending with migration concerns that each nation and citizen in the Union can be understood and accepted as an entity with multiple, often contradictory, affinities.

For Adnan, embracing affinity requires holding oneself open to multiple locations and multiple feelings, a balance the narrator practices while navigating Paris on foot. She sees herself as "walking simultaneously on many tracks: standing on Aleppo's Citadel, I'm also standing by this red light, getting wet, and I'm walking the streets of Beirut where a snow storm is raging" (98).[6] The narrator envisions herself in multiple spaces so powerfully that she can be attentive to the panoramic view in one space and the weather in another. Because of the wetness she feels from the Parisian rain, her body roots her in space even as she extends her sensibilities elsewhere. Affectively, the speaker also recalibrates her feelings about Paris, a constant process that forces her to exist in the discomfort of knowing that some affinities contradict each other:

> Paris is beautiful. But in that word beautiful there are centuries of lives, of wars, of work, of faith, of deaths ... it's harder for me to say so, it's also more poignant. It tears me apart. Paris is the heart of lingering colonial power, and that knowledge goes to bed with me every night. When I walk in this city I plunge into an abyss, I lose myself in contemplation, I experience ecstasy, and an ecstasy which I know to be also a defeat.
>
> (7)

The speaker points to a destruction of the self, a sense of the overwhelming pain, loss, exhaustion, and exertion that her movement through Paris demands. She does not propose the contradiction between her love for Paris' beauty and her knowledge of its violence as a solvable problem. Every day, every night, and every walk requires a new commitment and willingness to open oneself up to painful histories. Affinitive relations are only possible in this attention to often painful dissonance.

Affinity and Geopolitical Order

Adnan's most significant contribution to transculturalism comes through her careful descriptions of the complex and often ambivalent feelings that arise for someone affiliated with multiple cultural backgrounds. Nordin, Hansen, and Llena (2013, xiii) describe how "in the current transnational, globalized context, migrants do not necessarily sever their ties to their home country, but rather maintain them along with a sense of allegiance to their place and community of origins, while incorporating new allegiances to the receiving society and culture into their sense of identity." While the description emphasizes the challenges of multiple allegiances, it sanitizes the guilt and pain—and also the intense love—that accompany the allegiances' development. *Paris, When It's Naked* is unabashed in its love for French culture and the Parisian streets. It is also unrelenting in its criticism that that culture emerges through and because of colonial histories that oppressed Adnan's fellow Arabs; she calls Paris "an imperial capital" and describes the French as people "who can break houses with impunity" (9, 10). Transculturalism highlights Adnan's commitment to multiple cultural interstices without erasing their challenges. *Paris, When It's Naked*'s narrator is transcultural both through her multiple geographic affiliations and through her ambivalent relationship to Paris—she loves the city while remaining critical of its history and politics.

By modeling amorphous, temporary, and constantly shifting affinities, Adnan pushes against the fixed forms of knowledge, citizenship, and cultural affiliation governing the borders of the EU. Adnan's understanding of affinity is related to the ability to see suffering and the painful aftereffects of history. Affective experience is important to affinity because, the narrator explains, "feelings are antennae, and they open up spaces there in front, not unlike snowmobiles in snowed-in territories" (11). If the EU establishes affiliations that are fixed and immobile, Adnan's speaker depicts herself as a trailblazer. She promotes an affinitive methodology that would allow the contemporary EU to recognize the suffering and physical presence of refugees seeking asylum today. Without recourse to the affective and fluid affinities Adnan illustrates, for example, the EU of the 2010s is unable to ward off the threats presented by reactionary nationalisms responding to increased migration.

While the narrator of *Paris, When It's Naked* obliquely references multiple geopolitical developments, including contemporaneous violence in Algeria, the aftereffects of civil war in Lebanon, and the recent collapse of the Soviet Union, the formation of the EU primarily draws her attention. The text responds specifically to the Treaty on European Union, which was signed in the Netherlands on February 7, 1992.[7] The treaty established the EU's modern incarnation, following previous forms beginning with the European Coal and Steel Community in 1951.[8] The treaty's language is notable not only in its call for economic unity—its primary goal—but also in its aims to foster European identity. Although the treaty leads to the Euro's development, as it proposes a common form of currency, it drops "economic" from the European Economic Community, focusing instead on a "European Community" at large, a union bound by more than just a shared financial future. The introductory resolutions (EU 1992, 3) frame participating countries as "desiring to deepen the solidarity between their peoples while respecting their history, their culture and their traditions." The resolution leads to the establishment of Union citizenship in Article 8, which states that "every person holding the nationality of a Member State shall be a citizen of the Union" (15). The treaty indicates European identity's importance to the Union, although it also claims that European identity supplements rather than replaces national identity. It scaffolds what is already in existence and grants additional rights and privileges of citizenship—including, most notably, the ability to move freely through the Union's now extended borders—to those who already have those rights in their home countries.

Adnan observes the way that the EU's formation extends citizenship without redefining it. As a predominantly economic body that gestures toward cultural affiliation, it retains citizenship as the community's foundation at the expense of other forms of relation. Extending citizenship makes claims about who belongs in the EU's borders and formalizes the communal relations between various places and groups. As the EU develops, for example, the narrator muses on the way that individual nations' currency, politics, sporting events, and even weather reports will merge. Through an obsessive focus on the television, Adnan describes weather reports and Olympics coverage, noting that "European unity is a panacea, and the average Frenchman wants to know how high the snow is in Russia" (1). Both increased media capabilities and European unity make even the smallest detail about life in another country significant. Identifying the EU as a "panacea," a curer of all ills, the narrator has no need to identify which specific ills the EU might cure. She suggests, however, that attention on weather elsewhere leads France to forget its own. While the French watch reports on Russian and German weather, Paris experiences rain, and the narrator imagines that "Europe brings out its umbrellas" (1). In the attention to weather events, the narrator suggests that the Union binds participants into caring about Europe's weather patterns, a focus that even extends to nonmember countries like Russia. Of course, weather is about as local a phenomenon as possible—the snow in Russia cannot directly impact the French, nor do Russians require umbrellas to fend off French rain.

By imagining the umbrellas of Europe emerging, then, Adnan's narrator performs two seemingly contradictory acts. In the first, Adnan's overemphasis on weather illustrates the limits of unity by stretching solidarity to its logical conclusion; there's ridiculousness embedded in the notion that a Russian would open an umbrella simply because of rain more than 1700 miles away. And yet, at the same time, weather for Adnan suggests a micro-political approach to the EU that contests the economic and social categories the Union incentivizes. Unlike the development of the Euro, the experience of weather here is intimate and physical. The emergence of umbrellas across the continent suggests a possible embodied affinity engendered by the EU and yet resisting the Union's dominant organizing categories.

As Adnan attempts to destabilize the organizing principles of the EU, she retains an awareness of how the body threatens the way noncitizens can develop and assert affinity with a range of places and people. Just as the EU layers European citizenship and identity over that of citizens already affiliated with EU nations, migration can also demand a layering and subsequent erasure of national identity. For example, in Germany, the European nation that received the most asylum applications in 2015, government agencies in conjunction with cultural and communication companies developed a mobile app called Ankommen for migrants needing access to information about German language, employment, and culture. *Quartz Daily* notes that "developers added information on, for example, freedom of religion in Germany, while an article on gender equality was added after a mass assault against women in Cologne" (Wong 2016). Not simply a virtual welcome wagon, the app reflects German anxieties about incoming populations as threats who will not understand concepts like religious freedom or equal rights. Ankommen equates assimilation and erasure of cultural difference with increased safety.

Though such technology was not available in the early 1990s, the emergence of the EU instigated increased limits on displaced populations' access to both their cultures of origin and the cultures they encounter in diaspora. In research on contemporary Arabic literature about Europe, Johanna Sellman (2013) argues that the EU's rise and extension of citizenship constrained migrants' and refugees' abilities to be in relation with multiple places and histories:

> European migration policies have gradually displaced the rights framework that is central to the Geneva Refugee Convention .... The post-Cold War migrant becomes a category to be managed, restricted, re-directed, and contained, according to an economic logic.
>
> (48)

Unlike the Geneva Convention's parameters, which asserted the rights of migrant and refugee populations, Europe in the EU era reified citizenship in such a way as to close off additional avenues of relation. Rather than allowing migrants to enter and transform the community, the policies of the EU prioritize containment.

Writing in 1993, Adnan is attuned to these shifts and uses the changes in citizenship and national identity to anticipate changes for noncitizen populations in EU communities expressing affinity with other places and pasts. For her, the EU's formation takes on apocalyptic undertones, arriving as it does just before the new millennia. Asking "How can we get ready for a century? It's not a party after all," the narrator suggests that the EU emerges in part to counteract the anxieties generated by Y2K and to account for shifting continental politics during the Soviet Union's dissolution (11). She begins to think of the EU as an anticipatory body and points to the contradictions in its goals: "European unity is being made to avoid that third World War. Of course, one never knows, it may very well bring about what it was meant to avoid" (12). Eerily adopting the language of prophetic and self-fulfilling destiny, Adnan describes the EU as an initiative intended to ensure safety and stability but that may enact its own destruction and threats. Both the EU's goals and its challenges are rooted in questions about belonging, namely, What threats can be defused through inclusion? In her anticipatory language, Adnan indicates that extending belonging to defuse some threats necessarily excludes affinitive relations with others—other people, other cultures, and other historical interactions.

Paris, When It's Naked demonstrates how the Union not only excludes but makes invisible people both within the borders of particular countries and in specific countries themselves. It also describes how Union membership minimizes the significance of other historical narratives and affinities. In a passing line, the narrator mentions the diversity of theater appearing in Paris: "Most of the plays are in foreign languages, European of course" (22). The presence of French, Italian, German, and Spanish gives the theater scene an aura of multiculturalism. It's a given, however, that these languages will be part of a European exchange; linguistic and cultural traditions of the Arab world, Asia, Africa, and the Americas go unrecognized and unrepresented. It's through these cultural, political, and even gastronomical developments that some countries—and the people who hail from them—begin "dropping out of History" (34). With the EU's arrival, France has an opportunity to reconfigure its globality, nominally distancing itself from its ongoing relationship with former colonies in favor of an internationalism that prioritizes the cosmopolitan and the illusion of mutual exchange and diversity.

Adnan's assessment of exclusion reads as a warning for the twenty-first century when the EU's structure makes it difficult for Syrians and other displaced populations to seek refuge in the region. She is also prescient in her awareness that official responses to expanding belonging will eventually become reactionary and nationalistic in tone. Adnan predicts that both expanding and contracting definitions of identity and citizenship will only provide an illusory sense of stability and security. If citizenship is extended rather than rearticulated as affinity, she suggests, nationalist groups will choose to reestablish firm boundaries and to withdraw from the Union's open borders, as has proven true with the 2016 Brexit vote in the United Kingdom, the reconfiguring of Schengen Zone border policies in the summer of 2015, and the ongoing rise of populist parties in France, Austria, and the Netherlands, among others.

Anticipating Union and Exclusion

Adnan's efforts to predict the EU's future stem from a desire to explore which cultural, geographical, and economic elements now link its citizens and how those elements reinforce the noncitizens' exclusion. Because of her own multifaceted position, Adnan is less interested in critiquing the EU than in assessing what types of relations it offers and precludes. Her analysis of the EU gives rise to an anticipatory, borderline prophetic project that connects in style if not content to conversations about migration and resettlement in the 2010s.[9]

The narrator of *Paris, When It's Naked* refuses to participate in the expanding and contracting narratives of citizenship espoused by EU policies, preferring instead to explore ever-branching communal and personal affinities. She traces her own ambivalent connections to her current hometown of Paris by envisioning herself as connected to a global history of suffering and holding France accountable for lingering colonial liabilities, while also describing in loving detail her ability to walk through Parisian streets. Adnan examines the past in order to articulate the affinitive relations that might be possible in the future. By doing so, she participates in a literature of futurity. The term

> marks the potential of literature to widen the language and to expand the pool of idioms we employ in making sense of what has occurred while imagining whom we may become ... futurity is tied to questions of liability and responsibility, to attentiveness to one's own lingering pains and to the sorrows and agonies of others. Futurity marks literature's ability to raise, via engagement with the past, political, and ethical dilemmas crucial for the human future.
>
> (Eshel 2013, 5)

Amir Eshel, who coined the term, describes "futurity" as introspective historical narration rather than futurism or science fiction. He describes contemporary German and Israeli writers developing new vocabularies and narrative structures not to better understand their histories but rather to expand the ways communities can and should discuss those histories in the future. Even a backward-looking text can be oriented toward the future.

Unlike the German writers in Amir Eshel's study, who write about the Second World War and the Third Reich at a remove of several decades, Adnan writes through her contemporary moment—the book was published just a few months after the EU's official formation—so her futurity reads like prophecy. She demonstrates, along with her fellow "Europeans," an anxiety about the future of the region and international politics. At the same time, Adnan's work falls under Eshel's definition because it aims to re-write the vocabularies already in place for discussing belonging. While the EU appears to promise the potential for new forms of belonging, the narrator suggests that a vocabulary other than that of belonging is needed. She explains that "I'm witnessing, and so are the cleaning lady and the Prime Minister of France, a nation-state's agony, and the merging of all national rivers into the European Ocean" (92–3). Initially, "witnessing" history might appear to erase the divides between the three individuals, people in France with different financial, political, and social statuses. They share not just the geography of France but the experience of being historical participants, people currently watching history unfold together. The shared experience, though, is illusory; because of political power, the prime minister will always experience unification differently than Adnan or a cleaning woman. Even the title "prime minister" suggests an importance to the project that the cleaning lady cannot access. It would be a mistake, though, to suggest that Adnan uses this example merely to critique the EU. Instead, recourse to affinity allows her to emphasize the tenuous relationship that does exist among the three witnesses. They are not together, but they are beside each other—not a collective but individuals in relation.

Affinity's willingness to see social divides and attempts at relation as co-extant problematizes the dichotomy of inclusion and exclusion on which notions of belonging rely, a dichotomy Adnan's narrator identifies particularly in the dilemma facing national or international projects incorporating migrant workers: "A lot of immigrants work in factories and create a major problem: how to make them work without having them breathe our air, live in our cities, or look at our wives and husbands?" (59). The national or international body looks for outsiders who will contribute labor without taking up space, who will inhabit the collective invisibly. While the cleaning woman in the previous example does not become equal with the prime minister through affinitive relation, affinity emphasizes her presence. Unlike those who seek to make migrants work without "breath[ing] our air," the narrator uses articulations of affinity to make those who perform labor visible, even in a framework that would erase them.

Adnan also highlights the history of French colonialism, occupation, and brutality in North Africa, the location from which many of the laborers she observes migrate. Adnan notes France's uncomfortable relationship to its Algerian involvement in particular even before the Union. "This Algerian turmoil," she writes, "made of France a nation with two faces" (10). She describes the history "haunt[ing] France … like veiled women," forcing it to confront the violence and control inflicted on the country's inhabitants. France had global economic and political ties prior to the EU. By becoming European, though, France can minimize its colonial identity. Rather than branching out to colonial outposts, it now branches to other European nations.

While France continues to align itself with Europe, Adnan bears witness to the ongoing resonances of the colonial period in Algeria and the brewing civil war in the country.[10] Watching what she calls "news from the Empire," the narrator receives updates about President Chadli Bendjedid's decision to resign:

> [He made] room for a military takeover against the Islamic parties which won handily their recent elections, because that's also Paris' wish. How can such a huge difference between cultures be tolerated by a dominant power? ... French women can bear to know that women in Algeria are starving, but they can't stand the knowledge that these Algerian women say their prayers at home while their French counterparts go to mass .... So in the night, sitting close to my T.V. set, I see tragedy getting ready to unfold. It's too late for phoning anybody, and what can anybody tell me which is not already told?
>
> (8–9)

The speaker draws a direct connection between France's colonial presence in Algeria and its current pressuring of the military to push back against popularly elected Islamic parties. She emphasizes the anticipatory nature of her text with the language of unfolding "tragedy" and things "already told," and the hypocrisy of French women whose feminist sensibilities collaborate with neoliberal rationales to perpetuate war and conflict abroad. The moment echoes Charles Hirschkind and Saba Mahmood's (2002, 341, 345) analysis of American women participating in the Feminist Majority Movement to "rescue" Afghan women from the Taliban in the early 2000s:

> In the crusade to liberate Afghan women from the tyranny of Taliban rule, there seemed to be no limit of the violence to which Americans were willing to subject the Afghans, women and men alike .... Why were conditions of war, militarization, and starvation considered to be less injurious to women than the lack of education, employment, and, most notably, in the media campaign, Western dress styles?

In both Adnan's description of French women responding to Algerian women's "oppression" and Hirschkind and Mahmood's assessment of the Feminist Majority, campaigns that masquerade as concerns about women's rights in fact reinforce the boundaries between a here and a there, an us and a them, often dictated by religious differences. These then justify continued violence and marginalization.

By contrast, Adnan's development of affinitive relations closes some of the distance between people. Because affinity is nonhierarchical and mutual (objects or people experience affinity for one another), affinity cannot be enacted by one party onto another party (as opposed to the "liberating" that Americans provided Afghan women). While the narrator experiences contradiction related to both her geographical location in Paris and her sense of solidarity with Algerians, she advocates for an ongoing practice of affinity. She proclaims herself connected to Algeria because "I got up one morning out of a long sleep, and found myself lying next to them, engulfed by their proximity" (10). The experience of being "engulfed by proximity," Adnan argues, is foundational for practicing transcultural affinity. By getting close to the television, by sitting in the moment of hypocrisy and tragedy,

Adnan's narrator practices the work of sitting alongside that identifies the other as inhabiting the same space and having the same agency as oneself. Her concerns and efforts here anticipate continued challenges of relating across the boundaries of the EU, challenges that were thrown into relief in the early 2010s with increasing arrivals from the Middle East and North Africa.

Implications for Current Approaches to Migration

The EU can only remain unburdened insofar as its definitions of belonging, hospitality, inclusion, and affiliation are not challenged—challenges contemporary readers have witnessed in spades in recent years as refugees seeking asylum in the EU have prompted member nations to reevaluate the Schengen Zone borders (Rankin 2016). The Union's attempts to appease its members by solidifying the zone's external border demonstrate how Middle Eastern countries continue to "drop out of the history" that the EU writes. Adnan demonstrates that expanding belonging in the EU context—even from the moment of its conception—would not be capable of encompassing a massive influx of refugees. From her perspective as an outsider—albeit a privileged one—the EU is still set up to deal with refugee crises as a nation would. Its borders extend without becoming more malleable and creative. Adnan's early observations note the hairline fractures in the system that crack once a group of newcomers challenges its inclusivity and unification.

Reading *Paris, When It's Naked* from a twenty-five-year remove—in a moment marked by unprecedented numbers of migrants and displaced persons seeking refuge globally—is in itself an exercise in futurity. Contemporary readers are encouraged to consider what a text about a privileged migrant navigating the EU's formation as an outsider but lover of Paris has to teach us about how we approach migration and belonging today. In October of 2016, for example, UK prime minister Theresa May delivered closing remarks at her Conservative Party's annual conference. In those remarks, she criticized the notion of global citizenship, presumably linking it to the EU's current refugee policies and prioritizing a return to a localized politics:

> Today, too many people in positions of power behave as though they have more in common with international elites than with the people down the road, the people they employ, the people they pass on the street. But if you believe you're a citizen of the world, you're a citizen of nowhere. You don't understand what the very word citizenship means.
>
> (qtd. in Bullen 2016)

May's comments reflect the logic that led to the United Kingdom's decision to leave the EU. She showcases the country's anxieties that the poor and rural in the country are being ignored in favor of both connections abroad and attention to international refugee populations. May argues that the EU's version of a global citizenship—which it has attempted but failed to extend in the wake of increased migration from the Middle East and North Africa—evacuates citizenship of its meaning. She sees the term as having been stretched too far and offers an ultimatum for reclaiming it: either reaffirm the citizenship of your nation or give up the benefits of citizenship altogether.

As May's rhetoric echoes through discussions about the EU's continued existence, *Paris, When It's Naked* reminds readers that citizenship need not be an either-or proposition, especially when it encounters the displaced and asylum seekers among us. In fact, the text is adamant that the "people [we] pass on the street" are often migrants themselves; many of the people May worries about ignoring are in fact migrant workers from the Middle East, North Africa, and Southeast Asia.

Anti-global rhetoric targets populations that have been forced into nomadic, global modes of belonging. Adnan's narrator is a more affluent and privileged example than most of the Syrians seeking refuge from the country's civil war, but she too has fled a war-torn country and looks to belong to spaces through a framework other than national or even international citizenship. In contrast to May, though, who sees the "citizen of the world" ignoring the people in her backyard, the narrator's globality is precisely what allows her to be a more committed resident of Paris—she can see into the dark spaces of the national history with open eyes. She becomes a "stranger more French than the French" not by rejecting her stranger-ness but by exploring what her distance allows her to see and understand (99). Because *Paris, When It's Naked* looks to articulate affinity rather than extending citizenship as the EU has done, it does not fall victim to May's slippery slope—citizenship here cannot be stretched until it has no meaning because affinity's meaning is constantly shifting and adapting so that participants hold themselves accountable to multiple people, places, and histories.

The reactionary politics emerging in the contemporary moment come from the sense that belonging can be either expanded or retracted—we either open our borders or build a wall, remain in the EU or leave it, gaze outward dreamily or tend to our own gardens. In those binary scenarios, leaders like Theresa May, Donald Trump, and Marine Le Pen choose the most exclusionary form of that decision. By contrast, and even after more than two decades of circulation, *Paris, When It's Naked* proposes an imaginatively oriented affinitive methodology. Writing like Adnan's prompts readers to see the links between narratives that borders attempt to separate, thereby realizing that Europeans, Americans, and other would-be hosts are already implicated in the forces that have displaced contemporary refugees and migrants. The text invites readers to imagine what could have happened if the Union had more willingly contended with members' colonial histories or reflected on the communities it would exclude from its formation. Would the Union now have systems in place to host refugees more effectively? There is no way to know for sure, but current political developments suggest that the EU has witnessed the rise of nationalist and exclusionary policies it sought to prevent.

Writing about the enormous challenges currently facing the EU, Giles Merritt (2016, xiii) argues that "we must acknowledge the profound structural handicaps that have developed—some through our own neglect, others through ineluctable global changes." Adnan's futurity contributes a literary, imaginative component to analyses like Merritt's, suggesting that often the sheer act of imagining possible alternative outcomes is a form of political activism and transformation. And while the text invites alternative imaginings, it itself does not seek a clear alternative to national belonging so much as it undermines current structures' fixity. Her engagement with affinity allows her to articulate branching, sideways, and nonhierarchical relations even in the midst of her current geopolitical climate. The narrator's experiences open up a broader range of ways in which people, places, and objects might encounter each other in urban, national, or even international spaces. Creative explorations of the past remind us that history was not always destined for the outcomes we now witness. Continued imaginative acts also expand our ability to talk about and interact with the designated "Other" populations, whether they migrate or are displaced. By envisioning shared and constantly changing histories more clearly, we begin to imagine the possibilities tied to a different sort of future.

Notes

1. In its catalogue, Post-Apollo terms *Paris, When It's Naked* a work of poetry.
2. Though the couple does not collaborate directly, Adnan notes in a joint interview that "you can't really know your influences, but you can't live with a person 40 years and have no give and take" (Roffino and Tome 2014). In the same interview, Adnan and Fattal reflect on their own continually fluctuating relationships to feminism and gender identity.
3. For more on the Post-Apollo Press' development and its role in Etel Adnan's work, see Fattal's interview with Karl Roesler (2000).
4. Because I will be quoting from *Paris, When It's Naked* frequently, future in-text citations will feature only the page number.
5. The siege and massacre at Tal el-Zaatar took place in the summer of 1976. According to the Civil Society Knowledge Centre (2019), Christian militias killed somewhere between 1,000 and 1,500 Palestinians on the day Tal el-Zaatar fell. An additional 11,000 to 15,000 were evacuated from the camp.
6. It is here that Adnan's prescience fails, although the contemporary reader feels the weight of the present; the views of Aleppo that Adnan envisions are now no longer possible. The Aleppo Project traces the war's effect on the city, noting that "all six sites classified as World Heritage Sites by UNESCO have been damaged badly or completely destroyed" (Strickland 2016). The staggering statistics still pale in comparison to the loss of life and suffering as sieges and bombardments of the city continue without reliable evacuation.
7. The Treaty on European Union—or the Maastricht Treaty—was signed by representatives from Belgium, Denmark, Germany, Greece, Spain, France, Ireland, Italy, Luxembourg, the Netherlands, Portugal, and the United Kingdom (Council of the European Communities 1992).
8. The ECSC had six members: Belgium, West Germany, Luxembourg, France, Italy, and the Netherlands. Later incarnations of the union included the European Economic Community and the European Atomic Energy Community ("A Brief History of the EU" 2010).
9. Though I focus in this chapter on Adnan's anticipatory work, she is by no means the only author to engage in prophetic analysis of Europe. Milan Kundera (1984) writes that "all of this century's great Central European works of art, even up to our own day, can be understood as long meditations on the possible end of European

humanity … a world without memory, of a world that comes after historic time." Before the formation of the EU, he suggests that Central European nations are most representative of the "vulnerability" that will come to define European states, and he wonders "what realm of supreme values will be capable of uniting Europe."

10   *Paris, When It's Naked* was written toward the beginning of the Algerian Civil War (1991–2002). For more on women's literature that engages that war and its aftermath directly, see Daoudi (2016), Flood (2017), and Mehta (2014).

References

"About" on Etel Adnan's official website, accessed November 22, 2016. http://www.eteladnan.com.

Adnan, Etel. 1993a. *Of Cities and Women: Letters to Fawwaz*. Sausalito: Post-Apollo Press.

Adnan, Etel. 1993b. *Paris, When It's Naked*. Sausalito: Post-Apollo Press.

"A Brief History of the EU." 2010. National Public Radio. July 8. http://www.npr.org/templates/story/story.php?storyId=128389419

Bullen, Jamie. 2016. "Theresa May's Speech Sparks Twitter Backlash over 'Citizen of the World' Remark." *The Evening Standard*. October 5. http://www.standard.co.uk/news/politics/theresa-may-sparks-twitter-backlash-over-citizen-of-the-world-remark-in-conservative-party-a3361701.html

Civil Society Knowledge Centre. 2019. "Conflict Incident Report: Fall of Tal el-Zaatar and Jisr el-Basha." https://civilsociety-centre.org/sir/fall-tal-el-zaatar-and-jisr-el-basha.

The Council of the European Communities and the Commission of the European Communities. 1992. "Treaty on European Union." February 7. https://europa.eu/european-union/sites/europaeu/files/docs/body/treaty_on_european_union_en.pdf.

Daoudi, Anissa. 2016. "Algerian Women and the Traumatic Decade: Literary Interventions." *Journal of Literature and Trauma Studies* (5) 1: 41–60.

Eshel, Amir. 2013. *Futurity: Contemporary Literature and the Quest for the Past*. Chicago: University of Chicago Press.

Flood, Maria. 2017. "Resisting Terror: Imaginaries of Violence in Algeria." *Journal of North African Studies* (22) 1: 109–31.

Harrison, Olivia C. 2009. "Resistances of Literature: Strategies of Narrative Affiliation in Etel Adnan's Sitt Marie Rose." *Postcolonial Text* (5) 1: 1–15.

Hirschkind, Charles, and Saba Mahmood. 2002. "Feminism, the Taliban, and the Politics of Counter-Insurgency." *Anthropological Quarterly* (75) 2: 339–54.

Kundera, Milan. 1984. "The Tragedy of Central Europe." Trans. Edmund White. *New York Review of Books*. April 26. http://www.bisla.sk/english/wpcontent/uploads/2014/03/Kundera_tragedy_of_Central_Europe.pdf

Mehta, Brinda. 2014. "Commemorating the 'Disappeared': Maternal Activism and the Algerian Civil War in Fatima Bourega-Gallaire's La Beauté de l'icône." *Research in African Literatures* (45) 2: 26–45.

Merritt, Giles. 2016. *Slippery Slope: Europe's Troubled Future*. Oxford: Oxford University Press.

Nordin, Irene Gilsenan, Julie Hansen, and Carmen Zamorano Llena, eds. 2013. *Transcultural Identities in Contemporary Literature*. New York: Rodopi.

Parsons, Deborah L. 2000. *Streetwalking the Metropolis: Women, the City and Modernity*. New York: Oxford University Press.

Rankin, Jennifer. 2016. "EU's Schengen Members Urged to Lift Border Checks to Save Passport-free Zones." *The Guardian*, March 2. https://www.theguardian.com/world/2016/mar/02/eus-schengen-members-urged-to-lift-border-checks-to-save-passport-free-zone

Robertson, Lisa. 2014. "Etel Adnan." *BOMB—Artists in Conversation*, accessed May 15, 2016. http://bombmagazine.org/article/10024/etel-adnan

Roesler, Karl. 2000. "Counting the New Age: An Interview with Simone Fattal of the Post-Apollo Press." The Post-Apollo Press, accessed November 22, 2016. http://www.postapollopress.com/about.

Roffino, Sara, and Anna Tome. 2014. "In Conversation with Etel Adnan and Simone Fattal." *The Brooklyn Rail*, September 4. http://brooklynrail.org/2014/09/art/eteladnan-simonefattal-with-sararoffino-annatome

Said, Edward. 1983. "Secular Criticism." *The World, the Text, and the Critic*. Cambridge: Harvard University Press, 1–30.

Sellman, Johanna. 2013. "The Biopolitics of Belonging: Europe in Post-Cold War Arabic Literature of Migration." PhD diss., University of Texas at Austin.

Strickland, Patrick. 2016. "Rebuilding Syria's Aleppo under Fire." *Al Jazeera Interactive*. http://interactive.aljazeera.com/aje/2016/rebuilding-syrias-aleppo/index.html

Wolff, Janet. 1985. "The Invisible Flâneuse: Women and the Literature of Modernity." *Theory, Culture & Society* (2) 3: 37–46.

Wong, Joon Ian. 2016. "There's an App for That: Germany Made an App to Help Refugees Integrate." *Quartz Daily*, January 14. http://qz.com/594570/germany-made-an-app-to-help-refugees-integrate/

4

The Fractured Music of Arab-Jewish Friendship in Waguih Ghali's *Beer in the Snooker Club* and Ismaël Ferroukhi's *Free Men*

Caroline Rooney

Don't forget, Cairo and Palestine were full of Jews. (Said 1999)

In this chapter, I wish to consider how Waguih Ghali's novel *Beer in the Snooker Club* and Ismaël Ferroukhi's film *Free Men* present us with the possibilities of imagining a common ground in excess of both nationalism and cosmopolitanism (often posited as each other's Other).[1] In particular, these two works engage with the vicissitudes of Arab-Jewish friendship in such a way as to contest identity politics (conservative or liberal) through configurations of ethics, creativity, spirituality, and utopianism that are affirmative of shared lives. Furthermore, the language appropriate to the displacement of what may be termed "a logic of the family"—as a way of defining identity politics—could be posited as a nonliteral one that can be explored in terms of musical analogies. In order to substantiate these assertions, I will offer a reading of *Beer in the Snooker Club* followed by a reading of *Free Men*, concluding with a reflection on the interrelated implications of these works.

Before embarking on a closer examination of the works in question, I wish to signal further their relevance to the question of contemporary transcultural concerns. While *Beer in the Snooker Club* and *Free Men* are historically distant from each other, as will be explored, they are yet very similar in their cultural and sociopolitical preoccupations where they respectively juxtapose different forms of togetherness that may be found at any one moment in history in order to explore their respective dynamics in relation to each other. As I have begun to indicate, these forms of togetherness may be designated in terms of nationalism, cosmopolitanism, and transcultural solidarities of a revolutionary or utopian cast (the latter as Other to the polarities constituted by the first two). In both works, it is Arab-Jewish friendship that metonymically and metaphorically serves to signify the possibility of counter-hegemonic, defiant, or heuristic transcultural affiliations that bear the promise of true universality.

The reason that I raise these questions in the light of the Arab uprisings is that the uprisings challenged certain nationalist legacies (those commandeered by their governments), while this challenge cannot adequately be explained in terms of cosmopolitan liberalism in the Western tradition. Rather, the uprisings can be seen, at least in some respects, to have brought to the fore what the nationalist/cosmopolitan binary eclipses—in particular, earlier liberationist or revolutionary moments in history. While it often seems that the very dynamic of revolutions is one of "setbacks," instead of interpreting this as failure, we can see a setback conversely in terms of retrieval, or a looping back to a previous moment in order to resume or reset what it initiated. In my view, the dynamics of this are neither teleological nor dialectical, and my suggestion is that we may think of the tempo of revolutionary times in the way that we experience music: for instance, as the unfolding of sonic aggregates that loop and resume, surge and recede, detour and coalesce.

Beer in the Snooker Club, a novel set in 1950s Cairo and London, is frequently associated with a celebration of cosmopolitanism. For instance, in "Drinking, Gambling and Making Merry: Waguih Ghali's Search for Cosmopolitan Agency," Deborah Starr summarizes her reading of the novel as follows: "I maintain that it is not through a nationalist lens, nor through the mediated binaries of post-coloniality, but rather through the notion of the cosmopolitan that the novel becomes 'readable'" (Starr 2006, 272). First published in 1964, *Beer in the Snooker Club* is also a novel that has attracted fresh attention in the light of the Egyptian Revolution. For instance, Susie Thomas blogs, "Having lost his faith in both Arab nationalism and Communism, Ram [the novel's protagonist] feels his is a wasted life. But as Egyptians gathered in Tahrir Square and the Arab Spring unfolds, Ghali's novel has never felt more timely" (Thomas 2011). In what is to follow, I will explore the tension between positions dramatized in *Beer in the Snooker Club*, in particular, between a liberal cosmopolitan "universality" and a more radical universality.

The narrative of the novel is divided into five sections. The first is set in the present time of the novel and concerns the narrator's reunion with the love of his life. He is a young Egyptian Copt called Ram (arguably an allusion to ram-headed deities or to Ramses, thus to Ancient Egypt) and his lover is a Jewish woman called Edna. The second section of the novel comprises a flashback that shows how Ram and Edna met and that tells the story of how Edna brought Ram and his best friend, a fellow Copt called Font, to England for an extended stay, the two young Egyptians being Anglophiles. The last three sections return us to the present, in which Ram realizes that his relationship with Edna is doomed and switches his attention to a woman from his own family background. This summary fails to convey what may be termed the novel's musical structure, which could loosely be associated with counterpoint, following Edward Said, if the emphasis were on the polyphony of its cosmopolitan texture—a matter of the interplay of disparate voices. However, in this chapter, I wish to attend to the music of the text in different ways, as will unfold.

Although Said's suggestions concerning the contrapuntal organization of literature and the literary analysis appropriate to such have been widely taken up, what has been overlooked is that counterpoint is an especially Western tradition and one not classically associated with Arabic music. The main difference here is that Arabic music is traditionally monophonic, following a single melodic line as opposed to interweaving two or more differing melodic-rhythmic lines. While this might imply that Arabic music is more diachronically linear, I would suggest that in actuality, the reverse is true: in not being polyphonic, Arabic music is played in unison or synchronically. We could thus say that its mode of attunement is more synchronic than the comparatively more diachronic mode of attunement of counterpoint. Alexander Honold, in considering the art of counterpoint in relation to Said's interest in it, speaks of "the dialectical process inherent in counterpoint" and of how the "virtual relations with the harmonic order entered into by individual voices as discrete melodic vectors are made visible in the form of their opposite number, whether it precedes or follows them" (Honold 2012, 197).

While Said appreciates the attention counterpoint gives to different voices, my interest lies in a musicality of the collective. In addition, classical Arabic music takes the form of *maqamat*, or tonic arrangements, which I will translate nontechnically in terms of "sonic emotional maps." While the music in question thus offers an emotional synchronicity, it also offers scope for improvisation and spontaneity, being less reliant on a "set text" than Western music.

Thus, beyond a cosmopolitanism heard polyphonically (i.e., as reflecting the crossings and disjunctions of different stories and histories), there are other questions of coexistence that I will explore in the following readings toward a possible explanation of how music and the arts may be understood less in terms of dialectics than in terms of a mediation between temporality and timelessness. This is a question I will return to at the end of the chapter.

The meandering or improvisatory movement of the narration of the novel, which could be considered in terms of an unresolved, digressive *maqama*, reflects the social lifestyle of the narrator. He is the poor relative of a rich and privileged extended family that supports him in his unemployed existence of hedonistic drifting. In this respect, the novel unfolds haphazardly as we follow the urban nomadism of Ram, who hangs out with his friends at cafés—especially the famous Groppi's—at the snooker club, at the Gezira sporting club in Zamalek, and at the houses of family and friends. Ram is a drinking, gambling, and flirting flaneur figure who introduces us to the world of Cairo's elite class continuing their privileged existence in Nasser's new nationalist Egypt, with Ram as a youthful member of this class particularly addicted to the responsibility-free good life.

The cosmopolitanism of the novel is mainly associated with this elite world in which Ram associates with Armenians, Americans, the English, German and Norwegian governesses employed by the club set, and Jews. Through Ram's family connections, he meets the Jewish Edna, who comes from a family enriched by a large supermarket chain. While Ram takes all this for granted, Edna has a sociopolitical awareness of their situation, which she offers to enlighten Ram, as he confesses in the following:

> It was Edna who introduced me to Egyptian people. It is rare in the milieu in which I was born, to know Egyptians. She explained to me that the Sporting Club and the race meetings and the villa-owners and the European dressed and travelled people I met, were not Egyptians. Cairo and Alexandria were

cosmopolitan not so much because they contained foreigners, but because the Egyptian born in them is himself a stranger to his own land.

(53)

What this implies is a cultural colonization of the metropolitan centers whereby foreign cultures export themselves without really engaging with the local culture. The fact that Ram is estranged through his cosmopolitanism is also a matter of his education, and while his family speaks French, he himself is British educated, and his sense of the world is shaped by the literature he reads. He tells us:

> The world of intellectuals and underground metros and cobbled streets and a green countryside which we had never seen, beckoned to us. The world where students had rooms, and typists for girlfriends, and sang songs and drank beer in large mugs, shouted to us. A whole imaginary world. A mixture of all the cities in Europe.
>
> (55)

With this, cosmopolitanism is posited as precisely an imaginary formation. This is the case not just for Ram but is implied universally. For example, some Americans he meets at the club have wanted to visit Egypt ever since they read a book that stimulated their imaginations.

Ram's questioning of his own liberal cosmopolitanism is set in motion through his increasing radicalization, which is in part brought about through his experience of historical events, in particular the Suez conflict, and in part informed by Edna's radical left view of the world. Ram states:

> When Edna began talking to us of socialism or freedom or democracy, we always said yes, that's what the Egyptian revolution was; everything good was going to be carried out by the revolution. To begin with Edna's politics were not noticed by us at all, but gently she talked to us about oppressed people in Africa and Asia and even some parts of Europe, and Font and I started to read political books with more interest …. We learnt for the first time, the history of British imperialism and why we didn't want the British troops in the Suez Canal area. Up to then we had shouted "evacuation" like everyone else, without knowing why evacuation was so important. Gradually, we began to see ourselves as members of humanity in general and not just as Egyptians.
>
> (53)

This question of being "members of humanity in general" is posited in counterpoint to a contrapuntal cosmopolitanism of cultural difference—paradoxically in counterpoint to counterpoint—in that what is at stake is how imperialism denies the very commonality of humanity. When Edna takes Ram and their friend Font to England, Ram learns that the English notion of "fair play" that he has imbibed is a hypocritical one, not only given the Suez conflict but also because of the difficulties he faces in obtaining a visa. That is, while the English feel that they can graft themselves onto

Egypt, and that they belong there, they do not welcome Egyptians as belonging in England. The visa problem is resolved through the connections of an Englishman, Dungate, whose brother, it is said, "had always loved Egyptians" (65), and Ram gets to meet the leftist middle-class Dungate family. As they are all set to go convivially to a pub, the following is narrated: "I put my coat on slowly and wondered whether meeting these people and receiving their hospitality was actually enjoyable" (68). He speaks of suddenly feeling himself split, aware from this point onward of his being pulled in two different directions.

This fracture is not only of concern to Ram's self-consciousness; it is also a fracture that runs throughout the novel between liberalism and communism, cultural difference and the common ground of the real. In the frivolity of his Cairo life, he especially loves Edna and Font because he sees them as authentic, honest, loyal, and true, as he repeatedly observes.

In speaking of his English education, Ram talks of swallowing supposed truths that turn out to be lies, as is hinted at by the name Dungate as suggestive of eating dung or bullshit. Ram gets to meet various members of the working class, who, unlike the polite Dungates, are rude to Ram, even calling him "wog," which he finds hilarious because of the upfront honesty in spouting prejudice. When he meets a working-class man called Vincent, who is honest and without prejudice, Ram reflects, "I felt instinctively that he was more real than John Dungate .... Vincent was essentially free from racial traits .... He was Vincent Murphy and no more" (87). He also meets a woman similar to Vincent called Shirley, and he asks himself what it is he particularly likes about the two of them, answering, "With them I forgot I was Egyptian and they English and I a stranger in their midst. No matter how hard the Dungates tried, they were never able to make me feel one and the same" (101).

The hospitality of the liberal Dungates is based on a logic of the family and the stranger, whereas the friendship he has with Vincent and Shirley affirms a radical sameness in which friendship may be said to override the family/stranger dialectic, as in the case of Ram's relationship with Edna.

Edna leaves Ram to return to Cairo, and it is only in the final section of the novel that we find out that Ram then joined the Communist Party in England but was forced to leave when he could not renew his visa. Back in Egypt, he resumes his rich playboy lifestyle, but we also learn that he becomes an undercover activist for radical dissidents who have been imprisoned and tortured by the Nasserites. At one point, he confronts a female journalist lover who is pro-Nasser with the accusation that she represents the "muzzled press" who disavow the concentration camps in Egypt (205). Given his relationship with Edna, it is striking that Ram calls the torture prisons "concentration camps" (205).

While anti-imperialist, Ram is clearly not an Egyptian nationalist. Influenced by his Jewish lover, he seeks the utopia of universal justice and dignity for everyone. However, there remain differences between Ram and Edna. We learn that Edna, although Jewish, feels herself to be Egyptian more than anything else due to the fact that her globe-trotting parents left her to be brought up by a Greek nanny who was married to an Egyptian, who spent time raising Edna in her husband's humble village. Edna, through experience, is part of the Egyptian *fellah* class or class of *fellaheen*, which Ram clearly is not. Nonetheless, Ram comes to assert that he is Egyptian in ways that Edna is not, arguing that Egypt is so many things to him, especially the sarcasm, the wit, and the broader sense of humor of the people, traits that he sees as lacking in Edna: "How can I explain to you that Egypt to me is something unconscious, is nothing particularly political" (190). For Ram, the authenticity and companionship he seeks is beyond the political, which is ever divisive, and what he terms the unconscious may be said to have no finite form—hence his inability to articulate it. The inexpressibility at stake here may implicitly concern the sacred, a point I will return to.

Although Ram wishes to marry Edna, she refuses, revealing the surprising fact that she is already married to an Israeli. Her husband turns out to have been an Egyptian communist Jew who had been imprisoned for ten years and then brutalized by Egyptian soldiers with Russian-donated weapons, leading to his disfigurement and castration. Edna explains, "He is in Israel because he is a Jew" (184). Ram says he and Edna can still live together, but she considers this impossible. While the novel does not elaborate on this impasse, we are invited to read between the lines.

When Ram reunites with Edna, she has a mysterious disfiguring scar on her face that she refuses to explain, but it is implicitly the result of an anti-Semitic attack upon her, probably by an Egyptian army officer. As with her radical Jewish husband, she is not wanted in Egypt in spite of her feeling herself to be Egyptian. It is implied that her Jewish identity would thus also make Ram, if he stayed with her, a persona non grata in his own land. What the novel does not address, however, is Israel's recruitment of Egyptian Jews to perpetrate terrorist acts, as discussed by Joel Beinin in his examination of Operation Susannah, a terrorist plot that was thwarted by Egyptian intelligence. Beinin states, "Operation Susannah was the most salient political event in the life of the [Egyptian] Jewish community from 1949 to 1956. The involvement of Egyptian Jews in acts of espionage and sabotage organized and directed by the Israeli military intelligence raised fundamental questions about their identities and loyalties" (Beinin 2005, 31).

While for Ram and Edna, cultural and ethnic differences don't actually matter as differences, they are embroiled in a world deeply invested in a divide-and-rule strategy based on identities, in relation to which cosmopolitanism emerges as the soft power mask of cultural diplomacy. The novel leaves these questions hanging in the air, unresolved. Ahdaf Soueif, however, informs us that Ghali, the author of the novel, committed the transgressive act of visiting Israel, which meant that he could not return to Egypt and thereafter had to live in England (where he eventually committed suicide) (Soueif 2004, 198–200).

The lesson of *Beer in the Snooker Club* is that the promise of universality that Egypt mutely yet undeniably bears for Ram is betrayed by the historical Egypt. In his novel, Ghali goes against the grain of the dissent of his times, both the liberal trend and the revolutionary nationalist trend, out of a utopian communism. In an interview with Philip Lopate, Edward Said states of Nasser, "He led a massive campaign against people who are my great friends today, left-wing intellectuals, many of whose lives were destroyed by their years in prison. It's still not entirely clear to me what he was doing, because he was very closely aligned with the Soviet Union and yet he destroyed the Egyptian Communist Party" (Said 1999). Two points may be made in relation to this statement. First, Nasser's ties with the Soviet Union were particularly over arms deals (rather than ideology as such) in that the West would not supply Egypt with arms given Egypt's pro-Palestinian position. Second, Nasser's crackdown on Egyptian communists came in the wake of the 1958 Iraqi revolution, during which General Qasim had the strong support of Iraqi communists in a complicated national and international context in which communism was being pitted against Nasserite and Ba'athist Arab nationalism. In this situation, Nasser (with the support of Washington) defended nationalism, and Robert Stephens quotes him stating, "If a Communist State is established [in Iraq], the communists will smite down all patriotic and nationalist elements" (Stephens 1971, 309). Nasser goes on to warn of a "Red terrorist dictatorship" emerging through the violent purging of the nationalists.

Ghali's association of his Jewish character Edna with radical politics is interestingly echoed by Jacqueline Kahanoff's autobiographical reflections on her upbringing in Egypt in which the utopian universality of communism is stressed. Kahanoff writes:

> We thought ourselves to be Socialist, even Communist, and in our school yard we ardently discussed the Blum government, the civil war in Spain, revolution, materialism, and the rights of women …. We wanted to break out of the narrow, minority framework (upper middle class) into which we were born, to strive toward something universal, and we were ashamed of the poverty of what we called the "Arab Masses", and of the advantages a Western education had given us over them.
>
> (Beinin 2005, 50)

Her voice sounds uncannily like that of Edna in Ghali's novel. This could suggest that Ghali accurately reflects predominant strands of Egyptian Jewish sentiments although it is also the case, according to Beinin, that prior to writing the above, Kahanoff had read *Beer in the Snooker Club* and reviewed it enthusiastically. That is, the intriguing question arises of whether her self-construction was somewhat influenced by Ghali's Jewish heroine. Either way, Kahanoff sees *Beer in the Snooker Club* as depicting a common cause between Jews and Copts, whom she sees as nostalgic for the more cosmopolitan nationalism of 1919, one overtaken by what Kahanoff terms "Muslim nationalism" (Beinin 2005, 54). It may be said that she projects her own concerns onto Ghali's work given that his novel very much downplays religious differences in offering a secular Cairean world. That said, Ram's communist leanings are bound up with his skeptical take on identity politics indicating that his deepest investments are in the chance of a common humanity.

When the 2011 Egypt revolution occurred, Ghali's novel came to mind, and I wrote about it in this context (Rooney 2011), going on to subsequently discover a number of internet postings that describe the novel, which first appeared in 1964, as coming across as particularly contemporary. Agamben defines the contemporary in terms of the fracture between the lifespan of the individual and his collective age, a matter of the exceptional individual's alienation from the society of his time (Agamben 2009). This typical Western avant-garde stance might vaguely seem to fit with Ghali's novel, except for the fact that the novel is not primarily concerned with an anachronistic, spectral relation to its own present but rather with precisely maintaining a fidelity to its present moment through lived coexistence (which is why it feels relevant to the 2011 revolution). Its utopianism is real—not imaginary—in the novel's celebration of the micro-society of authentic, if unlikely, friendships: this constancy. In fact, what is at stake is an inversion of Agamben's understanding of the contemporary; the fracture is not between the individual and his or her collective age (the sensitive intellectual and the mindless common masses) but between those in solidarity with each other and the self-interest of those who have a stake in maintaining social divides, mainly on the basis of class but also on the basis of ethnicity, religion, and gender.

The novel, however, is not at all hostile to cosmopolitanism. My reading of the work left me with a certain thought, one not actually expressed in it but rather arriving from the silence of its aftereffect. The silent or unsayable thought is this: cosmopolitanism is a joke. It is a joke in positive and negative, comic and painful ways. It is a source of amusement and fun; it is not for real.

The above observation serves to provide an opportunity to reengage with the question of the novel's musical aesthetic. In fact, Ram explicitly connects the Egyptian sense of humor with music when he explains to Font, "Jokes to Egyptians are as much culture as calypso is to West Indians, or as spirituals and jazz to American Negroes" (19). There could certainly be a tangent between Ghali's novel and a novel such as Sam Selvon's *The Lonely Londoners* (Selvon 2006), which first appeared in 1956 and stands out for its ironic and witty take on multiculturalism, its calypso ethos, and its episodic structure. However, this fails to address the sensibility of Ghali's novel specifically enough.

The ironic fissures between the imaginary and the real that *Beer in the Snooker Club* engages with and its sense of cosmopolitanism as a kind of travesty (viewed in terms of the Egyptian sense of humor Ram endorses) give rise to a sensibility that could be termed burlesque. The term "burlesque" derives from the Italian word *burla*, meaning joke or mockery. Some of the novel's burlesque features include its humorous sociopolitical commentary, its carnival style in which social hierarchies are caricatured, its flirtation with human desires for sophistication, hedonism, and glamour combined with a self-deflating populism and a live-and-let-live spirit, sometimes racy or risqué. As such, it is a work that could be compared with the film *Cabaret* (Fosse 1972), based on Isherwood's *Goodbye to Berlin* (1939). What the film *Cabaret* does is to juxtapose the world of Weimer cabaret, what was deemed decadent culture by the Nazis, reaffirmed in the film as "divine decadence," with the growing fanatical nationalism of fascism. The musical conviviality and live-and-let-live spirit of the burlesque underworld contrast starkly with the self-righteous and sinister death drive of militant German pride.

The cabaret ethos that I am trying to address is wonderfully expressed in a recent Lebanese production called the *Hishik Bishik Show* (*hishik bishik* is an Egyptian term that refers to cabaret), which pays tribute to the kind of Egyptian popular culture that Fahmy draws attention to in *Ordinary Egyptians* (Fahmy 2011), and Iain Aikerman's review of the show captures its spirit:

> Musically, it is a curiosity. It has taken its cue from the weddings and cabaret shows of early 20th century Egypt and re-imagined what is an Egyptian pop cultural

experience via a Lebanese lens. When the stage curtains are opened, they reveal a wheelchair-bound general playing the violin, a whirling Sufi who frequents bars, and Roaring Twenties flapper girls intent on having a good time. It is a sometimes mesmerising spectacle, weaving together exquisite musicianship with song and dance, although its comic word play and numerous visual gags may well be lost on those who do not speak Arabic.

(Aikerman 2014)

More specifically, the show offers a pastiche of Egyptian popular music covering the very popular Sayyid Darwish and Um Kulthum, as well as songs listed by Fayid (2015), including Shadia's "Ya Hasan Ya Khouly al-Geniena" from *Leilat al-Hanna* (Night of Joy, 1951), Hind Rostom's "Habibi ya Re2a" from *Atrafat Zog* (Confessions of a Husband, 1964), and Leila Nazmi's revival of Egyptian folk in 1970s. The show (which I saw produced by Metro al Madina in 2014) does not have much of a plot, although it transports us from Cairo's nightclubs to the countryside of Upper Egypt, connecting the populism of the urban street with so-called folk culture. The term "folk" is an inadequate translation given its connotations in English; the Lebanese term *darwish* (*darwich* or *darwiche* in French) would be more precise in that this term refers less to clannish kinsfolk than to the decent though sometimes gullible and foolish common man. Although *darwish* is related to dervish, this is not a narrow reference to Sufism as a religion but rather to a certain Sufi spirit of anti-elitism. An example of this type of everyman could be Habiby's character Saeed in his novel *The Secret Life of Saeed the Pessoptimist*, a character humorously based on Voltaire's Candide. The important point is that this type of character precisely transcends cultural divisions in that all cultures have their common man or common woman types, as discussed by Raouf Rifai in the documentary *White Flags* (Rooney and Sakr 2014). That is to say, the populism at stake is transnational, since it refers to the everyman figure or the one who represents our common humanity.

Ismail Fayid's review of the *Hishik Bishik Show* offers a contemporary (post-revolution) Egyptian perspective of its implications for current audiences (Fayid 2015). He writes:

What I found extraordinary and bewildering was how enthusiastically the audience received the music and performance (they knew the songs almost word for word) when the show is not just a simple reenactment. It is a pastiche, a cynical reinterpretation that makes fun of the originals and makes fun of itself making fun of the original. The performers use exaggeration, slapstick moves and all kind of insinuations, both obscene and absurd.

I felt as if *Hishik Bishik* and the audience reactions were a manifestation of a sinister fascination for a past that refuses to let go. A past that is holding all of us, Egyptians and Lebanese as well as other Arabs, hostage to grandiose post-colonial fantasies that failed spectacularly.

The reference is particularly to the Nasserite past, which Fayid considers the show to trivialize at the same time that he sees this past as something that Arab audiences invest in too nostalgically. In a way, this touches on what I tried to address earlier concerning *Beer in the Snooker Club*'s depiction of cosmopolitanism as a joke, as something both funny and upsetting or troubling. For instance, it's a joke that Ram and Font play at being English, while what underlies this are serious anxieties over Egyptian nationalism. However, that said, I do not see the *Hishik Bishik Show* as hopelessly nostalgic. What I speak of in terms of the burlesque aspects of cabaret, Fayid sees as offensively kitsch. Regarding Fayid's postrevolutionary perspective, it could alternatively be said that Sisi-mania is kitsch (the strongman posters and superman trinkets, for instance), because it is based on a kind of nostalgia for Nasser that turns out to be inauthentic, kitsch being precisely failed authenticity in my view. However, the kitsch of Sisi-mania does not thereby make Nasser kitsch as if he had been retrospectively remodeled in the image of Sisi-mania.

In her review of the *Hishik Bishik Show*, Ellie Violet Bramley argues that although it might appear nostalgic in that it draws on the past, it is really forward looking. She states, "For all its accessibility, this is an artistically valuable show. For all of its theatricality, its magic lies in the details of the staging and the costumes. And, for all of its nostalgia, its relevance is in its direction: forward-facing" (Bramley 2013). I agree with this and propose that the reason why this is the case is because the show celebrates its rediscovery of *the forward-looking moments in the past*, or the Egyptian popular avant-garde. Bramley quotes Ziad Al Ahmadiye, responsible for the musical orchestration of the show, as affirming,

> We were trying to be as honest as we could, and as correct as we could in presenting these songs. If you don't have this special feeling and spirit in the Arabic music—it is not a kind of classical music that anyone can play—you have to understand the spirit of Egypt so that you succeed in presenting these songs in the correct way.
> (Bramley 2013)

It is this *spirit* that is seen as relevant to the present by the show's creative cast, who speak of the show's honest celebration of the feminine (as ranges from Sufi mysticism to female singers and dancers) in the context of the puritanical Muslim Brotherhood.

What is interesting about burlesque or cabaret culture is that it often emerges as a response to situations of fascist or racist forms of what may be termed tribal nationalism and the authoritarianism of its norms as ideals. Thus, *Cabaret*, as mentioned, pits its sardonic musical theater against the rise of Nazi Germany, while the film *The Grand Budapest Hotel* makes use of a thoroughly burlesque aesthetic to celebrate the life-affirming culture of Mittel Europa (that *mezzaterra* or common ground) in the context of the rise of thuggish fascist elements in 1940s Hungary. I will turn now finally to an analysis of *Free Men* with the above considerations in mind.

Free Men is a 2011 film that revisits the Nazi occupation of France in order to explore the role of a Paris mosque in providing sanctuary and escape for Jews in danger of persecution or execution. It is based on true stories that are covered by Robert Satloff in his book *Among the Righteous*. Satloff's research makes the case that "at every stage of the Nazi, Vichy and Fascist persecution of the Jews in Arab lands, and in every place that it occurred, Arabs helped Jews." Satloff further observes, "There were occasions when certain Arabs chose to do more than offer moral support to the Jews. They bravely saved Jewish lives sometimes risking their own in the process" (Satloff 2006, 99).

Satloff gives the following reason for his research project: "I decided that the most useful response I could offer to 9/11 was to combat Arab ignorance of the Holocaust" (5). That is, Satloff sees 9/11 as a protest against American support for Israel. Yet Satloff's response is rather lopsided in that he seems to think that reminding present-day Arabs of how earlier generations of Arabs helped Jews resist persecution is likely to promote acceptance of Israel as a place of refuge; in this light, Israel would not be conceived of as a settler colony but rather as one donated by Arab charity. What Satloff does not really consider is that if Arabs came to the aid of racially persecuted Jews, then today Jews should in turn come to the aid of racially persecuted Arabs such as the Palestinians (as some do). I will come back to this question later.

In his book, Satloff draws our attention to the writings of a North African Jew named Albert Assouline, a captive in a German prison camp. Assouline escaped and made his way to Paris, where he received sanctuary in a mosque. He claims that the mosque's imam, Si Mohmmed Benzouaou, issued certificates of Muslim identity to Jews to save them from deportation and death and that as many as 1732 resistance fighters found refuge in the caverns of the mosque. Satloff also refers to the surfacing of the story of Jewish singer Salim Halali, in that Salim was one of those who received help from the mosque. Satloff informs us:

> Assouline's story received a boost in June 2005, when Salim (Simon) Halali, a world-renowned singer, died in Cannes. Born in 1920 to a poor Jewish family in Annaba (formerly Bône), near the Algerian-Tunisian border, Halali hailed from a local Jewish Berber tribe. When he was just fourteen he made his way to France, where he was eventually discovered singing in a cabaret. It was not long before Halali became France's most celebrated "oriental" singer. For the next forty years, he was a fixture of Andalusian music, predecessor of today's rai trend.
>
> (145)

Halali's story inspired a French documentary short, *A Forgotten Resistance* (Berkani 1991), and is at the core of *Free Men*. What *Free Men* does is to provide a wider political dimension to Halali's story through entwining it with the fictional creation of a friendship between Halali and a young Algerian economic migrant, Younes. Younes first arrives in France to join his cousin Ali in a factory. When he contracts tuberculosis, Younes loses his job, and while jobless, he is reduced to selling goods on the black market. The Vichy police arrest him for this criminal activity but offer him his freedom if he agrees to spy for them at the local mosque to report on any suspicious activities there. Younis meets Salim at the mosque and starts to frequent his cabaret performances in Paris. Salim had already been given Muslim identity papers by the mosque, but the Germans have begun to suspect the racket. Aware of the Germans' suspicions, the rector and leader of the Muslim community, Si Kaddour Ben Ghrabit, tells Salim that if he is arrested, he should say that his father is buried in the Muslim cemetery in Bobigny. Meanwhile, Younes discovers that the mosque is a refuge not only for Jews but also for Algerians who have joined the French resistance movement, among whom is his cousin Ali.

Whereas Satloff's account of the Arabs who helped Jews stresses the humane and selflessly ethical aspects of this, Ferroukhi's film deliberately politicizes the situation. This is particularly underscored when the Algerian fighters link the anti-fascist resistance with anti-colonial resistance, chanting, "Down with colonialism, down with fascism!" While Younes is initially apolitical, seeing the political struggles of others as not his business, he is increasingly politicized into understanding that the various fights for freedom from racist power regimes are interconnected, where the fight to free Europe from fascism is offered as a prelude to the Algerian liberation struggle.

The film was released in early 2011, and so while it implicitly addresses questions of Islamic militancy, the making of it would not have been influenced by the Arab Spring. It positions Islam (with the mosque as refuge not only for Jews but for freedom fighters too) on the side of revolution and as inclusive, and the Islam it addresses is one that is humanist rather than intolerant in its worldly involvements. Some have seen the film as a response to Islamophobia, in its restoring the memory of Muslims and the French Resistance as having once shared a common cause (Monji 2015), while this could not be seen as a mere gesture of appeasement in that the film also raises the memory of the Algerian liberation struggle.

It is almost as if the film offers us something like a partnership between the revolutionary humanist Fanon, a widely embracing Islam, and a cabaret culture of joie de vivre as its utopian horizon. However, more problematically, the politicization of Younes is accompanied by his induction into committing violence. First, in a scene where he is trying to escape German soldiers who have identified his resistance group through an Algerian informer, he kills a German soldier in self-defense. Shortly after this, he kills the Algerian sellout in cold blood. This violence is presented as understandable in its context, and even inevitable. That said, Si Kaddour Ben Ghrabit upbraids Younes for his rashness, not really over the violence per se but for endangering the reputation of the mosque. The rector is presented as someone who tries to work pragmatically with authorities in power, trying to outwit them through the weapons of intelligence and cunning.

The style of the film is that of an art house Second World War espionage thriller, set to the jazz riffs of contemporary Lebanese trumpeter Ibrahim Maalouf and punctuated with cameo cabaret scenes that present the cabaret world as very much the alternative to the political one. In terms of the musical arrangements, Halali's own song "Andalusia" features as typifying his romanticism, while *tarab* features strongly in the vocals, inducing ecstasy in the audiences. The film also includes a surprising meeting between the Salim character and the great Egyptian musician Mohamed Abdul Wahab, each as an ardent admirer of the other. Mohamed Abdul Wahab (born 1907) was a singer who initially composed songs in praise of King Farouk, changing his allegiance to Nasser after 1952, a trajectory similar to that of singer Umm Kulthum. In brief, what is at stake here is music more in the service of patriotism (love of country) than politics, and the songs of Abdul Wahab, who wrote the national anthems of Libya, Tunisia, and the United Arab Emirates, are indeed strongly characterized by pan-Arab patriotism.

I can find no evidence of Mohamed Abdul Wahab's having visited Vichy Paris, so it may be that the film invents this scene. However, it is the case that he came to Paris in the 1930s to study French film music, going on to become a composer of Egyptian film scores and to incorporate Western influences and instruments in his work. For instance, as with Hilali, some of his music makes use of Spanish or Latin rhythms. More broadly, Paris in the 1930s and 1940s was a locus of a buzzing Franco-Oriental culture that brought together Catholics, Jews, and Muslims, often around Arab and North African music, as documented by Ethan B. Katz in his book *The Burdens of Brotherhood: Jews and Muslims from North Africa to France*. Salim Halali was, of course, a part of this wider musical culture, and Katz comments, "It was in Paris's Latin Quarter around rue de la Huchette that a host of Oriental cabarets, including 'El Djazair' ... 'Le Kasbah', 'Tam Tam' and 'Nuits de Liban' created a dynamic music scene with Jewish-Muslim co-operation at its heart" (Katz 2015, 168). Katz goes on to mention that when Salim Halali moved to Casablanca after the war, he opened his own cabaret, Le Coq d'Or, with an orchestra of Jewish and Muslim musicians, and "it quickly became a legendary regional draw." Katz also points out that "Arabic music greats Umm Kulthum and Mohamed Abdul Wahab came from Egypt just to watch" (168).

Whether or not Abdul Wahab came to Paris during the war and met Halali then, *Free Men* seeks to draw attention to their historical connection in a particular way. At the same time that the two singers meet in the film, Salim is warned of an imminent roundup of Jews in the area and is advised to flee. However, he refuses to heed the warning because it is a dream of his to sing with Abdul Wahab. When the two take the stage, soldiers break in, and Salim is arrested. The scene thus indicates that on an affective and spiritual level, music has the power to transcend religious and national differences, while it is yet helpless in the face of fanatical militancy. Not only that, it is as if the targets of fascism are not simply Jews but more widely those who resist the separatist identity politics of divide and rule.

After his arrest, Salim's last resort to validate his Muslim identity is to claim that his father is buried in the Muslim cemetery at Bobigny, as he was advised to do. He is taken to the cemetery and there, with German guns pointed at him, told to identify his father's grave. Eventually he finds a gravestone bearing his family name, as arranged by the mosque, and he is thus saved from execution. This powerful scene makes use of the Joycean identification of paternity as a "legal fiction," to evaporate it as charade at the same time that another kind of belonging is enabled. That is, the legal fiction is one of authoritarian branding and sectarian ownership of people. As Salim kneels before the gravestone under a cloudy sky, a far-off rumble of thunder is heard, as if to suggest that his salvation is rooted in the truth that Muslims and Jews both are sanctioned as children of the divine. This moment in the film, one of deliverance through compassion, has a sacred feeling.

The above moment in the film may be juxtaposed with a scene toward its ending, when Younes and Salim have a brief reunion after parting ways. The rift between them is partly due to Younes's discovery that Salim is gay. When they meet again, however, there is a charged moment in which they gaze at each other in a way that silently expresses the emotional connection between them given their common cause against

Nazism, with not only its racism but its homophobia. Although the title *Free Men* might sound vaguely masculinist, the film makes clear that the freedom at stake extends to men who are feminine, as Salim is. The actor who plays Salim (Mahmoud Shalaby) has an androgynous beauty but is not camp, while the actual Salim Halali's performances (which can be seen on YouTube) have camp or dandified aspects to them in keeping with the cabaret world more generally.

Earlier I spoke of kitsch in terms of failed authenticity, while Sontag describes camp in terms of failed seriousness (Sontag 2009). While there may be overlaps here, there is a significant difference. It may be said that it is kitsch that takes itself seriously in a literal-minded manner leading to an unpersuasive sentimentality, whereas with camp, there is an understanding of the game as a game or a joke, as in the dandified sensibility of Ram or as in Yurid's account of the *Hishik Bishik Show* as a show that makes fun of itself making fun. That is, camp plays on the distinction between knowing what is and is not real, where gender is real but divisive gender norms are unreal stereotypes. Whereas kitsch invests in the stereotype as real, camp sends up the stereotype for what it is, precisely in appreciating the difference between what is real and what is not. Of course, reality is much more fluid than typologies, epistemologies, and ideologies.

The final meeting between Younes and Salim seems to suggest that the emotional bond between them exceeds their differences as Muslim and Jew, straight and gay, while the two men are yet committed to different trajectories of freedom, Younes presumably going on to fight for Algerian liberation and Salim bound for cabaret life in Morocco. In *Beer in the Snooker Club*, Edna's heritage appears to be more bound up with European Jewish legacies in that her parents come to base themselves in South Africa while her relatives are scattered around America and Europe. In "On Orientalist Trajectories," Ella Shohat addresses how "the Zionist project paradoxically involved a de-Semitisation of the Jew ... even while simultaneously claiming an originary Semitic lineage" (120). In the light of this, while Salim is able to affirm that he is an Arab Jew, Edna is pressured into taking the path of de-Orientalization as her Egyptian identity is called into question. Thus, at stake is also an unresolved fracture between European Jew and Arab Jew.

What do *Beer in the Snooker Club* and *Free Men* contribute to understandings of transnationalism of relevance today? *Beer in the Snooker Club* may be said to challenge the foreclosure of a common humanity by a liberal cosmopolitanism that bases itself on the differences between self and other, family and stranger, at the same time that the novel opposes the authoritarian and right-wing tendencies of nationalism that pit self-determination against a cosmopolitan liberalism seen as fake. In a way, *Beer in the Snooker Club* embraces the fakeness of cosmopolitanism, cosmopolitanism as a joke, while holding out for something more authentic, prefiguring the Egyptian Revolution. The novel, however, remains haunted by its silences. One such silence is the Palestinian question, which is bracketed off in the foregrounding of Arab-Jewish friendship. Similarly, the novel brackets off questions of religion as a concern with the sacred as opposed to matters of identity. I think that the communism of Ram is, beyond what he can say, not a secular formation but ultimately sacred in its implications: it touches on what he speaks of as an Egyptian unconscious beyond the political. Furthermore, the novel runs up against a troubling flippant callousness in

Ram (or seeming inability to feel) that is, in inexpressible ways or ways not addressed, in danger of tipping into the cruelty that he fears.

Free Men does introduce questions of the sacred through the role played by the mosque concerning how religion can and should transcend national identities, while it also brackets off the question of Palestine in creating alliances between Jews fighting fascism and Algerians fighting colonialism. At this point, it is worth pointing out that Satloff speaks of how he tried to present Yad Vashem, the Israeli Holocaust Museum, with evidence of Arabs who had helped Jews so that at least one Arab be inscribed among the righteous. However, to this day, Yad Vashem refuses to acknowledge any of the Arabs who intervened against the Nazi persecution of the Jews. This amounts to a shocking politicization of the Holocaust, either because the Holocaust loses its significance as a violation of the sacred or because the sacred is transferred to a self-promoting national cause.

With the above in mind, it may be said that while liberal cosmopolitanism forecloses the sacred so that its forms of togetherness are merely performative enactments, like the polite rituals of hospitality offered by the Dungates in Ghali's novel, right-wing nationalism attempts to reappropriate the sacred for its own political ends, denying thus the value of other lives. Both *Beer in the Snooker Club* and *Free Men* serve to raise the question of whether the cabaret aesthetic and milieu constitute a *political* resistance to the theater of identity politics or whether they constitute instead a resistance as *limit to the politicization* of human relationships. This is open to debate, but on the whole, the cabaret or burlesque ethos implicitly sends up the deadly earnestness of the political through an awareness of human realities that exceed political determinants.

What I would like to suggest further is that the Egyptian Revolution may be seen on the one hand as hinged on political resistance to authoritarianism and on the other hand as a creativity that resists the all-pervasive politicization of human relationships. Burlesque is more generally related to the carnival or the carnivalesque, which itself borders on the religious festival. This brings me to the Egyptian Revolution as a *mulid* (Keraitim and Mehrez 2012; Elmarsafy 2015; Rooney 2015), that is, experienced as a radiantly joyful togetherness. Mona Prince, in her firsthand account of the revolution, speaks of it in such terms and ends her testimony with the following:

> We danced and sang until a friend came back with a big cassette player.
> We inserted a cassette and pressed play.
> We cheered and sang along.
> Pink
> My life is pink ...
> Pink, pink
> My life is pink without you, Hosni.
> Without you Hosni, life is now pink.
> Pink, pink, pink. (191)

The revolution is presented as a song (somewhat camp) that we can all sing in unison (Arab style as opposed to contrapuntally), and it is a song that can only come into its own by deposing the figureheads of illusory unity (political leaders and their causes) through a demonstration of real unity, a human solidarity that borders on the sacred, here in a festive way. As such, the song mediates between its moment in history and the timelessness of what cannot be dated. In fact, tellingly, this song comes from an Egyptian film, *Khallī Bālak min Zouzou* (Watch out for Zouzou), with Suad Hosni (here, the alternative to Hosni Mubarak) in the leading role and with Salah Jahine, a leading Egyptian poet, as its lyricist. In the film, Hosni plays a student whose humble origins are revealed through her mother's belonging to a belly-dancing troupe. In brief, the film celebrates both unapologetic femininity and the cabaret world of the belly dancers.

While nationalism and cosmopolitanism each posit themselves as progressive in relation to the regressive, respectively, the dialectics of progression and regression are ultimately irrelevant to the true common ground, which is why works such as *Beer in the Snooker Club* and *Free Men* are able to present us slices of history that have the potential to seem always contemporary as they musically resist the foreclosure of the synchronic, upon which dialectical histories of assimilation and expulsion are otherwise predicated. That said, the valences of nationalism, cosmopolitanism, and revolutionary friendships often coexist in any one historical moment, in which can reside the symbolic (nationalism), the imaginary (cosmopolitanism), and the real (solidarity that is dependent on neither the symbolic nor the imaginary). With respect to the Arab uprisings, the fraught question of Arab-Jewish friendship remains pertinent. I say this because the thwarting of the Arab uprisings—their being put on hold, so to speak—can be attributed in part to the fact that the Israeli-Palestinian conflict continues, where Israel fears genuine anti-neoliberal and antiracist democracy in the region and where American support for Israel makes its liberal cosmopolitanism a joke.

Finally, why music? In a conversation between the conductor and pianist Daniel Barenboim and Edward Said, Barenboim asks Said to explain, from his perspective as a cultural critic, why, as globalization spreads and intensifies, "political conflicts and national conflicts are deeper and pettier than ever before" (Barenboim and Said 2004, 14). Said responds that this is, first, a reaction to global homogenization and, second, a case of the imperial advocacy of "partition" as a solution to "the problem of multiple nationalities" (14). Said goes on to say:

> It's like someone telling you, "Okay, the way to learn a musical piece is to divide it into tinier and tinier units, and then suddenly you can put it all together." It doesn't work that way. When you divide something up, it's not so easy to put it all back together.
>
> (14)

For both Barenboim and Said, music both inspires and entails a pluralistic and unified collaborative ethos, one that may sometimes entail—as exemplified by their friendship and professional partnership—co-creative and mutually supportive visions across official enemy lines. It is as if in music, we are able to find our way around the destructive forces that exploit our differences by turning them into fractures and partitions.

Note

1 An early version of this chapter was presented at the Mediterranean Fractures conference organized by Norbert Bugeja and Abdulrazak Gurnah (University of Kent, April 2014). I am grateful to Ayman A. El-Desouky and Eid Mohamed for the opportunity to present a longer version at the Doha Institute (January 2017) and to all those who responded to both versions of the work in progress at these events.

References

Agamben, Giorgio. 2009. "*What Is the Contemporary?*" *What Is an Apparatus? and Other Essays*. Translated by David Kishik and Stefan Pedatella. Stanford: Stanford University Press, 39–54.

Aikerman, Iain. 2014. "Journey into Hamra." *Gulf Business*. Review of Hishik Bishik Show, January 11. https://www.pressreader.com/uae/gulf-business/20140101/281646778044201. Last accessed May 24, 2017.

Al Imam, Hassan. 1972. Dir. *Khallī Bālak min Zouzou* [Watch Out for Zouzou].

Anderson, Wes. 2014. Dir. *The Grand Budapest Hotel*.

Barenboim, Daniel and Edward Said. 2004. *Parallels and Paradoxes: Explorations in Music and Society*, edited by Ara Guzelimian. London: Bloomsbury.

Beinin, Joel. 2005. *The Dispersion of Egyptian Jewry: Culture, Politics and the Formation of a Modern Diaspora*. Cairo: American University in Cairo Press.

Berkani, Derri. 1991. Dir. *Une Résistance Oubliée: La Mosquée de Paris* [A Forgotten Resistance: The Mosque of Paris].

Bramley, Ellie Violet. 2013. "Egyptian Cabaret in Beirut." NOW. Review of Hishik Bishik Show, February 27. https://now.mmedia.me/lb/en/features/egyptian-cabaret-in-beirut. Last accessed May 27, 2017.

Elmarsafy, Ziad. 2015. "Action, Imagination, Natality, Revolution." *Journal for Cultural Research* 19 (2): 130–8.

Fahmy, Ziad. 2011. *Ordinary Egyptians: Creating the Modern Nation through Popular Culture*. Stanford: Stanford University Press.

Fayid, Ismail. 2015. "Death of a Hegemon: Mid-Century Egyptian Music in Beirut." *Mada Masr*. http://www.madamasr.com/en/2015/04/03/opinion/culture/death-of-a-hegemon-mid-century-egyptian-music-in beirut/. Last accessed May 24, 2017.

Ferroukhi, Ismaël. 2011. Dir. *Free Men* [Les hommes libres].

Fosse, Bob. 1972. Dir. *Cabaret*.

Ghali, Waguih. 2010. *Beer in the Snooker Club*. London: Serpent's Tail.

Habiby, Emile. 1974. *The Secret Life of Saeed the Pessoptimist*. Translated by S. Jayyusi and T. LeGassick. Northampton, MA: Interlink.

Honold, Alexander. 2012. "The Art of Counterpoint: Music as Site and Tool in Postcolonial Readings." In *Edward Said's Translocations: Essays in Secular Criticism*, edited by Tobias Döring and Mark Stein, 187–204. London: Routledge.

Isherwood, Christopher. 1998. *Goodbye to Berlin*. London: Vintage.

Katz, Ethan B. 2015. *The Burdens of Brotherhood: Jews and Muslims from North Africa to France*. Princeton: Harvard University Press.

Keraitim, Sahar and Samia Mehrez. 2012. "Mulid al-Tahrir: Semiotics of a Revolution." In *Translating Egypt's Revolution: The Language of Tahrir*, edited by Samia Mehrez, 25–68. Cairo: American University Press.

Monji, Jana. 2015. "'Free Men', Islamophobia and Liberty." http://www.rogerebert.com/far-flung-correspondents/free-men-islamophobia-and-liberty. Last accessed May 25, 2017.

Prince, Mona. 2014. *My Name Is Revolution: An Egyptian Woman's Diary from Eighteen Days in Tahrir*. Translated by Samia Mehrez. Cairo: American University in Cairo Press.

Rooney, Caroline. 2011. "Egyptian Literary Culture and Egyptian Modernity: Introduction." *Journal of Postcolonial Writing* 47 (4): 369–76.

Rooney, Caroline. 2015. "Sufi Springs: Air on an Oud String." *CounterText* 1 (1): 38–58.

Rooney, Caroline and Rita Sakr. 2014. Dir. *White Flags*.

Said, Edward. 1999. Interview with Philip Lopate. *Bomb Magazine*, 69. http://bombmagazine.org/article/2269/edward-said. Last accessed May 24, 2017.

Satloff, Robert. 2006. *Among the Righteous: Lost Stories from the Holocaust's Long Reach into Arab Lands*. New York: Public Affairs.

Selvon, Sam. (1956) 2006. *The Lonely Londoners*. London: Penguin Books.

Shohat, Ella. 2018. "On Orientalist Genealogies: The Arab/Jew Figure Revisited." In *The Edinburgh Companion to the Postcolonial Middle East*, edited by Anna Ball and Karim Mattar. Edinburgh: Edinburgh University Press.

Sontag, Susan. 2009. "Notes on 'Camp.'" In *Against Interpretation and Other Essays*, 275–92. London: Penguin Books.

Soueif, Ahdaf. 2004. *Mezzaterra: Fragments from the Common Ground*. London: Bloomsbury.

Starr, Deborah. 2006. "Drinking, Gambling and Making Merry: Waguih Ghali's Search for Cosmopolitan Agency." *Middle Eastern Literatures* 9 (3): 271–85.

Stephens, Robert. 1971. *Nasser: A Political Biography*. New York: Simon and Schuster.

Thomas, Susie. 2011. "Waguih Ghali: *Beer in the Snooker Club*—1964." *London Fictions*. http://www.londonfictions.com/waguih-ghali-beer-in-the-snooker-club.html. Last accessed May 24, 2017.

Part Two

Migration and the Challenges of Subjectivation

5

Poetics of the Virtual: Technology and Revolution in the Poetry of Sghaier Ouled Ahmed

Hager Ben Driss

> *I was about to write a new poem,*
> *I found Mohamed Bouazizi's funeral.*
> *As I followed the procession,*
> *I realized I was participating in the creation of a whole Revolution.*
> —Sghaier Ouled Ahmed, *The Poetic Leadership*[1]

Sghaier Ouled Ahmed (1955–2016) posted this graffiti-like text, which operates on the frontiers of poetry and prose, on his Facebook wall on January 15, 2011.[2] The words "poem" and "revolution," which close the first and the last lines of the text, define Ouled Ahmed's belief in a poetic agency capable of leading revolutions. Poetry, which maneuvers as a revolutionary act, has also accommodated to a new space: the internet. The Tunisian uprising has enacted a spatial revolution that accommodates hitherto incongruent geographies, namely the virtual space of social media and the real space of the street. Poetry, revolution, and technology lace together and negotiate a new aesthetics wherein poetics and politics engage a dialogue in a porous virtual space.

Dubbed the "Revolution of shabab al-Facebook" (the youth of Facebook), the political uprisings of the Middle East and North Africa region have taken the world aback. These revolutions have forged a new spatial continuum wherein the virtual spaces of social networks and the contested space of the street meet in leaky boundaries. The first sparkle of the so-called Arab Spring took place in the street. On December 17, 2010, the young Mohamed Bouazizi, a Tunisian street fruit vendor, immolated himself in front of the municipal headquarters in Sidi Bouzid, a socially and politically marginalized region in the south of the country. It was a desperate act of protest against confiscating his merchandise by a municipal official. Soon, the incident set the social network ablaze, and Bouazizi became the symbol of social and economic injustice in Tunisia.

Facebook in particular played a significant part in awakening a dormant discontent, inflaming feelings of spurned dignity and spreading dissent. The ripple of protest that mounted on Facebook culminated in a wave of angry people flooding Habib

Bourguiba Avenue in Tunis on January 14, 2011, and asking for justice, freedom, and dignity. Social networks mediated between two seminal moments in the modern history of Tunisia: Bouazizi's self-immolation and thousands of people occupying the street. Asef Bayat's theorization of "street politics" can be recuperated in the case of "online politics." Indeed, "streets serve as a medium through which strangers or casual passersby are able to establish latent communication with one another by recognizing their mutual interests and shared sentiments. This is how a small demonstration may grow into a massive exhibition of solidarity." Such "an epidemic potential of street politics" (2010, 12) reverberates in social networks, albeit in more rapid and escalating proportions. The anonymity and ubiquity of online street users facilitate subversion and transgression.

The conjunction between the virtual (social networks) and the real (the street) is at the heart of the story of the Arab Spring. The "most consistent narratives," claim Philip Howard and Muzammil Hussain, ascribe to the internet and social media a fundamental, active role in these uprisings. Indeed, "digital media helped turn individualized, localized, and community-specific dissent into a structured movement with a collective consciousness about both shared plights and opportunities" (2013, 25). The technical side of these revolutions has been addressed in a plethora of studies looking mainly into their sociopolitical aspects (Salvatore 2011, Howard and Hussain 2013, Amira 2014, Jamshidi 2014, Jamoussi 2016).

The artistic facet of the Arab revolutions, however, remains underresearched and still needs a more profound examination. Samia Mehrez's edited anthology *Translating Egypt's Revolution: The Language of Tahrir* (2012) offers a pertinent research of the textual side of Egypt's revolution. Within the same vein, Anna M. Agathangelou's "Making Anew an Arab Regional Order" (2013) examines the "poetics-agonistiki," or struggle poetry (31), of the Arab Spring and claims that these revolutions were invigorated by an artistic *energeia*. Mohamed Salah Omri's "A Revolution of Dignity and Poetry" (2012) is the first, and so far the most pertinent, essay cogently relating the Tunisian Revolution to poetic expression. His comparative reading of Ouled Ahmed's and Palestinian Mahmoud Darwishe's texts explores the poetics of resistance in their writings. Other studies focused on the ascent of hitherto marginalized or underground artistic forms such as rap music (Gonzalez-Quijano 2013) or the emergence of new artistic expressions like slogans (Colla 2012).

This chapter looks into the spatial continuum created by the Tunisian Revolution and examines the poetics of the virtual. It addresses the work of the late Tunisian poet Sghaier Ouled Ahmed, who offered a fascinating case of using Facebook as a poetical platform of resistance. The tension between the literati and the digerati complicates the interface between literature and the internet. Accordingly, literary writers who make use of social networks are often accused of self-aggrandizement and egocentrism. The case of Ouled Ahmed provides a counterexample, for his use of the social network circumvents the personal and the private to encompass the political and the collective. More than a mere Facebook user, he engaged in political cyber-activism, addressing a transnational online community. His awareness of a global readership is clear in his attempt at interrogating and rectifying the Western grammar of revolutions. The porous space of the internet engenders further spatial leakages, this time between the national and the transnational. Based in Tunisia, Ouled Ahmed's politicized poetry posted on Facebook offers a pertinent case of border-crossing activity. Facebook is a subversive site that fuses and confuses the poetry of revolution and the revolution of poetry, yielding thus new poetics of the virtual.

Literature and Social Networks

As several writers have indulged in an intensive use of social networks, a camp of literati has raised angry, often reprimanding, voices against the use and abuse of Facebook and Twitter. In her essay review of *The Social Network* (2010), a film that charts the story of Facebook and its creator Mark Zuckerberg, Zadie Smith launches a harsh attack on digital life. She describes this social network as a reductive space wherein "everything shrinks. Individual character. Friendship. Language. Sensibility. In a way it is a transcendent experience: we lose our bodies, our messy feelings, our desires, our fears." She also cautions that "our denuded networked selves don't look more free, they just look more owned" (Smith 2010). Within the same vein, Pulitzer Prize winner Jennifer Egan believes that social networks have transformed people's lives into "a huge apartment block, [in] which everyone's cell looks exactly the same" (qtd. in Schuessler 2013). Such discontent is also directed to famous novelists and poets who use social networks as a podium for self-publicity.

A new type of literary feud has emerged between "disconnected" literati and "connected" ones. A notorious example is offered by American novelist Jonathan Franzen, a fierce opponent of the internet. In his essay "What's Wrong with the Modern World?," he speaks about his "disappointment when a novelist who ought to have known better, Salman Rushdie, succumbs to Twitter" (2013). Rushdie's retaliation on Twitter was as much acerbic as sarcastic: "Dear #Franzen, @MargaretAtwood @JoyceCarolOates @nycnovel @NathanEnglander @Shteyngart and I are fine with Twitter. Enjoy your ivory tower" (qtd. in Schuessler 2013). Rushdie's list of literary writers whom he tagged in his tweet could have been much longer, as a growing number of novelists and poets are using social networks and even making a case of it. Turkish writer Elif Shafak, for instance, has difficulties "understanding the widely held criticism among the literati that the Internet is a fake world which novelists and poets should refrain from if they want to preserve their intellectual depth, focus, and integrity." Shafak ends her essay, "Storytelling, Fake Worlds, and the Internet," by claiming social media to be an effective "political platform" (2015). Shafak's understanding of the subversive power of technology—that belonging to a country where the word becomes a weapon in the struggle against oppression and dictatorship—is quite similar to that of Sghaier Ouled Ahmed.

Ouled Ahmed's use of Facebook as a space of protest finds explanation in the long years of silencing and censorship that characterized the two governments of Habib Bourguiba (1956–87) and Zine al-Abidine Ben Ali (1987–2011). With a state-policed media, the freedom of expression was nullified in Tunisia. Ben Ali's policy of beautifying the country by circulating an image of an open modern society to attract foreign investments resulted in a growing rate of connectivity. The government encouraged and even subsidized internet cafés, implemented the internet at universities, secondary schools, and primary schools, and enhanced the purchase of computers. In 2001, out of a population of 10.5 million, the estimated number of Tunisian internet users was around 4 million, with 2.5 million subscribers to Facebook (Amira 2014, 45). By 2010, Tunisia had the highest rate of connectivity among the Arab countries, with 34 percent of all internet users (Kallander 2013, 7).

The story of the internet in Tunisia was steeped in dramatic irony. While encouraging connectivity, the government prohibited and persecuted any type of digital dissent. More than six hundred cyber officers regulated internet traffic (Amira 2014, 45) and prohibited access to sites deemed dangerous to the national security. The situation, however, veered toward the farcical as the "father" of the nation, who bestowed knowledge upon his people, was not aware that he was to be ousted with that knowledge. Digital dissent generated a type of "Caliban digerati," who circumvented the government's tactics of internet censorship. The result was similar in its dramatic irony to Caliban's use of Pospero's language in Shakespeare's *The Tempest*: "You taught me language; and my profit on't/Is I know how to curse" (1986, 33). In the Tunisian context, Caliban's words would outline the addendum: "You gave me the internet, and my profit on it is to throw you outside the country." My catachrestic use of Caliban's subversive use of language and knowledge in a colonial situation finds resonance in Ouled Ahmed's statement, "We are the victims of this independent colonization" (2013a, 10). The foreign colonization only ceded place to a local one. Indeed, Tunisia was colonized for over fifty years by two repressive governments.

It was within this Caliban-like digital performance that Ouled Ahmed launched his guerillas during and after the revolution. Contrary to Zadie Smith, who accused Zuckerberg of creating "something like a noosphere, an Internet with one mind" (2010), Ouled Ahmed praised the creator of Facebook for this technology, "a wonderful tool of communication that facilitated fast revolutions" (Ouled Ahmed 2014). In several interviews, he hailed social networks as new tools of dissent. "We have to understand that technological and digital development have by now the final word," he stated in an interview. "This development has contributed in launching revolutions and changing regimes. What happened to Ben Ali is the best example. Before the digital turn, revolutions used to last for years; today, revolutions start and finish quickly" (Ouled Ahmed 2016). Ouled Ahmed found in Facebook a free and unrestrained space against censorship and regimented creativity.

Before the revolution, artistic creation in Tunisia was as restrained as freedom of speech. Ouled Ahmed had a long story of struggle against repression, which he described in a 2012 essay, "Waiting for the Second Round":

> I came to Tunis from Sidi Bouzid by the end of the last century, precisely in 1981. Since then, I have been fighting oppression with two weapons: pen and language. I used language, my unique weapon, to fight Bourguiba and Ben Ali as well as the one party, which became the only one. I also fought those who were once in the opposition and ended up in the oppressor's camp. I fought legions of writers and intellectuals who were the police arm of the regime. And I am still fighting. (2013a, 115–16)

In 1984, *Nachid al-Ayyam al-Sitta* (Song of the Six Days), his poetic response to the violent events of the Bread Upheaval in Tunisia, was immediately censored, and he was incarcerated. The poem is a long elegy to a nation betrayed by its rulers and to a population living under siege and perpetual surveillance:

They were behind the door,
in the train, inside the walls,
and the green blood cells.
They were transcribing
his words and his traits.
Stripped was he of secrets and underwear! (Ouled Ahmed 2015a, 310)

Ouled Ahmed was imprisoned twice and fired from work between 1987 and 1992. His poems were banned and he was prohibited from appearing in the media. His short truce with Ben Ali's regime resulted in the founding of the House of Poetry, an intellectual space for poets. He explains in *The Poetic Leadership* (2013a) that the government benefited from this short peaceful relationship: "My poems were allowed to be published, albeit in a mutilated way, so that the government could boast: 'the regime is democratic because Ouled Ahmed can write'" (162). Very quickly, he resumed his antagonist relationship with the state. His feelings of bitterness and frustration remained as acute as ever. He translated them in dark poems about censorship and death.

"The Mouse" is a short poem that illustrates Ouled Ahmed's ironic attitude toward a censorship apparatus that he continually challenged with a perseverant act of writing:

O homeless mouse:
be less greedy than the censor.
Nibble those books steeped in certainty,
and take care of my manuscripts. (2015a, 297)

The ironic image of the mouse, who becomes a more sensible figure than the censor, is Ouled Ahmed's way to lament a poetic wasteland where poetry piles in mountains of rubbish that is only good for feeding mice.

Death as related to poetry is a compulsive image in Ouled Ahmed's texts. The act of writing has an obituary quality, for the poem is doomed to death as soon as it is composed (Ben Driss 2016). In "Maqam al Wuquf" (Shrine for Standing), he bitterly mourns the death of his texts:

Standing up
and words,
like a coffin,
walking
to their grave
in
the
poem. (2015a, 295)

In this tomb-like land, the word is immediately executed, as he illustrates in "Uktub" (Write):

Write whatever you want.
Get ready for the two angels
and be a forgotten text
under Gabriel's wings. (2015a, 152)

It is not surprising, therefore, that the revolution was Ouled Ahmed's long-awaited moment for poetic revenge. He found in Facebook a space of defiance and a means to curse the oppressor.

Poetry and Revolution

Ouled Ahmed started his Revolution on Facebook on December 17, 2010, the day Bouazizi immolated himself. In a small room in his apartment located in Rades, a southern suburb of Tunis, he created a virtual space of rebellious writing. He bestowed upon himself the title of the "poetic leader of the revolution," and he called this space the "poetic headquarters of the Tunisian Revolution," or, as he suggested, the "Tunisian headquarters of the poetic revolution." This way or the other, revolution and poetry lace together, exchange meaning, and negotiate agency. "All the political parties said they did not start the Revolution. Who did it then?," he wonders. "The answer: poetry and young people" (Ouled Ahmed 2013a, 278). Accordingly, he made it a point to obfuscate the lines between poeticizing politics and politicizing poetry.

Ouled Ahmed's poetry offers a terrain of entente to the edgy relationship between politics and poetics. "What's poetry in the end?," he asks in his poem "By Way of Keeping Spirits Up." His trenchant answer would become his motto in his poetic revolution: "It is a linguistic speculation/whose aim is to assist power in its downfall" (Trans. Omri 2012, 159). In his discussion of the role of writers and intellectuals, Edward Said astutely captures the paradox in the "unresolved tension" between politics and art. "We might as well ask," Said contends, "whether non-political writer or intellectual is a notion that has much content in it" (2002, 20). Said's theorization of the public role of the intellectual perfectly chimes with Ouled Ahmed's vision: "There are intellectuals who have not realized yet that we are living in a political stage *par excellence*, a stage that necessitates resistance and clear stands" (Ouled Ahmed 2016). On December 24, 2010, he took a rather precarious stand at that time: he openly and publicly sided with the burgeoning revolution, a position he defiantly posted on Facebook:

It is high time I chose between home [*mawtini*] and homeland [*watan*].
The first, which is really the first, is Sidi Bouzid,
the second, which could have been the first, is Tunisia.
I start immediately my choice, leaving to the custodians of patriotism the pleasure to bark and the leftovers they gain from lavishing their flatteries on the regime via official TV channels. (2013a, 9)

Ouled Ahmed's use of Facebook provided him with a channel to emerge as a public intellectual whose role, according to Said, is "to challenge and defeat both an imposed silence and the normalized quiet of unseen power wherever and whenever possible" (Said 2002, 31). Indeed, "those who keep silent, are not poets" (2016), Ouled Ahmed contends.

Poetry, the poet insists, is the ultimate legitimate leader of the revolution. "The label 'poetic leadership,'" he explains, "is not a stylistic embellishment. It rather demonstrates that the Revolution was a poetic demand" (2013a, 47). Poetry was liberated from classrooms, literary salons, or official cultural spaces and brought to the street. It became a galvanizer of rebellion. Tunisian poet Abu al-Qasim al-Shabbi's poem "The Will to Life" (1955) offers the best example of the poetic impulse energizing Arab revolutions. Al-Shabbi's "was perhaps the first poetry to be appropriated by protesters that infused the term al-sha'b with revolutionary connotations among the narratives of revolutions sweeping across the Arab world" (Sanders and Visona 2012, 229). The two famous opening lines of his poem, "If, one day, the people will to live/Then fate must obey," were chanted not only during the Tunisian Revolution but during the Egyptian as well. The slogans derived from these two lines, like "the people want to collapse the regime," testified to "the presence of poetry as well as the intimate relationship between people and poetry" (Ouled Ahmed 2015c).

The undecided relationship between politics and aesthetics still raises doubts over the agency of art. In his essay "Revolution, Transformation and Utopia: The Function of Literature," Bill Ashcroft discusses the active role of literature in times of revolutions. He contends that literature has the important function of inspiring hope because it dwells in the realm of imagination and dreams: "Creative works confirm a fundamental truth of revolution; that no future is achieved unless it is first imagined" (2014, 24). That was exactly what Ouled Ahmed purported to achieve in his poetic leadership. "Poetry is in reality an ensemble of imagined images asking for liberty and trying to make life possible," he declares in an interview, "like art, poetry operates on the frontiers of dreams. Revolution is a dream because it is based on cutting the ties with an oppressive past and heralding a better life. Revolution, therefore, is a poetic act" (Ouled Ahmed 2015c). Poetry and revolution exchange meaning and urgency in a process of mutual fertilization: the poetry of revolution is also a revolution of poetry.

Poetics of the Virtual

Ouled Ahmed's anthology of collected texts, *Al-Qiyada al-Shi'riyya li al-Thawra al-Tunusiyya: Yawmiyyat* (The Poetic Leadership of the Tunisian Revolution: A Diary), affirms new aesthetics of the virtual. It especially upsets the dividing lines between online writings and printed works. The book assembles Ouled Ahmed's posts on Facebook between 2010 and 2012. The elocutionary quality of his online texts, often midway between verse and prose, obfuscates another boundary, the one between the oral and the written. He infuses his texts with Tunisian dialect, the language of the marginalized grassroots who made the revolution. "Ya Sidi 'Arfinik" (Sir, We Know You), a poem posted on Saturday January 8, 2010, is fully written in Tunisian dialect, something rather unusual for Ouled Ahmed, who had hitherto kept to standard Arabic:

Ya sidi we know you're a policeman
and we know those who know you're a policeman.
By God, we know you're a policeman,
even the director knows it.
Ya sidi we know you're a director
and we know those who know you're a director.
By God, we know you're a director,
even the minister knows it.
Ya Sidi we know you're a minister
and we know those who know you're a minister.
By God we know you're a minister,
even the President knows it.

Ya sidi we know you're a President
and we know those who know you're a President.
By God we know you're a President,
even the policeman knows.

The poem ironically enumerates in an ascending hierarchy the different agents of oppression in the country: the policeman, the director, the minister, and the president. The mounting irony in the poem culminates in amalgamating "president" and "policeman" in the fourth stanza to describe a police state. The exasperation and escalating anger of the speaking voice transpires through the reiteration of the phrase "*ya sidi,*" literally "my master." The exact meaning of this phrase, however, depends on the tone of the speaker, as it can be used in a polite, friendly, or mocking way. The speaker's annoyance is clear through the excessive repetition that governs each stanza, as well as the whole poem. The eloquence of the text is based on Tunisian idiomatic language. The ironic "*ya sidi*" is emphasized by the sarcastic "we know you," which in Tunisian Arabic is an invitation to stop lies and hypocrisy.

The poem ends with a stanza midway between Tunisian dialect and standard Arabic, testifying to the linguistic continuum that characterizes social networks:

Ya sidi just let us
draw dots
on the letters,
in the middle of letters,
under the letters.
Ya sidi just let us
draw the wing of freedom. (2013a, 205–6)

The poem closes with the power of language to liberate people from an institutionalized oppression. Language, contends Ouled Ahmed, shows the aesthetic side of this technological revolution. Social media, he states, "has molded a telegrammatic and communicative language anchored in immediacy. All these features convey the essence of poetry itself as it is a linguistic condensation attempting to seize a running and unruly moment" (Ouled Ahmed 2016). The linguistic negotiation between the internet and poetry destabilizes an elite-regulated cultural life. It also liberates minds from ossified, often institutionalized, spaces of producing and consuming poetry.

Because it was initially produced online, the soft version of Ouled Ahmed's *Poetic Leadership* testifies that the virtual generates its proper aesthetics, which is capable to compete with traditional channels of literary productions. In his description of this work, Ouled Ahmed points out its new poetics:

> I started writing a volume of poetry that will be published soon. It is a collection of revolutionary diaries entitled *The Poetic Leadership of the Revolution*. I was aware that it was the first postmodern Revolution in the twenty-first century; a savvy revolution that used new technology. The texts I wrote, diaries, poetry or prose, replicated the new forms of the revolution. Some poems took the shape of short Facebook posts, sometimes with a military-like headlines. In the absence of political leadership, poetry takes the lead. (Ouled Ahmed 2012)

Ouled Ahmed's book, which he insists on calling "a volume of poetry," is a potpourri, a textual space amalgamating poetry, prose, and journalism. He chronicles in this work the Tunisian everyday revolution, hence the subtitle "Yawmiyyat," a diary. It is divided into three parts: "Texts of the Revolution," "Poems of the Revolution," and "Telegrams and Letters from the General Headquarters." The book powerfully captures the revolutionary euphoria of the beginning and the subsequent disappointment and malaise after the first elections (October 23, 2011) won by the Islamist party, al-Nahda.

Ouled Ahmed's combination of wry humor and serious political activism is clearly manifest in his epigraphic introduction to the first part of his book: "With God's blessing, while benefiting from Satan's expertise, I give myself the license to publish this fifty-word daily newspaper whose public slogan is: 'Helping power to collapse'" (2013a, 13). Facebook offers a rebellious medium apt to deface power. The "carnivalesque" overtones of the virtual space supply "contested strategies through which space and time are inverted through parody and grotesque symbols, imageries and languages" (Rahimi 2011, 3). Masquerading as a military leader of the revolution provides Ouled Ahmed with a carnivalesque power to undermine the oppressive regime. The following excerpt from "A Free Speech to a Free People" offers a pertinent example of both the creative and the subversive gestures in such online politics:

> The Headquarters of the Poetic Leadership of the Tunisian Revolution.
> Wednesday 19 January, the fifth day of the Revolution.
> Mr. Mohamed Bouazizi,
> Young People,
> Free people:
> Now that we have liberated ourselves from the independent colonization and become the way we want: fully human beings, our duty is to lead a life worth of living …
> Now that the Dictator has run away, testifying once more, that any dictator will ineluctably run away to a tomb outside his country—he ran away leaving behind his party, gangs, and militias …, we ought to cut the road before them.

Occupy the streets ...
The free people of the world lay heavy expectations on you. If we disappoint ourselves, we'll fail all of them.
Hail to the Revolution. (2013a, 32)

This parody of an inflaming speech proffered by a revolutionary leader obfuscates the lines between digital mutiny and street protest. People are encouraged to occupy public space while the poet himself is occupying an online street. Ouled Ahmed offers here a pertinent example of the fluid boundaries between street politics and online poetics.

The revolution invigorated Ouled Ahmed with a renewed hope in homeland and poetry. His 1984 lines "I'm still inhabiting a shroud/Still looking for a homeland" ("Song of Six Days") fade in front of an elated optimism like the one he chanted in both verse and prose a short time before the 2011 elections:

I'm writing a new poem. It seems to be a good one. I think that the people who are still continuing the revolution against the "ministers of God" will take one of its lines as a slogan to topple down oppression and backwardness. O Tunisian People, it seems that my life is still possible among you:
If you were a great people,
Vote for yourself in the nick of time.
If you still crave for humiliation after degradation,
Cheer up and prepare yourselves for the ultimate blow. (2013a, 285)

The virtual space of Facebook provides him with a strong sense of poetic justice: it is here that he, as well as his poems, can finally survive. The term "revolution" is the linking thread between Ouled Ahmed's online poetic rebellion and people's street mutiny. This is why he was adamant about using no other label but "revolution" to name what happened in Tunisia between December 17, 2010, and January 14, 2011. "Scribbling is written with ink; Revolution is written with blood," he admonishes his Facebook followers. "To those who circulate the label 'Jasmine revolution,' please get educated a little more during curfews. Lift your heads and say: the Tunisian Revolution" (2013a, 216). Such a reproof aims at claiming an authentic revolution made in Tunisia.

Ouled Ahmed's refusal of labels and coinages describing the Tunisian Revolution marks a transnational moment wherein he negotiates the Western grammar of revolutions. Tags such as "Arab Spring," "Arab Awakening," or "Arab Tsunami" are all steeped in "terminological schizophrenia" (Browlee and Ghiabi 2017) stemming from the perception of the Arab world as stagnant and unable to change. Arab exceptionalism, argues Asef Bayat, "informs the whole edifice of the 'democracy promotion industry' in the West, which pushes for instigating change through outside powers, one that does not exclude the use of force" (2010, 3). The label "jasmine revolution," first circulated by Western media, corroborates the exotic image of a country whose economy relied heavily on tourism. Mohamed Salah Omri believes that it is "a reassuringly safe way of referring to Tunisia's upheaval: it caters to the exotic imaginary, and invokes lab-incubated revolts" (Omri 2011). The word "revolution" destabilizes the occidental myth of the sleeping Mediterranean beauty waiting for the Western kiss.

Facebook, a transnational space par excellence, accommodated the poet's negotiation and retrieval of the Tunisian Revolution. While aware of its potential disfiguring, he continued to urge his online followers to translate his posts into all possible languages: "Read and translate simultaneously to your languages, for they are continuing their massacres ... out of cruelty?" (2013a, 17). This excerpt, taken from a long text titled "The Lesson of Tunisia," posted on January 12, 2011, is translated into both French and German (19–22). Translation inscribes the text into a transnational collective action, a "process through which individuals, nonstate groups, and/or organizations mobilize jointly around issues, goals, and targets that link the domestic and international arenas" (von Bulow 2010, 5). His detailed online transcription of the revolution offers not only a sense of immediacy but also a new mode of transnational poetics. His ability to capture every moment of the revolution and diffuse it online goes beyond Henri Lefebvre's "Let everyday life become a work of art" (1984, 204). Ouled Ahmed proposes, "Let every moment of the revolution become a work of art."

The term "revolution" in Ouled Ahmed's work has a spatial resonance; it is a rebellion that redefines spaces and makes places. Transforming the virtual space of Facebook into a poetic place cannot be severed from the geo-poetic concerns in his work wherein Tunisia is loved and celebrated. The virtual exudes a "sense of place" demonstrated, according to Yi Fu Tuan, when people "apply their moral and aesthetic discernment to sites and locations" (1979, 410). Even though disappointed, silenced, and ostracized, Ahmed kept a strong passion for a country he cherished the hope to liberate one day. In "Love of Country," he boasts his love for Tunisia:

> We love this country
> As none has done.
> Morning
> Evening
> Before morning
> After evening
> On Sunday again.
> Should they kill us,
> As they have done;
> Should they expel us,
> As they have done,
> Conquerors to this country we shall return. (Trans. Khalifa 2015b, 55)

"Love of Country" is Ouled Ahmed's most famous poem. The simple rhythm and the proverbial quality of its style make it vie in popularity with al-Shabbi's "The Will to Life." This poem, as well as all Ahmed's poetic texts about Tunisia, are anchored in a strong topophilia.

The solid affective bonding to homeland is at the heart of Ouled Ahmed's poetic revolution. His love for the country tolerated no negotiations or concessions. In "Tunisian All at Once or Never," he writes:

> I am writing my song with my blood
> To a martyr who was my mouth and voice,

To a future, O friend that has not come for centuries
   Tunisian once.
   Tunisian all at once or never shall I be. (Trans. Khalifa 2015b, 57)

Ouled Ahmed equates in these lines writing poetry and dying for one's country. Poetry in his revolutionary glossary is another word for homeland. "Write!," he braces himself in his poem "Write": "Write!/so that you prevent them/from destroying home [*beit*]" (2015a, 159). The word *beit* in Arabic has a double meaning: "home" and also "a line in a poem." The oppressive regime in Tunisia destroyed both—homeland and poetry. It is through a virtual home (social network) that Ahmed retrieved his country and his poetic power.

Technology versus Ideology

Ouled Ahmed rebelled against all types of political oppression and ideological regimentation. His war against what he called "the ministers of God" or the custodians of religion started long time ago with a 1988 poem, "Supplications," a poem that ignited the wrath of religious zealots:

   O God,
Help me against them.
They gored my camel
And sanctioned my blood
In places where you bade no blood
Be spilt on the prayer rag.
   O God
I seek protection in you from my kinsmen.
They sell cheap wine in day light,
And ruin the drunk's innocent night!
   O God
The tickets for the afterlife are sold out.
But no money, no time, no reason could I afford.
Please tear their tickets, O God,
And let my heart rejoice.
Did you not promise us your grace? (Trans. Khalifa 2015b, 59)

The poem, with its high insurgent overtones, mocks blind religiosity and its utilization to orchestrate people's lives. Because of this poem, Ouled Ahmed was accused of heresy and was pronounced an infidel.

His highly controversial article "Ideology and Technology," originally published in *al-Mawkif* (September 4, 1984), intensified his image as an opponent of religion. In this article, he ironically criticizes the use of loudspeakers to call for prayers. "Between the ideological enthusiasm and the technological stupidity," he states, "there is ample room to make of the muezzin a topic for modern writing." According to him, the ideological enthusiasm starts with shouting "*la ilaha illa allah*" (there is only one God), which is a matter of fact for all Muslims and does not need to be proved. This enthusiasm, however, morphs into "stupidity" when the technology of the loudspeaker is used and abused to propagate a fundamental truth. His point against such use of this technology is that it disturbs the sleep "of children, ill people, seculars, tourists, and those who believe in God but do not pray" (2013b). Ouled Ahmed's semiotic reading of the loudspeaker challenges the sacred and the taboo. This technology used in the call to prayer has become for many people a part of Islam that should not be criticized or questioned.

The poet's war against the guardians of religion gained momentum before and after the elections of October 23, 2011. The internet became the poet's savvy technology to fight a new way of life insidiously propagated by Islamists whose social agenda was based on "the regimentation of the ways of eating, drinking, dressing, and fornicating" (Ouled Ahmed 2013a, 59). Between March and October 2011, his posts on Facebook targeted mainly the Salafists. On March 10, for instance, he wrote, "Anyone who hasn't read five different and contradictory writers has no right to create a political party. On the other hand, when we say 'we refuse any foreign intervention in our affairs', we also mean the intervention of the sky!" (2013a, 226). On October 10, he posted eleven short messages, all of them criticizing al-Nahda's politicization of religion and the Islamists' aversion to art and freedom (250). In subsequent posts, a few days before the elections, he admonished Tunisians to remember that they made an ideology-free revolution and they should keep it free from all ideologies, including religion (251).

Ouled Ahmed was concerned not only with the Islamists' infiltration in political life but also their attempt at changing the social model of Tunisia. "Those people who have never ever watched a film or a play, never wrote one single poem worthy to be chanted by revolutionary people" (Ouled Ahmed 2013a, 250) cannot be trusted with the future of the country. Women are often the first target of Salafist thinking, and Ouled Ahmed warned against this gender-oriented ideology. The poet's celebration of women is articulated in one of his most famous and often quoted poems, "Women":

> I wrote
> and wrote again
> till I exhausted all letters.
> I described
> and described again
> till I consumed all images.
> I wrap it up, then,
> and carry on:
> women of my country
> are truly women. (2015a, 180)

"*Nisau biladi/nisaun wa nisf*" became a feminist revolutionary slogan during and after elections. He believed that "women's votes will be decisive in the elections because it simply means the choice of a social model. It is not a political question; it is rather a structural and strategic matter" (2013a, 247). Accordingly, he intensified his Facebook guerillas against a social model in which women were nullified. In his poem "Qawsaqab," wherein he juxtaposes the creative power of the pen (poetry) to the violent authority of the sword (ideology), he vents his apprehensions over a potential society shrouded in black: "Is that a woman or a female?/What's her name?/A woman with a *niqab* is just nameless" (2015a, 83).

One day before the elections, Saturday, October 22, 2011, Ouled Ahmed posted a poem addressing Tunisian women voters: "A Last Letter to the Women of Tunisia":

> In the heart of time
> In the polling booth,
> Remember that men have ruled you for twenty centuries.
> You were their things,
> their shadows.
> Do not count on doubt despite your clear vision,
> But read the book of poetry before politics and religion. (Trans. Khalifa 2015b, 63)

It is significant that in this poem, too, Ouled Ahmed advances poetry as a tool of revolution, this time a revolution against patriarchy and misogyny. Because poetry comes before "politics and religion," it acquires the legitimate role of the leader. Poetry, according to Ouled Ahmed, is a revolutionary medium to collapse ideology.

Conclusion

The Tunisian Revolution, as well as the other uprisings that swept the Arab world, offered new spatial parameters. The spatial turn, inaugurated by Michel Foucault and Henry Lefebvre in the 1970s, is defined by Edward Soja as a move to retrieve space from the Bergsonian time-oriented vision of human affairs (Soja 2009). The new spatial turn started up by *Shabab al-Facebook* in the beginning of the new millennium effaced the fissure between the virtual and the real. The overlapping boundaries between social networks and the street engendered a nomadic revolution transgressing the front lines of digital and physical topographies. It created in the process, to use Soja's words, an "ontological parity ... with neither being extrinsically privileged" (2009, 18). The dialectical relationship between social media and physical spaces was crucial in enacting fast revolutions.

Social networks, offering new technological spaces of protest, were also an apt artistic medium. These revolutions were marked by one major feature: an energizing poetic strain. Sghaier Ouled Ahmed was the first poet to seize this opportunity and declare poetry as the leader of the Tunisian Revolution. In fact, Ouled Ahmed started his proper poetic revolution long time ago. His 2015 volume of poetry *Muswaddat Watan* (Draft of a Homeland) is a collection of pre- and post-revolution poems testifying to his own continuous rebellion. A great number of his old poems, like "Love of Country" (1988), which, significantly, opens the collection, or "Song of the Six Days" (1984) which records an important social upheaval in Tunisia, still sound fresh and timely.

The new and innovative turn in Ouled Ahmed's work, starting from December 17, 2010, and continuing until his death on April 5, 2016, was his unremitting use of Facebook as a channel of writing and protest. It was a space to write/right old and new wrongs. As he blurred the lines between the private and the public, the personal narratives about his oppression by the old regime became a testimony of a collective trauma. Facebook was his headquarters, a location of poetical and political activism. The term "headquarters" was not a mere metaphor, for he used it literally as it is clear in this statement posted on Facebook on January 16, 2011, addressing his followers: "Your private messages on Facebook hinder my work for the Revolution" (2013a, 214). In other words, Facebook was not a site to indulge in private socialization; it was an official place for militant activities.

As a place maker, Ouled Ahmed transformed the virtual space of social network into a place of poetry and revolution. As he complicated the lines between poeticizing the revolution and revolutionizing poetry, he created a poetics of the virtual, a new geo-poetics combining virtual geography with poetry. The result is a type of writing that trespasses across the traditional borders between prose and verse, online texts and printed ones.

Notes

1 Unless otherwise indicated, translations from Ouled Ahmed's texts and interviews are mine.
2 For a full biography of Sghaier Ouled Ahmed and a survey of his work, see Hager Ben Driss, "Mohamed Sghaier Ouled Ahmed," *The Literary Encyclopedia*, October 13, 2016, https://www.litencyc.com/php/speople.php?rec=true&UID=13853.

References

Agathangelou, Anna M. 2013. "Making Anew an Arab Regional Order." In *Arab Revolutions and World Transformations*, edited by Anna M. Agathangelou and Nevzat Soguk. London: Routledge. 31–44.
Amira, Aleya-Sghaier. 2014. "The Tunisian Revolution: The Revolution of Dignity." In *Revolution, Revolt, and Reform in North Africa: The Arab Spring and Beyond*, edited by Ricardo René Larément. London: Routledge. 30–52.
Aschroft, Bill. 2014. "Revolution, Transformation and Utopia: The Function of Literature." In *IAFOR Keynote Series*, edited by Joseph Haldane. Australia: University of NSW. 1–26.
Bayat, Asef. 2010. *Life as Politics: How Ordinary People Change the Middle East*. Amsterdam: Amsterdam University Press.
Browlee, Billie Jeanne, and Ghiabi, Marziar. 2016. "Passive, Silent and Revolutionary: The 'Arab Spring' Revisited." *Middle East Crit*. July 2 25: 3. Accessed May 9, 2017.
Colla, Elliot. 2012. "The People Want." *Middle East Report* 263: 8–13.
Franzen, Jonathan. 2013. "What's Wrong with Modern World?" *The Guardian*, September 13, https://www.theguardian.com/books/2013/sep/13/jonathan-franzen-wrong-modern-world

Gonzalez- Quijano, Ives. 2013. "Rap, an Art of the Revolution or a Revolution in Art?" *Orient-Institute Studies* 2: 1–9.
Howard, Philip N., and Hussain, Muzammil M. 2013. *Democracy's Fourth Wave*. Oxford: Oxford University Press.
Jamoussi, Jawhar. 2016. *Al-Iftiradi wa al-Thawra: Makanat al-Internet fi Nashat Mojtama' Madani 'Arabi*. Doha: Arabic Center for Research and Policy Studies.
Jamshidi, Maryam. 2014. *The Future of the Arab Spring: Civic Entrepreneurship in Politics, Art, and Technology*. Amsterdam: Butterworth-Heinemann.
Kallander, Amy Aisen. 2013. "From TUNeZine to Nhar '3la '3ammar: A Reconsideration of the Role of Bloggers in Tunisia's Revolution." *Arab Media and Society*, 17: 1–28.
Lefebvre, Henri. 1984. *Everyday Life in the Modern World*. Translated by S. Rabinovitch. New Brunswick: Transaction Publishers.
Mehrez, Samia. Ed. 2012. *Translating Egypt's Revolution: The Language of Tahrir*. Cairo: The American University of Cairo Press.
Omri, Mohamed Salah. 2012. "A Revolution of Dignity and Poetry." *Boundary* 239, 1: 137–55.
Omri, Mohamed Salah. 2011. "Tunisia: A Revolution for Dignity and Freedom That Cannot Be Colour-coded." *TNI*, January 29, https://www.tni.org/es/node/12503
Ouled Ahmed, Sghaier. 2012. "Ana Tunis al-okhra … ramadun mobtakir" (I Am the Other Tunisia … a Creative Ash). *France* 24, December 28, http://www.france24.com/ar/20121228
Ouled Ahmed, Sghaier. 2013a. *Al-Qiyada al-Shi'riyya li al-Thawra al-Tunusiyya: Yawmiyyat* (The Poetic Leadership of the Tunisian Revolution: A Diary). Tunis: Manshurat Ouled Ahmed.
Ouled Ahmed, Sghaier. 2013b. "Al-Tiknolujiya wa al-Idyulujia" (Technology and Ideology). *Al-Shahid*, March 30, http://www.turess.com/achahed/25395
Ouled Ahmed, Sghaier. 2014. "Sha'ir mina al-Maghrib" (A Poet from Morocco). *Al-Quds al-Arabi*, July 18, http://www.alquds.co.uk/?p=194406
Ouled Ahmed, Sghaier. 2015a. *Muswaddat Watan* (Draft of a Homeland). Tunis: Al-Dar al-Arabiyya li al-Kitab.
Ouled Ahmed, Sghaier. 2015b. *Ouled Ahmed: Selected Poems*. Tunis: Nirvana.
Ouled Ahmed, Sghaier. 2015c. Interview with Ahmed Zakarna. *Alhadath*, March 10, http://www.alhadath.ps/article/13300/
Ouled Ahmed, Sghaier. 2016. Interview with Mohamed Moncef Ben Mrad. *Al-Jomhuriyya*, April 13, http://www.jomhouria.com/art51496_%D8%AE%D8%A7%D8%B5
Rahimi, Babak. 2011. "Facebook Iran: The Carnivalesque Politics of Online Social Networking." *Sociologica* 3: 1–17.
Said, Edward. 2002. "The Public Role of Writers and Intellectuals." In *The Public Intellectual*, edited by Helen Small. Oxford: Blackwell. 19–39.
Salvatore, Armando. 2011. "Before (and After) the 'Arab Spring': From Connectedness to Mobilization in the Public Sphere." *Orienté Moderno* 1: 5–12.
Sanders, Lewis, and Visona, Mark. 2012. "The Soul of Tahrir: Poetics of the Revolution." In *Translating Egypt's Revolution: The Language of Tahrir*, edited by Samia Mehrez. Cairo: The American University of Cairo Press. 213–48.
Schuessler, Jennifer. 2013. "Jonathan Franzen Assails the Internet (Again)." *The New York Times*, September 16, http://artsbeat.blogs.nytimes.com/2013/09/16/jonathan-franzen-assails-the-internet-again/

Shafak, Elif. 2015. "Storytelling, Fake Worlds, and the Internet." *World Literature Today*, January, http://www.worldliteraturetoday.org/2015/january/storytelling-fake-worlds-and-internet-elif-shafak

Shakespeare, William. (1623). 1986. *The Tempest*. London: Methuen.

Smith, Zadie. 2010. "Generation Why?" *New York Review*, November 25, http://www.nybooks.com/articles/2010/11/25/generation-why/

Soja, Edward. 2009. "Taking Place Personally," in *The Spatial Turn: Interdisciplinary Perspectives*, eds. Barney Warf and Santa Arias, 11–35. London: Routledge.

Tuan, Yi-Fu. 1979. "Space and Place: Humanistic Perspective," in *Philosophy in Geography*, eds. Stephen Gale and Gunnar Olsen, 387–427. London: D. Reidel Publishing Company.

Von Bulow, Marisa. 2010. *Building Transnational Networks: Civil Society Networks and the Politics of Trade in the Americas*. Cambridge: Cambridge University Press.

6

Identity Politics and Digital Space: Adel Abidin's *Abidin Travels: Welcome to Baghdad*

Jenna Altomonte

Being politically correct is almost like being a hypocrite. History is all about manipulation; as Napoleon said, it's like a set of lies we all agreed upon. I always ask myself [about] how we could live without history. And how can we rely on a history which is written by the victor?[1]

—Adel Abidin

Introduction

At the 2007 Venice Biennale in Italy, Iraqi-born artist Adel Abidin premiered his interactive installation, *Abidin Travels: Welcome to Baghdad*. The multifaceted exhibition space consisted of reservation kiosks, travel pamphlets, and an information center. Located at a reservation kiosk computer, participants accessed a travel booking webpage at www.abdintravels.com. Similar in design to popular travel sites like Expedia or Orbitz, abidintravels.com invited participants to explore the cultural and historical sites of Baghdad via interactive video links. Rather than show *souqs* or open-air cafés, viewers witnessed footage of burning buildings, bloated corpses, and US Coalition troops cavorting at checkpoints. The narrator warned about kidnappings and recent execution sites, using a body-count tracker to keep potential travelers informed of the most recent casualties. After viewing the travel videos, participants could reserve flights to Baghdad from the United States, Western Europe, and Scandinavia. Using violent content and imagery from the aftermath of the 2003 US invasion, the piece served to inform potential visitors about the limitations of travel to and from Iraq.

Using *Abidin Travels* as a conduit for critical inquiry, I challenge several frameworks used to understand post-invasion identities as collective congeries formed by displacement. In particular, *Abidin Travels* works as a critical device that urges viewers to consider how diasporic identities are represented via mediatized intervention. Abidin uses a "sharp palette of irony and humor" to recognize limitations imposed on Iraqis living in diasporic regions.[2] Using an amalgamation of both lived and collective experiences, his work serves as a complex instrument for promoting social and political change in regions affected by war.

Three frameworks will be used to articulate the creation, premise, and effect of *Abidin Travels*. The first approach examines the events, both personal and collective, that inspired the creation of the installation. Work by fellow Iraqi artist Wafaa Bilal will complement Abidin and serve to demonstrate common tropes used by Iraqi artists working to create post-invasion content in their oeuvres. Bilal's *Virtual Jihadi* will be discussed to explicate the various prejudices Iraqis encounter while residing in regions or nations outside the homeland.

The second approach examines the premise and execution of the installation, focusing primarily on the videos and website content. This section extrapolates on the affective use of humor as a critical device. The travel-agency format incorporates humor to placate the viewer before revealing violent footage and images.

The third approach contests the original intention of the installation, specifically how Abidin critiques the relationship between the Iraqi civilian and the American occupier. Supported by a discussion on the development and dissemination of digital identities, I position *Abidin Travels* as a device used to explore the limits, issues, and fallacies of online identity politics. Abidin's installation will be posited in conjunction with *Hometown Baghdad*, a post-invasion video series created by students in Baghdad from the mid-2000s.

Abidin: Reflections from the Diaspora

Abidin's artwork combines lived experience with contemporaneous commentaries on Iraq.[3] Born in Baghdad in 1973, Abidin describes his childhood as "ideal," impervious to the volatile regime change affecting the political landscape of Iraq. He reflects, "Like all children, I used to think the only way to grow up is the way that I did. Iraq was an ideal place, as I did not have an alternative vision. When I traveled the world, I viewed my upbringing as conservative but still beautiful."[4]

Framed by the Iran-Iraq War and the invasion of Kuwait in 1990, the "ideal place" of Iraq succumbed to the volatile political regime of Saddam Hussein. Witness to the aftereffects of American airstrikes during the Persian Gulf War, Abidin recalls the following about the 1991 bombing of the Al-Jumhuriyya Bridge in Baghdad:

> On that day I heard that American air forces had bombed the Al-Jumhuriyya Bridge, one of my favorite bridges in the city. The bridge—located in the heart of downtown Baghdad—is the most important and frequently used bridge that connects the two banks of the Tigris River …. Devastated and in shock, I did not know how to react. The next day, I cycled downtown, to see if it was true. As I approached the bridge, which had been broken off completely in two places, I saw a strange scene: a dead cow on one piece of the fallen bridge. I pushed aside my sorrow for the bridge as the unexpected image occupied my mind, as it was unusual to see a cow in central Baghdad. I started imagining different scenarios about the death of this poor cow. Why was she there in the first place? Where had

she come from? Why was she alone? Lately, I have been consumed with thoughts on our human need to gather, to feel connected and be assured that we are not alone.[5]

Themes pertaining to connectivity and collaboration remain central to many of Abidin's works, specifically, the use of the digital platform. This media form encourages connectivity between users and the artist, addressing the desire to reach a diverse audience outside the stationary environment of the museum or gallery.

After the Persian Gulf War, Abidin studied industrial management at Mansour University and painting at the Academy of Fine Arts in Baghdad. His transition to the digital platform started after graduating from the academy. In 2000, he left for Finland to study at the Academy of Fine Arts in Helsinki.[6] With regard to his graduate training in Helsinki, Abidin states, "Real education comes from being aware and perceptive of the surrounding world. It is based on the information that we constantly gain from our environment."[7] Living as a diasporic artist, his work comments on the shifting political and social environments affecting individuals residing outside the homeland.

In *Shoot an Iraqi: Art, Life, and Resistance under the Gun*, fellow Iraqi-born artist Wafaa Bilal reflects on the political environment of Iraq in the late 1980s and early 1990s. Born in Kufa, Iraq, in 1966, Bilal grew up in a difficult environment that paralleled the shifting political regime. While a student, Bilal denied allegiance to the Ba'athist Party and refused to "volunteer" for service. In 1991 he fled Iraq, and by the end of 1992, Bilal immigrated to the United States after spending nearly two years in refugee camps in Kuwait and Saudi Arabia. In an interview in 2008, Bilal explained:

> Though my consciousness and memories are forever connected to the conflict zone and is Iraq (and so many other war-torn countries across the world), my present reality has become the same comfort zone. I have a warm bed in a comfortable apartment, a hot cup of coffee …. I live in complete comfort and security, even when I am constantly worried about my family and my people.[8]

The demarcation between these two "zones" signifies a separation of space: one based in violent and traumatic experiences, and the latter as a space for recall. Although Abidin and Bilal work from various "comfort zones," they bifurcate between their homeland of Iraq and diasporic spaces abroad. Abidin and Bilal work to negotiate the complexities of defining post-invasion identity, merging experiences from the "conflict zone" of Iraq to the "comfort zones" of Finland and the United States.

Abidin's *Cold Interrogation* and Bilal's *Virtual Jihadi*

In 2004, Abidin created *Cold Interrogation* in response to prejudicial comments received about his Iraqi identity. Originally located in the Gallery Huuto in Helsinki, *Cold Interrogation* combines humor with interactive play, encouraging participatory interaction. Against a white wall in the corner of the gallery, Abidin placed a medium-sized refrigerator. Using common tropes found in many American kitchens, he covered the surface of the refrigerator with magnets, personal photos, pictures, and a "Support Our Troops" ribbon decal in red, white, and blue. Centered on the top portion of the refrigerator, a small eyehole provided access to the interior freezer space. Instead of seeing frozen TV dinners or leftover condiments, viewers gazed upon the visage of a man on a television screen. After several seconds, the man asked the following questions:

> Where are you from?
> How did you end up in Finland?
> Do you think there will be a war on Iraq?
> Where were you during the first war?
> What do you think of Saddam Hussein?
> Did you see Baghdad burning?
> What do you think of George Bush? What about Tony Blair?
> Tell me about Bin Laden.
> What do you think of 11th of September?
> Do you drink any alcohol in Iraq?
> You don't look like one from Iraq.[9]

The actor quickly moves from one question to another, rapidly "interrogating" the viewer. The questions and comments made by the actor reflect actual conversations between Abidin and Finnish citizens. According to the artist, these types of questions are still asked in interviews and casual conversations about his art and his position as a diasporic artist. Concerning the overall intent of *Cold Interrogation*, participants learn about the invasive line of questioning affecting immigrants and refugees. Though the satirical format of the installation attempts to defuse the seriousness of ethnic and racial profiling, it fosters a critical discussion concerning Iraqi identity in the post-invasion era.[10]

In a similar thematic vein, Bilal's work addresses responses to post-invasion, diasporic identities. In 2008, Bilal created *Virtual Jihadi*, an online interactive gaming experience. Bilal's game uses schematics from *Quest for Saddam*, a first-person shooter game developed by Petrilla Entertainment.[11] In the game, the user hunts down a cyber version of Saddam Hussein and executes military avatars.[12] At the start of the game, the user enters cyber-Iraq and performs the role of an American soldier. The user maneuvers terrain designed to mimic actual military training facilities.[13] The final objective: find cyber-Saddam and assassinate him using a cache of weapons collected throughout the game.

By the mid-2000s, the Al-Qaeda media faction known as the Global Islamic Media Front obtained a copy of *Quest for Saddam* and changed the tonal appearance, visage, and clothing of the American soldiers. The role of protagonist changed from US troops to members of Saddam's guard. The title also changed to *Quest for Bush*, reflecting the role reversal of the game's characters and objective.[14] Instead of executing cyber-Saddam, the new goal centered on the assassination of cyber-President George W. Bush.[15] In Bilal's version, the participant plays an avatar of the artist. Dressed in a thobe and strapped with a belt of orange explosive sticks, the user maneuvers the terrain to recruit members before assassinating President George W. Bush.[16]

Virtual Jihadi critiques the hypocrisy of the gaming platform. Bilal extrapolates on the intention behind the piece, stating:

> Because we inhabit a comfort zone far from the trauma of the conflict zone, we Americans have become desensitized to the violence of war. We are disconnected and disengaged while many others do the suffering. The game holds up a mirror that reveals our own propensities for violence, racism and propaganda. We can close our eyes and ears and deny that it exists, but the issues won't go away.[17]

When the perpetrator/victim dynamic changed, the shift caused public furor. Rather than fostering a conversation about the relationship between violence and digital games, *Virtual Jihadi* was met with opposition and criticism. During the first exhibition of the game at Rensselaer Polytechnic Institute (RPI) in Troy, New York, administrators censored the show and forcibly shut down the venue because of the "pro-terrorist message." Bilal, hired as an artist-in-residence at RPI, was banned from entering campus buildings and teaching courses.[18] What prompted the censorship of *Virtual Jihadi*? Considering the year in which the piece was created (2008) and the proximity of the exhibition to New York City, protestors argued that *Virtual Jihadi* glorified terrorism and the killing of American troops. Interviews with local politicians echoed anti-Iraq and anti-Arab sentiments, referring to Bilal as a "terrorist" and "anti-American." When confronted, many protestors admitted they did not know the content of the exhibition or the artist's intention behind the work. Their opinions of the piece relied solely on the title of the game and Bilal's Iraqi identity.

When audiences criticized the content of *Cold Interrogation* or protested at the opening of *Virtual Jihadi*, they reinforced the marginalization and subjugation of the Iraqi. Though commentary on the relationship between "two unequal halves, the Orient (East) and the Occident (West)" was detailed in *Orientalism* by Edward Said, the legacy of the marginalized Arab body reinforces centuries-old stereotypes.[19] In the visual arts, works by nineteenth-century artists like Eugène Delacroix and Jean-Auguste-Dominique Ingres captured Western ideals of the East by presenting Arab culture as "Europe's collective day-dream of the Orient."[20] According to Said, they "are the lenses through which the Orient is experienced, and they shape the language, perception, and form of the encounter between East and West."[21] Paintings of women, in repose, surrounded by turbans and hookahs signified the "exotic East." Travel journals, literature, and historical records also added to the "day-dream" of Westerners looking East. Linda Nochlin described such scenes:

> [The paintings act] as a visual document of nineteenth-century colonialist ideology, an iconic distillation of the Westerner's notion of the Oriental couched in the language of a would-be transparent naturalism.[22]

Represented in these paintings, figures appear idle, consumed by sloth, sexual licentiousness, or in some artworks, forced servitude.[23]

Since the Persian Gulf and Iraq Wars, the vision of Iraq no longer reflects the "exotic" imagery depicted in paintings by Delacroix or Ingres. Instead, the violent figure of the Iraqi perforates online and print sources. In many of these popular media forms, the

Iraqi body correlates with words like "terrorist" and "anti-American."[24] Specifically, after the fall of the Twin Towers, equating Iraqis with terrorism grew exponentially in online spaces, furthered by the dissemination of misinformed news reports and xenophobic rhetoric from online internet trolls and Arabophobes.

In "Disjuncture and Difference in the Global Cultural Economy," Arjun Appadurai critiques the dissemination of images, text, and data through digital networks like the internet.[25] He explicates how identities of the marginalized become part of a "digital accumulation," lacking context and points of reference.[26] He states,

> The Internet is the bastion of the diasporic body. Diasporic politics, as opposing, antagonising and competing with national politics, is part of the growing culture of cyberpolitics, which in turn is largely transnational and which adopts tactics of connecting offline locations (and politics) with online transnational networking activities.[27]

Evident in artworks by Abidin and Bilal, the digital platform provides access to geographical regions suppressed and restricted by war, government censorship, and free speech regulations. Originally defined as the movement of displaced bodies, the concept of the diaspora serves to categorize exiles and refugees "scattered" from the homeland to a host land.[28]

In "Diasporas," James Clifford suggests that "modern technologies of transport [telephones, satellites] reduce this distance" between homeland and host land.[29] The digital diaspora serves as a transnational network for promoting connectivity and accessibility. Digitally constructed media, like the internet, serves to redirect connectivity of the displaced body back to the homeland. As framed by Michael Laguerre,

> A digital diaspora is an immigrant group or descendant of an immigrant population that uses IT connectivity to participate in virtual networks of contacts for a variety of political, economic, social, religious, and communicated purposes that, for the most part, may concern the homeland, the host land, or both, including its own trajectory abroad.[30]

Diasporic artists harness digital spaces to reach vast audiences of connected users. Outlined by Appadurai, the propagation of information via media outlets like the internet, cable television, and radio serves to connect users from across geographical spaces. Considering the transference of information through these mediascapes, individuals of the diaspora may harness technological spaces to expound issues associated with marginalization, racism, and ethnocentrism. Suspended within cyberspace, physical bodies do not have to be removed from the homeland to exist within the digital diaspora, although many users perform outside their geographical space of origin.[31]

In "Defining Diaspora, Refining a Discourse," Kim Butler suggests that "diasporas intersect and overlap," positing that a diaspora is not a singular experience enacted by many but a multitude of interactions, exiles, and traumas.[32] Online users may find commonality with other participants of various diasporas. For the diasporic artist working in digital media, the internet serves as a platform for resistance, providing the opportunity to subvert stereotypes, challenge hegemony, and share lived experiences. In *Abidin Travels*, the installation fosters a space for sharing the effects of marginalization, inviting participants to experience the frustration of attempting to connect between homeland and host land.

Tourism during War: *Abidin Travels: Welcome to Baghdad*

In response to the aftereffects of the 2003 invasion, Abidin debuted *Abidin Travels* at the 2007 Venice Biennale. Touted as the premier event in contemporary art, the Venice Biennale occurs every two years.[33] Select artists from around the world exhibit artworks based on a general theme developed by the Biennale curatorial staff. Nations are granted space in prestigious exhibition zones located in the Giardini and the Arsenale pavilions. Since the early twentieth century, legacy and tradition dictate the location of these national pavilions. At the 2007 iteration, Abidin exhibited in the Nordic Pavilion.[34] Participants entered the installation and walked through a series of rooms designed to mimic a travel agency. Above the entrance, the sign "Abidin Travels" in hot pink and blue neon welcomed visitors. Juxtaposed with the text, the silhouette of a fighter jet brightly illuminated the entryway. Once inside the installation, the space diverted into several sections. In one space, pamphlets adorned the gallery walls, offering historical information about the city of Baghdad (Figure 6.1). Inside the pamphlets, stock photos of ancient Iraqi artifacts juxtaposed military tanks and incinerated city streets. When describing the National Museum of Iraq, the text line reads, "All the beautiful places that you might have read about are either destroyed or have been looted. There really are no sights left."[35]

In another room of the installation, participants encountered a computer kiosk guiding visitors to "BOOK NOW" at www.abidintravels.com. Located on the site's main page, a selection menu provided visitors the option to plan trips to the city of Baghdad.[36] Similar to popular travel pages, the website included a flight booking section and informational links to tourist sites (Figure 6.2). Instead of photos depicting luxurious hotels and spas, a blindfolded hostage surrounded by men in black face masks welcomes the viewer. Superimposed on the image, a blue sign touts "free-sightseeing!" (Figure 6.3).[37] In the upper right corner, a body counter informs viewers of recent executions. The reservation section displays departure locations and date options. Users input the number of travelers with the option of adding travel insurance for an extra 399,999 USD.[38] Recommended as a precaution against the occasional roadside bombing or rocket-propelled grenade attack, users are encouraged to rent a tank or armored Humvee.

To complement the pamphlets and webpage, Abidin included informative travel videos in various languages, including English, Arabic, French, and Swedish.[39] In one of the videos, a female narrator describes the top tourist sites of Baghdad. As she narrates, footage of mourning women, public executions, and car bombs play in the background. A transcribed excerpt announces the following:

108 Cultural Production and Social Movements after the Arab Spring

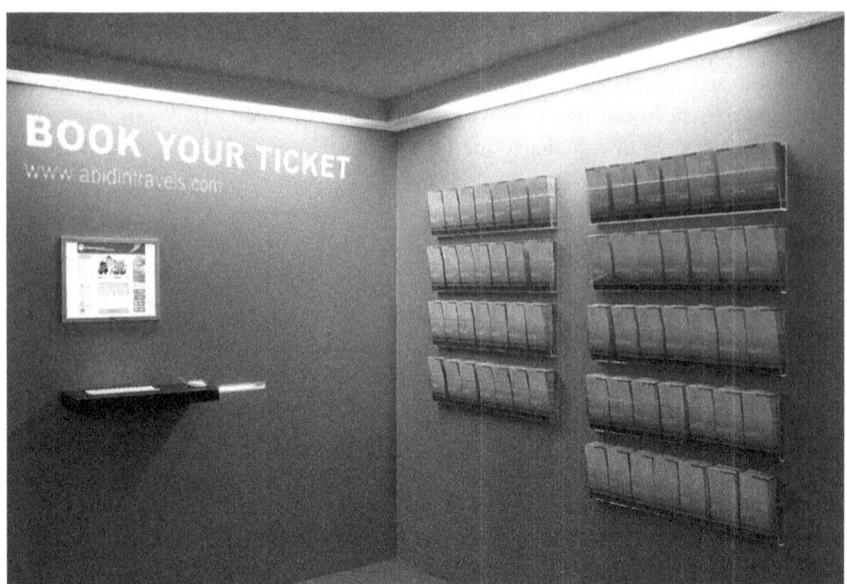

Figure 6.1 Display wall with travel pamphlets and booking kiosk, *Abidin Travels*, 2006–7. Courtesy of Adel Abidin.

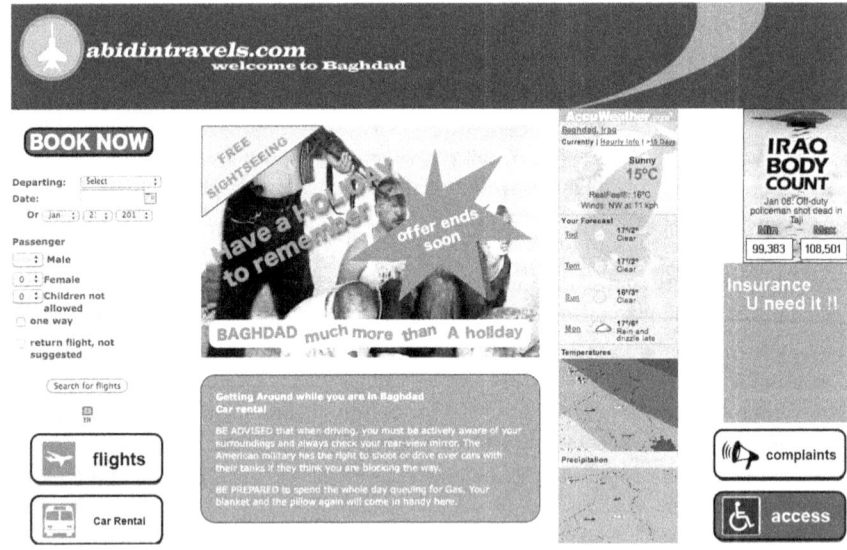

Figure 6.2 Mainpage to www.abidintravels.com, *Abidin Travels*, 2006–7. Courtesy of Adel Abidin.

Figure 6.3 Video still, *Abidin Travels*, 2006–7. Courtesy of Adel Abidin.

You can find wonderful souvenir shops and boutiques and cafés. And at the end of Nahir Street is Al-Khesa, where the old Ottoman rulers were situated. And don't forget the beautiful churches and mosques with their elaborate signs and intricate arches ... all part of the rich heritage of this city. And don't forget the museum and galleries that reflect the great history of this city.[40]

The violent footage contradicts the narrator's enthusiastic description of pre-invasion Baghdad. Instead of souvenir shops, weapon venues filled with assault rifles dominate market booths and kiosks. Rather than show busy street vendors selling goods on Nahir Street, the footage displays burned-out cars and skeletal remains. When describing museums and galleries, images of broken Assyrian vessels and plunderers escaping through side doors replace footage of pristine galleries and pavilions. Represented in the videos, American soldiers laugh and frisk Iraqi civilians at checkpoints (Figures 6.4 and 6.5).

Why use the satirical venue of a travel agency? How can humor be used to confront traumatic events associated with war? The relationship between humor and trauma seeks to defuse political, religious, and social tensions.[41] *Abidin Travels* confronts the violent effects produced by the Iraq War. The content—especially the merger of humorous, satirical components with serious content—provokes uncomfortable

110 Cultural Production and Social Movements after the Arab Spring

Figure 6.4 Adel Abidin, still from *Abidin Travels* video, 2006–7. Courtesy of Adel Abidin.

Figure 6.5 Adel Abidin, stills from *Abidin Travels* video, 2006–7. Courtesy of Adel Abidin.

reactions from viewers. First referenced in *Jokes and Their Relation to the Unconscious*, Sigmund Freud examined how humorous anecdotes act as forms of suppression, often concealing deep, traumatic experiences. A joke or satirical reference may reveal past traumas, serving as a therapeutic device.[42] In *Trauma Treatment Techniques: Innovative Trends*, Jacqueline Garrick uses a variety of case studies involving traumatized patients exposed to abuse, violence, or high stress environments. Humor diffuses stress and alleviates symptoms associated with post-traumatic stress disorder. Even though the humor or joke may be viewed as inappropriate due to the content, it may aid in the healing process.[43] In *Abidin Travels*, the choice to juxtapose violent images with the narrator's commentary reflects Abidin's satirical approach to confronting trauma.

Unlike *Cold Interrogation*, which combined a humorous format (the refrigerator) and the language of interrogation, *Abidin Travels* takes a different approach to satire and violence. The installation uses actual footage of corpses, blown-up cars, and violent street footage from Baghdad. According to Giselinde Kuipers, the use of violent imagery in satirical or humorous works serves as an aggressive political statement about the war in Iraq. Satirical or humorous jokes or cartoons about the Twin Towers falling or the execution of terrorist victims act as disaster jokes, or "sick jokes based on an incongruity between the gruesome and the innocuous."[44] In this paradigm, the joke or satirical reference is linked to a real event, often gruesome or incomprehensible (9/11, the 2003 invasion of Iraq, etc.). When the gruesome event and the harmless reference combine, it creates a humorous anecdote to an otherwise serious situation.[45] By using graphic imagery coupled with the satirical atmosphere of the travel agency, the installation provides an environment that fosters a critical dialogue about the Iraq War and the travel limitations affecting individuals returning to regions in conflict.

In critique of *Abidin Travels*, Laura Marks states,

> Abidin is more intimately aware than are most of his Western interlocutors of the specific suffering of Iraqi people; and on the other, he can only describe this suffering in generalities that his audience will grasp.[46]

Aware of the demographic of Venice Biennale visitors, Marks references an inherent issue with how the audience views and experiences the installation. Since most of the participants experienced the Iraq War via Western-based news outlets, the representations of pain and suffering correspond with familiar tropes. Abidin represents these common media tropes to reference the iconic symbols of the post-invasion Iraqi stereotype.

Dereck Gregory positions these representations of the Iraqi as "collections of objects not congeries of people."[47] In *Abidin Travels*, a commodification of the Iraqi body is placed in opposition to the American occupier. How does Abidin present the American occupier in *Abidin Travels*? The bodies of the American soldiers serve as fetishized objects, presented as stereotypical icons of occupation. The edited footage shows troops blocking roadways with tanks and Humvees, laughing at the demise of Iraqi civilians, consuming alcohol near sacred mosques, and launching weapons. They become coded objects associated with occupation, rather than liberation and protection. Abidin's attempt to subvert the bodies of the Westerner as the "barbaric occupiers" of his homeland fails to adequately succeed in fostering a dialogue centered on Middle East–West relations.

Although the appropriated media footage used in *Abidin Travels* satirizes the Iraqi as Other, the footage also reinforces mediatized constructions of the Iraqi as subordinate. In *Virtual Orientalism: Asian Religions and American Popular Culture*, Jane Iwamura considers how the media represents the Other or marginalized body in online space. Iwamura specifically examines the role of the online Other via the theory of virtual Orientalism, a contemporary approach to Said's Orientalism. Virtual Orientalism may be defined as "cultural stereotyping by visual forms of media [that] rely heavily on new seemingly uninterrupted flows of representations and their easy access."⁴⁸ For example, images of the gun-wielding Iraqi male exemplify a type of stereotyping associated with virtual Orientalism. In a recent Google search from 2019 of the term "Iraqi," the first several lines of images still display militant troops wielding assault rifles, US troops interrogating a male figure, and recommended sub-searches of associated terms linked with Humvee, AK-47, tea, special forces, and soldier.⁴⁹

Hometown Baghdad

To subvert negative visual tropes associated with virtualized Orientalism, *Hometown Baghdad* documents and archives the daily lives of three Iraqi civilians living in Baghdad (Figure 6.6).⁵⁰ Created in the mid-2000s during the onset of the Iraq War, *Hometown Baghdad* serves as a response to mediatized stereotypes of the Iraqi. Rather than focus on violent footage, the series documents hobbies, conversations, and daily activities of Saif, Ausama, and Adel.⁵¹ Using hand-held cameras and Flip devices, the participants capture pedestrian footage.

In one segment, titled "Symphony of Bullets," Adel attempts to travel to his university to study for exams (Figure 6.7). He becomes trapped in his dorm because of the barrage of gunfire occurring outside his room. He jokes about his ability to differentiate between American and insurgent bullets.⁵² In another short film titled *Market Boom*, the men visit a local open-air market to purchase travel gear for a month-long trip (Figure 6.8). One of their friends enters the apartment, stating that a sniper has shot pedestrians and police, killing several in the process. A bomb also destroys part of al-Arabi market in downtown Baghdad. As these events unfold, the men comment on how the violence is more nuisance than threat.⁵³ Compared to footage edited by American news networks like CNN and Fox News, *Hometown Baghdad* subverts the violent and victimized body of the Iraqi civilian by showing its subjects engaged in mundane, routine activities while a war occurs around them. Abidin's piece fractures the romanticized aura of the spice market and bazaar by displaying the markets as ruined spaces, a by-product of US raids and insurgent car bombs.

Figure 6.6 Footage from *Hometown Baghdad,* 2005–7.

Identity Politics and Digital Space 113

Figure 6.7 Still from the "Symphony of Bullets" segment, *Hometown Baghdad*, 2005–7.

Figure 6.8 Still from the "Market Boom" segment, *Hometown Baghdad*, 2005–7.

Conclusion

The works presented throughout this chapter use satire and humor as both a means of provocation and an attempt to understand the nuances of post-invasion identity. *Abidin Travels* exemplifies a unique method of informing audiences about post-invasion politics, stereotyping, and the reality of displacement during an active war. The various approaches to Abidin's work originate from a need to examine the post-invasion marginalization and restrictions/limitations imposed on Iraqis since 2003. *Abidin Travels* exposes these issues using humor to placate the viewer. However, elements of the video and webpage components reinforce negative tropes associated with the Iraqi civilian and American occupier.

Since *Abidin Travels* debuted, US military operations have steadily declined in Iraq. However, the images produced in the years after 9/11 remain fixed as iconic constructions, by-products of the Western interpretation of the Iraqi. As Iwamura postulates, these images remain caught in digital spaces and disseminated in continuum through the internet and online networks.[54] However, projects like *Hometown Baghdad* remedy issues involving the subversion of the Iraqi as Other by capturing relatable moments in the lives of the Iraqi civilian. Each work serves to expose and problematize the representation of the Iraqi since the 2003 invasion. Once viewers bypass the veneer of humor and satire, each piece reveals the limitations and prejudices imposed on Iraqis living within the borders of Iraq and diasporic communities abroad.

Notes

1. Megan Miller, "'History Wipes' and Other Ambiguities: Iraqi Artist Adel Abidin at Ateneum Art Museum, Helsinki," *Art Radar*, April 17, 2018, http://artradarjournal.com/2018/04/17/history-wipes-and-other-ambiguities-iraqi-artist-adel-abidin-at-ateneum-art-museum-helsinki/.
2. Adel Abidin, "Biography," http://www.adelabidin.com/biography.
3. Adel Abidin, interview by Erin Joyce, "The Beauty of Conflict: Adel Abidin," *UltraUltra*, December 7, 2012, http://www.ultraextra.org/interviews/2012/12/7/the-beauty-of-conflicts-adel-abidin.
4. Abidin, "The Beauty of Conflict," http://www.ultraextra.org/interviews/2012/12/7/the-beauty-of-conflicts-adel-abidin.
5. Adel Abidin, "Memorial," *Adel Abidin*, last modified 2016, http://www.adelabidin.com/component/content/article/16-video-installation/14-memorial.
6. Abidin, "The Beauty of Conflict," http://www.ultraextra.org.
7. Ibid., http://www.ultraextra.org.
8. Wafaa Bilal and Kari Lydersen, *Shoot an Iraqi: Art, Life, and Resistance under the Gun* (San Francisco: City Lights Books, 2008), 68.
9. "Works/Cold Interrogation," *AV-ARKKI*, http://www.av-arkki.fi/en/works/cold-interrogation_en/. The actor portraying the interrogator is Mika Hannula, an artist and curator and former director of the Academy of Fine Arts, Helsinki, Finland.
10. Abidin, "The Beauty of Conflict," http://www.ultraextra.org. After the creation of *Cold Interrogation*, Abidin sought to return to Baghdad. However, due to post-9/11

travel sanctions imposed by the United States, Abidin could not gain permission to reenter Iraq. According to the artist, "The threat of Mr. Bush kept him in Finland."
11 Zach Whalen, "Quest for Bush/Quest for Saddam: Content vs. Context," *Gameology*, last modified September 26, 2006, http://www.gameology.org/reviews/quest_for_bush_quest_for_saddam_content_vs_context.
12 Brian Boyko, "Interview: Wafaa Bilal Casts Himself as Terrorist in Virtual Jihadi," *Geeks Are Sexy*, last modified 2012, http://www.geeksaresexy.net/2008/03/03/interview-wafaa-bilal-casts-himself-as-terrorist-in-virtual-jihadi/.
13 Whalen, "Quest for Bush/Quest for Saddam," http://www.gameology.org/.
14 Ibid., http://www.gameology.org/.
15 Boyko, "Interview," http://www.geeksaresexy.net. An hour before Bilal gave his talk at the opening of *Virtual Jihadi*, police shut down the exhibition for "code violations." A month later, the exhibition lasted one day before Rensselaer Polytechnic Institute closed the exhibition.
16 Kate McKiernan, "Cease Fire: A Look at Virtual Jihadi," *The Escapist*, last modified August 18, 2009, http://www.escapistmagazine.com/articles/view/issues/issue_215/6393-Cease-Fire-A-Look-at-Virtual-Jihadi.
17 Ibid., http://wafaabilal.com/virtual-jihadi/. Typical of first-person shooter games, participants witness the perspective of the digital character they are "playing" within the space of the game.
18 The Sanctuary for Independent Media, *Art ≠ Terrorism*, YouTube video, 2008.
19 Edward Said, *Orientalism* (New York: Pantheon, 1978), 5.
20 V. G. Kiernan, quoted in Edward Said. *Orientalism: Western Conceptions of the Orient* (New York: Pantheon, 1978), 52.
21 Said, *Orientalism*, 51.
22 Linda Nochlin, *The Politics of Vision: Essays on Nineteenth-Century Art and Society* (New York: Harper-Row, 1989), 35.
23 Ottoman painter and "revisionist" of European Orientalist art Osman Hamdi Bey sought to represent Arab figures performing tasks of intellectual inquiry, devoid of lustful poses, violent interactions, or passive indolence. In two pieces by the artist, *Two Musician Girls* (1880) and *Theologian* (1907), the figures remain fully clothed, displaying expressions of concentration and focus. In *Two Musician Girls*, the figures appear in richly patterned tunics, hyper-focused on the stringed tamboura and the brass tambourine. In *Theologian*, a male figure concentrates on a Qur'anic manuscript. In these examples, Hamdi Bey favors practicality over desire, intellect over garishness. See Emine Fetvaci, "The Art of Osman Hamdi Bey," in *Osman Hamdi Bey and the Americans: Archeology, Diplomacy, Art*, eds. Renata Holod and Robert Ousterhout (Istanbul: Pera Museum Publications, 2011), 119.
24 Raymond Pun, "Digital Images and Visions of Jihad: Virtual Orientalism and the Distorted Lens of Technology," *CyberOrient* 7, no. 1 (2013): www.cyberorient.net/article.do?articleId=8391.
25 Arjun Appadurai, "Disjuncture and Difference in the Global Cultural Economy," in *The Globalization Reader*, eds. Lechner, Frank J. and John Boli (Oxford: Blackwell Publishing, 2008), 99.
26 Pun, "Digital Images," www.cyberorient.net/article.do?articleId=8391.
27 Appadurai, "Disjuncture and Difference in the Global Cultural Economy," 39.
28 Andoni Alonso and Pedro J. Oiarzabal, "The Immigrant Worlds' Digital Harbors: An Introduction," in *Diasporas in the New Media Age: Identity, Politics, and Community*, eds. Andoni Alonso and Pedro J. Oiarzabal (Reno: University of Nevada Press, 2010), 3.

29   James Clifford, "Diasporas," *Cultural Anthropology* 9, no. 3 (1994): 304.
30   Michael S. Laguerre, "Digital Diaspora: Definition and Models," in *Diasporas in the New Media Age: Identity, Politics, and Community*, eds. Andoni Alonso and Pedro J. Oiarzabal (Reno: University of Nevada Press, 2010), 50.
31   Aini Linjakumpu, *Political Islam in the Global World* (Reading, NY: Ithaca Press, 2007), 116–17.
32   Kim Butler, "Defining Diaspora, Refining a Discourse," *Diaspora: A Journal of Transnational Studies* 10, no. 2 (2001): 211.
33   David Neustein and Grace Mortlock, "The Venice Biennale's Many Inequalities, in Map Form," *Metropolis*, 2016, http://www.metropolismag.com/cities/the-venice-biennales-many-inequalities-in-map-form/. Critics David Neustein and Grace Mortlock describe the division of space at public art events like the Biennale: "Marooned on its tourist island, the Biennale is an idealized world-in-miniature, free of the realities, confusions and conflicts of the world-at-large. The environment is timeless, picturesque, serene: hardly representative of the world's 'increasing complexity.'" Increasingly viewed as a space of privilege, the Biennale caters to art connoisseurs, collectors, and art enthusiasts afforded the opportunity to travel to the event.
34   Amanda Duhon, "Contemporary Art of Iraqis and Categorical Assumptions of Nationality: An Analysis of the Art and Narrative of Hana Mal Allah, Adel Abidin, and Wafaa Bilal" (thesis, Louisiana State University, 2008), 31–2. It is important to understand why Abidin exhibited at the Nordic Pavilion rather than the Iraqi. Due to political and social limitations, Iraq did not have a national presence at the Biennale until 2011. At the 2011 event, Abidin exhibited under the nation of Iraq rather than the Nordic area.
35   Marks, "Adel Abidin's 'Baghdad Travels,'" http://universes-in-universe.org/content/view/print/9014. Note: This was created after the infamous looting of the Baghdad Museum in 2003.
36   "Abidin Travels, 2006," http://www.adelabidin.com/video-installation/abidin-travels.
37   Ibid.
38   Women are not permitted to book flights alone on the webpage without a male chaperone, and children are prohibited.
39   "Abidin Travels, 2006," *Adel Abidin*. Accessed March 27, 2014, http://www.adelabidin.com/video-installation/abidin-travels.
40   Marks, "Adel Abidin's 'Baghdad Travels,'" http://universes-in-universe.org/content/view/print/9014.
41   "Gargantua," *Brandeis Institutional Repository*, http://bir.brandeis.edu/handle/10192/3930. In the nineteenth century, humorous undertakings in the arts were often found in print media. Honoré-Victorin Daumier dominated political satire through his etchings of Louis Philippe as Gargantua in the French weekly publication *La Caricature* in 1831. Francisco Goya also captured political and social discrepancies in his nineteenth-century etchings, depicting outrageous displays of human suffering with exaggerated, corporeal renderings. In these works, the role of humor and satire among dark political events served as a didactic tool for understanding moments of destabilization and social decline.
42   Sigmund Freud, *Jokes and Their Relation to the Unconscious*, trans. James Strachey (New York: W. W. Norton, 1960), 5–6.
43   Jacqueline Garrick, "The Humor of Trauma Survivors: Its Application in a Therapeutic Milieu," in *Trauma Treatment Techniques: Innovative Trends*, eds. Jacqueline Garrick and Mary Beth Williams (New York: Routledge, 2014), 173–4.

44 Giselinde Kuipers, "The Functions of Laughter after 9/11," in *A Decade of Dark Humor: How Comedy, Irony, and Satire Shaped Post-9/11 America*, eds. Ted Gournelos and Viveca Greene (Jackson: University Press of Mississippi, 2011), 21.
45 The role of community also plays a major role in *Abidin Travels*. Rather than experience the traumatic images alone, the installation provided participants a public space to view and screen the images. In this sense, the piece provides the opportunity to experience violent images with other participants, sharing in a universal experience associated with the war in Iraq.
46 Marks, "Adel Abidin's 'Baghdad Travels,'" http://universes-in-universe.org/content/view/print/9014.
47 Dereck Gregory, *The Colonial Present* (Oxford: Blackwell Publishing, 2004), 201.
48 Pun, "Digital Images," www.cyberorient.net/article.do?articleId=8391.
49 Jane Iwamura, *Virtual Orientalism: Asian Religions and American Popular Culture* (Oxford: Oxford University Press, 2011), 7–8.
50 "Hometown Baghdad," *Chat the Planet*. Accessed April 3, 2014, http://chattheplanet.com/index.php?page=about&cat=82.
51 "Hometown Baghdad," http://chattheplanet.com/index.php?page=about&cat=82.
52 Ibid., http://chattheplanet.com/index.php?page=about&cat=82.
53 Ibid.
54 Iwamura, *Virtual Orientalism*, 7.

References

Abidin, Adel. "The Beauty of Conflict: Adel Abidin." By Erin Joyce. *UltraUltra*, December 7, 2012. http://www.ultraextra.org/interviews/2012/12/7/the-beauty-of-conflicts-adel-abidin.

"Abidin Travels, 2006." *Adel Abidin*. Accessed March 18, 2019. http://www.adelabidin.com/video-installation/abidin-travels.

"Adel Abidin." *Musee d'Art Contemporain du Val de Marne*. Accessed November 1, 2017. http://www.macval.fr/english/residences/residence-archives/article/adel-abidin-5042.

Appadurai, Arjun. "Disjuncture and Difference in the Global Cultural Economy." In *The Globalization Reader*, edited by Lechner, Frank J., and John Boli, 95–104. Oxford: Blackwell Publishing, 2008.

Bilal, Wafaa and Kari Lydersen. *Shoot an Iraqi: Art, Life, and Resistance under the Gun*. San Francisco: City Lights Books, 2008.

Butler, Kim. "Defining Diaspora, Refining a Discourse." *Diaspora: A Journal of Transnational Studies* 10, no. 2 (2001): 189–217.

Coronil, Fernando. "Beyond Occidentalism: Toward Nonimperial Geohistorical Categories." *Cultural Anthropology* 11, no. 1 (February 2006): 51–87. doi: http://www.unc.edu/~aparicio/WAN/CoronilBeyondOcc.pdf.

Duhon, Amanda. "Contemporary Art of Iraqis and Categorical Assumptions of Nationality: An Analysis of the Art and Narrative of Hana Mal Allah, Adel Abidin, and Wafaa Bilal." Thesis, Louisiana State University, 2008.

Fetvaci, Emine. "The Art of Osman Hamdi Bey." In *Osman Hamdi Bey and the Americans: Archeology, Diplomacy, Art*, edited by Renata Holod and Robert Ousterhout, 118–38. Istanbul: Pera Museum Publications, 2011.

Gregory, Dereck. *The Colonial Present*. Oxford: Blackwell Publishing, 2004.

"Hometown Baghdad." *Chat the Planet*. Accessed November 3, 2016. http://chattheplanet.com/index.php?page=about&cat=82.

Iwamura, Jane. *Virtual Orientalism: Asian Religions and American Popular Culture.* Oxford: Oxford University Press, 2011.

Kuipers, Giselinde. "The Functions of Laughter after 9/11." In *A Decade of Dark Humor: How Comedy, Irony, and Satire Shaped Post-9/11 America*, edited by Ted Gournelos and Viveca Greene, 20–46. Jackson: University Press of Mississippi, 2011.

Kierman, V. G. Quoted in Edward Said. *Orientalism: Western Conceptions of the Orient.* New York: Pantheon, 1978.

Laguerre, Michael S. "Digital Diaspora: Definition and Models." In *Diasporas in the New Media Age: Identity, Politics, and Community*, edited by Andoni Alonso and Pedro J. Oiarzabal, 49–64. Reno: University of Nevada Press, 2010.

Marks, Laura U. "Adel Abidin's 'Baghdad Travels.'" *Nafas Art Magazine.* 2007. http://universes-in-universe.org/content/view/print/9014

Malcolm, Daniel. "Photographers in Egypt." In *Heilbrunn Timeline of Art History.* New York: The Metropolitan Museum of Art, 2000. http://www.metmuseum.org/toah/hd/treg/hd_treg.htm.

Miller, Megan. "'History Wipes' and Other Ambiguities: Iraqi Artist Adel Abidin at Ateneum Art Museum, Helsinki." *Art Radar.* April 17, 2018. Accessed March 12, 2019. http://artradarjournal.com/2018/04/17/history-wipes-and-other-ambiguities-iraqi-artist-adel-abidin-at-ateneum-art-museum-helsinki/.

Modarresi, Mona and Ata Anbarani. "Feminist Glimpses to Oriental Culture: The Study of Lady Mary Montagu's Travel Letters." *International Journal of English Language and Literature Studies* 1, no. 2 (2012): 47–56.

Neustein, David and Grace Mortlock. "The Venice Biennale's Many Inequalities, in Map Form." *Metropolis.* 2016. http://www.metropolismag.com/cities/the-venice-biennales-many-inequalities-in-map-form/.

Nochlin, Linda. *The Politics of Vision: Essays on Nineteenth-Century Art and Society.* New York: Harper-Row, 1989.

Pun, Raymond. "Digital Images and Visions of Jihad: Virtual Orientalism and the Distorted Lens of Technology." *CyberOrient* 7 (2013): 1–11. Accessed October 5, 2016. www.cyberorient.net/article.do?articleId=8391.

Said, Edward. *Orientalism: Western Conceptions of the Orient.* New York: Pantheon, 1978.

Said, Edward. "The Last Interview." By Brigitte Caland. *Al Jadid.* 2004. http://www.aljadid.com/content/%E2%80%98-last-interview%E2%80%99-edward-said.

Slavick, Susanne. *Out of Rubble.* Milan: Edzioni Charta, 2011.

The Sanctuary for Independent Media. *Art ≠ Terrorism.* YouTube video, 2008.

"Works/Cold Interrogation." AV-ARKKI. Accessed November 20, 2016. http://www.av-arkki.fi/en/works/cold-interrogation_en/.

Part Three

Transcultural Dimensions in Contemporary Arab Literature and Culture

7

Transcultural Identity Formation among Canadian-Arab Youth: Nurturing Self-Knowledge through Metissage and Blunting Canadianness as an Alterity

Melissa Finn and Bessma Momani

Overview

While cultural reductionists and right-wing populist politicians point to the incompatibility of Western and Arab identity or cultural values, we speak to young Arabs living in Canada to understand how they eschew such discursive narratives by nurturing self-knowledge through hybridity. This nurturance allows for transcultural identity formation. It is made possible when youth embrace their multiple cultures, identities, and senses of belonging through open-minded exploration. In this chapter, we investigate the transcultural identity formation of Arab youth through an epistemology of metissage that challenges the idea that Canadianness is an alterity to them. We draw upon survey results from over 860 Canadian-Arab youth and structured focus groups with two hundred youth. We ask them how art, music, culture, and social media shape their conceptions of the world, and explore how Arab youth in Canada navigate their identities and stay translocally and transnationally connected to the people, spaces, and objects associated with their home country cultures. We find that Arab youth hybridize their lives by balancing attachment and longing, living in Arabic culture, demarcating the inside and outside of cultural boundaries and choosing positions on an issue-by-issue basis, and pursuing Arab-Western metissage as an identity.

The authors would like to thank Eid Mohamed and Ayman A. El-Desouky for their insights which helped us to refine this chapter.

Introduction

> But you know, if you're dedicated enough and feeling nostalgic, you're going to want to go back to Arabic music ... and get sense of Arabic roots ... [it's] not something you can buy, [or] something you get from you and your parents; it's something a lot of people here forget you know, like white washing is a big problem. I'm going to say it proudly, people need to know where their roots come from, can't let that go![1]

As many chapters in this volume attest, transcultural Arab identity mobilization is not simply an expression of transnational citizenship engagement, nor is it necessarily a form of pan-Arab reclamation that might mirror a pan-Arabism of the past; if it is pan-Arab at all, it would do it justice to see it as a novel form of pan-Arabism that is multicentered and reflexive (e.g., open to how agency has the capacity to be dominating, carrying awareness of how the peripheries of Arab knowingness are multifariously expressed). Such a novel conception of pan-Arabism eschews older generations' rejection of Western cultural values for the sake of preserving cultural sensitivities or revolts against cultural colonialism for the sake of cultural redemption. Arab cultural identity formation is not currently a reaction "to" or a reaction "for" but rather an expression of an unfolding yet to be fully crystalized. Contemporary transcultural Arab identity formation and production(s) are thus not expressions of coagulated and globalized cultural values where Arab identity moves transnationally into Western cultural spaces and vice versa, thus prompting a cultural amalgamation that necessarily unifies or affixes the cultures together, but where Western values are accepted on a case-by-case basis, down to the individual level, through personal forms of hybridity and collective forms of Arab cultural glocalization in a Western milieu. This transculturation is not a cultural expression alternative between the binary options of exporting Arab culture or keeping it protectively located in the home country (Hannerz 1996) whose "either/or" might be ostensibly relieved by circular and ongoing cultural performances (Cho and Westley 2002). It is also not reducible to a binary between uncoerced and privileged physical and imaginary mobility (cultural identities that experience zero "check-stops" while passing borders) and coerced and marginalized displacement (cultural identities that only experience stoppages while passing borders, as well as dislocation/dispossession) (Inda and Rosaldo 2002). Transcultural identity is prompted, as Eid Mohamed and Ayman A. El-Desouky note in the Introduction, from the seismic action that rocked Arab states multiple times before and after 2011 and from ongoing Arab subject formation. This is not to say that everything is in flux, but much is undergoing significant renegotiation, especially in terms of acculturation or transculturation, language and creativity in public spaces, collectivizing mobilizations, and Arab self-perception. As the editors ask, what new dynamics are emerging, what new modes of expression are being expressed, and what forms of knowing are being transmitted that transcend or subvert those traditionally determined by the politics of institutions, the national and postcolonial histories, and discursive expert opinions in and on the Arab world?

We interject in this conversation by asking questions about how Canadian-Arab youth as a transnationally situated and moving set of Arab subjectivities articulate their epistemological and cultural connections to the Arab world, what they prioritize in their struggle to reclaim themselves in the face of what Mohamed and El-Desouky call the "irreducible heterogeneity" of the public sphere, which is true in the Arab world as it is in Canada, and how do they express their views on cultural loyalty and belonging to Canada and the Middle East? How does metissage or hybridity create cultural emergence from interaction?

What one typically finds in this literature are various attempts to link the stories of immigrant experiences in the North American context with questions of social identity formation and social belonging with an inquiry into the parameters and norms surrounding multiculturalism, assimilation, and prejudice. Immigrant populations in the American context have some cultural idiosyncracies that they are expected to abandon in a bid to locate the Anglo-American values they are expected to adopt. Any type of "heterolocalism without integration" (Zelinsky and Lee 1998) is often seen as subversive because it might involve a stable love and yearning for homeland cultural reference points that might impede assimilation which would therefore be seen to impede the Americanization of them as a new entrant to a system expecting sameness. Keeping ties to the homeland cultures might be seen as loyalty to one set of values that are at odds with the new set of values and groups that require protection in the American context.

Nagel and Staheli (2005) are among those scholars who point out that cultural retention and citizenship mobilization in the new society are not mutually exclusive processes. They argue that the perceived impossibility of immigrants to fully assimilate into American culture stems from "the fusion in public debate between particular understandings of assimilation and citizenship as all-or-nothing conditions. One is assimilated or not. One is citizen or not. Yet immigrants and other marginalized groups often move between sameness and difference in ways that challenge those constructions" (10). The authors mention their surprise in discovering that between 2003 and 2004, Arab-American activists preferred strategies of assimilation over multiculturalism that were modeled on the Irish immigration experience. Assimilation tactics were seen by those interviewed to build loyalty, credibility, and normalize their difference(s) vis-à-vis a mythic mainstream American society. With hard work, patience, public education, and time, the activists of their study believed that Arabs would become fully accepted members of the American polity and would become "white." "Their comments represent an attempt to situate Arab immigrants with respect to American society and citizenship, even as they attempt to broaden and challenge mainstream understandings of what it means to be an American as an immigrant" (Nagel and Staeheli 2005: 4).

> The expectation and reality of assimilation was so common that many organizations had to teach Arab language and culture to the second and third generations, and indeed, teaching those generations about their own culture was an important goal for many groups. To some degree this was necessary to counteract the negative

images of Arabs and Islamic cultures the children would face ... many activists were also worried about being swallowed into an American culture. Some second generation activists worried that unfamiliarity with their own culture would mean they would never be fully American, even as being raised in the US meant they would never be fully Arab.

(Nagel and Staeheli 2005: 15)

Interest in how Arab cultures evolve and transpose themselves around the world will continue to increase as new social networks, rapid labor mobility, and new modes of global idea exchange continue to expand. As transnational spaces open up for intercultural understandings, the influences of the West in the Arab region and the impact of Arab/Islamic culture on Western societies cannot be ignored. After all, the Arab region is a growing source for Western immigration, and a large number of Arab students are flocking to learn in Western universities. What these youths learn abroad and take home with them can be a valuable part of understanding the future trajectory of their societies (Momani 2015). More and more Arabs now hold dual citizenship, particularly from the Western world, and Arab communities in Europe and the Americas are increasing their ties to the Arab region. In many parts of the West, the migration of Arabs and Muslims is rapidly increasing and accelerating due to the Syrian refugee crisis. Among incoming immigrants, Arabs and Muslims now comprise one of the largest ethnocultural and religious groups in the Western world. In Canada, immigrants hailing from Arab countries have become the second largest immigrant group for several years. This is particularly evident in major Western cities, such as in Toronto where nearly 10 percent of the population is Muslim.

Transcultural identity development is not just how local actors might think and work globally, how they might be Canadian, but continually projecting their Arab-ness, for example, in every facet of their engagement with the world or how they forge multiple networks of social relations between Canada and the Arab world (Schiller et al. 1995). It is also not just how identities might be, in a counterintuitive sense, simultaneously boundary-defiant, rooted, and cosmopolitan but also socially networked and geographically situated (Mercea and Bastos 2016). What we mean by this is that identities, especially of immigrants qua transnationals, are neither entirely local nor global, they are neither entirely a hybrid of these two things, and in many cases identities are the result of a complex interplay of seemingly contradictory forces including statelessness, dispossession, grounded-ness, worldliness, parochialism, being socially constituted, and yet individually and communally idiosyncratic. We have focused in other academic works on how actors, identities, and political technologies move in A ↔ B "return-trip" forms transnationally, but also in meshwork forms, from A to various points on a spider-web-like trajectory in disparate directions and then back to A again. We have theorized how these mobilizations and movements encompass different forms of circular citizenship capacity-building (Finn and Momani 2017, 2019; Finn, Opatowski, and Momani, 2018).

In this chapter, we investigate how a growing number of Arab transnationals, particularly young people living in Canada, connect to and frame their cultures based on lived interactions in Canadian society. We also study how their metissage or hybridity is expressed by them, as they work to navigate complex spaces of being distinctly Canadian, and yet decidedly also Arab. This analysis problematizes the idea that Western and Arab identities are incompatible for we find in Canadian-Arab youth a lived hybridity that carries visceral meanings and claims-making to origination and identity emergence in both Canada and the Arab world. We find also an internal struggle in these youth who feel mostly "at home" in Canada but who face discursive narratives and questions about the capacity of Arabs to be Canadian. In this study of Arab émigrés, we describe their affiliations using the language and reference points of transnationalism rather than diaspora. Although diaspora helps capture Arab settlement in the Western world because it connotes the physical diffusion of immigrants across a landscape, state, or region, transnationalism better explains youth connections to homeland because it denotes exchange, which is an important concept for theorizing political and civic agency and identity development. Regarding transcultural identity formation among Canadian-Arab youth, we find four patterns in our qualitative and quantitative methods of inquiry: (1) pursuing belonging in Canada by strengthening connections to circles of Arab friendship and the Arabic language in ways that fulfill an intrinsic longing for homeland while forming attachments in a Canadian land; (2) seeing cultural artifacts and productions as core to living in Arabic culture which manifests itself in an appreciation for Arab music as the most consumed cultural product; (3) interweaving cultural threads in complex and novel ways presented in a strong appreciation for family ties, and criticism and/or disavowal of misogyny, patriarchy, and collective shaming found in Arab culture; and (4) engaging in active reflexivity of cultures and expressing cultural loyalty by (re)claiming Arab-Western hybridity as an identity. In all of these expressions, we find Canadian-Arab youth, in their pursuit for belonging and home, making epistemological claims about how to ground self-knowledge through metissage and blunt "Canadianness" as an alterity (Zuss 1997; Baumann and Gingrich 2005).

Home and Metissage

Home means different things to ethnic and religious minority youth, particularly those originating from immigrant families; their views are highly divergent based on complex and at times idiosyncratic outlooks, experiences, and practices. In many cases, immigrant minority youth straddle or multifariously invest themselves in multiple "homes." What is politically interesting about transnationally connected youth is that they are culturally and politically connected to two or more different countries (Nagel and Staeheli 2005; Tarrow 2005). Kenneth Wald (2008) found in a study on Middle East heritage groups in the United States that transnational migrants feel that they actively pursue issues in their "home" countries by participating in their "resident" country's politics, and that "micro-level" political consciousness among transnationally connected communities, locally in places of residence, affects individual connections and impact abroad. We see throughout our study several instances of "micro-level" political consciousness among Canadian-Arab youth built around Arab popular culture, hybridized social values, and friendship building. Wald argues that ethnic identities of diaspora communities can become politicized, wherein members are variously attentive to homeland issues despite being in diaspora, depending on the priority or prominence of the "homeland" in minority peoples' political thinking, behavior, and connections which he measures. He finds that the "more individuals participate in culture-forming organizations, maintain endogenous social life, and develop powerful symbolic ties to the ethnic community, the greater the probability that ethnic identity will spill over into other aspects of social behavior" (2008, 276). Collective consciousness building among individuals that connect back to homeland concerns or orientations depends on the particular experiences of their families in how they exited the home country and how well they were received in the country of current residence (Wald 2008). For example, many early Arab immigrants to Canada are Christian and migrated to pursue work opportunities—in many respects, their connection to their specific homeland countries is more important to them than their connection to the Arab world; alternatively, many (not all) current Arab immigrants to Canada are Muslim and migrate as refugees fleeing war and social unrest and therefore build a collective consciousness around Arab-ness as a way to cope, survive, and stay connected to their homelands.

Looking at cultural citizenship, or cultural belonging in a society, Sunaima Maira (2008) explores how Muslim youth in the United States connect to the concept of (cultural) citizenship in multiple ways. For the purposes of this particular chapter, Maira's analysis of flexible citizenship is highly relevant. Flexible citizenship is the use of transnational connections among migrants because a single nation-state does not provide all of the political and material resources they need. Flexible citizenship is enabled when migrants keep transnational ties (bridge home and residence countries) for economic reasons (e.g., to send or receive remittances to family), when they stay connected to "home country" popular culture because of its convenient prominence in their homes, and by their willingness to act as flexible labor in neoliberal societies. For Maira, polycultural citizenship, though more about political contestation in the public sphere, refers to how youth navigate their complex political affiliations that are not reducible to a discrete culture (Ewing 2008; Maira 2008). Since citizenship is not just what people have (in terms of status) but also what they do (Turner 2016), the attempts of Canadian-Arab youth to consolidate their hybridity by building translocal and transnational connections among other Arab peoples, spaces, and objects are forms of citizenship mobilization (Finn and Momani 2019).

Shain and Barth (2003) find that the effectiveness of transcultural connectedness among what they call diaspora is affected by the foreign policy choices of host country to "home" country politics and the openness of the "home" country to domestic influence. Gans (1997) found that assimilation among immigrant communities into the culture and lifestyles of resident communities does not necessarily follow a straight line. In many cases, third-generation members of transnationally connected communities can be found embracing core aspects of the groups' particular practices, views, and customs. Alba and Nee (2003), on the other hand, have found that connectedness to group particularities tends to erode over time as generations settle in a new locale.

We contribute to this growing literature by building further knowledge about the Canadian context for Arab youth and this demographic's core priorities as first-, second-, or third-generation immigrants. We find that although their transnational ties to the MENA are prominently cultural, especially as they relate to "home country" popular culture, as Maira (2008) has found, they also have competing ideas about how to navigate multiple identity affiliations, tend to reject affiliation to a single discrete culture, and are openly critical of some Arab cultural practices that contradict what they see as Canadian values, especially how they relate to gender and the collective surveillance and regulation of the individual in his or her own choices. We argue that these decisions are related to the epistemological lens they use to see their identity (what they see and why) and that this lens is founded centrally on metissage. Hybridity is the kaleidoscope through which Canadian-Arab youth tend to read their world and govern their practices in it.

Methodology

In order to explore and theorize Canadian-Arab youth transcultural connections to home countries and in the process contribute to the literature looking at transcultural identity formation, we conducted both quantitative and qualitative methods with this demographic. We first went across Canada to twelve large and medium-sized cities to ask Arab youth to fill out a survey. We were able to bring youth to fill out the survey by wearing t-shirts saying, "Arab and under 29? Earn $25." For their participation, youth were issued a $25 gift card as a reimbursement. We went to places where Arab youth hang out including shish bars, cafés, restaurants, Arab supermarkets, and some universities. We did not approach places of worship in order to avoid selection biases, preferring instead to convenience sample from the street. From this survey, we gathered over 860 responses for a population size of 380,620 Canadians of Arab ancestry and 661,750 of partial Arab ancestry (Census 2011). When we factor in our goal to speak to Arab youth, the representativeness of the sample size we attained was extremely high.

After completing the surveys, we conducted further research using focus groups in two major Canadian cities to get more qualitative data and to triangulate our findings. Participants for the focus groups were recruited using Facebook and other social media platforms. We did not advertise the theme of our discussions in order to avoid selection bias of those who are culturally connected. Instead, we advertised the meeting as social events supporting research-based discussions. To incentivize participants and ensure attendees, we offered dinner and raffle prizes composed of gift cards to popular retailers. The specific topic was revealed while we gathered participant consent at the start of the discussions. Focus groups were composed of approximately six to eight youth at a time and a total of 100 participated in each city.

At our focus groups, we asked four questions that garnered discussions that lasted an hour to an hour and a half for each group. We had both English and French discussions; French discussions were translated into English transcripts. Few youths opted to have discussions in Arabic, as all felt more comfortable in English or French. Our questions were designed to uncover potential connectivity to and interweaving with Arab culture and values. Our four questions were as sterile as possible so as to not have suggestive questions that lead to predictable answers, but at the same time, we could not sustain youth interest if we did not have some focused questions. Finally, we asked the same questions of all of our 200 youth to standardize the process.

Based on structured focus groups with 200 Arab youth, split evenly, in Montreal and Toronto, we asked them four questions: (1) How are you connected to Arab culture around the world? (2) Do you consume Arab media, film, music, theater, literature, or art? If so, by which means do you have access? (3) What Arab cultural values do you want to retain in the diaspora or pass on to your children? What Arab cultural values do you not want to pass on? and (4) In your opinion, can your Arab identity be compatible with Western identity (in any way you would interpret either)? In both settings, focus groups lasted a few hours and were combined with dinner in small groups of six to eight individuals, with one note taker at each table. For those readers who would like to know more about the details of our findings beyond the analysis, we have provided the raw data findings for this study in the Appendix of this chapter.

Transcultural Identity Formation of Arab Transnationals

Among Canadian-Arab youth, there is an epistemological privileging of Arab self-identification over Canadian self-identification in their formations of hybridity. We consistently found, for example, that majority of first-, second-, and third-generation Canadian-Arab youth in our study preferred seeing themselves as "Arab" or "Arab-Canadian" rather than "Canadian-Arab" or "Canadian."[2] The majority of surveyed youth are highly connected to individuals from their home countries not living in Canada. Arab youth are also connected with their home countries often using WhatsApp and Facebook on a weekly basis. Specifically, 83 percent use at least one of the following methods of communication at least once a week: Skype, phone, Facebook, text, BBM, FaceTime, email, Tango, Viber, WhatsApp, Instagram, or Snapchat. Further, approximately 70 percent of respondents use the aforementioned methods daily to communicate with people from their home country who are not living in Canada (see Table 7.1).

Moreover, from our survey findings, we tested the relationship between sense of belonging to Canadian society and level of connectivity to individuals from home countries. We ran a linear regression and found supporting evidence that a lower sense of belonging to Canadian society translated to higher connectivity to home countries and vice versa. Respondents who feel isolated or marginalized in Canada were more likely to reach out to home country networks for support.

Significant differences were also found between respondents who identified as "Canadian" and those who identified as "Canadian-Arab," whereby Canadian-Arabs were significantly more likely to exhibit high connectivity to home countries. On the flip side, Arabs were more likely than Arab-Canadians to have high connectivity levels. When dual identities ("Arab-Canadian" vs. "Canadian-Arab") were compared in isolation, no significant differences in high connectivity levels were found. Self-identity similarly affected likelihood of high engagement in MENA media, such that

Table 7.1 Most and least frequently used methods of communication with home country.

	At least once a week		At most once a year	
	Total number of respondents	Percentage of respondents	Total number of respondents	Percentage of respondents
Skype	207	28	251	34
Phone	458	61	86	11.5
Facebook	518	69	89	12
Text or BBM	377	52	223	30.5
Facetime	210	29	341	47
Email	251	35	311	43
Tango or Viber	277	38	292	40
WhatsApp	523	71	101	14
Instagram	387	53	251	34
Snapchat	389	53.5	276	38

respondents who identified as "Arab" or "Arab-Canadian" were more likely to be highly engaged in MENA media (news, TV, music, and film) than those respondents who identified as "Canadian" or "Canadian-Arab."

When dual identities ("Arab-Canadian" vs. "Canadian-Arab") were compared in isolation, a significant difference in high MENA media engagement was also found. Namely, Arab-Canadians were more likely to be highly engaged in MENA media than Canadian-Arabs. And, while levels of MENA media engagement between Canadians and Canadian-Arabs were significantly different at $p < .05$ (with Canadians being less engaged), a significant difference in MENA media engagement did not exist between Arabs and Arab-Canadians.[3]

The Metissage Complexities of Attachment Formations and Longings

The epistemology of metissage (the lens of hybridity that affects what the people see and why) grounding Canadian-Arab youth self-understandings of identity is found in the complex interplay between attachment and longing. The lens through which Arab youth view their lives, and the politics they rely upon to reinscribe hybridity into their lifeworlds, emerges in their pursuit of local Arab friendships and language development. Friendships and language are central to their grounded belonging in Canada. Canadian-Arab youth "become" Canadian by weaving Arab threads into their lives. Their Canadian houses are built on an Arab foundation.

Many Arab youths yearn to be "more connected" to Arab culture but recognize that living in the diaspora is a disconnecting experience. Those who have just come from the Arab region felt less disconnected than those who had been in the West longer. For many young people, they gravitated toward friendships with other Arabs to increase cultural connections and to help them integrate into Canadian society from familiar starting points. As one youth noted,

> I think that a part of living abroad sort of makes you more connected and intertwined in your Arab culture because you're coming somewhere and would like to see someone who has similar habits, similar cultural background, similar language, it just makes it easier to navigate the city. So I found that right when we came here, that's the first thing that we wanted to meet, lots of Arabs, and then you will eventually integrate within the city. But that first starter point, you need to meet a lot of Arabs.[4]

A prominent method of attachment formation in Canada was the practice of entering, inculcating, and nurturing friendship circles with other Arabs. Such friendships help youth boost their confidence and self-understanding as Arabs. As one youth noted, [in Arab friendships/communities] "You don't feel embarrassed to pronounce your name because everyone is familiar with that name. [For example, non-Arabs say] 'Akhmed' [instead of Ahmed]. So yeah, it's a good idea being surrounded by Arabs."[5] Some of the most oft-repeated words used to explain why youth befriend other Arabs were "warmth" and "familiarity." Emerging from this emphasis on the warmth and familiarity we read a longing for their Arab identity as a place of comfort, security, and clarity of self in the world.

This is one aspect of the metissage or hybridization process for Canadian-Arab youth: building an epistemology (or lens to read the world) through self-knowing in one cultural space grounded by attachment and longing to a different ancestral cultural space. An oft-cited prerequisite or precursor to this process is self-awareness about how multiple network channels can be strategically advantageous. Many youths noted that they actively gravitate toward Arab friendships, and that this is encouraged and preferred by their parents, but that they actively pursue friendships with non-Arabs as well. Both forms of friendship building are their way of expanding attachments to Canadian society and youth construct strategies to make that possible. Part of the reason youth develop friendships with non-Arabs was due to a natural and genuine interest in their cohort, and part of the interest was built around an appreciation of the social benefits of having non-Arab friendship networks. Youth recognized that they would experience difficulty integrating into Canadian society and would face difficulties in the workplace if they only had Arab friends. Some of the social benefits that Arab youth identified in having non-Arab friends included helping people in society understand Arab culture better and *ipso facto*, helping their social and political communities overcome discrimination and prejudice, participating in a community outside of their ethnic circles, avoiding the social losses that accompany isolation, and building hybridity as a social good. As one youth noted, "If you don't have that integration, you miss a whole link with the culture especially living in a western community. If you seclude yourself to a group of Arab friends, other people don't learn about you! [Hence] You see the whole antagonizing [of] Islam and Arabs. Mixing is essential."[6]

Arab youth come to know better who they are by building cultural loyalties with different Arab groups and communities in order to expand their sense of belonging in Canada. Arab youth are not connected to Arab culture in exactly the same ways, and we found that the variations were often based on national or geographical origin. Many North Africans living in Montreal expressed greater ambivalence about their Arab identity compared to Levant Arabs living in Ottawa. Nevertheless, when pressed, many of the Montreal youth noted that what binds North Africans is the same attributes that binds them to Levantine Arabs. We frequently heard that being Algerian, Moroccan, or Tunisian youth, they often made friends to Levantine Arabs because of the same feelings of transcultural connectedness. Moreover, many youths explained that Montreal had a large Arab community of people from various national backgrounds that facilitated high interaction and comfort with other Arabs.

Living in Arabic Culture

Through metissage or hybridity, Canadian-Arab youth see cultural artifacts and productions, particularly Arabic music, as core to living in Arabic culture, and in the process, feel more grounded living in Canada feeling like their cultural cups are full. Canadian-Arab youth actively consume Arab music, films, and television shows, and tend to passively consume news media from the Middle East. Thus, in sum, Arab music is a very important part of their lives and news media is less likely to be pursued for its own sake even though parents actively consume it. The news was deemed by some of the participants to be too depressing, and for that reason, they avoided it. As one respondent noted, "I always try to avoid that, just because being raised in an Arab surrounding, you're always surrounded by news. So, as a kid, I just wanted to run away from that, it was always a noise and just a headache. I didn't understand it and I wasn't interested. I tried to just drift away from that."[7]

From our quantitative survey, we found that the most popular form of MENA media is music and film, followed by news and television. Frequency of reading/watching MENA media does not appear to be correlated with age (within the 18–29-year-old bracket). However, frequency of reading/watching one type of MENA media is significantly positively correlated with watching/reading other types of MENA media at p <.000, which is to say a respondent is significantly more likely to frequently watch MENA TV if they frequently watch MENA news or listens to MENA music/watches MENA films. The majority of survey respondents are highly engaged in media originating from the MENA region. Specifically, 63 percent watch/read MENA news, TV, music, and/or films at least once a week. Further, approximately 36 percent of respondents watch/read MENA media daily (see Table 7.2).

For Arab youth, there is an apparent passion for Arab music. They often consume this at events like weddings and festivals, but also download music through YouTube and Facebook sharing. As one youth noted,

Table 7.2 Frequency of reading/watching MENA media.

	At least once a week		At most once a year	
	Total number of respondents	Percentage of respondents	Total number of respondents	Percentage of respondents
MENA news	361	50	205	27
MENA TV	318	44	265	36
MENA music/films	425	58	158	22

I may not watch a lot of TV, I will go online though and watch talk shows every once in a while or like comedy skits. But one thing I have noticed that will always be is Arab music, as much as I listen to English western music, I will always kind of go back to Arabic music because it was what I was raised on, it's just very different and sometimes you need that little dose of it.[8]

The music of Arab pop-stars is particularly favored and enjoyed by many Arab youth. They listen to artists such as Wael Kfoury and Amr Diab via music videos or by playing such music at home with their parents or in their cars with their friends and cousins. Classic Arab singers, such as Fairouz and Umm Kuthum, are also popular. Sometimes the music is consumed for its own sake, sometimes it is used by youth to help them reconnect to their culture, and sometimes it is used to help youth connect to other Arabs who are not from their national origin. For example, one youth noted that "I am Algerian, but I really like Egyptian music and so, yes, I love listening and I access it through YouTube. It's mostly the music that connects me to the Arab culture, mostly Egyptian and Lebanese, Algerian music if it's modern music groups."[9] While pop-stars are popular, some noted they listened to alternative Arab music as well. For example, one youth said: "I'm a big fan of Arabic music, especially Arabic rock, the new bands of rock music, there are a lot in Jordan. Also, I sometimes watch mostly through YouTube. I really like Moroccan drama and movies, they're really good, and it's a way to connect with my background, it's really nice."[10]

While alone, Arab youth, like many other Canadian youth demographics, consume popular media online. They listen to music and watch TV skits frequently via internet downloads. One youth said, "For films, I think the Internet mostly [is where I go to get them], as in YouTube, Sound Cloud, music streams, especially living in the West you'd have to pay quite a bit to have the regular TV service to come. So out of falling on Internet, YouTube videos are the best."[11] Arab youth are especially fascinated by Arab soap operas or "Syrian dramas"[12] on satellite which they watch with their parents. Soap operas are watched with greater intensity during holiday celebrations such as Ramadan.

Canadian-Arab youth's hybridity is also cemented through multilingual practices. Advanced use of English and French is met with an attachment to and longing to develop skills in the Arabic language and be connected to the Arabic accent. For one participant, connecting to home meant staying connected to the accent of Arabic people made accessible through popular media:

I do miss my country, and the people and the accent so I do find myself watching shows from that country so I can see and be surrounded and listen to that accent and feel more connected in that sort of way. Because, personally, I barely find Jordanians here, or Palestinians from my nationality, so I don't really hear the accent. I do find myself listening to songs and watching shows with that accent just to feel more connected.[13]

Another links language survival to watching TV shows:

I watch a lot of series, and a part of watching Arab shows is just to keep some type of Arabic language in the daily life, because I speak English with almost everyone I know, and everyone speaks it. So, I like to just have shows every now and then to hear the different dialects and keep in touch with the culture. If we're watching English TV, and talking English, we'll eventually start losing our Arabic.

Arab cultural products like film, literature, and poetry are not as interesting to Arab youth in the West. Some youth noted that if their Arabic was stronger, they would read more Arabic literature because they hear that it is quite rich. A number of youth were fascinated by Arabic calligraphy as an art form and turned to social media to access it.

The Epistemological and Social Significance of Boundaries

In the process of hybridizing, Canadian-Arab youth actively demarcate social boundaries. The nuances of this social boundary making are unique to them. If family is imagined as a space, Arab youth draw borders around it to emphasize its importance and their desire to "own" family as a value. Youth in our study expressed great appreciation and love for strong family ties which they linked back to Arab culture. Very strong emphasis on family and close familial relations was one value that Arab youth felt distinguished Arab culture from Western culture, which they regarded as more individualistic. As one participant put it, "We are very family oriented, most Arab families are very close, and not only between our first family but our further family members too."[14] Others echoed comparisons between Arab cultural values and non-Arab values: "The respect in the family is definitely something I've noticed in the non-Arab community [that] is not prominent, and I do not want that. The whole respect and family staying close, like I'm connected to my cousins, my great aunts, uncles and everyone. That would be such a nice thing to keep."[15]

Nagel and Staeheli (2005) found that Arab-Americans believed they shared values with American culture on such areas as family, religion, and justice, but that Arab culture differed from American culture in the degree to which they acted upon these values. In explaining why Western families are less close-knit than Arab families, many identified a perceived individualism and business-orientedness to Western culture:

> I feel like in the West it's mostly, it's more of like individualistic society. I really like our sense of community in Arab countries where like your neighbours are your friends and you visit each other and talk to people ... I really like that sense of belonging and going out. I feel like here it's more about your professional life and career, and you sort of work on yourself and it's not about working together as a community.[16]

Similar sentiments were shared by others. For example, one youth noted:

> People here aren't really attached to family, it is very different from our culture and I don't want to pass that on to my children ....[also, in Canada] we live in an open country and religious values aren't really present in society, which is different from Algerian culture. We have certain convictions in Arab culture and I want to pass that on and they aren't here in Western culture.[17]

While the importance of family was resoundingly the most important characteristic of Arab culture that participants wanted to pass on to their children, others included generosity, hospitality, food and culinary practices, respecting elders, pushing for academic success, altruism, and charity.

Arab youth build knowledge about their identities through self-awareness and re-evaluation. Contrary to how they might be perceived, Arab youth do not take their cultures, values, and practices at face value or accept them as they have been socialized to accept them. This is profound because many youth are taught not to question the values of their upbringing. In conservative Muslim circles, values of patriarchy remain strong and children are encouraged to never challenge their parents out of respect for them, except if parents ask their children to act against the religion. In the wider Arab community, people take an interest in other people's affairs and it is considered normal, even an obligation to intervene when a person feels another is going in the "wrong" direction. Arab youth, instead, make claims about who they are through an open-minded hybrid exploration; it is an exploration of self-understanding regarding the limits of what they consider acceptable and unacceptable, some of which involves deviation from inculcated practices. The epistemology of their particular hybridization process therefore includes boundary making around Arabic cultural spaces and practices that do not define them. In this way, they live outside of particular parts of the cultural space instead of inside of them. Youth may be then in a Canadian space or a decidedly new one that may or may not pay deference to Canadian values. While many young Arabs noted that they like the collective nature of Arab culture, they criticized it as well.

> As for values [that] I don't want to pass on, one thing I feel we have in the Arab community that is slowly diminishing is the whole kind of parents choose your way of life for you when you grow up. That's definitely not something I want to give to my kids. I want to let them [make choices], make it more open for them, but definitely sneak in my advice here and there, but ultimately I want it to be their choice of what they do in life. We can be very controlling sometimes; there is also a whole stigma with things in religion. I was raised up in a moderate to strict, not

the most strict like I do have my freedoms but, I definitely want to pass that on. I don't want to be too strict because to grow up you need to make your own mistakes in life and learn from that.[18]

Cognizant of the misogyny prevalent in their community, many put themselves outside of that cultural space, on the other side of the boundary that they had drawn. Arab Muslim youth argued that their parents confused religion with culture. Religion, in their opinion, is often more progressive on gender issues than Arab culture. For example, one participant noted:

You see a lot of Arab families usually have the wife staying at home and is a stay-at-home mom always. I feel that that responsibility should be shared among both, *and religiously it should be shared among both*. It just culturally it's not shared among both. I want to bring to light where it's okay for the wife to work, the husband can work and they can both share the raising of the kids. It would be much better as a family. It could also lead to less marriage problems.[19]

Arab youth widely echoed and rejected sentiments that conflated cultural taboos with religious mores. This was often most reflected upon when discussing gender roles. Many of the youth participants made this connection to women working outside the home. They often defended a woman's right to work outside the home on religious grounds and noted that in Western society with the cost of living, it was difficult financially for women to stay home. Others also criticized what they perceived as hypocrisy in Arab culture concerning the appropriate roles for men and women. As one noted,

Basically some [Arab] parents and older generations would think that a girl is not well seen when she comes late at home. But when it is a guy, it's fine? This is something I don't want my kids to grow up with! A guy can do whatever he wants and you can't do whatever you want and because you're a girl, and since you're not married, you can't. I feel like that a girl can respect herself coming home at the same time as a guy, that does not change. The gender should not make a difference or be a factor to discriminate about.[20]

This boundary making is not without push-back. Many youths had a strong sense of individual self-expression and self-identity, but still confronted social challenges related to collective shaming for having independent thoughts or values that ran contrary to Arab culture. Arab youth who challenged ideas for being illogical or irrational would often experience elders who disregard their concerns or who painted such ideas as "aib" (shameful). Thus, many parents support and encourage girls and women to pursue higher education partly to increase their perceived marriage potential, but only support women's educational ascension to a point because of the perceived cultural taboo of women holding a higher level of education than their husbands. It was upsetting to many Arab youths that felt pressure to keep limits on their educational ambitions in order to ensure their ability to get married in the community. Arab youth frequently cited shaming others, laziness, lack of punctuality, gossiping, and materialism as characteristics of Arab culture that they wanted to disavow and not pass on to their children.

(Re)claiming Arab-Western Hybridity as an Identity

Canadian-Arab youth engage in active reflexivity about culture and express their cultural loyalty through Arab-Western hybridity as their identity. Arab-Western hybridity was natural to many youths who took offense in being asked whether their Arab identity is compatible with being Western. We left what "being Western" might mean in abeyance and allowed the focus group participants to address or imply what it might mean to them. For Arab youth, "being a westerner" refers to more or less adopting a liberal social and political values framework on a spectrum, pursuing individual aggrandizement, leaning more toward a secular outlook, being respectful (or tolerant) of others and of differences, being privileged in terms of material comforts, and adhering to values of civility and civil society including the pursuit of peaceful resolutions to conflict. Being "Canadian" meant, for some, being part of a nation of peoples whose common linking bond is their multicultural differences and thus being allowed to be fluid in the expression of identity. Given that we found in Arab youth a desire to be inside and outside of Arab cultural boundaries, the fact that some might embrace the identity fluidity premised on metissage is not surprising. The resounding opinion of the groups was that Arabs can still retain their cultural attributes while being Western. This sentiment is shared by one youth which was typical of other responses.

> I think the question separates the two identities and I don't see it as two different identities. I see right now, that I am a little bit of here, and a little bit of there, and [those two things] came together and I am what I am right now because of [my] experiences within the Middle East and experiences in the West, that forms my identity. It has a bit of both in it. I am not 100% there, and I am not 100% here either. I am hyphenation; in the middle.[21]

A youth responded to the last statement with this: "I agree. Of course our identities can come together as one, but I mean obviously there are some differences. Compare one Western person to another Western person; they won't be compatible as well. We can be compatible, but not 100%. No one is perfect."[22] Again, we heard the view that their identities do coexist, and that one does not have to choose one or the other. As one youth noted, "The Arab identity, or Algerian identity, is very attached to religion. The western identity is very just open to everything and there is no religion. They are not necessarily fully compatible, but you can still mix both together."[23] Another youth noted, "I think that being Arab or Canadian is not contradictory. You can be one and the other at the same time. Canadian, Arab, Muslim, occidental, these don't contradict each other. I think each identity has a different colour on the personality. The stronger colour will show, but it doesn't define the entire image."[24] Again, we heard this appeal to superimposed layers (upon layers) or a multi-circle Venn diagram to understand their hybridity of identities. One youth eloquently noted,

> I don't think you can identify solely as one nation, but as a bunch of nations. I think I'm Québécois, a Montrealer, Canadian, Arab. So yes, but how does one define what Arab and Muslim culture is? Western values are compatible with Arabs. Because it's the same values. But, for example, the Arab political culture is garbage, but our arts are amazing. The two can be compatible, just depends what values I look at like "liberty, fraternity, equality."[25]

A number noted that the flexibility of Canadian multiculturalism (which expects people to respect others) allowed Arabs to make their identity compatible with Western identity because they could be genuine in individually self-expressing themselves. For example,

> Arab identity is very compatible with western identity because western identity is actually a broad concept, so, as long as you respect other people you can be yourself and act according to your Arabic identity and still fit in the Canadian society. Western society is very open and inclusive so you can be yourself and still be part of the western world in some way.[26]

Similarly, another youth noted that hybridity might manifest itself in identity bifurcation (or multi-furcation) to make belonging possible:

> I can comfortably, at least in Canada, express my Arab identity along with my Western identity in a society that is very multicultural. I can come to events like this and speak only in my home language. At the same time, I can walk 30 seconds outside and be in a completely different Western world, and express my own Western, or Western adopted identity simultaneously. I don't think it can really be exclusive to one or the other.[27]

Others reflected on the idea that their hybridity through mixing and interacting with others allowed them to take the best of the Western and Arab cultures and leave what they did not want to adopt:

> Even the West can learn things from Arab culture and the Arabs can learn lots of things from the West. ... You can be a person that agrees to aspects from Arab culture and the Western culture. I don't see any of us here agreeing fully with the Arab culture or fully with the western culture. We have a little bit of both.[28]

Similarly, another youth added, "I always try to take the best from like Arab identity and best of Western, and try to have a mix of both as much as I can. Try to think what is best and mix ... I think I'm a mix of both."[29]

Many Arab youths did not want to have to choose between being either Arab or Western identities or cultures. On the contrary, they often advocated for the value and merit of their hybridity. Some reflected on how Canadian multiculturalism had also given non-Arab Canadians an opportunity to learn from Arab culture:

> Even if you look at an average white person who has had some experience with Arabs, he does himself have an Arab identity in him because he's just observing something from us. You absorb something from everyone you meet and that forms who you are in the end. In the end, your identity comes down to whom you interact with, and just how you are, and what your values are.

Similar views about being Muslim in a social environment where encounter is a form of exchange were also echoed. Arab youth are also cognizant of religious fundamentalism in their community. The youth that we spoke to were often supportive of having strong spiritual faith but did not want fundamentalist values in their lives.

While many youths noted that although they feel that Arab and Western values can coexist in this hybrid identity space, there was an acknowledgment that their identities can be in conflict. For example, one young person who was part Egyptian and Palestinian but born in Canada noted,

> I am proud to say, I am half Egyptian, half Palestinian, but when you go back there [in Egypt, it] is always this feeling that you're not really integrated. Why? Because the language barrier, yes it's the same, but they have some dialects that you'll not understand, or some insides you won't understand because it's not the same thing. You feel [like] a visitor in your own home country while you're born here. You also feel as not necessarily an immigrant, but you're not Canadian-based like as a real Canadian because you have [a] background and origin [different] than other people here.[30]

Similar views were expressed about how their hybrid identity was not always understood by others. One youth noted, "When I'm in Algeria, they'll ask you where you're from, and when you're in Canada, they'll ask you where you're from. So, I don't belong anywhere. Being in Canada I feel like there's different values. And they'll hear you're Algerian or Muslim, so on the exterior I see that I have a difference." The idea that Arab youth felt both Arab and Western was repeated, but that both family in the Middle East and North Africa and other Canadians, always ask "where are you from?" was frustrating. As one noted, "Yes, my Arab identity can become compatible with my western identity. I feel like I don't really have to choose. But when I go to Morocco, people are like where are you from? And like here in Canada, they're like, 'where are you from?' and I'm like 'Morocco.'"[31]

Another youth added a similar sentiment,

> I live in a really Québécois neighborhood, and I didn't have a lot of Arab friends, mainly Québécois friends. But I do carry forth from my parent's culture and my language …. Yes, I am very connected by my Arab parents. [] When I'm in an Arab country it's different though, I am not Arab enough for them. You cannot answer whether I am Arab or Canadian; like I feel attached to both, you have the

Canadian part and the Arab part, it combines both of them and it makes "you". You can't feel just Arab or Canadian, I feel both. I feel happy and proud of my country and I feel happy and proud of Canada.[32]

A number of youth reflected on how rising global populism and Islamophobia were raising a binary trope between being Arab/Muslim and Western. One youth went further to say, "there is a policy of division telling us we can't have both [Arab and Western identity], but we can have both!"[33]

Many youths wanted to visit the Middle East or North Africa or "back home" more often if they could. But most youth acknowledged that they preferred to raise a family in the West: "When we talk about going back to these countries and not mixing in, it is because the values we have adopted here in the West aren't there, like being open, pushing for feminist agendas, all these things are really present here in the West and we can't find them there."[34]

Conclusion and Analysis

Canadian-Arab youth use a number of tactics and strategies to stay translocally and transnationally connected to their Arabic culture which is widely adored by them. In exploring these Canadian-Arab youth translocal and transnational connections to their "home" countries, we observed four main themes: transnationally connected Arab youth long for stronger Arab connections in friendships and language, they appreciate Arab music and consume it with enthusiasm, they love having family ties but are critical of the misogyny, patriarchy, and collectivism, where it exists, in Arab cultures, and they have strong feelings of Arab-Western hybridity as an identity. Self-identity was shown to affect respondents' connectivity to home countries, whereby those who identified as Arab or Arab-Canadian were more likely to have high connectivity (at least weekly communication with individuals from home countries) than those respondents who identified as Canadian or Canadian-Arab. Our findings support the work of Maira (2008) that shows how popular culture prominently characterizes Arab youth's connections to the MENA culture and that they are vocal in criticizing gender relations and collective suppression of their desire to determine their destiny, while still respectful of collectivism as it relates to respecting family connectedness. Nurturance of a hybridity or metissage (as a lens for seeing their world and explaining their "why" in the world) is a core precursor for Canadian-Arab youths' transcultural identity formation and helps them to blunt the idea that Canadianness is an alterity to them.

Notes

1 Focus group respondent. Ottawa. June 20, 2016.
2 Among Canadian-Arab youth not born in Canada, 40.2 percent identify as "Arab," 30.2 percent identify as "Arab-Canadian," 2.5 percent identify as "Canadian," and 13.1 percent identify as "Canadian-Arab" (10.6 percent identify as "Other").

3   Note: In these findings, we discover that whereas earlier studies had identified differences in "connectivity" between Arabs and Arab-Canadians, but had overlooked differences between dual identities themselves, we provide evidence that such differences between dual identities exist. Youth media engagement with the Arab world might have more to do with knowledge of language, and therefore Canadians (who may not speak Arabic) are less engaged than all other groups who do speak Arabic. Thus, the difference between Canadian-Arabs and Arab-Canadians in media consumption is likely a consequence of the fact that Canadian-Arabs are not as fluent, whereas Arab-Canadians and Arabs are equally fluent and therefore have a similar prevalence of higher engagement.
4   Focus group respondent. Ottawa. June 20, 2016.
5   Ibid.
6   Ibid.
7   Ibid.
8   Ibid.
9   Focus group respondent. Montreal. July 18, 2016.
10 Focus group respondent. Ottawa. June 20, 2016.
11 Ibid.
12 Ibid.
13 Ibid.
14 Ibid.
15 Ibid.
16 Ibid.
17 Focus group respondent. Montreal. Translated from French. July 18, 2016.
18 Focus group respondent. Ottawa. June 20, 2016.
19 Ibid. Emphasis added.
20 Focus group respondent. Montreal. July 18, 2016.
21 Focus group respondent. Ottawa. June 20, 2016.
22 Ibid.
23 Focus group respondent. Montreal. Translated from French. July 18, 2016.
24 Focus group respondent. Montreal. July 18, 2016.
25 Focus group respondent. Montreal. Translated from French. July 18, 2016.
26 Focus group respondent. Ottawa. June 20, 2016.
27 Ibid.
28 Ibid.
29 Focus group respondent. Montreal. July 18, 2016.
30 Ibid.
31 Focus group respondent. Montreal. Translated from French. July 18, 2016.
32 Focus group respondent. Montreal. July 18, 2016.
33 Ibid.
34 Ibid.

References

Alba, Richard and Victor Nee (2003). *Remaking the American Mainstream: Assimilation and Contemporary Immigration*. Cambridge, MA: Harvard University Press.

Baumann, Gerd, and André Gingrich. Eds. (2005). *Grammars of Identity/Alterity: A Structural Approach* (Vol. 3). New York: Berghahn Books.

Cho, Sumi and Robert Westley (2002). Historicizing Critical Race Theory's Cutting Edge: Key Movements That Performed the Theory. Francisco Valdes, Jerome McCristal Culp, Angela P. Harris (Eds.). *Crossroads, Directions, and A New Critical Race Theory*. Philadelphia: Temple University Press, pp. 52–4.

Ewing, Katherine Pratt. Ed. (2008). *Being and Belonging: Muslims in the United States since 9/11*. New York: Russell Sage Foundation.

Finn, Melissa and Bessma Momani (2017). Voting in Controversy: A Critical Analysis of the Canadian Arab Youth Vote in the 2015. *Canadian Political Science Review*. Vol. 11. Issue 1: 61–89.

Finn, Melissa and Bessma Momani (2019). Transnational Citizenship Mobilization among Canadian Arab Youth: An Engaged Social Movement for Change in the Middle East. *Canadian Ethnic Studies*. Vol. 51. Issue 1: 25–68.

Finn, Melissa, Michael Opatowski, and Bessma Momani (2018). Transnational Citizenship Capacity-Building: Moving the Conversation in New Directions. *International Political Sociology*. Vol. 12: 291–305.

Gans, Herbert J. (1997). Toward A Reconciliation of "Assimilation" and "Pluralism": The Interplay of Acculturation and Ethnic Retention. *International Migration Review*. Vol. 31. Issue 4: 875–92.

Hannerz, Ulf (1996). *Transnational Connections: Culture, People, Places*. New York: Routledge.

Inda, Jonathan Xavier and Rentao Rosaldo (2002). Introduction: A World in Motion. In *The Anthropology of Globalization: A Reader*. Malden, MA: Blackwell Publishing.

Maira, Sunaima (2008). "Citizenship, Dissent, Empire: South Asian Muslim Immigrant Youth." In K. P. Ewing (Ed.). *Being and Belonging: Muslims in the United States since 9/11*. New York: Russell Sage Foundation.

Mercea, Dan and Marco T. Bastos (2016). Being a Serial Transnational Activist. *Journal of Computer-Mediated Communication*. Vol. 21. Issue 2: 140–55.

Momani, Bessma (2015). *Arab Dawn: Arab Youth and the Demographic Dividend They Will Bring*. Toronto: University of Toronto Press.

Nagel, Caroline R., and Lynn A. Staeheli (2005). "We're just like the Irish": Narratives of Assimilation, Belonging and Citizenship amongst Arab-American Activists. *Citizenship Studies*. Vol. 9. Issue 5: 485–98.

Schiller, Nina Glick, Linda Basch, and Cristina Szanton Blanc (1995). From Immigrant to Transmigrant: Theorizing Transnational Migration. *Anthropological Quarterly*. Vol. 68. Issue 1 (January): 48–63.

Shain, Yossi, and Barth, Aharon (2003). Diasporas and International Relations Theory. *International Organization*. Vol. 57. Issue 3: 449–79.

Tarrow, Sidney (2005). *The New Transnational Activism*. Cambridge: Cambridge University Press.

Turner, Joe (2016). (En)gendering the Political: Citizenship from Marginal Spaces. *Citizenship Studies*. Vol. 20. Issue 2: 141–55.

Wald, Kenneth D. (2008). Homeland Interests, Hostland Politics: Politicized Ethnic Identity among Middle Eastern Heritage Groups in the United States1. *International Migration Review*. Vol. 42. Issue 2: 273–301.

Zelinsky, Wilbur, and Lee, Barrett A. (1998). Heterolocalism: An Alternative Model of the Sociospatial Behaviour of Immigrant Ethnic Communities. *International Journal of Population Geography*. Vol. 4. Issue 4: 281–98.

Zuss, Mark (1997). Strategies of Representation: Autobiographical Metissage and Critical Pragmatism. *Educational Theory*. Vol. 47. Issue 2: 163–80.

Appendix

CAYS STATA Workbook

LEGEND

Never	1
Yearly	2
Special occasions	3
Once a month	4

Total number of valid observations: 814
- 564 respondents are between 18 and 24
- 250 respondents are between 25 and 29

Self-identification
- 237 respondents identify as Arab
- 43 respondents identify as Canadian
- 183 respondents identify as Canadian-Arab
- 233 respondents identify as Arab-Canadian
- 72 respondents identify as Other
- 46 missing responses

What is your age range?	Freq.	Percent	Cum.
1824	564	69.29	69.29
2529	250	30.71	100.00
Total	814	100.00	

How do you self-identify?	Freq.	Percent	Cum.
1	237	30.86	30.86
2	43	5.60	36.46
3	183	23.83	60.29
4	233	30.34	90.62
5	72	9.38	100.00
Total	768	100.00	

Frequency and Methods of Communication with Home Country

Frequency of Home Country Communication - Skype	Freq.	Percent	Cum.
1	186	25.14	25.14
2	65	8.78	33.92
3	191	25.81	59.73
4	91	12.30	72.03
5	104	14.05	86.08
6	103	13.92	100.00
Total	740	100.00	

. tab Phone

Frequency of Home Country Communication - Phone	Freq.	Percent	Cum.
1	53	7.08	7.08
2	33	4.41	11.48
3	110	14.69	26.17
4	95	12.68	38.85
5	142	18.96	57.81
6	316	42.19	100.00
Total	749	100.00	

Frequency of Home Country Communication - FaceTime	Freq.	Percent	Cum.
1	310	42.64	42.64
2	31	4.26	46.91
3	94	12.93	59.83
4	82	11.28	71.11
5	109	14.99	86.11
6	101	13.89	100.00
Total	727	100.00	

. tab Email

Frequency of Home Country Communication -Email	Freq.	Percent	Cum.
1	278	38.56	38.56
2	33	4.58	43.13
3	85	11.79	54.92
4	74	10.26	65.19
5	57	7.91	73.09
6	194	26.91	100.00
Total	721	100.00	

Frequency of Home Country Communication - Facebook	Freq.	Percent	Cum.
1	73	9.76	9.76
2	16	2.14	11.90
3	52	6.95	18.85
4	89	11.90	30.75
5	149	19.92	50.67
6	369	49.33	100.00
Total	748	100.00	

. tab TextBBM

Frequency of Home Country Communication -Text or BBM	Freq.	Percent	Cum.
1	194	26.61	26.61
2	29	3.98	30.59
3	66	9.05	39.64
4	63	8.64	48.29
5	102	13.99	62.28
6	275	37.72	100.00
Total	729	100.00	

Frequency of Home Country Communication -Tango or Viber	Freq.	Percent	Cum.
1	257	35.35	35.35
2	35	4.81	40.17
3	65	8.94	49.11
4	93	12.79	61.90
5	120	16.51	78.40
6	157	21.60	100.00
Total	727	100.00	

. tab Whatsapp

Frequency of Home Country Communication -WhatsApp	Freq.	Percent	Cum.
1	91	12.35	12.35
2	10	1.36	13.70
3	40	5.43	19.13
4	73	9.91	29.04
5	106	14.38	43.42
6	417	56.58	100.00
Total	737	100.00	

```
. tab Instagram

Frequency
of Home
Country
Communicati
   on
-Instagram |   Freq.     Percent      Cum.
-----------+--------------------------------
         1 |    235       32.15      32.15
         2 |     16        2.19      34.34
         3 |     31        4.24      38.58
         4 |     62        8.48      47.06
         5 |     91       12.45      59.51
         6 |    296       40.49     100.00
-----------+--------------------------------
     Total |    731      100.00

. tab Snapchat

Frequency
of Home
Country
Communicati
   on
-Snapchat  |   Freq.     Percent      Cum.
-----------+--------------------------------
         1 |    260       35.71      35.71
         2 |     16        2.20      37.91
         3 |     25        3.43      41.35
         4 |     38        5.22      46.57
         5 |     80       10.99      57.55
         6 |    309       42.45     100.00
-----------+--------------------------------
     Total |    728      100.00
```

Most and Least Frequently Used Methods of Communication with Home Country

```
. ttest Snapchat, by(whatisyouragerange)

Two-sample t test with equal variances

  Group  |   Obs      Mean    Std. Err.   Std. Dev.   [95% Conf. Interval]
---------+-------------------------------------------------------------------
   1824  |   518    4.069498   .0969944   2.207556   3.878946    4.26005
   2529  |   210    3.166667   .1566602   2.270222   2.85783    3.475503
---------+-------------------------------------------------------------------
combined |   728    3.809066   .0838202   2.261593   3.644507   3.973624
---------+-------------------------------------------------------------------
    diff |          .9028314   .1820844              .5453565   1.260306
---------+-------------------------------------------------------------------
    diff = mean(1824) - mean(2529)                           t =   4.9583
Ho: diff = 0                                  degrees of freedom =      726

    Ha: diff < 0            Ha: diff != 0             Ha: diff > 0
 Pr(T < t) = 1.0000      Pr(|T| > |t|) = 0.0000      Pr(T > t) = 0.0000

. ttest Phone, by(whatisyouragerange)

Two-sample t test with equal variances

  Group  |   Obs      Mean    Std. Err.   Std. Dev.   [95% Conf. Interval]
---------+-------------------------------------------------------------------
   1824  |   524    4.53626    .0704017   1.611569   4.397955   4.674564
   2529  |   225    4.702222   .100104    1.50156    4.504956   4.899488
---------+-------------------------------------------------------------------
combined |   749    4.586115   .0577379   1.580164   4.472767   4.699463
---------+-------------------------------------------------------------------
    diff |         -.1659627   .1258844             -.4130921   .0811667
---------+-------------------------------------------------------------------
    diff = mean(1824) - mean(2529)                           t =  -1.3184
Ho: diff = 0                                  degrees of freedom =      747

    Ha: diff < 0            Ha: diff != 0             Ha: diff > 0
 Pr(T < t) = 0.0939      Pr(|T| > |t|) = 0.1878      Pr(T > t) = 0.9061
```

Transcultural Identity Formation

At Least Weekly Communication with Home Country	Freq.	Percent	Cum.
0	141	17.32	17.32
1	673	82.68	100.00
Total	814	100.00	

Daily Communication with Home Country	Freq.	Percent	Cum.
0	246	30.22	30.22
1	568	69.78	100.00
Total	814	100.00	

Independent variable: Sense of belonging to Canadian society

Dependent variables: Very high connectivity (daily communication with individuals from home country); very low connectivity (at most, yearly communication with home country individuals)

```
. regress veryhighconnectivity feelingofbelongingincanada
```

Source	SS	df	MS			
Model	2.27049648	1	2.27049648	Number of obs	=	778
Residual	153.760352	776	.198144783	$F(1, 776)$	=	11.46
				Prob > F	=	0.0007
				R-squared	=	0.0146
				Adj R-squared	=	0.0133
Total	156.030848	777	.200811903	Root MSE	=	.44513

veryhighconnectivity	Coef.	Std. Err.	t	P>|t|	[95% Conf. Interval]	
feelingofbelongingincanada	-.0548007	.0161889	-3.39	0.001	-.0865799	-.0230215
_cons	.9353694	.0649166	14.41	0.000	.8079363	1.062802

```
. reg verylowconnectivity feelingofbelongingincanada
```

Source	SS	df	MS		Number of obs	=	778
					F(1, 776)	=	4.24
Model	.211240005	1	.211240005		Prob > F	=	0.0397
Residual	38.6280916	776	.049778469		R-squared	=	0.0054
					Adj R-squared	=	0.0042
Total	38.8393316	777	.04998627		Root MSE	=	.22311

verylowconnectivity	Coef.	Std. Err.	t	P>|t|	[95% Conf. Interval]	
feelingofbelongingincanada	-.0167153	.0081142	-2.06	0.040	-.0326437	-.0007869
_cons	1.012271	.0325376	31.11	0.000	.9483991	1.076143

Interest in MENA TV, Music, Film, etc.

Read or watch news from MENA	Freq.	Percent	Cum.
1	76	10.41	10.41
2	119	16.30	26.71
4	174	23.84	50.55
5	202	27.67	78.22
6	159	21.78	100.00
Total	730	100.00	

Watch satellite TV from MENA	Freq.	Percent	Cum.
1	117	16.05	16.05
2	148	20.30	36.35
4	146	20.03	56.38
5	183	25.10	81.48
6	135	18.52	100.00
Total	729	100.00	

Watch Music/Film from MENA	Freq.	Percent	Cum.
1	64	8.77	8.77
2	94	12.88	21.64
4	147	20.14	41.78
5	202	27.67	69.45
6	223	30.55	100.00
Total	730	100.00	

High Engagement in MENA Media	Freq.	Percent	Cum.
0	298	36.61	36.61
1	516	63.39	100.00
Total	814	100.00	

Very High Engagement in MENA Media	Freq.	Percent	Cum.
0	520	63.88	63.88
1	294	36.12	100.00
Total	814	100.00	

```
. reg MENAPol WatchMENANews

      Source |       SS           df       MS      Number of obs   =       706
-------------+----------------------------------   F(1, 704)       =     68.38
       Model |  108.436366         1   108.436366  Prob > F        =    0.0000
    Residual |  1116.33417       704   1.58570195  R-squared       =    0.0885
-------------+----------------------------------   Adj R-squared   =    0.0872
       Total |  1224.77054       705   1.73726317  Root MSE        =    1.2592

     MENAPol |      Coef.   Std. Err.      t    P>|t|     [95% Conf. Interval]
WatchMENANews|   .2401488   .0290405     8.27   0.000     .1831325    .2971651
       _cons |   2.385338   .1282812    18.59   0.000     2.133479    2.637198
```

High Interest in MENA Politics	Freq.	Percent	Cum.
0	452	55.53	55.53
1	362	44.47	100.00
Total	814	100.00	

High Interest in International Politics	Freq.	Percent	Cum.
0	429	52.70	52.70
1	385	47.30	100.00
Total	814	100.00	

```
. reg veryhighconnectivity highMENAmediaENGAGE

      Source |       SS           df       MS      Number of obs   =        814
-------------+----------------------------------   F(1, 812)       =      80.04
       Model |  15.402703         1    15.402703   Prob > F        =     0.0000
    Residual |  156.253317      812     .192430193 R-squared       =     0.0897
-------------+----------------------------------   Adj R-squared   =     0.0886
       Total |  171.65602       813     .211139016 Root MSE        =     .43867

------------------------------------------------------------------------------
veryhighconnectiv~y |      Coef.   Std. Err.      t    P>|t|     [95% Conf. Interval]
-------------------+----------------------------------------------------------
highMENAmediaENGAGE |   .2855471   .0319165     8.95   0.000     .2228984    .3481957
              _cons |   .5167785   .0254114    20.34   0.000     .4668988    .5666583
------------------------------------------------------------------------------
```

```
Two-sample t test with equal variances
------------------------------------------------------------------------------
   Group |     Obs        Mean    Std. Err.   Std. Dev.   [95% Conf. Interval]
---------+--------------------------------------------------------------------
       0 |     226    .7610619    .028429     .4273814    .7050408    .8170831
       1 |     470    .8978723    .0139827    .3031388    .8703957    .9253489
---------+--------------------------------------------------------------------
combined |     696    .8534483    .013415     .3539128    .8271094    .8797871
---------+--------------------------------------------------------------------
    diff |           -.1368104    .0281946               -.1921673   -.0814535
------------------------------------------------------------------------------
    diff = mean(0) - mean(1)                                  t =  -4.8524
Ho: diff = 0                                  degrees of freedom =      694

    Ha: diff < 0                Ha: diff != 0                Ha: diff > 0
 Pr(T < t) = 0.0000         Pr(|T| > |t|) = 0.0000         Pr(T > t) = 1.0000

. ttest highconnectivity, by (MixedIdentity)

Two-sample t test with equal variances
------------------------------------------------------------------------------
   Group |     Obs        Mean    Std. Err.   Std. Dev.   [95% Conf. Interval]
---------+--------------------------------------------------------------------
       0 |     233    .8583691    .0228914    .3494218    .8132675    .9034707
       1 |     183    .8032787    .0294661    .3986104    .7451395    .8614178
---------+--------------------------------------------------------------------
combined |     416    .8341346    .0182588    .3724076    .7982434    .8700259
---------+--------------------------------------------------------------------
    diff |            .0550904    .036729                -.0171081    .1272889
------------------------------------------------------------------------------
    diff = mean(0) - mean(1)                                  t =   1.4999
Ho: diff = 0                                  degrees of freedom =      414

    Ha: diff < 0                Ha: diff != 0                Ha: diff > 0
 Pr(T < t) = 0.9328         Pr(|T| > |t|) = 0.1344         Pr(T > t) = 0.0672
```

```
Two-sample t test with equal variances

    Group |       Obs        Mean    Std. Err.   Std. Dev.   [95% Conf. Interval]
        0 |       226    .5486726     .033175     .49873     .4832991    .6140461
        1 |       470    .706383     .0210293    .4559038    .6650597    .7477062
 combined |       696    .6551724    .0180296    .4756539    .6197734    .6905715
     diff |              -.1577104   .0380626               -.2324421   -.0829787

    diff = mean(0) - mean(1)                                      t =   -4.1434
Ho: diff = 0                                    degrees of freedom =       694

    Ha: diff < 0                 Ha: diff != 0                 Ha: diff > 0
 Pr(T < t) = 0.0000       Pr(|T| > |t|) = 0.0000           Pr(T > t) = 1.0000

. ttest highMENAmediaENGAGE, by (MixedIdentity)

Two-sample t test with equal variances

    Group |       Obs        Mean    Std. Err.   Std. Dev.   [95% Conf. Interval]
        0 |       233     .72103     .029445    .4494583    .6630163    .7790438
        1 |       183    .5846995    .0365268   .4941257    .512629     .6567699
 combined |       416    .6610577    .0232358   .4739202    .6153831    .7067323
     diff |              .1363306    .0463861               .0451489    .2275123

    diff = mean(0) - mean(1)                                      t =    2.9390
Ho: diff = 0                                    degrees of freedom =       414

    Ha: diff < 0                 Ha: diff != 0                 Ha: diff > 0
 Pr(T < t) = 0.9983       Pr(|T| > |t|) = 0.0035           Pr(T > t) = 0.0017
```

8

Reshaping Social Practice in Post–Arab Spring Egypt: Expression of Identity and Affiliation in New Media

Mohamed ElSawi Hassan

Introduction

This chapter analyzes the construction of a virtual community for social action through the discursive practices of the Egyptian Facebook group AlMawkef AlMasry (MM; the Egyptian Stance) that communicates through the new media across traditional geographic, social, institutional, and linguistic boundaries and in so doing negotiates communal identity and expressions of transcultural communication in the post–Arab Spring world. Social media—AlMawkef AlMasry notable among them—had an undeniable effect on the promotion of written dialect, particularly during the events that led to, accompanied, and followed the Arab Spring in 2010, 2011, and the following years. The study argues that the type of code-mixing or code-switching of Arabic that the group uses, mainly dialectal elements of Egyptian Arabic (EA) with features of Standard Arabic (SA), is an intermediate register that represents a form of "crossing" or "stylization" (Rampton 2009) that enabled the group members to ideologically reference their commitments, position themselves, and build their own community across the Arab world with respect to group identity through the functional use of language that represents its own type of social action in a culturally and linguistically diverse Arab world. Cohen (1985) maintains that people construct community symbolically, making it a resource and repository of meaning and a referent of their identity (118). The use of EA establishes the group as locally Egyptian, while the employment of SA features that are made to appear "natural" establishes the wider ties to all Arab recipients with which the SA forms are associated. The MM text is to be analyzed for the way it draws on and transforms social practice by creating a collectivizing mode of verbal expression. A critical discourse analysis (CDA) approach (van Leeuwen 1995, 1996, 2008; Fairclough 2003, 2013) will be used to bring these elements together in a descriptive framework for critically analyzing this mode of social practice in post–Arab Spring Egypt and examining how transcultural it can be.

The activism of the Facebook group represents a decentralization of cultural and social practice that transcends dialect borders and serves as a collectivizing mode of verbal expression and discursive action of online writing and circulation in a global system. AlMawkef AlMasry aims to shape a post–Arab Spring social perception of pertinent democracy-related issues in the Arab world through linguistic choices that form a social and political bond among Arab readers. The online group is therefore discursively empowered through social media as an agent of change with the purpose of constructing social action, and possibly a new more democratic reality, as a conscious motive or intention. This dynamic is emphasized by van Leeuwen who states that "the discursive distribution of purposefulness has everything to do with the distribution of power in concrete social practices" (135). In a connection between online and offline practices, the localized posts of the group that uses Facebook as a catalyst explore and intertwine present-day modalities of writing practices and activism and are interwoven with delocalized social-practice purpose of raising awareness of, and criticizing, the bill under discussion. As indicated in utterances 40 and 41 in the analyzed text below, all Arab readers as recipients of the posts constitute a wider transcultural epistemic community that can be motivated to further intercommunicate, to act, and to speak out against the bill and against any similar practices in their own local contexts in any possible way after they have collectively shared this knowledge and its attendant power.

Comparing it to the "linguistics of community" that is built on the idealization of the nation-state, Rampton and Charalambous (2012) provide an empirical illustration of the relevance of Mary Louise Pratt's (1987) concept of "linguistics of contact" as a field of research in sociolinguistics that investigates the impact of media culture—not just the impact of home socialization—and looks beyond intragroup language to the use of language across social boundaries (Rampton and Charalambous 2012, 842). They maintain that as a concept, "crossing" is tightly linked to boundaries and the renegotiation of traditional interethnic relations (Rampton and Charalambous 2012, 494). They continue to add that in "crossing," people foreground the socio-symbolic connotations/indexical values of particular linguistic forms, implying that they have special relevance to some aspect of interaction in the here and now. As defined by Rampton (2009), "stylization" involves "reflexive communicative action in which speakers produce specially marked and often exaggerated representations of languages, dialects, and styles that lie outside their own habitual repertoire …. Crossing … involves a stronger sense of social or ethnic boundary transgression" (149). Crossing can be mocking, admiring, an end in itself, or the first step in a longer journey, and it may strengthen boundaries, undermine them, or assert their irrelevance (Rampton and Charalambous 2012, 486).

To that end, the chapter attempts to examine and analyze how language and identity can be fruitfully conceptualized for the analysis of this aspect of Arabic transcultural communication of this Facebook group that draws on a common store of linguistic resources to achieve the goal of its social practice. It seeks to address several questions. Given the online nature of the group and its strategies to define its Egyptian and Arab identity through discursive practices, how was it able to communicate on a transcultural level to include collectives of people through a process of inclusion without a challenge?

When crossing recipients encounter such discourse, the interactional question "Why this linguistic choice?" is supplemented with more political questions, such as "In what capacity?" and "How am I included?" Such questions help align recipients from different Arab representations to interact with this special framing of the discourse that licenses the use of SA and EA in a written form that would otherwise seem unaccountable.

AlMawkef AlMasry is an online group with more than six hundred thousand followers (as of December 25, 2016) that defines itself as non-aligning with any particular political group. It utilizes language choices in its efforts to find solutions for recurrent societal needs after the Arab Spring through certain discursive structures. The group's mission was stated on their Facebook page as "AlMawkef AlMasry: the opinion of every Egyptian who believes in a change for the better. With the support of experts, we will help formulate an opinion that reflects change to create a better 'alternative' and we will organize ourselves to make this alternative a reality" (AlMawkef AlMasry, "Timeline," December 25, 2016). The linguistic resources that they have at their disposal here as politically determined have important identity functions. The group negotiates its own self-reference with respect to others and their virtual community. Auer (2006) argues that in code-switching, participants belong to one bilingual community in which a common repertoire of linguistic resources is shared. Crossing, he says, always implies three parties: a speaker who crosses, the owner of the language or variety into which the crossing is done, and a recipient in the bilingual encounter in which the crossing occurs (490). Crossing, in the case of MM's discourse, is not a form of appropriation—as opposed to some definitions of crossing that emphasize "entitlement" as a factor. It is a strategy of building social borders with all Arabic-language speakers and readers as it makes the social and political issues discussed relevant to the interaction. Group boundaries are not usually a topic of talk in and of themselves. In this particular situation, speakers employ the mixed varieties as their own and at the same time enable the recipients to receive such linguistic resources also as owners. Identity factors are maintained through the EA choices while also being extended beyond the Egyptian context through SA crossing strategies. As members of the internet community, they position themselves with respect to group identity and cohesion through an examination of the uses of inclusive and exclusive linguistic resources to build a shared target culture. Data will be represented by a long post for the group on their Facebook page, dated November 16, 2016, that explains and comments on a bill to regulate Egyptian NGOs that had been recently approved by the Egyptian Parliament (AlMawkef AlMasry, "Timeline," November 16, 2016).

Theoretical Framework

This section surveys the theoretical framework informing the analyses of the discourse of MM's Facebook posts. Generally, discourses can be analyzed in combination with social theories to obtain a critical view on the relation between discourses and other aspects of social practice. Miller (2000) acknowledges that individuals belong to varied groups and so take on a variety of identities defined by their memberships in these groups. These identities, however, are not fixed but rather are "multifaceted in complex and contradictory ways; tied to social practice and interaction as flexible and contextually contingent resources; and tied to processes of differentiation from other identified groups" (72). The discourse theories employed in the forthcoming analysis elucidate interrelationships between identity, language, and the media to determine to what extent the linguistic contributions are institutionally and transculturally determined. Theories in CDA have proven to be effective in taking up social scientific questions and claims about social and institutional change and exploring how these changes may be taking place at the micro level of texts and interactive events (Fairclough 2013, 418). Fairclough's vision of CDA offers a way of conceptualizing social and institutional practices in terms of three dimensions: discourses, which are ways of representing the world from particular perspectives; genres, which are ways of acting and interacting with other people; and styles or voices, which are ways of identifying, constructing, or enunciating the self, including both social and institutional identities (Fairclough 2013, 218–20). These are designed deliberately to conceptualize the more sociological concepts of discourse, actions, and identity in terms that can be explored empirically through repertoires of linguistic analysis (Fairclough 2013, 220). In the CDA theoretical framework used in this chapter, discourse is seen as differentiated into discourse, genres, and styles. Following Fairclough (2003, 2013) and van Leeuwen (1995, 1996, 2008), the categories of discourse that represent elements of social practice are social actors, social action, and social circumstances. The interactional processes will be looked at as a type of communication where the special framing of the activity involves crossing and stylization strategies (Rampton 1999, 2009).

Social actors are people involved in the discursive practice who have roles, relative positions, and groupings. Van Leeuwen's (1996, 2008) framework for the analysis of the representations of social actors in discourses is a network of abstract social and discursive categories into which social actors can be placed. The second element that gives similar advantages to the representation of social actors is the representation of social action (van Leeuwen 1996, 32). The framework of discourse as the recontextualization of social practice attempts to relate sociologically relevant categories of action to their grammatical and rhetorical realizations in discourse in what van Leeuwen refers to as a "sociological grammar or the representation of social action" (van Leeuwen 2008, 4–6). Fairclough (2003) describes social circumstances in terms of interconnected space, time, and the intersection of the two in different space-time. He expounds that space, time, and "space-times" are routinely constructed in texts through the chaining of texts and genre chains that contribute to linking different scales of social life—the local, national, regional, and global—which is currently a matter of linking different "space-times" (Fairclough 2003, 151). Furthermore, Coupland (2007) argues that variationist sociolinguistics has worked with a limited idea of social context—and styling is precisely the contextualization of social styles. The survey designs of variationist research, which have been remarkably successful in revealing broad patterns of linguistic diversity and change, have not encouraged us to understand what people meaningfully achieve through linguistic variation (Coupland 2007, 5).

Background

The debate about the Arabic language and its dialects as crucial factors in identity formation with deep sociocultural bearings has been going on for a long time. Given the extremely wide range and the whole set of mixed varieties that Middle Arabic may encompass, Kees Versteegh (2014) defines Middle Arabic as the collective name for all texts with deviations from classical grammar and generalizes the use of the term to literary texts with dialectal elements and to texts that are found as early as the seventh century and as late as the twenty-first century (155). Tracing the history of Middle Arabic, Versteegh states that in the archives of Aphrodito (present-day Kum Ishqaw in Upper Egypt), a large number of papyri have been found, dating from the end of the first to the third centuries of the Hijra and containing official correspondence with the governor of Egypt. Most of the papyri stem from Egypt, written by Muslims, and most of them contain nonliterary administrative or commercial texts. The significance of the papyri, in Versteegh's opinion, lies in the fact that their language exhibits more or less the same traits as later Middle Arabic texts, which confirms the fact that from the very beginning, these linguistic changes had been present in colloquial language (Versteegh 2014, 157). During the twentieth century, and in line with many intellectuals and authors at that time, in his 1938 *Mostaqbal Al-Thaqafa fi Misr* (The Future of Culture in Egypt), Taha Hussein argued that dialect is unworthy of being called a language and is unfit to fulfill the aims of intellectual life. He maintained that language is not only a means of communication among fellow citizens but also a vital part of national identity (Hussein 2013, 193). On the other hand, writers like Salama Musa, Luwis Awad, and Mustafa Musharrafa tried to challenge the then existing canon by introducing the Egyptian dialect as an accepted form of expression in literature. Musa opined that efforts should be made to give splendor to the Egyptian dialect. Since the vernacular language is the commonly used living language, it represents the only idiom that can be functional for the nation's progress (De Angelis 2016, 197). After such attempts, the shift toward pan-Arabic nationalism in the sixties rendered the use of the colloquial in literature controversial once more.

In his work *Language and Symbolic Power* (1991), Pierre Bourdieu analyzes the production and reproduction of legitimate langauge and maintains that language is not merely a tool of communication but also a medium of power. Legitimate language, according to Bourdieu, is the dominant language that assumes official status through asserting its legitimate competence in the linguistic market. He maintains that "speakers lacking the legitimate competence are de facto excluded from the social domains in which this competence is required, or are condemned to silence" (Bourdieu and Thompson 1991, 55). Acquiring the necessary legitimate competence in the conversation with the official language confers upon one a capital, a cultural capital of knowledge, skill, and other cultural acquisitions and a symbolic capital of accumulated prestige or honor that optimizes the standing of the individual or group in the commonly shared and coveted market or field (Bourdieu and Thompson 1991, 60–2). The field here is the cultural-political space of Facebook posts, where different groups enter into trade exchange with the aim of sharing information with a wide range of readers and inviting them to participate in the discussion.

156   *Cultural Production and Social Movements after the Arab Spring*

De Angelis (2016) maintains that a democratic language context should guarantee each member of the speakers' community the right to speak up. In Egypt in particular, a democratic language context should guarantee citizens the right to write, in the face of the grievous issue of diglossia (199). The use of the Ammiya, or local dialect, is in direct response to social needs. De Angelis continues to pose the question, If everything in Egypt is written in a language that is not accessible to the majority of the community, or in a language that only few can master, how could we claim that contemporary Egypt lives in a context of linguistic democracy? (2016, 199). As an advocate of vernacularization, Safouan states that writing in vernacular does not mean reproducing the language of the street but creating new language from literature, a possibility that exists in any language (2007, 62–3). The data in this chapter represent a different register, however, since it utilizes features from SA in a written-dialect form. Research in premodern Middle Arabic focused on how much the texts deviated from the "correct" form of SA, or overcorrections, pseudo-corrections. The text here is one that deviates from both EA and SA norms to reach out and highlight a form of activism across the Arab world. According to Lentin (2016), forms of Arabic language that do not belong to classical, dialect, or mixed spoken Arabic, like "hybrid" and "symbiotic" forms, position Middle Arabic as a separate variety. Lentin further adds that "Middle Arabic has taken upon itself the glorious and obscure task of pragmatically dealing with Arabic diglossia, by filling the space of the linguistic continuum between both polar varieties, thus preventing it from becoming a 'no language's land' with all the consequences of such a situation" (2016, 216). Comparing spoken contemporary mixed Arabic and modern and premodern written Middle Arabic, Mejdell (2012) notes that the Arabic colloquial-oriented style in print is here to stay and concludes, "Above all, the new electronic media provide arenas for new written practices—unedited and uncontrolled by language authorities, literary as well as purely communicative" (244–5).

Analysis

The generic structure of the post provides some evidence of what the group is trying to achieve with this recontextualization (van Leeuwen 2008, 11). The social actions represented and performed here are as follows:

1. MM states the problem of the initial approval of the law and possible ramifications and consequences (utterances 1–5).
2. MM expounds some articles of the proposed law and its dire effects (utterances 6–4).
3. MM compares the new law to the existing one (utterances 25–27).
4. The Egyptian Parliament passes a bill (utterances 28–30).
5. MM comments on the procedures of passing the law (utterances 31–37).
6. MM counsels an alternative framework for cooperation between the state and NGOs (utterances 38–39).
7. MM invites readers to spread the news and respond by sharing their opinion or personal experience (utterances 40–41).

Social circumstances reflect a pattern of inclusion and exclusion. To discuss this pattern, it is necessary to bring the various ways in which each category of social actors is represented under a common denominator—for example, those who impose the law and those who oppose the law (we)—as representations rearrange the social relations between the participants. Discursive strategies of crossing establish the association practice.

Activation occurs when social actors are represented by the active, dynamic forces in an activity, passive when they are represented as undergoing the activity or as being "at the receiving end of it" (van Leeuwen 2008, 33). Utterances 40 and 41 (40: "If you like what you read on our page, tell your family and friends about it and come and participate with your reactions"; 41: "If you have any experience or information about corruption in Egypt, or international initiatives to fight it, write to us in the comments section, post it on our page or email us … and we will publish whatever is useful for our members") clearly foreground the active role of the readers in the social action. EA is the register used in the two utterances. Hence, the choice between generic and specific reference is another important factor in the representation of social actors; the generalized class of citizens addressed here constitutes the real, in which specific participants are "specimens" of these classes (van Leeuwen 2008, 35).

The post in general draws on the representation of the social practice of giving an opinion on social issues in Egypt and beyond. All of these practices involve specific sets of social actors or participants. Some actions are objectified through nominalization while others are spatialized. The text here will include some of these actors—bearing in mind that recontextualization into discourse may exclude some of the participants from the practice they recontextualize that can be retrieved by the reader or the writer. In van Leeuwen's terms, the participants here can be realized as *a group of Egyptian activists* reporting to *all readers* of the Facebook community, the counsel of *expert analysts* regarding an action taken by *Egyptian legislators (whose nomination is realized by proper nouns)*, and, in this way, indirectly counseling *all readers* across Arab communities who may also be concerned about *NGOs* and the future of its regulations in Egypt and the Arab world as *categorized* social actors. Hence, we notice a shift to SA in the two utterances that express the "counseling" act:

(٣٨) ز ي ما فلنا قبل كده الدولة الجادة هي اللي تستفيد من الجهد اللي ممكن تقدمه هذه المنظمات وتضع الأطر القانونية والإدارية العادلة.. الدولة محتاجة اعادة النظر في علاقتها بالمجتمع المدني، خصوصا في ظل ظروف اقتصادية صعبة وزيادة سكنية متسارعة.
(٣٩) الحلول الأمنية دائما سهلة ولكنها لها تكلفتها، واللي منها فعلاً الاساءة لسمعة مصر، بالاضافة الي فقدنا مزايا وجهود كثيرة اقتصادية واجتماعية.
(AlMawkef AlMasry, "Timeline," November 16, 2016)

Like we said before, the state that takes things seriously is the one that utilizes any effort of these organizations and introduces fair legislative and administrative frameworks. The state needs to reconsider its relation to the civic society, specially under the current economic hardships and the accelerated population rate. (38)

Security-based solutions are always the easier choice, but they come with a price—which may include smearing Egypt's reputation in addition to the loss of a great deal of social and economic efforts and advantages. (39)

The combination of linguistic elements here is treated as unmarked. The move from one variety or style to another has significance in the moment-to-moment development of the talk itself. Arab readers as social participants share identities and functions with the group of Egyptian activists. The key participants (activists and readers) are not directly realized in and by the text. The text only realizes the group's action (analyzing/describing/commenting) while the other elements of the practice are seen as "context." Some participants are "particularized" and "nominated," like the speaker of the parliament and the parliament member who proposed the law, while others are "generalized" and "aggregated," like large numbers of NGO members in Egypt and beneficiaries of the social work who will be negatively affected. The most frequently included social actors are "legislators," who are invoked by quoted law articles as their social action, and "us" readers and citizens, also represented as active participants who are invited to share and react to the post.

Analyzing dialectal versus oral features, Doss (2014) observes that "oral features are not necessarily nor exclusively to be found in the written representation of the dialect. An author can proceed to write the dialect while adopting the constraints of writing and using its code, he can do so by making his text explicit …, non-redundant and far from improvisation, or well-planned" (52). We have to note that the written dialect is not identical with the spoken variety as exemplified in this sequence in the beginning section of the post:

(٥) ياريت واحنا بنقرا كل الكلام الجاي منفكرش بس في منظمة حقوقية بتدافع عن مواطن اتعرض للتعذيب مثلا، مع ان ده حق ضروري جداً طبعاً.. لكن نفكر مثلاً في جمعية تعليمية بتتلقى تبرعات لتعليم الأطفال، أو جمعية غرضها صحي زي أصدقاء مستشفى أبو الريش مثلا، واللي وارد تلاقي جمعية خيرية طبية أجنبية من سويسرا مثلا عايزة تتعاون معاها، أو مواطن عادي في قرية بآخر الصعيد جمع كام واحد يعرفهم من وبيعملوا جمعية لمساعدة أهل البلد.

(AlMawkef AlMasry, "Timeline," November 16, 2016)

Hopefully, while reading all of the following account, we would not limit our scope to one human rights organization that defends a citizen subjected to torture for example—though this is of course an extremely necessary right. But we also need to think about an educational organization that receives donations to help educate children or an organization that works in the health sector, like "Friends of Abu-Errish Hospital" for instance, that may receive cooperation offers from a Swiss medical charity organization, for instance; or an ordinary citizen in a remote village in southern Egypt who united efforts with a number of his acquaintances to establish an organization to help his fellow villagers. (5)

The use of EA in this sequence is meant to represent not an oral thought but a written one that is meant to be widely read and identified as a specific type of social practice. A feature like subordination (as opposed to coordination) is an example of crossing to SA. Auer (2007) maintains that with code-mixing, the combination of words, phrases, and longer sequences from different lexico-grammatical codes is more conspicuous, making it easier for linguists to classify the speech involved as more than just a subvariety of the national language, but the changes from one code to another do not reframe the ongoing interaction or impact on its unfolding (15). Doss (2014) summarizes Ong's (1982) account of the features of oral thought and expression and their difference from the written one by identifying the following features: exhibiting a larger number of subordinate elements, being more aggregative than analytic with a higher use of epithets and formulaic expressions, and being more redundant and repetitive than the written (Doss 2014, 49–50). As a form of stylization, the speakers here shift into varieties that are seen as lying beyond their normal range, beyond what participants ordinarily expect of them in terms of EA or SA. This type of disjunction of speaker and voice draws attention to the speakers themselves, temporarily positioning the recipient(s) as spectator(s) who participates in the social act and at least momentarily reframing the talk as nonroutine. The style is elaborate, analytic, and organized with discursive expressions of identity and affiliation.

Syntactically, crossing throughout the text saliently occurs in syntactic constructions like relative and subordinate clauses that follow the SA syntax, though EA vocabulary is being used. Tense and verb constructions and negative constructions are introduced in EA.

Discussion and Conclusion

Two processes could be observed taking place here. One is a process of constructivism, where SA features especially are adopted as one's own and at the same time used as a tool for crossing to all Arab readers who will associate with the activists' social practice, and by association, constructing a collective identity. The other is the preference for EA in the discourse, even while SA is recognized for its instrumental and functional benefits. Variation in the use of styles/codes in this case can be framed as constitutive of social life. As such, the language here is perceived as an embodiment of a collective social identity that is manifested in and supported by ideological beliefs and practices. Representational choices here play a key role as they form part of the affiliation discourse in rhetorical realizations. Bakhtin (1986) developed the concept of the inherent "dialogicality" of language; he describes talking as a dynamic reciprocal process that engages an active listener and a responsive speaker who codetermine each other. The speaker designs the utterance, including the choice of variety and discursive strategies as crossing or stylization as a dialogue with a listener in mind.

Farrrelly (2015) stresses that language is not the only social system and discourse is not the only element of social practice. Holding this distinction, one can ask critical questions about the relationship between the discourse associated with a social practice and the other elements of the social practice (43). Based on the work of Fairclough (2013), social structures such as language and the political structure constrain and enable a certain kind of action, but they do not determine action (210–12). Chouliaraki and Fairclough (1999) clearly mark out this position in confirming that neither CDA nor other forms of critical social science are in the business of "prescribing" alternative practices but rather helping to clear the ground for those engaged within a social practice to seek the changes they want. In this social practice, we need a set of participants in certain roles—"instigator, agent, affected or beneficiary" (Chouliaraki and Fairclough 1999, 35). Eligibility conditions are the "qualifications" participants must have in order to be eligible to play a particular role in a particular social practice (van Leeuwen 2008, 10). The most obvious feature in this text is its variation and linguistic inconsistency between SA and EA. Throughout the text, the word order varies between the colloquial and the standard order and the agreement rules of CDA are applied in one sentence and not applied in another. The drive to maintain code-mixing is equally ideological in terms of working up within the social network. The strategic style shifting in this text creates and leads to a certain communicative effect and outcome that is achieved cross-culturally through the Arab world. Explorations of "crossing" and "stylization" features in the above text exemplified contextualization mechanisms by which AlMawkef AlMasry strategically reached out to commonly shared social meanings and meaning-making process among all Arab readers. This tenet was achieved through the post's linguistic choices and variation between the Egyptian Arabic dialect and the Standard Arabic variety in an example of the dynamic relationship between linguistic communication and culture. All Arab readers were here enabled to align themselves with this social group for different purposes at different times in acts of social construction within a linguistic frame of social meaning.

References

AlMawkef AlMasry. 2016. "Timeline." Accessed December 25. https://www.facebook.com/almawkef.almasry/posts/924303884336176.
Auer, P. 2006. "Sociolinguistic Crossing." In *Encyclopedia of Language & Linguistics*, edited by E. K. Brown, Anne Anderson, and R. E. Asher, Second edition. Boston: Elsevier.
Auer, P. (Ed.) 2007. *Style and Social Identities: Alternative Approaches to Linguistic Heterogeneity*. Berlin, NY: Mouton de Gruyter.
Bakhtin, M. M. 1986. *Speech Genres and Other Late Essays*. Edited by Michael Holquist and Caryl Emerson. University of Texas Press Slavic Series: No. 8. Austin: University of Texas Press.
Bourdieu, Pierre, and John B. Thompson. 1991. *Language and Symbolic Power*. Cambridge, MA: Harvard University Press.
Chouliaraki, Lilie, and Norman Fairclough. 1999. *Discourse in Late Modernity: Rethinking Critical Discourse Analysis*. Edinburgh: Edinburgh University Press.
Cohen, Anthony P. 1985. *The Symbolic Construction of Community*. Key Ideas; Variation: Key Ideas. Chichester: E. Horwood; London; New York: Tavistock Publications.
Coupland, Nikolas. 2007. *Style: Language Variation and Identity*. Key Topics in Sociolinguistics. Cambridge, UK; New York: Cambridge University Press.
De Angelis, Francesco. 2016. "The Egyptian Dialect for a Democratic Form of Literature: Considerations for a Modern Language Policy." In *Arabic Varieties: Far and Wide. Proceedings of the 11th International Conference of AIDA, Bucharest 2015. Ed. George Grigore and Gabriel Bițună*, 193–201. Bucharest: Editura Universității din București.
Doss, Madiha. 2014. "Some Remarks on the Oral Factor in Arabic Linguistics." *Studia Orientalia Electronica* 75: 49–62.
Hussein, Taha. 2013. *Mostaqbal Al-Thaqafa fi Misr*. Cairo: Supreme Council for Culture.

Fairclough, Norman. 2003. *Analysing Discourse: Textual Analysis for Social Research.* London; New York: Routledge.
Fairclough, Norman. 2013. *Critical Discourse Analysis: The Critical Study of Language.* Second edition. New York: Routledge.
Farrelly, Michael. 2015. *Discourse and Democracy: Critical Analysis of the Language of Government.* Routledge Critical Studies in Discourse: 6. New York: Routledge.
Lentin, Jerome. 2016. "Middle Arabic." In *Encyclopedia of Arabic Language and Linguistics*, edited by C. H. M. Versteegh, Mushira Eid, Lutz Edzard, and Rudolf Erik de Jong. Leiden: Brill. Accessed December 27. http://ezproxy.amherst.edu/login?url= and http://referenceworks.brillonline.com/browse/encyclopedia-of-arabic-language-and-linguistics.
Mejdell, Gunvor. 2012. "Playing the Same Game? Notes on Comparing Spoken Contemporary Mixed Arabic and (Pre)modern Written Middle Arabic." In *Middle Arabic and Mixed Arabic: Diachrony and Synchrony*, edited by Liesbeth Zack and Arie Schippers. Leiden, NL: Brill.
Miller, Jennifer M. 2000. "Language Use, Identity, and Social Interaction: Migrant Students in Australia." *Research on Language and Social Interaction* 33 (1): 69–100.
ONG, Walter J. 1982. *Orality and Literacy: The Technologizing of The World.* London.
Pratt, Mary Louise. 1987. "Linguistic Utopias." In *The Linguistics of Writing: Arguments between Language and Literature*, edited by Nigel Fabb, Derek Attridge, Alan Durant, and Colin MacCabe. New York: Methuen.
Rampton, Ben. (Ed.) 1999. "Styling the 'Other.'" Special issue of *Journal of Sociolinguistics* 3 (4): 421–7.
Rampton, Ben. 2009. "Interaction Ritual and Not Just Artful Performance in Crossing and Stylization." *Language in Society* 38(2): 149–76.
Rampton, Ben, and Constadina Charalambous. 2012. "Crossing." In *The Routledge Handbook of Multilingualism*, edited by Marilyn Martin-Jones, Adrian Blackledge, Angela Creese. London; New York: Routledge.
Safouan, Moustafa. 2007. *Why Are the Arabs Not Free?: The Politics of Writing.* Critical Quarterly; Variation: Critical Quarterly (Book Series). Malden, MA: Blackwell Pub.
Van Leeuwen, Theo. 1995. "Representing Social Action." *Discourse & Society* 6 (1): 81–106.
Van Leeuwen, Theo. 1996. "The Representation of Social Actors." In *Texts and Practices: Readings in Critical Discourse Analysis*, edited by Carmen Rosa Caldas-Coulthard and Malcolm Coulthard. London; New York: Routledge, 1996.
Van Leeuwen, Theo. 2008. *Discourse and Practice: New Tools for Critical Discourse Analysis.* Oxford Studies in Sociolinguistics. Oxford; New York: Oxford University Press.
Versteegh, Kees. 2014. *The Arabic Language.* Edinburgh: Edinburgh University Press.

9

Syrian Refugees as a Hybridizing Force in the Jordanian Society

Barkuzar Dubbati

Introduction

This chapter examines the sociocultural impact of the influx of Syrian refugees to Jordan. Several studies have examined the economic and political effects of the sudden and colossal demographic presence of Syrian refugees in Jordan. However, little attention has been given to its sociocultural impact. The neglect of this aspect can be attributed to the supposition that there is proximity between the dominant cultures of the refugees and their new host country that does not warrant investigation into any cultural consequences. This chapter argues the opposite and starts from the assumption that cultures are political compositions and their perception and reproduction rely on political needs rather than cultural and social realities.

Homi Bhabha (1994) has theorized that the cultural hybrid troubles the cultural differences that have created it. For example, an Anglo-Indian individual presents an opportunity to question the stability of the cultural binary opposition of British/Indian that created the hybrid who represents a living example of the blurry differences between cultures. Bhabha turns the binary on its ear and starts with the two ends of the binary (British vs. Indian) and melds them into the hybrid who hybridizes both. Instead of the outcome of cultural perception being difference, it becomes ambivalence. One criticism of Bhabha's deconstruction of the binary is that it presupposes difference before it questions it. It establishes the stability of difference (between being British or Indian) before it destabilizes it.

This study does not join in the criticism but exploits it. What if the binary opposition is created by the hybrid rather than deconstructed by it? If cultural differences between Jordanians, on the one hand, and Syrians, on the other, were not visible or noticeable when they were neighboring nations but have become striking and even threatening when Syrians have been relocated to Jordanian cities, then can't one argue that the hybrid has created the binary (Jordanian vs. Syrian) when the socioeconomic needs emerged? This study looks into the effects of refugees' resettlement in Jordan on Jordanians' cultural perceptions of the refugees as either different/Other or a hybridizing force. It will observe changes to the representation of Syrian refugees, attitudes toward refugees, and any reconceptualization of difference. The research examined consists of a quantitative analysis of two surveys, one among Jordanians and a second among Syrian refugees.

Theories on Cultural Hybridity

Since the publication of Bhabha's seminal work *The Location of Culture* in 1994, the conceptualization of the cultural hybrid has taken center stage in debates in the postcolonial field, representation studies, race studies, and transcultural and transnational fields. His reconceptualization of Frantz Fanon's black man's performance of inferiority into a performance of a hybridizing force has reinvigorated the discourse over the ways in which colonizers and colonized identities interact and the hierarchy of power that this interaction destabilizes. In *Black Skin, White Masks* (1967), Fanon introduces the "negro" who perfects a performance of whiteness to conceal his black identity. By "acting white," the black man recreates an identity as a space in which he renounces his black identity and puts on a white mask. Fanon employs the mask as a metaphor not only of concealment but also of self-deception on the part of the black man and the white French society. The deception is that by speaking white man's language, desiring white women, and acquiring knowledge institutionalized by the white man, the black man has finally become white. Fanon argues that the black man's integration into white society is not just a masquerade but a farce revealed by a young white child pointing at the black man and exclaiming, "Look at the nigger!" (113). The masquerade for Fanon ends there as the masks fall and the curtains are drawn on a play performed by the black man with the white mask and performed on him by a white society that has misled him into believing that negritude can be unperformed. This moment of realization is what DuBois (1903) and Gilroy (1993) describe as the double consciousness of the racial Other who view themselves through their own internal perception of the self and the external gaze of a hegemonic society built on a binary opposition of which the racial Other is one end.

Bhabha, however, reads the black man's performance as an indication of the failure of the stability of the racial identity rather than the failure of the black man's white performance. Whereas Fanon sees in the white mask a confirmation of the white gaze's ultimate power in constructing the identity of the black Other and the latter's internalization of his racial inferiority, Bhabha reimagines this performance as a destabilizing force that renders both the binary and the binarizing "pure" identities of black and white as ambivalent. For Bhabha, what the black man with the white mask achieves is the creation of a "third space," which

> makes the structure of meaning and reference an ambivalent process, destroys this mirror of representation in which cultural knowledge is customarily revealed as an integrated, open, expanding code. [The intervention of the third space]

quite properly challenges our sense of the historical identity of culture as a homogenizing, unifying force, authenticated by the originary Past, kept alive in the national tradition of the People.

(54)

The third-ness of the hybrid as neither one identity nor its Other, but both allows the hybrid to function as a force that denaturalizes the binary of self/Other, blurs the difference between the two ends of the binary and deems the homogeneity of identities and the discourse of power that constructs it as false, irrelevant, and self-contradictory. If the Other is the creation of the self, it is inseparable from it, as both Lacan (1977) and Said (1978) underline in their theorization of the interdependency of the construction of the binarized self and Other identities. Lacan argues that the ego is formed through the binary opposition of presence and absence in which the self is present through its absence in the Other, and the Other's presence is constructed through the absence of the self in it. In his debunking of Orientalism as a science, Said reveals that Orientalists constructed the Orient as an Other for a homogeneous West. The Orient in their discourse is silent but also fictional; however, if the identity of the homogenous and essentialized West relies on a fictional Orient, then both are fictional and constructed. This interdependency of identity construction, though, is meant to weaken the Orient as the projection of the West's otherness, it empowers the Other in making it indispensable in the process of the creation of the ego and the Western self. The instability of the identity of the Other renders the identity of the self unstable as well, which is the "equation" that Bhabha uses to represent the hybrid and hybridity as an empowering force. His theorization of the creation of the hybrid moves the debate from regarding it as a site of erasure of the identity of the Other, the colonized, or the indigenous and toward reconceptualizing it as a site in which the hybrid negotiates rather than negates its mixed identity. Thus, negotiation becomes a form of interrogation of the discourse of identity (43) rather than an acceptance of construction of identity by the colonial power.

Other writers have highlighted the importance of the hybrid within the emergent transnational and globalization discourses. Kraidy (2008) deems hybridity as "the cultural logic of globalization" and denies its celebration as evidence of "posthegemonic" times (148). Smith and Leavy (2008) view hybridity in a globalized world as an inevitability and a "benefit" (4). They recognize the hybrid's unique location as

> simultaneously members of the community and not members of the community. The stranger is one new identity that might emerge by combining two identities that were previously discrete and now overlap. They are not seen as individuals, but as a particular type that is a combination of the stranger's identity and the local identity. One resolution to the problem of having two identities, or being identified by types and labels, is to create a new identity. It is the hybrid identity that includes a local and global identity form, merged to create the hybrid identity.
>
> (4)

Pieterse (2001) underlines that hybridity is "to culture what deconstruction is to discourse: transcending binary categories" (238), while Bakhtin (1981) identifies two kinds of hybridity: unintentional/organic, which occurs naturally when cultures integrate, and a second type that is intentional and conscious.

Criticism of Bhabha's Theory of Hybridity

Bhabha's use of hybridity and hybridization has met its share of criticism. Friedman (1997) regards Bhabha's theorization of hybridity as elitist. The power to negotiate and interrogate is exclusive to elite intellectuals who have the luxury of engrossing themselves in the discursive negotiation of the hybridity of identity. Less privileged groups, such as workers or racially profiled immigrants, are less likely to be inclined to see the empowering aspect of their hybridized identity or to be in a position to negotiate or interrogate it. Bhabha's focus is on the enunciation of hybridity, which locates the discussion of the diversity of cultures within discourse and discursive production rather than tangible realities, such as actual discrimination. However, the assumption that negotiating discourse is a "privilege" is the cause of the discriminatory realities of the migrant, who Friedman argues is locked out of the debate. Realities cannot exist outside of discourse, or what Bhabha calls the enunciation of identities. Kraidy (2008) is also critical of the celebration of hybridity as an empowering force while neglecting its central role in legitimizing globalization's commodification of transculturation. He does not view the hybrid as the destabilizing factor of structured binary opposition of power/powerless, dominating/dominated, but rather as an instrument used by those in power to commodify the transcultural impact of the hybridization of the homogeneity of cultures.

Another aspect of criticism made against Bhabha's theory of hybridity is the assumption of purity that precedes the creation of the hybrid (Young 1995; Friedman 1997). The hybrid destabilizes the difference within a binary opposition and multiplies the possibilities of difference and similarities. However, critics of hybridity theory argue that hybridization starts from the assumption that cultures are distinctly different before being hybridized. Black and white are seen as purely different and are then hybridized by the hybrid, which blurs the boundaries between the two.

If the binary opposition divides the self and Other through the dichotomy of presence and absence as suggested by Lacan, then the hybrid's merging of the two becomes a pool mirror image of the pyramid and not a disruption of it (Figure 9.1). Other critiques question the whole idea of the assumption of purity, suggesting that colonial cultures were never essentialist to begin with (Young 1995) and that hybridity theory emerges as only a discursive response to essentialism. Hybridity theory responds that regardless of whether cultures have always been mixed, in colonialist discourse, conceptualization of reality overpowers its factuality. For instance, in a racist discourse in the United States, white and black are represented as distinctly different identities, even if in reality, centuries of miscegenation under the system of slavery has rendered neither race pure.

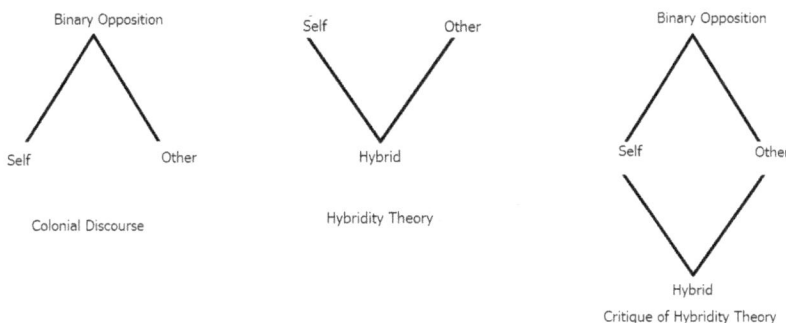

Figure 9.1 The binary opposition of Self/Other according to colonial discourse, Bhabha's hybridity theory, and its critics.

This study does not engage in either side of the discursive argument on the validity of the hybrid as a hybridizing force or as an affirmation of the assumption of purity and difference. It rather builds on this debate to suggest a third but interrelated structure at whose center is the hybrid. Looking at Figure 9.1 with the three models—colonialist discourse, hybridity theory, and critique of the hybridity theory—I propose the emergence of a fourth structure in which a hybrid is created in order to split a homogenous culture (Levant culture) or similar cultures (Jordanian, Syrian) into binary cultures (Jordanian vs. Syrian cultures). Syrian presence in Jordan, thus, is reconceptualized as a form of hybridity that entails an othering of Syrians and Syrian culture as different from their host culture, a distinction that was not prevalent before the eruption of the conflict in Syria in 2011. As Syrians' presence in Jordan becomes increasingly visible and conceived as visibly threatening as a result of the sharp rise in the numbers of refugees and the density of their location in some Jordanian governorates, cities, and towns, an alteration of the collective perception of Syrians emerges in order to preserve the host culture by distinguishing it from the "invading" culture.

Therefore, another factor to consider besides the demographic changes is the public discourse that accompanied the relocation of Syrians into Jordan. Media representation and construction of the nature of the Syrian refugees' stay in Jordan play an important role in seeing Syrians as a threat. Bhabha reminds us that "culture only emerges as a problem, or a problematic, at the point at which there is a loss of meaning in the contestation and articulation of everyday life, between classes, genders, races, nations" (50). Whereas the hybrid is used to destabilize the hegemonic culture's production of knowledge about the othered culture, in my examination of the case of Syrians in Jordan, I argue that the Syrian-as-hybrid is invoked to render Syrians as Other rather than to destabilize the difference between Jordan and Syrian cultures. Looking at Syrians as hybrid by location (living in Jordan) or as children of Syrian-Jordanian marriages recreates the binary opposition from bottom to top (Figure 9.2) and locates Syrians and Jordanians at opposite sides of the binary. It is

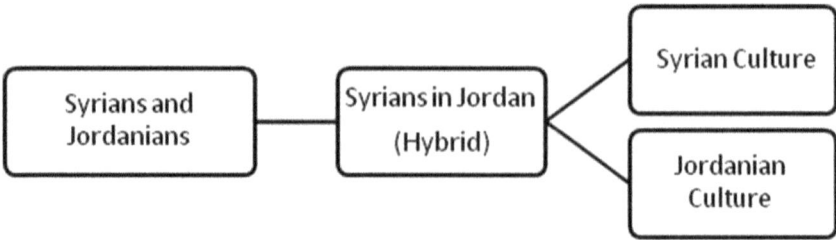

Figure 9.2 Bhabha's hybridity in reverse.

Bhabha's hybrid model but read in reverse, where the starting point is homogeneity rather than binarist difference, and the end result is the binary.

The Quantitative Study

Two different surveys were distributed among two samples of Jordanians and Syrians.[1] The surveys were randomly distributed based on the controlled variable of location. They were conducted as part of interviews during which respondents answered survey questions, and their answers were entered by the researcher. Additionally, some discussions or comments made by respondents during the interviews were recorded and used to frame the analysis of the survey results. Most questions aimed to capture respondents' perceptions of Syrians rather than test their knowledge of actual facts. Sociocultural impacts and identities are based on subjective knowledge, which is often influenced by economic and political realities. This study aims to explore the Jordanian respondents' attitudes and perception of the cultural difference of Syrians after their relocation to Jordan. The Syrian survey is used only to explain the context and results of the Jordanian sample survey; it is not analyzed extensively as an independent survey, and only responses related to the Jordanian survey results were selected for inclusion.

The Samples

The Jordanian survey was distributed to a stratified random sample of 192 Jordanians with a response rate of 100 percent. The sample was not meant to be representative of Jordanian society but was used as an instrument to detect and analyze trends emerging from the sample's answers. Though not representative, the sample mimics the demographic distributions related to the density of the Syrian population in Jordan. There was one controlled variable, as the surveys were distributed equally among three regions based on the density of Syrian presence. Region 1 is high density and consists of the cities of Mafraq and Irbid. Region 2 is medium density and consists of Zarqa and selected neighborhoods of Amman. Region 3 is low density and consists of Ma'an and selected neighborhoods of Amman. To determine the number of Syrians living in Jordan and their demographic distribution, I relied on the results of a 2015 national census conducted by the Jordanian Department of Statistics, which released the results in 2016. Amman was included in both Region 2 and Region 3 because of the density of Syrians relative to the general population (42 percent of the overall population), its size as the largest city in Jordan, and the variety of its residents' income.[2] The sample from Amman constituted 37.5 percent of the overall Jordanian sample, which is comparable to both the density of Syrians in the Jordanian population (37 percent) and the Syrian population (34 percent) in the capital. The Ammani sample was larger because of the diversity of income unique to the capital. It was difficult to find a sizable sample of high-income respondents in other governorates selected for this study because of the lower income levels there. In Amman, I was able to include a random sample of high-income respondents. The income division in the sample taken from other governorates was middle and low incomes only (Table 9.1).

Figure 9.3 shows the distribution of the percentage of the density of Syrian population in the governorates of the selected cities for the study and their geographic distribution.

Table 9.1 The distribution of the sample based on density and income.

		Regions			Total
		High density	Middle density	Low density	
Income (JD)	–350	31	26	26	83
	350–600	33	26	26	85
	600+	0	12	12	24
Total		64	64	64	192

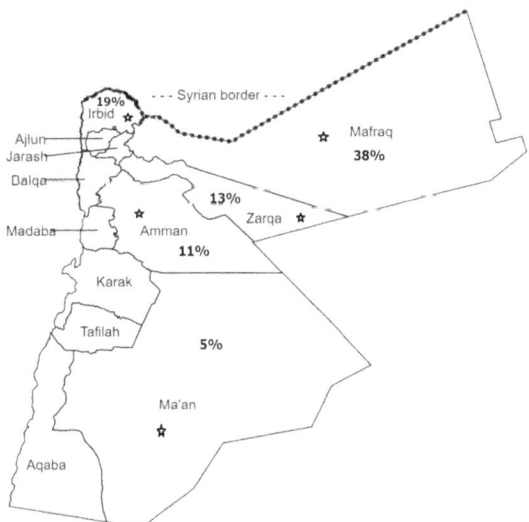

Figure 9.3 Percentages of Syrians out of the overall population in the selected cities (2015 national census).

The selection of these regions was also motivated by a desire to cover northern, midland, and southern parts of Jordan with their distinct diversities; northern governorates are more proximate to Syria, the midland is more urban, and the southern region is closer to Saudi Arabia, and the Bedouin culture is more dominant there.

The regional and income variables were selected to allow the study to examine whether economic concerns are really the contributors to hostilities toward Syrians. The first variable is the density of the Syrian population in Jordanian governorates, which was selected to explore any differences between the responses of Jordanians who have actual and daily interpersonal contact with Syrians and those who have less frequent daily contact with them and may base their perceptions on public discourse rather than actual interaction with Syrians. Additionally, regions with high densities of Syrian populations might feel more threatened, which can be translated into the cultural hybridization of Syrians. This study attempted to determine if there were significant differences in attitudes based on regions and the different degrees of Syrian visibility in them to test the theory that economic challenges posed by the refugees were the central cause for their alienation by the host communities.

A major concern for Jordanians has been the economic impact of Syrians' relocation to Jordan. Numerous studies show Jordanians' disdain for Syrians over job and housing competition. Sampling Jordanians of different income levels was meant to determine if there was a difference between actual and perceived economic impact of refugees on Jordanians' living standards and whether the ways in which Jordanians' reaction to the Syrian presence might have been influenced by their economic status and income.

Other uncontrolled variables are examined as shown in Table 9.2:

As for the Syrian sample, it was randomly selected among 121 Syrians residing in Mafraq and Irbid (Region 1) and Amman (Region 2), which was the controlled variable. Only Syrians living among Jordanians were included in the study, and refugees in camps were excluded as their contact with Jordanians is minimal and controlled, which does not benefit the aim of this study.

Table 9.2 Other variables in the study.

Variables	Type	Number	Percentage
Gender	Female	102	53
	Male	90	47
Employment	Employed	83	47
	Unemployed	92	53
Familial relations with Syrians	Have Syrian in-laws/relatives	40	21
	No Syrian relatives or in-laws	153	79

The Syrian Presence in Jordan

The number of Syrians entering and living in Jordan is continuously changing as the political and security situation in Syria develops. The information and figures presented in this section were compiled in the months of April and May of 2017. They were collected from the United Nations High Commissioner for Refugees (UNHCR) through the Jordanian Syrian Refugees Affairs Department.[3] Other figures related to the number of marriages between Jordanians and non-Jordanians have been collected from the Department of the Supreme Justice in Jordan.

According to the general census conducted in 2015, 31 percent of the population in Jordan was non-Jordanian. Almost half of those were Syrians (Table 9.3) and 34 percent of them lived in Amman.

According to UNHCR figures accessed on May 31, 2017, there were around 660,000 Syrians registered as refugees in Jordan, 21 percent of whom lived in refugee camps while the rest lived in cities and villages among Jordanians. These numbers do not represent the overall population of Syrians in Jordan, since only half of them registered as refugees, which is not mandatory. The largest number of Syrians in Jordan came from the border city of Daraa (Table 9.4). The distribution of the places of origin for the refugees reflects their hometowns' war and conflict situation. For example, there were more refugees from Daraa, Homs, rural Damascus, and Aleppo than from Damascus, which was relatively calmer than those regions. Geographic proximity is not a determining factor for refugees seeking asylum in Jordan; for instance, more Syrians from Aleppo, one of the most northern cities in Syria, have sought refuge in Jordan than have Syrians from Damascus and its suburbs, which are much closer.

As for the number of Syrian refugees according to their year of arrival, 2013 and 2012 witnessed the largest influx, as indicated in Table 9.5.

In terms of gender and age, around 51 percent of the refugees were female, 29 percent were aged eighteen to thirty-five, and 15.5 percent were infants (newborns through age four).

Table 9.3 The distribution of population in Jordan based on nationality.

Nationality	Number (in millions)	Percentage
Jordanian	6,613,587	69
Syrian	1,265,514	13
Egyptian	636,270	7
Palestinian	634,182	7
Iraqi	130,911	1
Other	251,248	3
Total	9,531,712	100

Source: The Jordanian Department of Statistics.

Table 9.4 The distribution of Syrians in Jordan based on place of origin.

Place of Origin	Number	Percentage
Daraa	276,114	42
Homs	104,954	16
Rural Damascus	78,388	12
Aleppo	67,319	10
Damascus	49,254	7
Other	84,125	13

Source: UNHCR.

Table 9.5 The numbers of Syrians in Jordan based on their year of arrival.

Year	Arrival Number	Percentage
Pre-2011	33,189	5
2011	22,555	3.4
2012	170,012	25.8
2013	292,261	44.3
2014	80,345	12.2
2015	33,325	5
2016	44,001	6.7
2017	7021[a]	1.1

Source: UNHCR.

[a] In the period between March 15 and May 31, 2017, 4577 Syrians have entered Jordan, at the rate of around fifty-eight people per day.

Analysis of the Jordanian Sample Survey Results

The majority of the respondents stated that they have not lived outside Jordan for more than six months (81 percent), have never visited Syria (67 percent), have not had any Syrian relatives or in-laws (80 percent), or have not had any interpersonal contact with Syrians before the conflict (62 percent). Of those who have had previous contact with Syrians, 84 percent believed that Syrians who lived in Jordan before the crisis were different from those who have come to Jordan after the crisis. They characterized the differences as primarily economic and secondarily as social, while cultural difference came a distant third. Respondents from Zarqa were the exception, as they ranked social differences first and economic differences second. The majority of the sample also indicated that their knowledge of Syrian culture before the crisis was basic, as half the sample rated their knowledge to be neutral or average while

Table 9.6 Sources of knowledge about Syrians before and after the Syrian crisis.

Sources of knowledge about Syrians before the crisis				Sources of knowledge about Syrians after the crisis		
Overall rank	Item	Score	Total respondents	Item	Score	Total respondents
1	What people say	787	193	Contact with them	832	181
2	Syrian TV drama	775	187	What people say	761	193
3	Contact with them	425	100	Social media	678	192
4	Books	366	126	Syrian TV drama	83	36
5	Other	51	25	Books	49	28

only 10 percent described their knowledge as very good to excellent. This changed after the influx of refugees into Jordan, as 44 percent of the respondents now rated their knowledge of Syrian culture as very good to excellent, and only 3 percent said their knowledge was nil or very weak. While respondents' source of knowledge of Syrian culture before the crisis was mainly non-interpersonal, this changed after the crisis, as the majority of respondents said they formed their opinions of Syrians on interactions with them (Table 9.6). Reliance on Syrian TV drama as a source of knowledge was strong before the crisis (ranked second), but it dropped to fourth after the crisis.

An analysis of the general results without looking at specific variables indicates that the general reaction of Jordanians toward Syrians' presence in their neighborhoods, towns, and cities was overwhelmingly negative. Their responses to questions related to perception of Syrian culture, its influence on Jordanian culture, and their presence in Jordan were negative. Sixty-eight percent of the sample described the Syrian presence in their country as very negative, while only 1.5 percent rated it as positive or very positive. When asked if they thought that the Syrian culture enriched the Jordanian culture, a majority of 92 percent rejected the idea completely. In response to a question about the effect of the Syrian culture on the Jordanian culture, the majority of respondents either negated the existence of any influence or labeled it as negative (Figure 9.4).

Even though a good majority of over 50 percent asserted that the Syrian presence has had no cultural effect on them, subsequent responses undermine this assertion. For example, 81 percent of those who denied the cultural effect said that Syrians had an impact on cuisine and the food industry in Jordan, and 46 percent of them said that Syrians affected them intellectually (thoughts and thinking). Answers to these questions were not required, and there was an "other" option to use to avoid stating any of these influences (Figure 9.5).

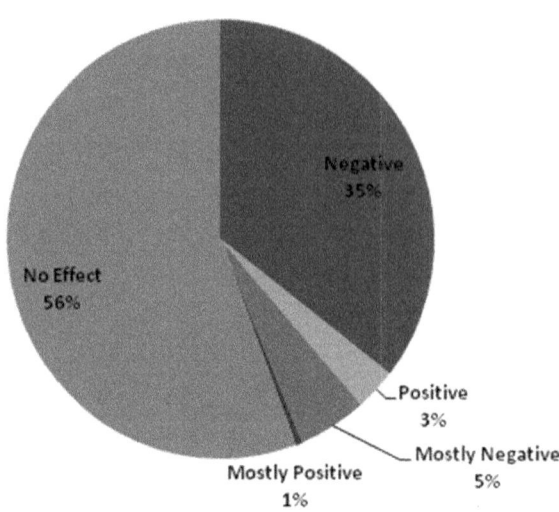

Figure 9.4 Effect of Syrian culture on Jordanian culture.

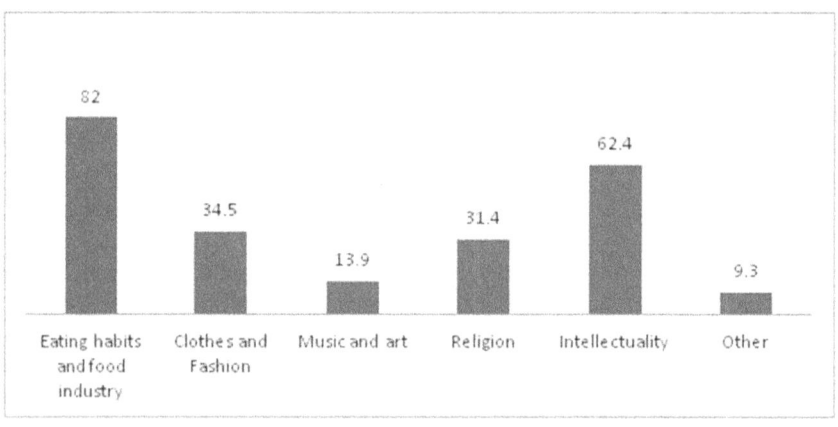

Figure 9.5 Areas of Syrian influence in Jordan.

Syrians' Influence on Marriage

Those who said that the Syrian culture had a negative or mostly negative effect expressed a major concern over their influence on local marriage habits and traditions and what they perceived as the growing trend of intermarriages between Jordanians and Syrians. When asked to name their concerns over Syrian presence, the words "marriage" and "norms and customs" were most frequently mentioned and "dialect" and "morality" to a lesser extent. The words "change" and "liberal" also featured in the sample's answers. Before discussing the sample's responses to questions on Syrians' influence on marriage, it is pertinent to compare facts with perception. Jordanians have often expressed concern over the rise of the number of marriages between Jordanians and Syrians following the 2011 crisis in Syria. Tables 9.7 and 9.8 compare the numbers and percentages of marriages between Jordanians and Syrians before and after the crisis. In the period of 2004–10, marriages between Jordanian men and Syrian women averaged 248 per year, with the highest number of marriages occurring in 2007. On average, marriage to Syrian women accounted for 11 percent of all marriages between Jordanian men and non-Jordanian women. For the same period, Jordanian women's marriages to Syrian men averaged 183 marriages per year, which was 6 percent of all their marriages to non-Jordanians. After the crisis, a natural increase of marriages took place, which accompanied the atypical growth of the Syrian population in Jordan since 2011. During the period of 2011–16, marriages between Jordanian men and Syrian women averaged 1030 per year, which was an average of 28 percent of all marriages to non-Jordanian women. The highest number of marriages occurred in 2015. For Jordanian women, the average number of marriages with Syrian men was 569 per year, which accounted for 15 percent of all marriages to non-Jordanian men. The year 2016 saw the highest number of marriages between Jordanian women and Syrian men.

The overall percentage of Jordanian-Syrian marriages for the period of 2004–10 was 0.7 percent of all marriages registered. After the crisis, the percentage increased to only 2 percent of all marriages in Jordan, which was still not a threatening increase considering that Syrians comprised 13 percent of the overall population. On the other hand, the Palestinian population in Jordan was half the Syrian population, yet they accounted for half of the registered marriages between Jordanians and non-Jordanians in Jordan. In view of the widespread fear among Jordanians of the possibility of establishing an "alternative homeland" for Palestinians in Jordan, one expected them to be more wary of the high number of marriages between Jordanians and Palestinians, posing a problem of nationalizing Palestinians; however, the survey results showed no concerns when it came to marrying Palestinians. In fact, when asked to indicate

Table 9.7 The number of Jordanian-Syrian marriages between 2004 and 2010.

Jordanian-Syrian marriages statistics before crisis							
	2004	2005	2006	2007	2008	2009	2010
Jordanian males	267	264	189	292	254	290	184
	10%	10.50%	10%	11.50%	13%	13%	10%
Jordanian females	196	188	186	179	162	225	146
	6%	5%	7%	7%	6%	8%	6%
Overall number of marriages between Jordanians and non-Jordanians	5630	5979	4532	5096	4553	4989	4252

Source: The Jordanian Supreme Judge Department.

Table 9.8 The number of Jordanian-Syrian marriages between 2010 and 2016.

Jordanian-Syrian marriages statistics after crisis						
	2011	2012	2013	2014	2015	2016
Jordanian males	270	495	1182	1389	1431	1412
	11%	19%	32%	34%	35.50%	36%
Jordanian females	155	280	499	791	795	895
	6%	10%	13%	19%	19.50%	23%
Overall number of marriages between Jordanians and non-Jordanians	4996	5475	7488	8137	8084	7805

Source: The Jordanian Supreme Judge Department.

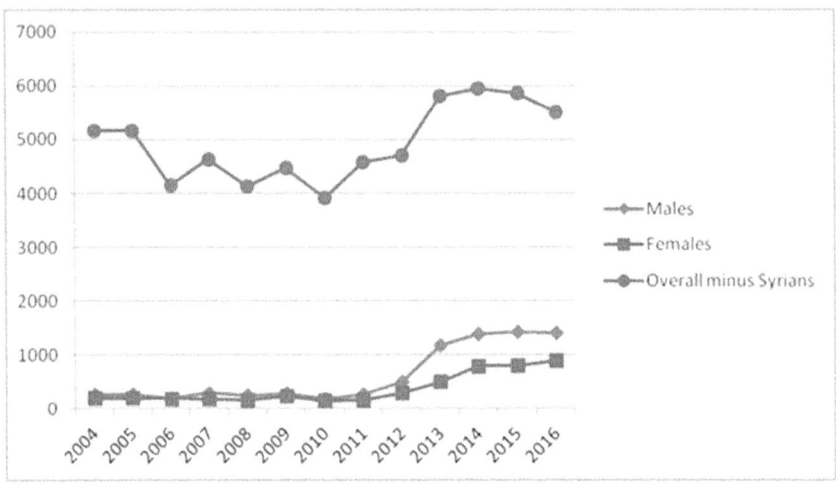

Figure 9.6 Numbers of marriages between Jordanian and Syrians between 2004 and 2016.

their degree of acceptance and rejection of marriages with Palestinians, Syrians, Iraqis, and non-Arabs whose religion was similar to that of the respondent, the majority of the sample—whether they were Jordanian or Palestinian-Jordanian—viewed marriage with Palestinians quite favorably while looked at the other marriages quite negatively. In fact, the degree of their rejection of marriages with non-Arabs was similar to their rejection of Syrian marital partners, even though one expected them to find Syrians to be more culturally compatible than non-Arabs. This suggests that fear over changing marriage values was based on a desire to alienate Syrians rather than on concerns based on tangible realities. Looking at Figure 9.6, one notices that even though there was a spike in the number of marriages between Jordanians and Syrians after the crisis, it fell far below the overall number of marriages between Jordanians and other non-Jordanians.

Table 9.9 Views on Syrian marriage customs.

		Syrian marriage customs are						Total
		Very similar (percent)	Somehow similar (percent)	Neutral	Little different	Somehow different (percent)	Very different (percent)	
Opinion on marriage with Syrians	Positive	7 (11)	7 (11)	7	8	19 (30)	15 (24)	63
	Negative	5 (4)	12 (9)	16	11	41 (32)	44 (34)	129
Total		12	19	23	19	60	59	192

In answering questions related to the issue of marriage, a third of the sample said Syrian marriage customs were very different from Jordanians', and a 10 percent said they were quite similar (Table 9.9). However, those who already had a negative opinion of marriage with Syrians were more likely to see them as different. A higher majority of 66 percent of them thought Syrian marriage customs were very different compared to a smaller percentage of 54 percent of those who held a positive opinion of marriage with Syrians. More of those who had a positive opinion (22 percent) thought marriage customs were somewhat similar to very similar compared to only 13 percent of those who had a negative opinion. Additionally, 68 percent of those who had a positive opinion of marriage with Syrians said they would accept their sons marrying a Syrian woman while only 12 percent of those who had a negative opinion said yes. When asked if they would accept their daughters marrying a Syrian man, most of the respondents on both sides said no, but with a significant difference of 88 percent of those who have negative opinions to 56 percent of a positive opinion. Consequently, it may be argued that the perception of difference was decided on the bias of opinion rather than actual difference.

Gender was also a factor when determining the degree of negative attitudes toward marrying Syrians. Female respondents were more opposed to it, with 73 percent of them describing such a marriage as negative compared to 61 percent of male respondents who were of the same opinion. This was consistent with how female respondents were more likely (53 percent) than male respondents (45 percent) to find Syrians to be socially different. This gender disparity was clearest in Region 1 (high Syrian population density; Table 9.10). Male respondents there were evenly divided in their position on marriage with Syrians, while females in the same region were decidedly against it (72 percent). It is also interesting that in Regions 2 and 3 (middle and low density, respectively), opinions were stronger against marriage with Syrians. The strongest rejection of marriage with Syrians was expressed by Region 2 respondents, and the least objection of 61 percent was in Region 1, which had the highest density Syrians. This suggests that demographic threats are not necessarily the determining factor on how the sample felt toward Syrians' integration into Jordanian society through marriage.

Table 9.10 Views on Jordanian-Syrian marriage based on region and gender.

Region			Marriage with Syrians		Total
			Positive	Negative (percent)	
High density	Gender	Female	9	23 (72)	32
		Male	16	16 (50)	32
	Total		25	39 (61)	64
Middle density	Gender	Female	9	27 (75)	36
		Male	9	19 (68)	28
	Total		18	46 (72)	64
Low density	Gender	Female	10	25 (71)	35
		Male	10	19 (66)	29
	Total		20	44 (69)	64
Total	Gender	Female	28	75 (73)	103
		Male	35	54 (61)	89
	Total		63	129 (67)	192

Region 3 consisted not only of low-density areas where Syrian visibility is minimal but also included a high-income community whose livelihood is least threatened by Syrians; in fact, the Syrian presence might have enhanced their lifestyle with the availability of Syrian delicacies and fashion trends. Looking at Table 9.11, one notices that there was no difference in opinion regarding the idea of marriage with Syrians across income. High-income respondents were as negative in their opinion as low-income respondents. The lack of significant impact of density of Syrian population and Jordanian income on diversifying respondents' opinions suggests that viewing Syrians as a sociocultural Other by rejecting marriage with them was not based on a threat of demographic and social invasion or economic competition but rather on perceptual threats created by a general climate of resistance to Syrians' influence and presence.

These cross-tabulated comparisons, coupled with the general concern over marriage, suggest that the preconceptions people already had about Syrian-

Table 9.11 Views on marriage with Syrians based on income and gender.

Income			Marriage with Syrians		Total
			Positive	Negative (percent)	
−350	Gender	Female	16	37 (70)	53
		Male	12	18 (60)	30
	Total		28	55 (66)	83
350–600	Gender	Female	8	26 (76)	34
		Male	19	32 (63)	51
	Total		27	58 (68)	85
601+	Gender	Female	4	12 (75)	16
		Male	4	4 (50)	8
	Total		8	16 (67)	24

Jordanian marriages were the significant factor that influenced the view of the degree of difference between Jordanian and Syrian marriage customs. The fear over the Syrianization of the Jordanian family informed how likely Jordanian respondents were to see customs as different. This begs the question of whether those customs are really different or if their difference is manufactured to justify the rejection of intermarriages with Syrians.

The sample's responses also suggest a consistent trend in alienating attitudes toward Syrians focused on cultural estrangement. When asked about the causes of Syrian underage marriages, unlike media reports that suggest that Syrian families are forced to do this as a result of economic hardships, respondents identified the causes as social traditions and norms (ranked first) over economic causes (ranked second). The majority of the sample believed that Syrians marry off their underage daughters in adherence to social norms and traditions rather than because of poverty. In the next question, the respondents predominantly (97 percent) expressed opposition to underage marriage. Read in juxtaposition, Jordanian respondents attributed the phenomenon of underage marriage among Syrians to social reasons while simultaneously rejecting the norm as unacceptable, which indicates a form of condemnation of a social norm and relocating it outside Jordanian culture and the current economic hardships Syrians face.

Coupling the consistent sense of threat the Jordanian sample has expressed toward Syrians' influence on marriage habits, trends, and norms in Jordan with the rejection of Jordanian-Syrian marriages, one sees a tendency to use family structures as a tool of othering and alienating Syrians and justifying the desire to remove them from Jordanian towns and cities. A clear trend emerges when cross-tabulating answers to questions regarding marriage with answers to the question of whether they wished to see Syrians leave their neighborhood or city. Those who held a negative opinion of Jordanian-Syrian marriages were more likely to express the wish to see them leave (83 percent) than those who were not opposed to this kind of marriage (57 percent). An overwhelming majority of 84 percent of those who opposed their sons' marriage to Syrian women wished Syrians to leave, compared to the smaller majority of 53 percent of those who approved their sons' marriage to Syrian women yet still wanted them to leave. On the other hand, a majority of 57 percent of those who said they would agree to their daughters' marrying Syrians said they did not want Syrians to leave their neighborhood, which is an exception to the trend in responses. This might be due to the acceptance of the Syrian son-in-law in the Jordanian family mirroring a larger acceptance of them within the nationalist family.

Another significant factor that influenced the Jordanian sample's responses to this question was whether they have Syrian relatives. Those who did indicate that they had Syrian relatives or in-laws were more divided in their response to this question, even if a majority said they wanted Syrians to leave (51 percent), while those who did not have Syrian relatives or in-laws overwhelmingly said they wanted them to leave (80 percent). This subgroup of respondents did not differ in their general negative responses toward Syrians from other subgroups, as the majority of them described Syrian culture as different and the impact of Syrian culture as negative even though they have Syrian relatives and in-laws. Surprisingly, the majority of them said that their view of Syrians had changed after the crisis, and an astonishing majority of 87.5 percent said the change was negative. One expected that their opinion of Syrians would have been influenced by their interpersonal and interfamilial relations with them rather than the impact of political changes. The only exception was in response to their evaluation of marriage with Syrians; since they already had Syrian relatives or in-laws, 59 percent of them described it as positive, 61.5 percent said they would agree to their sons' marrying Syrian women, but 61.5 percent opposed their daughters' marrying Syrians.

Answers Based on Regions

This section examines the responses based on their place of residence. The sample was divided based on a controlled variable of regions of Syrian population density. In response to the question of how they evaluated the impact of the Syrian presence in Jordan, the majority of respondents across the three regions called it very negative (Table 9.12).

As shown in the table, the different degrees of the density of Syrians in the five regions chosen for this study had a minimal impact on the negative view that Jordanians in the sample held against Syrians. Seventy percent of those living in

Table 9.12 Views on Syrian presence based on region.

City/Density		Very negative (percent)	Negative	Neutral (percent)	Positive	Very positive	Excellent	Total
Amman	Middle density	26 (72)	4	5	1	0	0	36
	Low density	21 (58)	5	9	1	0	0	36
	Total	47 (65)	9	12 (17)	2	0	0	72
Zarqa	Middle density	21 (75)	3	2	0	1	1	28
Irbid	High density	22 (69)	3	4	3	0	0	32
Mafraq	High density	23 (72)	3	5	1	0	0	32
Ma'an	Low density	20 (71)	4	3	0	0	1	28
Total	High density	45 (70)	6	9	4	0	0	64
	Middle density	47 (73)	7	7	1	1	1	64
	Low density	41 (64)	9	12 (19)	1	0	1	64
	Total	133 (69)	22	28	6	1	2	192

regions with high densities of Syrians expressed very negative views of their presence, which is a lower percentage than those living in middle-density regions who expressed the same opinion (73 percent). A slightly but not significantly lower percentage of 69 percent of respondents who lived in low-density regions said the Syrian presence was very negative. This indicates that neither fears over jobs or economic opportunities nor great exposure to Syrians and Syrian culture were determining factors in how Jordanians in the sample evaluated the impact of Syrians among them. The negative perception is based on preconception and not on actual experiences.

When asked about their opinion of intermarriages with Syrians, respondents across the three regions opposed it, with the exception of those living in Irbid. A majority of 56 percent expressed a favorable opinion on the subject. However, all respondents consistently opposed their children's marrying Syrians. Regarding issues of difference, only respondents in low-density regions differed significantly from respondents in other regions when they expressed their opinion about Syrians' social difference. While respondents of the other two regions of high (58 percent) and middle density

(53 percent) rated Syrians' social difference as high, only 37.5 percent of respondents in low-density regions shared the same opinion. Their opinions were more diverse, with 19 percent saying Syrians were not socially different and 17 percent expressing a neutral view on the subject.

A high 66 percent of respondents from Mafraq and 50 percent from Irbid found Syrians to be socially different (which meant 58 percent of Region 1 were of the same opinion). This is noteworthy because this region is one of the closest to Syria geographically and culturally, where they have so many social commonalities with residents of the Syrian city of Daraa, sharing similar dialects and cuisine, intermarrying, and many having the same family name. Only Zarqa residents showed a majority (61 percent) who shared the same opinion as residents of Mafraq and Irbid about Syrian social difference. On the other hand, only 39 percent of respondents from Ma'an found Syrians to be socially different, even though in the study, it is the most southern city, the farthest from Syria, has the lowest per capita density of Syrians, and is the most different socioculturally from Syria. Amman also had a low percentage of those who thought Syrians were socially different, which might be attributable to its status as the capital with a diverse social structure.

In response to the question of whether they want Syrians to leave their neighborhoods, there was no significant difference across the three regions; the majority of respondents from all regions said they wanted Syrians to leave. Whether living in areas of high, middle, or low density of Syrians, respondents consistently wanted them to leave even when they posed no tangible threat or competition to their livelihood or presence in public spaces. Whether living in Mafraq, where 38 percent of the population is Syrian, or in low-density areas, respondents opposed the Syrian presence. A majority of 86 percent of respondents in Ma'an said they wanted Syrians to leave, even though only 5 percent of the residents there were Syrian. The view of Syrians as the Other that needs to be removed is motivated by perceptual rather than economic reasons. The general sense that Syrians are demographically "invading" the country, which is perpetuated by mainstream and social media, motivates the manufacturing of Syrians as socioculturally different which warrants their departure even from regions where they live in very small numbers.

When asked to describe Syrians in a few words, respondents from high- and middle-density regions tended to use overwhelmingly negative words, while respondents from low-density regions provided mixed words (negative and positive), since they recognized the hardships and ordeals Syrians have faced (Table 9.13). Additionally, most of the negative words they used have social values, which suggests that the negativity Jordanian respondents have toward Syrians was caused by social rather than financial or political interactions with them. For example, absent from the list are words such as "greedy," "beggar," "thief," and "terrorist." Many respondents used the word "Other" (*ghir*), which is the equivalent of the prefix "un/ir" in English as in "uneducated" or "irreligious." However, in a study about othering Syrians as the cultural hybrid, I think it is significant that one of the first words to occur to them when they thought of Syrians is "other." "Little" (*qalil*) is another word that respondents used, mainly in the context of having "little faith/religion"; however, like "Other," it is indicative of respondents' unconscious opinion of Syrians as being "little."

Table 9.13 Words most commonly used by the Jordanian sample to describe Syrians.

Ranking region	1	2	3	4	5
High density	Selfish *anani*	Hypocrite *munafiq*	Little (little religion/morals) *qalil*	Liar *kadhab*	Poor fellow *miskin*
Middle density	Selfish *anani*	Stingy *bakhil*	Other *ghir*	Poor fellow *miskin*	Hypocrite *munafiq*
Low density	Selfish *anani*	Oppressed *mazlum*	Liar *kadhab*	Other *ghir*	A fighter *mukafih*

Income and Employment

More high-income respondents (75 percent) than middle-income (66 percent) and low-income (67 percent) respondents described the Syrian presence as very negative. On the other hand, high-income respondents were less opposed to their sons' marrying Syrians (54 percent) than were middle-income (72 percent) and low-income (72 percent) respondents. A little over half of middle-income respondents (55 percent) found Syrians to be socially different, which is the highest percentage compared to high-income (46 percent) and low-income (45 percent) respondents. A higher percentage of 55 percent of middle-income males than low-income males (33 percent) said they found Syrians to be socially different. Significant differences based on income were few and inconsistent, suggesting that there was not an economic impact on the sample's view of Syrians. It should be expected that in regions where Jordanians' livelihoods were threatened (among middle- and low-income respondents), negativity should be higher. But the results suggest that either there was no difference or that in some cases, high-income respondents—the least vulnerable group—were more negative toward Syrians.

As for employment, almost identical percentages of both employed and unemployed respondents thought the Syrian presence was negative (66 percent and 68 percent, respectively). Even those working in government and military institutions where Syrians cannot compete with them for employment did not differ in their opinions toward Syrians. Fifty-three percent said the Syrian presence was very negative, 47 percent of them said Syrian culture affected Jordanians negatively, 53 percent said marriage with Syrians was negative, 70.5 percent opposed their sons' marriage to Syrians, 76 percent said their views of Syrians had changed after the crisis, and 100 percent said the change was negative. They also thought Syrians' culture and marriage customs were different. Those working in the sales sector, where Syrians pose the greatest threat in terms of job competition, understandably held negative attitudes toward Syrians, with 83 percent saying the Syrian presence is very negative, and of those who said their opinion of Syrians changed after the crisis, 100 percent said the change was negative. However, unlike those with government jobs, respondents were split in their opinion of marriage with Syrians and whether they would support their sons' marrying Syrians. Business owners who were likely to benefit from the arrival of Syrian laborers were also negative in their views. In response to the question of whether they wanted Syrians to leave, the majority of the respondents, regardless of their employment status and nature of their employment, said yes (Table 9.14). Respondents in sectors where job security was high (government sector) did not differ greatly from those who work in sales sector in their answers to this question. The analysis of the results based on income and employment status suggests that economic factors and job competitions are not the determining factors in shaping opinions of Syrians as a threat or an undesirable alien entity.

Table 9.14 The desire to have Syrians leave Jordan based on employment.

		Do you want Syrians to leave?		Total
		Yes (percent)	No	
Work	Yes	58 (70)	25	83
	No	71 (77)	21	92
	None applicable	13 (81)	3	16
Total		142 (74)	49	191
Government sector		11 (65)	6	17
Sales		8 (67)	4	12
Business owner		22 (76)	7	29
Private sector		7 (58)	5	12
Freelance		14 (87.5)	2	16
Professional		3 (60)	2	5
Housewives		34 (77)	10	44
Retired		5 (71)	2	7
Student		5 (55.5)	4	9
Looking for a job		21 (81)	5	26
Doesn't want to work		6 (100)	0	6

Implications of Findings

Reading the results of the survey distributed among Jordanians in juxtaposition with the results of the survey distributed among Syrians raises several pertinent questions regarding the hybridization of Syrians' identity as the Other. Whereas the Jordanian sample expressed an overwhelmingly negative attitude toward the Syrian presence and the possibility of their integration into society through marriage and their cultural influence on the Jordanian society, Syrians surveyed expressed a vastly positive opinion of their lives in Jordan. A great majority of 92 percent of the Syrian sample said they wanted to obtain Jordanian citizenship, even though according to Jordanian law they would have to rescind their Syrian citizenship in exchange. When asked if their opinion of Jordanians has changed after the crisis, 59 percent said it did not change, and 33 percent said it became positive or somewhat positive. Only 8 percent said it became negative and blamed it on Jordanians' treatment and the Syrian crisis. Unlike Jordanians who opposed marriage with Syrians, 62 percent of the Syrian sample approved of marriage with Jordanians, 92 percent said they would approve their sons' marriage with Jordanians, and 84 percent said they would consent to their daughters' marrying Jordanians. The latter percentage presents a jarring contrast with Jordanians' position on the subject. This can be interpreted as indicative of Jordanians' resistance to the integration of Syrians through their daughters, while Syrians showed a significant interest in integration through marriage. In an Arab culture that expects wives' mobility to be tied to their husbands', Syrians' acceptance of their daughters' and consequently the whole family's permanent resettlement in Jordan shows their willingness to adapt to life there not as refugees but as citizens.[4] The majority (59 percent) said Jordanian and Syrian cultures are not different, and 61 percent expressed a desire to stay in Jordan, which is a significant result for this study. It represents a possible context for Jordanians' negative response.

Based on the results of the two surveys, this study argues that the hostility Jordanians feel toward Syrians is motivated by the fear that Syrians are permanently resettling in their country and that there might be a possibility of nationalizing them. Many Jordanian respondents while answering the survey questions made a side comment in which they contrasted Syrians with Egyptians who live and work here. They said in praising Egyptians, *"Ma kunna nhis fihum,"* which literally translates as "we never felt their presence." They made the same comment when comparing Syrians who were living in Jordan before the eruption of the crisis and those who came afterwards. The choice of phrasing is quite telling. "Never feeling" the presence of someone indicates invisibility. Egyptian workers' and pre-crisis Syrians' invisible sociocultural status maintained their place as guests with a temporary presence that poses no challenge to the dominant culture. The post-crisis Syrians do not act like guests, and the Syrian sample's responses to the survey questions support this hypothesis that the connection they are forging with Jordan is one of an alternative homeland. When asked if they agreed with the statement that Jordan has become their new home, 93 percent said they agreed completely and only 3 percent disagreed. When asked if they felt they belong in/to Jordan, 82 percent said yes. They ranked Jordan's significance to them as first "a place to live in," then "neighbors to live next to," while "a place to work" came last. Again, this shows that for the Syrian sample, Jordan is not only a source of livelihood but also a community.

Reading the two surveys' results as providing a comprehensive understanding of the Othering of Syrians in Jordan allows us to look at economic factors such as job competition not as a determining cause but as a pretext for the hybridization of Syrians and their culture. The surveys' questions intended to scratch the surface of the public discourse over Jordanian-Syrian relations and the causes of the growing negative feelings among Jordanians toward Syrians. The surveys' central result showed that regardless of the distribution of the Syrian presence in Jordan—whether in Mafraq, where over a third of the population is Syrian, or in the wealthy neighborhood of Abdoun in Amman, where the Syrian presence is minimal—the negative attitude was the same and was motivated by the fear of Syrian sociocultural integration into Jordanian society, an integration that was also apparent in Syrians' responses to the second survey.

However, it is significant to note that even though the majority of the Jordanian sample expressed negative feelings toward Syrians and their presence in Jordan, this attitude has not had an impact on the way Syrians in the sample feel toward their lives in Jordan. The Syrian respondents described their lives in Jordan as overwhelmingly positive, particularly praising human rights, dignity, and freedom of expression as qualities of life they most appreciated. When asked if they encountered any harassment—physical, verbal, or sexual—a majority of the respondents said they had not encountered any. This suggests that the general resentment Jordanians feel toward the Syrian presence is either not translated into action or has not had an impact on how Syrians feel toward Jordan or their lives there. Whereas Jordanians in the study felt that Syrians had become increasingly different, particularly socioculturally, the surveyed Syrians felt that they were becoming more "at home."

Concluding Remarks

This study aimed to examine the transformation of the Jordanian perception and representation of Syrians from seeing them as Arab brethren to perceiving them as a cultural hybrid. Following their displacement to Jordan, Syrians and their culture have been alienated and othered by their Jordanian hosts, who have felt threatened by their presence. As shown by the surveys' results, by transforming Syrians into a site of difference, Jordanians inadvertently create a binary opposition that distances them from Syrians and their customs, which before the crisis and the mass movement of Syrians into Jordan were not viewed as being foreign. Concerns over marriage and changes to Jordanian family structure betray territorial fears as economic and political concerns are manifested as sociocultural estrangement of Syrians. Since the family is the microcosm of the nation, the desire to protect it reflects a deeper sense of political insecurity.

However, this binarization of the Syrian and Jordanian cultures does not have to be deemed as only a form of xenophobia and an ultra-nationalism that is prone to breeding hatred and prejudice. There is always the possibility of returning to Bhabha's hybrid as a tool of empowerment. Seeing Syrians as cultural hybrids could push Jordanians further into a cultural exclusivity of identity but might also initiate a debate over the potentials of diversifying the Jordanian culture and all its cultural manifestations. This has to begin with the admission that Syrians are culturally different, and that in itself is an opportunity for an empowering diversification of the Jordanian social norms, cultural tendencies, and trade. The counter approach to growing anti-Syrian sentiments within the Jordanian society has been to retreat into the fiction of pan-Arabism and to erase cultural differences that are seen as divisive. The other approach, however, can be to embrace this difference and translate it into an acceptance of the sociocultural difference that Syrians can bring. Creating Syrians as the hybrid can open opportunities to allow influence into what seems to be a culturally homogenous Jordanian society.

Notes

1 The surveys were conducted in 2017.
2 Since Syrians living outside camps have freedom of movement, it was difficult to get statistics on their distribution within cities. Therefore, my determination of the distribution of Syrians in Amman's neighborhoods was based on estimate and visibility.
3 The Jordanian Syrian Refugees Affairs Department uses UNHCR's refugees statistics
4 Jordanian nationalization laws allow non-Jordanian women married to Jordanian men to acquire a Jordanian passport after five years of marriage. Jordanian women cannot pass their nationalities to their husbands or children.

References

Bakhtin, Mikhail. 1981. *The Dialogic Imagination. Four Essays*. Austin: University of Texas Press.
Bhabha, Homi. 1994. *The Location of Culture*. London: Routledge.
DuBois, W. E. B. 1903. *The Souls of Black Folk*. Chicago: A.C. McClurg & Co.
External Statistical Report on UNHCR Registered Syrians as of 31 May 2017. 2017. UNHCR. http://data.unhcr.org/syrianrefugees/download.php?id=13552.
Fanon, Frantz. 1967. *Black Skin, White Masks*. Translated by Charles Lam Markmann. New York: Grove Press.
Friedman, J. 1997. "Global Crises, the Struggle for Cultural Identity, and Intellectual Porkbarrelling: Cosmopolitans versus Locals, Ethnics, and Nationals in an Era of De-hegemonisation." In P. Werbner and T. Moddod (Eds.), *Debating Cultural Hybridity: Multi-cultural Identities and the Politics of Anti-racism* (pp. 70–89). London and Atlantic Heights, NJ: Zed Books.
Gilroy, Paul. 1993. *The Black Atlantic: Modernity and Double Consciousness*. London: Verso.
Kraidy, Marwan. 2008. *Hybridity: The Cultural Logic of Globalization*. Philadelphia: Temple University Press.

Lacan, Jaques. 1977. *The Four Fundamental Concepts of Psycho-Analysis*. Translated by Alan Sheridan. New York: W. W. Norton.
Pieterse, Jan N. 2001. "Hybridity, So What?: The Anti-Hybridity Backlash and the Riddles of Recognition." *Theory, Culture, & Society*. 18: 219–45.
Said, Edward. 1978. *Orientalism*. New York: Vintage Books.
Smith, Keri E. and Patricia Leavy. 2008. *Studies in Critical Sciences 12: Hybrid Identities: Theoretical and Empirical Examination*. Leiden: Brill.
The Annual Statistical Report. 2016. The Supreme Judge Department. Amman: Supreme Judge Department Press.
The Annual Statistical Report. 2015. The Supreme Judge Department. Amman: Supreme Judge Department Press.
The Annual Statistical Report. 2014. The Supreme Judge Department. Amman: Supreme Judge Department Press.
The Annual Statistical Report. 2013. The Supreme Judge Department. Amman: Supreme Judge Department Press.
The Annual Statistical Report. 2012. The Supreme Judge Department. Amman: Supreme Judge Department Press.
The Annual Statistical Report. 2011. The Supreme Judge Department. Amman: Supreme Judge Department Press.
The Annual Statistical Report. 2010. The Supreme Judge Department. Amman: Supreme Judge Department Press.
The Annual Statistical Report. 2009. The Supreme Judge Department. Amman: Supreme Judge Department Press.
The Annual Statistical Report. 2008. The Supreme Judge Department. Amman: Supreme Judge Department Press.
The Annual Statistical Report. 2007. The Supreme Judge Department. Amman: Supreme Judge Department Press.
The Annual Statistical Report. 2006. The Supreme Judge Department. Amman: Supreme Judge Department Press.
The Annual Statistical Report. 2005. The Supreme Judge Department. Amman: Supreme Judge Department Press.
The Annual Statistical Report. 2004. The Supreme Judge Department. Amman: Supreme Judge Department Press.
The Official Results of the National Population and Housing Census in Jordan. 2015. The Department of Statistics. Amman: DOS Press.
Young, Robert J. C. 1995. *Colonial Desires: Hybridity in Theory, Culture and Race*. London: Routledge.

10

Ontological Citizenship: A Realignment of Rights and Responsibilities between the Individual and the State(s) in Twenty-First-Century Migration and Transnationalism

Saeed Khan

Migration and transnationalism in the twenty-first century are catalyzing the emergence of "poly-citizens" possessing legal-judicial relations in more than one state and capable of multiple spaces in which the interaction of rights and responsibilities may occur. This phenomenon may facilitate the process whereby a citizen may derive the benefits of one state—for example, where he or she resides—while fulfilling the obligations of being a citizen in another state, often the country of origin or ethnocultural affiliation, thus altering the conventional reciprocity of rights and responsibility within a single state and creating an asymmetrical exercise of citizenship and redefining it beyond merely its ontological or legal categories. Moreover, tangible impacts on the allocation of resources and their transfer between states by such citizens may affect perceptions of national allegiance and loyalty, as well as notions of belonging and nationality-based identity.

Examining second-generation Indians in the Persian Gulf region, this chapter analyzes the evolving morphology and ethos of the citizen within the global space as transnationalism and increased migration redefine the relationship of the citizen with the state or with multiple states. It will also explore and distinguish between single-state citizens and citizens claiming citizenship in multiple states and how the exchange of rights and responsibilities vis-à-vis the state is affected in each category. Finally, this chapter will offer a functional definition of these emerging expressions of citizenship that allows for the development of new models of sociocultural engagement, inclusion, and integration, in both national and transnational contexts (i.e., ontological citizenship). While anticipation for the demise of the nation-state may be premature, there is an emerging and burgeoning discourse whose focus is on a post-Westphalian paradigm. With the crystallization of the myriad effects of the era of globalization, transnationalism and increased migration abound, and new modalities of political, economic, and cultural expression often outpace the ability to fully comprehend their consequences. Post-national and supranational entities, whether corporations, nongovernmental organizations (NGOs), or associations like the European Union, have precipitated the need to assess and reassess the role and relationship of the citizen with the citizen's nation and toward additional entities to which the citizen may claim membership.

Transnational or multiple citizenship is generally based on two premises: being situational to a single geographic space or agency or between a choice of two spaces; and the status of various parties/groups of different politically and legally based categories. Much of the current discourse regarding citizenship resides within the context of the political and, more specifically, the relationship of the citizen to the state. In its simplest form, this relationship involves an individual with a single political entity, the nation-state.

Citizenship, whether political or ontological, creates identity; specifically, it allows the individual to be situated within a collective identity. How this identity informs one's notion of citizenship, or membership within a broader collective, may be understood through an examination of various typologies of identity. Pries, for example, proffers no fewer than six different identities: global, macro-regional, national, micro-regional ethnic, diasporic, and transnational (2013).

Citizenship, argues Seyla Benhabib, "is becoming disaggregated." She defines the component parts of citizenship as "collective identity, privileges of political membership and social rights and benefits" but notes that these components do not always go together. For example, she adds that under some circumstances, an individual might identify himself or herself as a member of one nationality by virtue of birth and culture and enjoy the social benefits of a host country—such as unemployment compensation—but has no right to vote in elections in that country. This situation occurs frequently within the European Union, she notes, especially in the case of foreign workers, where there is the existence of "porous borders" (Benhabib 2006). However, Benhabib presumes that this citizen would have dual identities based on birth/culture and host country. But what about the citizen who has no second tie? Can he or she not have a similarly disaggregated sense of citizenship? How does exposure to the dual-identity citizen affect this idea? How is globalization consciousness an impetus to disaggregation? Kymlicka's focus is on citizenship—cosmopolitan citizenship (2001), or examining whether transnational entities or organizations are equipped to facilitate democratic citizenship in a globalizing world. His notion of multicultural citizenship is generally focused on a single country and the dynamics of contestation and negotiation within that single space (2007).

Kymlicka's focus is on multicultural citizenship; more specifically, the study involves the heterogeneity of a population within a single political entity. A country may be composed of a multitude of ethnic and racial communities, immigrant and indigenous; it is the sum total of a variety of politically and legally determined categories: citizens, resident aliens, temporary workers, asylees, and refugees. Mere residence and engagement within a common public space do not, of course, confer equal status within that space. Furthermore, notions of belonging and perceptions of being "full citizens," that is, members of the dominant ethnic community, are highly contested issues. These issues achieve greater complexity in societies where demographics are a fluid phenomenon, as is seen in the United Arab Emirates (UAE).

Political participation is seen by some to be a function and marker of citizenship (Baubock). Within the context of dual citizenship, there is participation in multiple sending and receiving centers. As a consequence, stakeholder citizenship arises, where transnational citizenship may be achieved through such mechanisms as external voting. Yet external voting must be seen through the lens of a cost-benefit analysis. While the ancestral country may welcome its "diaspora" being engaged in its electoral processes, the citizens of the domiciled country may view such activity with suspicion, evoking inquiries and indictments of opportunism and a lack of national investment. External voting also runs the risk of affecting, even impeding, assimilation or the ability of citizens to perceive themselves as "full citizens" of the country where they reside. The challenge, therefore, is in coming to terms with the dialectic of "self vs. other," as such a line of demarcation is clearly more ambiguous with the "diaspora" individual and the "home" state: "Somewhat perplexing that something is as that which, at the same time, it is not."[1] How the nation balances its own interests and efforts to "repatriate" its diaspora members is as much a function of how the individual perceives this binary as how the society within the respective country sees the individual.

Nations operate with a certain modicum of jealousy when it comes to their citizens. They are well aware that their citizens comprise their most valuable assets and resources; sharing these with other countries, irrespective of the connections these individuals may bear, is not always or easily presumed. Moreover, the strength of a country coming from its citizenry is reason enough for the state to ensure that the state maintains as much control over the citizen as possible. Foucault, for example, recognizes the metanarrative of power inherent in the state-citizen relationship. In particular, issues of governmentality and bio-power influence the state's treatment and the categorization of individuals, especially citizens, and also affect the self-perception of these individuals, as well as the individuals' perception of their relationship to the state and, by necessity, other states. Often, the state will impose restrictions upon its citizens under the guise of national security. This ranges from limitations on maintaining multiple citizenship to placing restrictions on the level of engagement one may have with a second country, even if it may be the country of birth or ethnic origin. Though such measures may impede, even inhibit, citizens from exercising political citizenship vis-à-vis another nation, it will not be an obstacle for those who seek to act as "citizens" in the most fundamental, qua apolitical, sense of the word. For them, it is not an issue of *whether* to act as citizens; more precisely, it is an issue of *where* to act like citizens and whether that can be in more than one place at the same time.

The phenomenon of bifurcated rights and responsibilities of citizenship may be best illustrated by the example of second-generation Indians in the Persian Gulf, a considerable demographic in a place like the UAE. This group, now in their twenties, are neither immigrants nor do they perceive themselves or are perceived by broader society as being fully indigenous. Moreover, they do not conform to the traditional definition of diaspora, as they are not dislocated from a central point of ethnic origin. At the same time, and despite occupying what Bhabha describes as "the third space," these Indians do not hold conventional notions of a split identity (Bhabha 1994). Born in the UAE, many have a connection to the homeland of their parents or grandparents only through an occasional trip to the country of ethnic origin. It is logical to infer that this attenuation with the "homeland" will increase over time and with subsequent generations. With an identity of being "transferred Indian citizens," these Gulf Indians regard their citizenship as a function of political and legal modalities displaced and undeployed; many would hardly see themselves voting in the Indian elections or particularly concerned with domestic policy issues in the country. At the same time, however, they bear a strong affinity to a transnational or supranational identity: citizen of the worldwide Indian community, or Indian diaspora. The notion of diaspora reminds Indians that they belong to a global community that transcends race, ethnicity, culture, language, or class. Irrespective of location or even piety, the connection of being a part of the diaspora is a compelling and magnetic force of identity construction, similar to the Voltairian concept of universalism and its concomitant phenomenon of civilization. In addition, the contemporary fluidity of the Indian world, with its myriad social, economic, and political instabilities, creates a high level of visibility of challenges facing fellow religionists for Indians in the UAE, even if their lives may be relatively secure.[2] Furthermore, as Fraser discusses transnationalizing the public sphere (Benhabib 2006), Indians in the diaspora already see themselves living within such a global architecture, with technology and communications facilitating their connectedness as a people with a common geographic and genealogical base. In addition, these immigrant communities represent and reflect part of the "un-detachable correlate of progressive 'diasporization' of the planet" that contributes to glocalization (Baumann 2013).

The diaspora also typifies the new emerging architecture of globalization, the post-national realignment of borders and identities. Unfettered by political strictures, the diaspora resides as a network to which its citizens can maintain an ontological sense of citizenship; they are citizens of the diaspora by the mere fact that they are Indian.

The focus upon an ontological conception of citizenship allows for recognition of the fluidity of political engagements and notions of political citizenship; acknowledgment of migration, diaspora communities, and their multiple political affiliations; and preparation by societies for multiplicity.

The concept of the modern nation-state, per the Peace of Westphalia of 1648, is not even five hundred years old. And yet contemporary geopolitical developments reveal many trajectories that indicate a shift toward a post-Westphalian model of nationhood and, by extension, a new conception of citizenship. If the essentialization of the nation-state is being contested, challenged, and reconstituted, then the notion of citizenship will similarly and naturally be affected. With globalization and migration creating new relationships and modes of engagement between individuals and polities, there needs to be an assessment and reassessment of the citizen's role in new, multiple locations and in a transnational or supranational space.

Countries and their citizens have to contend with the prospect of membership in more than one polity. In the case of Portugal and Cyprus, each has citizens who belong to a nation and also to a supranational entity, the European Union, and both illustrate examples of what Baubock would call vertical citizenship. At the same time, current economic pressures in these countries may affect the identity construction of their citizens, who profess a deeply rooted national identity, yet equivocation, even hostility, about membership in the Eurozone, where financial autonomy is subsumed to the general will of the EU, and perhaps the perceived usurpation of fiscal agency by other, more powerful nations within the EU. Such hierarchal citizenship, based on economic as well as political realities, may cause disillusionment among a citizenry already perceiving disenfranchisement from critical decision-making processes.

As the nation-state is often considered a sine qua non and hallmark of Western modernity, certain other presumptions are made to reinforce the essential nature of this particular polity. Charles Taylor contends that Western modernity has the characteristics of a market economy, a public sphere, and a self-governing people. Of course, this is a rather privileged, Eurocentric construction of what constitutes being modern, and it is far from being uniquely a marker of the Occident. Singapore, India, Japan, and Turkey are but a few countries that will assert their inclusion in a list that Taylor would perhaps keep more limited in its membership or, to be charitable, allow for consideration but only because their "enlightenment" was the result of either Western conquest or colonization. If financial prosperity and integration in the global economic system are markers for modernity, several other countries will claim their right to inclusion in the "international premier league" of nations.

Clearly, democracy, market capitalism, and a public discursive space do not necessarily guarantee a successful and functional society or demonstrate political citizenship's perfection. After all, current economic maladies that plague many a Eurozone country must be viewed in comparison and contrast to China's prosperity, despite its severe central-planning model.

There is the growing phenomenon of individuals bearing multiple citizenship, either with two or more nations or simultaneously with a national and supranational entity, who possess political relationships with these entities and their constituents that are not always harmonious or readily compatible. Add to this the phenomenon of migrant and/or so-called diaspora communities and the consciousness and accusations of disloyalty to a particular state, spasms of nativism, and discrimination that often ensue.

Even Vertovec, who focuses on transnationalism, presumes, as do other scholars (e.g., Kymlicka and Benhabib), that citizenship is a primarily, if not exclusively, political phenomenon. In addition, it presumes tensions or focus on migrants, that is, on diaspora communities or individuals. As borders shift and globalization erases previously calcified barriers and boundaries, political limitations must yield to the new realities of permeability along economic, legal, and even sociological modes of engagement.

One ought to pay attention, therefore, to the growing visibility and importance of the so-called displaced generation within diaspora communities. How do they perceive citizenship? Is it solely a political phenomenon? If so, what will be the impact on the reconstitution of those political relationships and engagements? Are these generations less ossified, more malleable in negotiating citizenship? Are there, in fact, areas of focus that extend beyond the mere political? Is political citizenship like the paint on the wall of a room, where as it is stripped off to reflect changing political affiliations, the dimensions of the room are also being changed? The focus, then, is less exclusively upon the political or the ontic—that is, on what a citizen is—than on the ontological, that is, that the individual is a citizen.

The concept of flexible citizenship examines the role of economics as the primary factor of the selection of citizenship, rather than group identification as a function of shared political rights (Ong 1999). In the case of Gulf Indians, economics indeed is the principal impetus for migration from South Asia, but it is not a true, "flexible" citizenship; since there are no political rights beyond the work and residency permits they receive, "privileges" can be revoked at any time and, arguably, even for arbitrary reasons.

Flexible citizenship may also be examined as the assessment and reevaluation of identity and belonging that occurs because of a trauma that recalibrates national identity, with new constructions of otherness or through a rise in patriotism and/or xenophobia (Maira 2009). In the case of Gulf Indian youth, the sense of belonging for this second-generation category exists sui generis; that is, their identity was formed out of their alterity from birth and in the absence of either a national trauma or the experience of dislocation concomitant with migration.

Heidegger's assessment of ontology includes the delineation of two forms of interaction: praxis (i.e., social interaction) and poiesis (i.e., cultural interaction). These forms of interaction transcend and may occur beyond a political construct. Furthermore, it also facilitates the development of a construct that includes otherwise marginalized groups, such as stateless people (Arendt) or those who assert denationalizing citizenship (Bosniak).

An ontological sense of citizenship is inherent, instinctive, and innate, as evidenced by a newborn's interaction with its mother, a function of both praxis and poiesis. It is difficult to categorize such an interaction as occurring within a political citizenship paradigm. Such a relationship is beyond mere belonging; it recognizes both a transactional component and a transcendent element. While this construction of the social contract exists between individuals, it may also apply in the aggregate, that is, to a larger collective.[3]

When a citizen exists in negotiation with other citizens, it implies an exchange of social rights and duties vis-à-vis one another. Whether this occurs between individuals or between the individual and the state, the social contract is a bedrock principle of citizenship. With new political realities and engagements emerging, it is now possible for political citizenship to be subsumed to ontological citizenship. How does ontological citizenship operate within trans-, supra-, and post-national spaces? What is its correlation to engagement of the individual citizen? Does it assume characteristics of cosmopolitanism, or is it more a reflection of Rousseau's moral patriotism?[4] One must also address the notion of the locus of citizenship where traditionally, rights and responsibilities of citizenship are discharged within the same space. Trans-, supra-, and post-national realities are affecting and will affect such spatial considerations; ontological citizenship may facilitate diffusion across existing borders and allow for the establishment of new modes of engagement irrespective of limitations caused by political and legal strictures. Ontological citizenship needs assessment vis-à-vis individuals who reside in Bhabha's "third space," that is, second and subsequent generations, for whom sufficient political and legal connections to the second country do not exist. Bhabha's third space suggests a hybridity between two cultures that have relatively equal forces of influence on the individual; the identity and sense of citizenship for an individual who resides outside such symmetry, and for whom such residence is ephemeral, will need to consider new liminal spaces in which to operate and operationalize his or her sense of citizenship.

Political citizenship implies the exchange of rights and duties within a single space or across related spaces, for example, a nation-state or a supranational entity. Now, more citizens, especially the 1.5 and higher generations, are comfortable asserting or claiming their rights of citizenship in one locus while discharging their duties of citizenship in another, irrespective of whether they maintain a political relationship with both locales.

Some scholars have already envisaged a world where the nation-state may have a finite lifespan as it enters a "terminal crisis" (Appadurai). Based on such a conceit, the focus on diasporic public spheres is at the crux of understanding the emerging postnational political orders. If that is indeed the case, how does citizenship as an ontological category locate itself in the new paradigm? How does such a conceptualization of citizenship differ from citizenship, qua political citizenship? How does it inform and affect, or how is it affected by, the political conception of citizenship? The disaggregation of rights and responsibilities within a single polity should not be seen as a diminution of loyalty or allegiance or as undermining sovereignty or security through resource redistribution. In fact, ontological citizens demonstrate a level of engagement arguably higher than "real citizens," individuals who operate their roles as citizens within a single nation.

Diaspora is a problematic term, one that suggests uprootedness, separation, and dislocation. "It allows dispersion to be thought of as a state of incompleteness or a state of completeness" (Dufoix 2008). But are Gulf Indian youth uprooted or dislocated in the conventional context? In general, the decision of parents to migrate to the Gulf was volitional and intentional, with few, if any, "push factors" from India informing their election to leave. There are three features of the Indian diaspora in the scholarly literature: the myth of return, nostalgia, and hybridity (Vora 2013). The Gulf Indian youth possess none of these, yet they still belong to a sizable local and global Indian *ethnoscape* (Appadurai).

Is the Gulf Indian diaspora an imagined community in Andersonian terms? If so, what are the parameters of its imagination? Many Gulf Indians regard a place like Dubai not as a foreign country but rather as an extended Indian city. In fact, most do not identify themselves with the UAE as a whole but rather see themselves as residents of a particular emirate—they are a Dubaite or a Sharjahite. For some, the flight time between the Gulf and their ancestral hometown may be shorter than a domestic flight within India. But temporal realities may supersede spatial ones in determining the ontology of such a community. The age of the youth is the critical factor in framing the community's stability and identity. Foreign children born in the UAE are included in their father's visa until the age of eighteen or until the age of studies, whichever occurs later. Girls from this category, however, are subject to some important variations; they are considered dependents until they marry or are able to secure employment with the necessary sponsorship procurement.

Non-citizens in the UAE are not entitled to the same guarantees made to Emiratis of welfare benefits, such as free education, subsidized medical care, and land and housing allowances. As Vora contends, the vast majority of the inhabitants of the Gulf are not citizens within a "social contract"; they are inhabitants with "a right to the city." They are "impossible citizens," who define their identity and sense of belonging not despite the legal structures and constraints but through these structures of continuous temporariness (Vora). Gulf Indian youth are not migrants in the classic sense of the meaning. Migration suggests movement; the Gulf Indian youth did not "move"; they were born in the Gulf and have ostensibly known no other home. Theirs is a migration of stasis.

Indians have lived in the UAE for well over a century. Currently, there are approximately 4.5 million Indians in the Gulf, comprising about 20 percent of the worldwide Indian diaspora. In the UAE and Saudi Arabia, they represent 70 percent of the population (Naujoks 2013). As a comparison, nearly 90 percent of the UAE population is non-Emirati.

Clearing adolescence and enjoying the acceptance and tolerance of multiculturalism that is a common part of the college experience do not affect Gulf Indians in the same manner that it would in locations where their citizenship is commensurate with their domicile. Graduation creates the usual anxiety of finding a job and/or preparing for the impending social and family expectations of marriage. Yet for Gulf Indians, such concerns are complicated with the prospect of departure. Upon completion of their degrees, visa status expires, unless they can secure local employment and its concomitant visa sponsorship. Marriage may be a device to maintain residency status to avoid being separated from immediate family, which still maintains its residency status. With an Indian passport, the Gulf Indians can at least avoid being stateless. But they face the prospect of migrating to a country with which they may have little physical contact and cultural immersion. At the same time, however, the India to which they might migrate differs greatly from the India that their parents vacated to establish life in the Gulf.

No longer just a nation of poverty in the "third world," India has become a producer of brainpower and was a supplier of tech capital, both human and scientific. Interest in all things Indian began to grow, a newfound desire to learn the languages of the subcontinent, an appreciation of cuisine, and even the promotion of Indian culture, be it *banghra* dances or feature-length movies. Having Indian heritage evolved beyond being seen as a liability, it was now a source of pride and promise. As India entered the twenty-first century as an emerging regional and global economic power, many Gulf Indians of the second and subsequent generations "discovered" an India with an "updated operating system," one with which they could relate more easily. While identifying themselves politically as citizens, second-generation Gulf Indians began to see India through a range of different facets. For some, India offered new and unexplored economic opportunities, with investment in the IT industry and beyond. Yet for many others, there was recognition that India had several challenges as it attempted its leap into a more prominent international position. Having an ethnocultural, religious, or genealogical connection to India, many became interested in a mode of engagement with the country on their own terms, free of the imposition of connectivity they may have felt from family in earlier times. The actual manner of engagement has developed in activity both in India and in the Gulf, depending upon the particular focus and priority of the individuals in question.

For those Gulf Indian youth being compelled to migrate to India, an issue of authenticity will invariably permeate their consciousness and the perception by which they will be viewed by Indians. But what does it mean to be "authentic"? Can a diaspora community be as authentically Indian as those who have resided their entire lives in India? Does an Indian passport alone confer authenticity? Radakrishnan contends that "if a minority group were left in peace with itself and not dominated or forced into a relationship with the dominant world or national order, would the group still find the term 'authentic' meaningful or necessary?" (Braziel 2003). According to Radakrishnan, the Gulf Indian youth may be seen as an authentic community. The social dynamics of the UAE allow the Indian diaspora to exist within a bubble of Indian culture and social intercourse. They do not interact in any meaningful manner with the Emirati society. Moreover, the Emiratis are dominant in a political and legal capacity but are neither demographically nor culturally dominant. There is no paucity of Indian foods, clothes, cultural events, or entertainment available for every linguistic, regional, and ethnic subgroup of the subcontinent. There is no challenge to be and/or remain as quintessentially "Indian" as one so desires.

While Indians may have access to a shared ethnocultural space in the Gulf, socioeconomic realities create some of the same subdivisions within the diaspora community as would be evident in the "home country," especially in matters of education (Vora). There are Indian primary and secondary schools available for most families; for those with the requisite desire and financial means, British and American schools offer a more rigorous curriculum and a space in which to interact with non-Indian, even Emirati peers. As a result, this "privileged group" is limited in its interaction with conationals. The current study is limited in its scope to Gulf Indian youth hailing from middle- to upper middle–class families, whose parents occupy positions within the technocratic fields. Children of migrant laborers, particularly those from the construction and domestic sectors, are not included, primarily as a result of their absence from the Gulf due to immigration regulations.

For Appadurai, diasporic public spheres are the "crucible of a postnational political order" (Appadurai 1996). In essence, Gulf Indian youth epitomize such a conceptualization. They constitute a demographic attenuated from the country of its political citizenship but yet detached from the political anchor that one's domicile would normally provide. According to Pries's typologies, Gulf Indian youth comprise of all six identity markers. They bear a national (Indian) identity; they often maintain their micro-regional ethnic identity, contingent upon the region of India to which they affiliate (Kerala, Punjab, etc.); they are macro-regional (South Asian); diasporic; transnational; and, given Dubai's cosmopolitanism, global as well. While they bear such multiplicity of identity, the Gulf Indian youth lack any connective citizenship with their domicile.

Yet the lack of political citizenship does not seem to trouble the youth, who do not see such engagement as critical to their ability to navigate life in the Gulf. There is a cultural citizenship that occurs by their presence; it is diffusive in spreading their Indian ethnic culture into the multicultural mosaic that defines UAE society. Their location as a diasporic public sphere is within what many would argue is the very apotheosis of globalization. Ironically, their Indian identity may be less susceptible to the seismic and disruptive forces of global commodification. The Gulf Indian youth are children of every culture—Hollywood, Bollywood, US hip-hop, K-pop, Euro techno-pop—every culture but that of their physical "homeland," which does not assert a particular, identifiable Arab/Emirati culture.[5] By contrast, their ancestral homeland's culture is under assault, with the Anglicization of Bollywood dialogue and commodification of yoga in Western society. It is an open question whether their engagement with *mimetic rivalry*, the pursuit of material markers of success and acceptance as defined and determined by globalization forces, is more corrosive than the impact upon their conationals in India (Mishra 2017).

Gulf Indian youth navigated an identity that is a particularly contested construction. It does not readily emerge as an example of dual consciousness (DuBois 1994), a frame predicated upon binaries such as West versus East and Euro-American versus Asian. Rather, the youth represent the epitome of multiple consciousness, but one that is an example of alterity, not an affirmative assertion of identity per se (Dabashi 2013). They defy the simplistic binaries by being not Indian, not Emirati, not South Asian. Their transnational identity, qua alterity, thus defines them as being what they are not more than what they may be in more conventional registers.

The acceptance of Gulf Indians in positions of cultural production and cultural authority is certainly a positive development for the Indian diaspora in the UAE, but how does it affect its relationship with India? One may reasonably infer that the greater the sense of acceptance in the UAE, the lower the incentive to feel a strong connection to India. After all, if cultural acceptance is regarded as the most serious obstacle to breach in order to gain a sense of belonging, and if it is in fact overcome, then the need to maintain a close affiliation with the "home" country becomes all the more attenuated. Clearly, one can belong to and/or maintain identity and connectivity with more than one space—both the UAE and India simultaneously—but the odds and impetus for doing so will doubtless be influenced by the viability and merits of keeping a balance or strong tie to one country, especially if it is neither the domicile nor the locus of sustained engagement. For many young Gulf Indians, language, cuisine, and customs are not barriers to navigating life in the UAE. There is an ample critical mass of Indian culture, with its various manifestations—cuisine, apparel, entertainment, and so on—in abundant supply. Being Indian is not a challenge in Dubai; if anything, it is encouraged as a way to promote the emirate's insistence on displaying its cosmopolitan bona fides to the world and by creating a de facto cultural bubble in which the Indian diaspora can operate and feel a sense of belonging.[6] In addition, Gulf Indians who face the prospect of leaving their domicile have choices. Notwithstanding their effort to remain in the UAE by securing their own residency permit, they may avail themselves, through employment opportunity or marital dynamics, to opt for North America, Europe, or Australia as possible locales for migration. While India may present itself as a default destination with their citizenship, it may not be the presumptive, automatic selection. How then can India incentivize Gulf Indians to become "neo-patriates" to their ancestral country? Apropos Anderson, all communities are by definition imagined, but there exists a certain morphology to such an imagined community based upon ethnicity, religion, and culture, as well as interaction with the country of residence. For Gulf Indian youth, the parameters of the imagined community are nebulous given the uncertainty of the destination of their next migration.

In general, there are three reasons why someone may seek a stronger connection to India while living as a member of the diaspora: economic, political, and emotional. Each of these rationales, however, brings with it a measure of unreliability in its ability to serve as an accurate predictor of one's motivation to enter into sustained engagement with India. Economic reasons, for example, may fluctuate with the same level of volatility and uncertainty as market forces themselves. Given the mercurial nature of financial ties, through either short- or long-term investment, offering enticements to a member of the Indian diaspora carries the twin risks of instability of capital infusion and sustained interaction, as well as overreliance on a financial source that may be ephemeral. In addition, there may be a fine line of perception between someone regarding India as the venue for a sound capital investment or as a charity case. An economic relationship with India absent a well-developed, well-informed understanding of the country's myriad and complex cultural, political, and financial tectonic plates has the potential to create more tensions and conflicts than what the engagement seeks to mitigate.

Political incentives are oftentimes concomitant with economic enticements. The notion of a quid pro quo is not only an expected framing of the interaction between an individual and the state or society, but is made all the more poignant when the individual is not a "full" citizen of the state. Moreover, the oeuvre of some form of consideration by the state for the individual's engagement may be viewed by both parties as a vehicle to solemnize and bind the "contract," obviating the doubts of commitment that may exist in a more illusory or unilateral intervention. The scope of the political benefit that the state offers the diaspora individual may range from a status that facilitates entry into the country to expedited and less cumbersome means of transactional interaction, commercially and otherwise, and perhaps even citizenship with voting rights or privileges.

The state's decision on the scope of incentives it seeks to confer upon the diaspora individual is a dilemma involving the typical choices of offering too much or too little incentive to trigger interaction. While some non-resident Indian economic or social entrepreneurs will appreciate "fast track" airport service and the ability to avoid additional layers of bureaucratic complexity usually reserved for foreigners, the prospect of having rights comparable or equal to domiciled citizens is enticing and desirable but not a sine qua non to working or investing in India. Some may be dissuaded from engaging with the country if they are denied the privilege of being full stakeholders, but there does not appear to be a compelling rationale why an investor, property owner, philanthropist, or social entrepreneur would require voting rights in the nation's elections. Furthermore, the debate of being a "full" citizen will assume new levels and volumes of rancor in the public and political discourse when Indians question why a diaspora individual, for example, in his or her mid-twenties and with no prior interaction with India suddenly has the same enfranchisement in the voting process as, say, a sixty-five-year-old person who has always lived in India, always paid taxes there, and has never even left the country. Likewise, issues of transparency regarding political access may arise if resulting laws and regulations are based on status, not source of funding, lobbying, and so on. Given the twin polemical specters of corruption and foreign influence, the potential for a volatile, divisive controversy emerging is quite real. A thorough cost-benefit analysis is critical in gauging not just the economic consequences but also the sociopolitical dimensions that, oftentimes, obfuscate and dominate the issue at hand.

Guilt can serve as a highly compelling force of influence in causing an individual to engage in a situation that may be new and unfamiliar. For the diaspora individual, particularly for one with few to no ties with the home country, a latent sense of connection may manifest itself later in life and gain strength as a function of such guilt. The level of engagement, and perhaps the incentivization to "return" to the country in question, may be the result of overcompensation, insecurity, and even a feeling of coercion, either self-perceived or from family or community. All of these motivations, however, are unreliable and therefore may frame the desire for engagement to be ephemeral. The emotional impetus, borne of less-than-rational foundations, can create an impulsive, reflexive interaction but may lead to an equally rash, rapid disengagement. The decision to confer a powerful benefit upon a recipient who may possess an uncertain commitment to a sustained interaction places the state in a dubious position; the potential benefits of interacting at this level with diaspora individuals must be tempered by the risks of unpredictable relations and outcomes therein.

A state seeking to enhance connections to its diaspora through increased enfranchisement with the home country must recognize and address the diaspora individual's economic and political motivations, along with emotional influences that may inform his or her impetus to engage as well as any expectations of results from maintaining such a relationship. While each of these factors brings different costs and risks, as well as the varying levels of complexity that accompany them, the ability to appeal to a more core, ontological sense of connection may mitigate uncertainty and amplify the strength of the interaction. A focus on the elemental notion of citizenship, an exchange of rights and responsibilities, and the latitude to have such an exchange occur outside conventional spaces of reciprocity is an important dimension to explore when fostering the ties between members of the Indian diaspora and India.

Second-generation Gulf Indians do not see themselves as fully enfranchised and vested UAE citizens, because laws and regulations preclude their ability to do so; they consider themselves to be part of a diaspora community, not completely "home" yet not sure where some other "home country" exists for them. Nonetheless, it is their notion of ontological citizenship that motivates them to engage with India and allows for the prospect of continuing a beneficial series of engagements both in India, to improve civil society, and in the UAE, where they endeavor to ameliorate the narrative about India and its citizens.

Notes

1   Martin Heidegger, *Plato's Sophist* (Bloomington: Indiana University Press, 2003), 580. The ontological perception of the self is mediated by how others situate the individual. Common ethnic, religious, cultural, or linguistic markers may not be sufficient to overcome a sense of otherness that may emerge through migration. Over

time, both the diaspora individual and people in the home country may see each other as distinctly different, that is, as the Other.
2   Voltaire, *Candide* (London: Penguin Classics, 2005).
3   Scholars such as Castoriadis theorize on the relationship between the imaginary and the ontological as a synthetic process. However, Habermas's criticism of Castoriadis's difficulty in demonstrating the mediation between the individual and society provides justification for his particular exclusion from further analysis or citation in the present study. See Jurgen Habermas, *The Philosophical Discourse of Modernity* (Cambridge, MA: MIT Press, 1987).
4   George Cavallar, "Educating Émile: Jean-Jacques Rousseau on Moral Cosmopolitanism," *The European Legacy: Toward New Paradigms* 17, no. 4 (2012): 485–99.
5   The geography of Gulf Indian youth in the liminal spaces of what were once well-defined boundaries of nation-state dynamics, and their interaction with the material in a place like Dubai, reflects the cautionary tone issued by Habermas of the multinational corporation filling the void left by the breakdown of conventional nation-state modalities of distinction and concomitant modes of "citizenship," along with the degradation of traditional forms of political integration (Habermas 1998). Dabashi similarly recommends an antidote to the "systematicity of that globalized destitution" to create new forms of transnational solidarity. Gulf Indian youth could represent an example of such an alternative, but simultaneously, they may typify the very discontents against which Dabashi warns, given their exposure and engagement with Dubai's hyperconsumerism. See Hamid Dabashi, *Iran without Borders* (London: Verso Books, 2016).
6   There is an important caveat, however, of cosmopolitanism, specifically its default construction as "unabashedly Eurocentric and self-indulgent, confident and self-sufficient and yet paradoxically parochial and provincial in its confidence that what it imagines as 'the world,' and the manner in which it occupies that world, is 'the' world and nothing else." See Hamid Dabashi, *Persophilia* (Cambridge, MA: Harvard University Press, 2015), 139.

References

Anderson, Benedict. *Imagined Communities*. London: Verso Books, 1983.
Appadurai, Arjun. *Modernity at Large*. Minneapolis: University of Minnesota Press, 1996.
Appiah, Kwame Anthony. *Cosmopolitanism*. New York: W. W. Norton, 2006.
Baubock, Rainier. "The Rights and Duties of External Citizenship." *Citizenship Studies* 13:5 (2009): 475–99.
Baubock, Rainer and Guiraudon, Virginie. "Introduction: Realignments of Citizenship: Reassessing Rights in the Age of Plural Memberships and Multi-Level Governance." *Citizenship Studies* 13:5 (2009): 439–50.
Bauman, Zygmunt. "Glocalization and Hybridity." *Glocalism: Journal of Culture, Politics and Innovation* 1 (2013): 15.
Benhabib, Seyla. *Another Cosmopolitanism*. New York: Oxford University Press, 2006.
Benhabib, Seyla, Shapiro, Ian, and Petranovic, Danilo. *Identities, Affiliations, and Allegiances*. Cambridge: Cambridge University Press, 2007.
Bhabha, Homi. *The Location of Culture*. London: Routledge, 1994.

Croucher, Sheila. *Globalization and Belonging*. Latham: Rowman and Littlefield, 2004.
Dabashi, Hamid. *Iran, the Green Movement and the USA: The Fox and the Paradox*. London: Zed Books, 2013.
Dabashi, Hamid. *Iran without Borders*. London: Verso Books, 2016.
Dabashi, Hamid. *Persophilia*. Cambridge: Harvard University Press, 2015.
DuBois, W. E. B. *The Souls of Black Folk*. New York: Dover Publications, 1994.
Dufoix, Stéphane. *Diasporas*. Berkeley: University of California Press, 2008.
Favell, Adrian. "Applied Political Philosophy at the Rubicon: Will Kymlicka's 'Multicultural Citizenship'." *Ethical Theory and Moral Practice* 1:2 (1998): 255–78.
Habermas, Jurgen. *The Philosophical Discourse of Modernity*. Cambridge: MIT Press, 1987.
Habermas, Jurgen. *The Inclusion of the Other*. Cambridge: MIT Press, 1998.
Kymlicka, Will. *Liberalism, Community and Culture*. Oxford: Oxford University Press, 1989.
Kymlicka, Will. *Multicultural Citizenship*. Oxford: Oxford University Press, 1995.
Kymlicka, Will. *Multicultural Odysseys*. Oxford: Oxford University Press, 2007.
Kymlicka, Will. *Politics in the Vernacular*. New York: Oxford University Press, 2001.
Kymlicka, Will, and Norman, Wayne. *Citizenship in Diverse Societies*. Oxford: Oxford University Press, 2000.
Maira, Sunaina Marr. *Missing: Youth, Citizenship, and Empire after 9/11*. Durham: Duke University Press, 2009.
Mishra, Pankaj. *Age of Anger*. New York: Farrar, Straus and Giroux, 2017.
Naujoks, Daniel. *Migration, Citizenship, and Development*. New Delhi: Oxford University Press, 2013.
Ong, Aihwa. *Flexible Citizenship*. Durham: Duke University Press, 1999.
Peled, Yoav. "Towards a Post-Citizenship Society? A Report from the Front." *Citizenship Studies*, 11:1 (2007): 95–104.
Phillips, Anne. *Multiculturalism without Culture*. Princeton: Princeton University Press, 2007.
Pries, Ludger. *New Transactional Social Spaces: International Migration & Transnational Companies in the Early Twenty-First Century*. London: Routledge, 2013.
Radakrishnan, R. "Ethnicity in an Age of Diaspora" in Braziel, Jana Evans and Mannur, Anita (eds.). *Theorizing Diaspora*. Malden: Blackwell Publishing, 2003.
Ronkainen, Jussi Kasperi. "Mononationals, Hyphenationals, and Shadow-Nationals: Multiple Citizenship as Practice." *Citizenship Studies*, 15:2 (2011): 247–63.
Taylor, Charles. and Gutmann, Amy. (eds.). *Multiculturalism*. Princeton: Princeton University Press, 1994.
Vertovec, Steven. *Transnationalism*. London: Routledge, 2009.
Vora, Neha. *Impossible Citizens: Dubai's Indian Diaspora*. Durham: Duke University Press, 2013.

Part Four

Occupying Interstices and the Aesthetics of Dissent

11

Echoes of a Scream: US Drones and Articulations of the Houthi *Sarkha* Slogan in Yemen

Waleed F. Mahdi

> *Our villages are poor—no education, no hospitals, no roads, nor any services. Of all the progress and advances in the modern world, only these deadly missiles reached us. Such strikes ... only invoke people's indignation of both the Yemeni government and America.*
>
> —a Yemeni whose village was impacted by US drones[1]

Introduction

The second decade of the twenty-first century both rejuvenated hopes and dashed aspirations of many Yemenis in producing past due political changes without jeopardizing national unity and societal cohesion. Masses and militias poured to the public arena in 2011 and competed for rescue narratives to secure the people's demands for livelihood and dignity. The unity of their demand for regime change forced long-term president Ali Abdullah Saleh out of his position in 2012 and resulted in a National Dialogue Conference (2012–14) under President Abdrabbuh Mansur Hadi. The outcomes of the concerted efforts to secure peaceful transition were a new constitution and a proposal for a Yemeni federal governance system of six semiautonomous regions. Houthis, a sociopolitical movement in the northernmost part of Yemen primarily from Saada Governorate—a.k.a., Ansarullah (Supporters of God)—utilized their growing alliances and disrupted the process through multisite armed confrontations with various tribal, partisan, sectarian, and military forces. They eventually controlled the Yemeni capital (Sana'a) on September 21, 2014, before advancing southward to impose their control over other governorates. On March 26, 2015, the Kingdom of Saudi Arabia—with initial support from some Arab states, the United States, and the United Kingdom—intervened in the Yemeni affairs through, what Isa Blumi calls, a "Saudi/Anglo-American coalition"[2] to restore the legitimacy of President Hadi.[3] Since then and until the moment of this writing, Yemen has been locked in a bloody civil war between the de facto rule of Houthis and their local alliances, backed by quasi support from the Islamic Republic of Iran, and a loose opposition block in support of Hadi, enacted by direct Saudi and Emirati military interreferences and supported by the US military-industrial complex along with local tribal, partisan, and sectarian power players.

This chapter predates the 2011 revolutionary moment and the turbulence of its aftermath and draws attention to certain post-9/11 destabilizing conditions in Yemen that contributed to the post-2011 collapse of concerted efforts to institute peaceful transition of governance. More specifically, the chapter examines the Houthi sensational slogan *Allāhu 'akbar; al-mawt li-'Amrīkā; al-mawt li-'Isrā'īl; al-la'nah 'alā 'l-Yahūd; an-naṣr lil-'Islām*, which roughly translates as "God is Great; Death to America; Death to Israel; Damn the Jews; Victory to Islam," within the context of a growing public search for agency from implications of the US drone program in Yemen. Locally known as *sarkha* (scream), this slogan, I argue, is paradoxical because it both represents a cry for territorial autonomy from the disruptive nature of the US-led "war on terror" campaign and serves as a political tool that has fueled the Houthis' monopoly of power. Since its inception in 2002 within the context of US-led enhanced militarized presence in several Arab and Muslim countries, the *sarkha* has transcended its rhetorical value and permeated calls to violence, further transpiring along tribal, sectarian, and partisan lines in Yemen. It transpired from a rhetorical chant in religious gatherings into an activist outcry at rooftops and mosques, and, later on, a battlefield tune played while blasting homes of the rivalry. Thus, this chapter points to how the *sarkha* has directly served the Houthis' solidification of power but not without rendering the *sarkha*'s context of struggle against violations of Yemen's sovereignty meaningless.

While it is tempting to draw on the *sarkha*'s religious sentiment and interpret it as a sensational continuation of radical Islamist Sayyid Qutb's polarization of Islam and the United States, this chapter cautions against conceiving the *sarkha* as one modeled on the Qutbian conception of religious struggle.[4] Paul Berman's and Lawrence Wright's popular reflections on the relationship between Qutb's religio-political narrative and Al-Qaeda violence, problematic and reductive as they may be, cannot constitute the only primary lens through which readers in the West could view the relationship between the *sarkha* and violence in the Yemeni context.[5] Relying on existing counterterrorism literature on religious radical narratives and politically motivated violence may risk writing off the *sarkha*'s local context as simply a manifestation of a people who hate Americans, Jews, and the West. With multiple audiences in mind, the *sarkha* not only reflects a critique of American and Israeli hegemony in the Middle East, but it also reduces complex geopolitics to simple religious identifications to win support from core Houthi supporters along with the broader Yemeni public. It is worth noting that Houthis hail from a different sectarian background, that is, *Zaydi Shia*, as opposed to Qutb's Sunni background. The Houthi revolutionary mission is based on reviving *Zaidiyyah* and pushing against the Sunnification of the Zaydi lands. If anything, Houthis have targeted Salafis, both quietists and Qutb-inspired radicals, as enemies of Islam and branded their religious mission as one based on the holy book of *Qur'an* as opposed to *Hadith* (Prophet Sayings), thereby shifting away from a key pillar of Sunni religious tradition. Nonetheless, the sensational but broad nature of the *sarkha* shows an attempt to reconcile this sectarian difference, at least rhetorically.

This is not to dismiss readings of the *sarkha*'s visible manifestation of Houthi-based sectarianism. It may be true that the *sarkha* has functioned as a tool for what appears to be sectarian violence in Yemen. The omnipresent flag decorating the machinery of the Houthis' quasi-military wing renders the *sarkha* emblazoned with words and colors that emulate the Iranian post-Islamic revolution flag (Figure 11.1). In their territorial advance throughout the country, Houthis used the *sarkha* as a sound track in sectarian-influenced treacherous battlefields, political marches, and religious gatherings. Blowing up the houses of their rivalry while reciting the *sarkha* has been traumatic for many Yemenis who have struggled to understand the relationship between the slogan's components—that is, "United States," "Israel," "Jews," "Islam"— and the very Yemeni identity of their victims. However, the *sarkha* transcends this sectarian undertone as it mediates a specific Yemeni sociopolitical context that has cultivated the Houthis' broader appeals to independence from foreign interference and demands for self-control during a political transformation process that has recycled grievance, disenfranchisement, and polarization. At the core of this context is the US drone policy in the country, which has obliterated the public faith in status quo politics and shaped venues for alternative narratives. Rather than simply reading the *sarkha* as a mere indicator of Iran's influence on Houthis, the slogan could also be read as a reflection of a transcultural search for anti-imperial resistance rhetoric inspired by the Islamic Revolution in Iran. This is not to discard Iran's expansionist strategy in the Arab world or Houthis' reception of this influence; it rather confirms Houthis' localized forms of identity and agency.

Therefore, rather than basing my analysis of the *sarkha* on such an early model of radical thinking of Islam and the West as Qutb's, I build on Mark LeVine and Bryan Reynolds's definition of "theater of immediacy" as a "cultural creation and performance for an intended audience that is not merely emergent—that is, in the process of formation—but ... 'emurgent' (emergent + urgent): developing rapidly and in the context of intense sociopolitical struggle that destabilizes and even reconfigures previously dominant, congealed structures and networks of power and identity."[6]

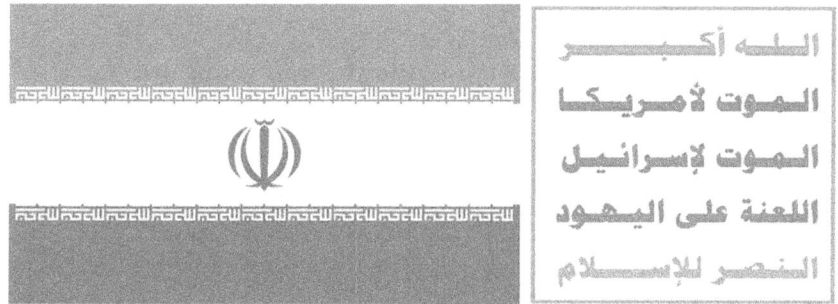

Figure 11.1 The *sarkha* slogan compared to the Iranian flag.

The Houthi *sarkha*, I argue, is emurgent because of its ability to simultaneously capture the public pulse of anxiety around US interventions in Yemen since 9/11 and forge a space for a growing consciousness (formed out of realignment of sectarian, tribal, and regional alliances) that legitimizes violence as a necessary revolutionary means toward independence and sovereignty. Hence, the theater of immediacy for the *sarkha*, as presented in this chapter, theoretically stretches at crossroads of two disrupting moments in Yemeni contemporary history, that is, *9/11* and *Arab Spring*. It promotes a postcolonial rescue narrative that critiques the post-9/11 "war on terror" articulations in US foreign policy toward Yemen and a post–Arab Spring state of lawlessness that envelops the country as a proxy for a regional sectarian conflict while pushing its citizens to coalesce around subnational and transcultural identity-based memberships.

US Drones, Yemeni Lives

The presence of tolerance in Yemen or its lack thereof is informed by the fragile nature of the political revolutionary process since February 2011, which has fractured state power through military division, sectarian unrest, tribal conflict, regional disunity, and partisan polarization. At the core of this process has been a rising anxiety around the country's sovereignty amid regional and international dictations, often guided by priorities unresponsive to local demands. In this context, the United States has advocated a paradoxical role in promoting peaceful transition of power through sustaining status quo politics in exchange for licensing its drone warfare against the threat of the Al-Qaeda in the Arabian Peninsula (AQAP). This is particularly articulated at the backdrop of a post-9/11 undefinable "war on terror" strategy that positions the United States as a prominent enemy of Yemeni indigenous rights to self-determination. The resulting sense of vulnerability among Yemenis has empowered certain localized critiques of the United States as an imperial power that does not necessarily occupy Yemeni territories but certainly employs technological advancements to dominate Yemen's skies. This "verticalization of power," to borrow Grégoire Chamayou's words, "implies a form of above-the-ground authority in which everything—every individual, every house, every street, even the smallest event"—is available for violation.[7]

Since the attack on the navy destroyer USS *Cole* on October 12, 2000, at Aden harbor, Yemen has become a site of US strategic interest for the "war on terror" campaign. Prior to its closure in 2015, the US embassy in the country operated as a front for both diplomacy and homeland security. Perhaps the launch of drone strikes would constitute the epicenter of such engagements, leading to unprecedented hard power involvement that dealt a serious a blow to the country's sense of sovereignty. In fact, it was in Yemen where the first drone strike was launched outside of a declared war zone back on November 3, 2002, which resulted in killing six al-Qaeda suspects.[8] In 2009, President Barack Obama authorized the launch of a systematic drone strike campaign in the country. It was not until June 15, 2012, when the administration disclosed its targeted killings campaign against the AQAP after consistent denial of the operations.⁹ One year later, the White House released a fact sheet laying the standards and procedures for conducting drone strikes. Five criteria were established as conditions for the authorization of lethal force: (1) "near certainty that the terrorist target is present;" (2) "near certainty that non-combatants will not be injured or killed;" (3) "an assessment that capture is not feasible at the time of the operation;" (4) "an assessment that the relevant governmental authorities in the country where action is contemplated cannot or will not effectively address the threat to US persons;" and (5) "an assessment that no other reasonable alternatives exist to effectively address the threat to US persons."¹⁰

There is an existing record that documents the inconsistencies between such drone-related standards and real-life practices.¹¹ The drone program has primarily relied on knowledge deficiency about Yemen's local complexities, flawed conflation between local resistance groups and groups sworn to threaten US homeland security, and outright faulty intelligence data. Despite emphasis on "near certainty" of no civilian casualty, the drone program has also placed a heavy toll on Yemeni civilians. On July 1, 2016, the Office of the Director of National Intelligence released official statistics of 473 strikes outside areas of active hostilities in the period January 20, 2009, and December 31, 2015, primarily in Pakistan, Yemen, and Somalia. The report estimated combatant deaths in the range of 2372–2581 and noncombatant deaths in the range of only 64–116.¹² The gross understatement of civilian causalities in addition to establishing statistical ranges in reporting deaths both confirmed critics' skepticism of the program's moral legitimacy and operational efficiency.¹³ On March 6, 2018, President Donald Trump restricted this move for transparency by issuing an executive order that banned the release of information about drone operations.¹⁴

Al-Ma'ajalah Massacre (December 17, 2009) was one of the earliest examples that articulated the indiscriminate nature of US strikes in Yemen. Tomahawk cruise missiles hit a camp in al-Ma'ajalah village in Abyan governorate, which resulted in the death of at least forty-five civilians, including fifteen women and twenty-two children. Yemeni activist Farea al-Muslimi recounted the traumatic nature of the incident in a testimony at the US Senate Judiciary Subcommittee on Constitution, Civil Rights & Human Rights, "The tribal leader and others tried to rescue the victims, but the bodies were so dismasted that it was impossible to differentiate between those of children, women, and their animals."¹⁵ The incident shocked the Yemeni community whose government initially rejected any US role in the attacks, but later on revealed that the operation was the spark of a momentum of a new war tactic adopted by the Obama administration as the most practical and least costly. *WikiLeaks* revealed messages from the ex-president of Yemen, Ali Saleh, demanding the US government to deny any active engagement in the waged war against the AQAP in an attempt to assure the public about the sovereignty of their state.¹⁶

In his speech on drone policy, President Obama acknowledged the civilian causality of the program:

> It is a hard fact that US strikes have resulted in civilian casualties, a risk that exists in every war. And for the families of those civilians, no words or legal construct

can justify their loss. For me, and those in my chain of command, those deaths will haunt us as long as we live, just as we are haunted by the civilian casualties that have occurred throughout conventional fighting in Afghanistan and Iraq.[17]

This important recognition of civilian loss was, however, presented in a framework that projected the United States as a humanitarian power set to save Americans and Yemenis alike. "To do nothing in the face of terrorist networks," President Obama argued, "would invite far more civilian casualties—not just in our cities at home and our facilities abroad, but also in the very places like Sana'a and Kabul and Mogadishu where terrorists seek a foothold."[18]

President Obama gained support from President Hadi, who praised the drone technology for its effectiveness.[19] Even Yemeni foreign minister, Abu Bakr al-Qirbi, described the drone strikes as a "necessary evil" and a "very limited affair."[20] The Yemeni parliament and public, however, rejected these views. On December 15, 2013, the Yemeni parliament issued a non-binding vote "to stop" violations of "Yemeni airspace" and stressed "the importance of preserving innocent civilian lives against any attack and maintaining Yemeni sovereignty."[21] This political measure was significant in its symbolic gesture to the disenchanted public. "I believe that America is testing its lethal inventions in our poor villages because [it] cannot afford to do so at any place where human life has value," once complained a Yemeni whose village was impacted by the drone program, "Here we are without value."[22]

A Human Rights Watch report investigating the drone attack of a wedding procession in Rad`a (December 12, 2013), which resulted in the death of twelve men and injury of fifteen others, illustrates the indiscriminate nature of this drone program.[23] Four Hellfire missiles hit a convoy of eleven vehicles during a counterterrorism operation in rural Yemen. Although initially celebrated as a successful strike against terrorists, ground reports verified that the procession consisted of civilians participating in a tribal event. Most civilian causalities in Yemen have been in part a result of such human errors in identifying potential targets; other cases are due to a double-tap practice that requires operators to follow the strike with another one to verify the elimination of the target, leading to the randomly killing civilian responders.

Echoes of the US strikes prompted the proliferation of resistance narratives against US violations of Yemen's sovereignty. Youth-based efforts were peaceful in nature and were geared into political and artistic advocacy. In the aforementioned congressional testimony, for instance, the US-educated al-Muslimi captured the public frustration with the US paradoxical approach to Yemen by reflecting on the contradictory nature of his own personal experience as a witness to hovering drones. "I was torn between this great country that I love [US]," he stated, "and the drone above my head that could not differentiate between me and some AQAP militants." Reflecting on the impact of drone strikes on Yemeni civilians, he continued:

> The drone strikes are the face of America to many Yemenis. I have spoken to many victims of US drone strikes like a mother in Ja'ar who had to identify her innocent eighteen-year-old son's body through a video in a stranger's cellphone; or that father in Shakrah who held his four-and-six-year-old children as they died in his arms.[24]

Mwatana for Human Rights is another important example of youth-based advocacy that has provided local-based reporting that has been critical of the US drone program.²⁵ Youth-based efforts have also advanced through art. Murad Subay's "12 Hours" graffiti campaign, for instance, invited fellow Yemeni graffiti artists to visually capture Yemenis' sufferings.²⁶ Perhaps the most iconic graffiti depicted was the one in which a little girl completed writing with her blood a question (in Arabic and English): Why did you kill my family? (Figure 11.2). This question gains more symbolic power if juxtaposed with Americans' post-9/11 most asked question "why did they hate us?," which rhetorically guided the US "war on terror" campaign.

Militants rushed to promote a rescue narrative that foregrounded an outcry against the intertwined deployment of US hard power and complicity of Yemeni ruling elite. The AQAP advanced a simplified response narrative that advocated violence. In February 2014, for example, their media outlet al-Malahim released Rad al-Idwan 3 (Repulsion of Aggression 3), a behind-the-scenes footage of four of the organization's 2013 coordinated attacks against several local military and security compounds, believed to host operation rooms for the US drone program. These were the Second Regional Military Command area in Mukala'a, Hadramout (September 30), the 111 Military Camp in Ahwar, Abyan (October 18), the Defense Ministry Compound

Figure 11.2 "Why did you kill my family" graffiti © Murad Subay.

in Sana'a (December 5), and the General Security building in Khour Maksar, Aden (December 31). The video highlights the impact of US drones on Yemeni civilians and promotes "martyrdom," a rhetorical tool of organized violence in the AQAP's literature, as Yemenis' salvation against the United States and its Yemeni allies.

Unlike the AQAP's one-dimensional critique, the Houthis' critique of the US role in Yemen invested in mobilizing the public to challenge perceived signs of Western hegemony in the country. Even though the movement has eventually failed in unifying the country as a result of short-sighted planning (e.g., 2015 coup) and inability to embrace pluralist politics (leading to civil war backed by Saudi-Iranian contestations), their outcry for sovereignty played an important role in their transformation from a socio-religious entity battling state atrocities into a well-organized political force that disrupted the country's post-2011 transition. The following section examines the Houthis' critique in light of their *sarkha*.

The Articulations of the Houthi *Sarkha*

The rapid disintegration of the 2011 revolutionary momentum in Yemen from concerted attempts to safeguard the political transition toward pluralism into a de facto constitutional declaration by Houthis was wrapped in multiple layers of disorder and violence. At the core of this transformation, Yemeni public anxieties around their country's sovereignty were constantly challenged by top-down interventions from US, UN, and regional power brokers. To codify this public anxiety, Houthi affiliates (fighters and politicians) advanced a rescue narrative that was already developing prior to 2011. This narrative sought to reclaim state agency through embattling the ruling elites, often presented as proxy agents to foreign interests. Key to the Houthis' efforts was their *sarkha*, which served as a recruiting slogan that advocated for a postcolonial grassroots religious militancy by framing the United States along with Israel as part of a Judeo-Christian composite dedicated to undermining Islam and Muslims.

The *sarkha* originated in a lecture titled *As-sarkha fi wajh al-mustakbreen* (A Scream in the Face of the Arrogant), delivered by the Houthi movement's founder Hussein Badreddin al-Houthi in 2002. In this lecture, al-Houthi offered the moral justification for the slogan by informing his followers that Islam and Muslims were "at the center of grave conspiracies woven by America and Israel." He reviewed the impact of the US-led "war on terror" on the lives of Muslims across the globe and inspired the audience to embrace the *sarkha* as a rejection of US hegemony.[27] Subsequently, the sensational *sarkha* rose as an empowering slogan for Houthi supporters, prompting more resistance against Saleh's US-backed government. Saleh's government perceived the Houthi slogan not as a demand for sovereignty but as a threatening local manifestation of Iran's increasing influence in the Arab world. The government ignored the root causes of the Houthi movement, that is, years of disenfranchisement, isolation, and disruption to the status quo tribal order in Houthis' stronghold governorate of Saada. The result was six wars against them in the period 2004–10, resulting in the death of the leader and the emergence of his younger brother's leadership, Abdul-Malik Bedreddin al-Houthi.[28] Marieke Brandt, author of one of the most comprehensive works on Houthis, locates these wars within a multilayered local context informed by several elements: post-1962 civil war "shifting internal power balances, the uneven distribution of resources and political participation, the accumulation of mutual grievances, [and] growing sectarianism and tribalisation."[29]

The government's violent approach against Houthis and openness to US violations of Yemen's skies only solidified the slogan's tenacity, which received much circulation through the Houthis' utilization of several communication tools in the country. Since mosques constituted a very critical popular culture site in the Yemeni culture, there were many accounts of Houthi members disrupting mosques in various parts of the country by abruptly shouting the *sarkha*. Houthi supporters were encouraged to yell their *sarkha* out loud from the rooftop of their houses. The message also disseminated through Houthi media outlets such as al-Maseerah (The March) television channel and *Nabth al-Masar* (*Pulse of the Path*) newspaper as well as alternative media tools, for example, internet websites www.ansarullah.com—which was later hacked and suspended—blogs, Facebook, Twitter, and YouTube. Both traditional and alternative media have served the movement organize their literature—lectures, statements, press conferences, poems, religious songs, *zwamil* (tribal chants), writings, and so on. The *sarkha*, in a sense, was a way for people to identify with Houthis but had a far more empowering appeal when screamed as it enabled individuals to personally participate in the rejection of status quo politics.

Although there is no immediate link between the origination of the *sarkha* and the US drone program, the premise of the *sarkha*'s anti-US and Israeli hegemony draws from popular sentiments at the core of Yemeni collective memory, most readily rendered through the Israeli-Palestinian conflict. In an interview with Hezbollah's television network al-Manar, on the International Day of Solidarity with the Palestinian people (November 29, 2013), the Houthi leader explained his movement's stance toward Israel and the United States. He criticized the success of imperial powers in disorienting Muslims from the Palestinian cause. This success, he added, was enabled by Arab and Muslim collaborating regimes that subjected media outlets, cultural products, educational curricula, and religious discourses to the service of the West.[30] In his response to a question about the Muslims' responsibility toward the Palestinian issue, al-Houthi reiterated the tenets of the movement's critique of America. He stressed the possibility of supporting the Palestinian cause through a number of measures that included utilizing media in "intensively spreading awareness" about the cause through feeding the public with slogans that denounce Zionism and America as two powers that have incurred aggression on Palestinians. The slogans, he argued, will "feed hatred" and "grow awareness" and the "feeling of responsibility" toward a firm stand on the issue. Hence, the *sarkha* could be understood in this context to serve as a recruiting instrument that transcends its rhetorical value and promises a uniting purpose for the public to rally around.

In the same interview, al-Houthi continued to argue that slogans could not operate in a vacuum. He called for enacting boycott measures against American and Israeli products. A Houthi supporter, Salah al-Shurqubi, captured the essence of this message, which had been central to the movement's demands since its inception, in a short clip titled al-Muqata'a (The Boycott, 2012). The clip starts with a screenshot of a list of American and Israeli brand products. Then, it features a Yemeni pushing a wheelbarrow to the market to buy American products, such as white flour, honey, and Coca-Cola. On his way, he reads a Houthi-endorsed road sign that roughly translates as "Boycott American and Israeli products" but chooses to completely ignore it. The camera moves to project interconnected images of the purchasing process of American brands and the arming of a drone at an American base with hellfire missiles. On his way back home, he stops by the board sign to catch his breath. As he starts drinking a Coca-Cola can, a drone fires the missile, the person falls dead while regretfully pointing at the boycott message. The clip functions within a continuum of Houthi critique that locates consumption of neoliberalism as a sign of complicity and acceptance of US aggressions against Yemenis.

Houthis have circulated fiery sermons, political speeches, and media reports denouncing targeted killing raids that claimed the lives of many civilians and violated Yemen's sovereignty. Their literature shows efforts to debunk US claims of liberty and freedom by showing how drone strikes impact Yemenis in populated areas, markets, refugee camps, and villages. During the GCC-brokered national dialogue process, Houthi representatives abstained from attending meetings involving the US ambassador Gerald Feierstein. In a *Yemen Times* interview with Ali al-Emad, one of the young representatives of the movement in the national dialogue shared the reason:

> We think that the US administration doesn't respect Yemenis and is managing everything in Yemen. The US ambassador wanted to hold the lead in the Yemeni scene ... Even his statement regarding military performance and army reorganizing indicates that he controls everything in Yemen.[31]

Al-Emad's assessment of the American ambassador role in Yemen echoes a public anxiety around the US visibility in the political transformation process given its "war on terror" investment in the country.

Al-Emad's rejection of the American ambassador was not because Houthis were necessarily uncompromising in their acceptance of American political interference. The rejection seemed rather mobilized by a sentiment at the time that swept US embassies in Egypt, Libya, Tunisia, and Yemen—to only name Arab Spring revolutionary spaces at the time—when they were swarmed by angry protests, in some cases resulting in acts of vandalism and even violence.[32] This was a result of a mixed sense of frustration and anger because of *Innocence of Muslims* (2012), a film that advanced denigrating images of the prophet of Islam along the lines of perversion and sadism.[33] "It seems that inviting the ambassador to the meeting was just to restore him after the American-made film mocking Prophet Mohammed," al-Emad stated. Houthis excelled in cultivating narratives that fed sensational perceptions of the United States in religious terms. The totality of post-9/11 encounters with Muslims in the United States and elsewhere fed a popularized critique of the United States as a neocolonial entity, bent on, what President Bush once called, a "crusade" against a conflated conception of Islam and terrorism. Using religious diction in describing the US "war on terror" was key in resurrecting a trauma in Islamic collective memory of Western "Christian" aggressions. The religious content of the Houthi *sarkha* became especially potent in such a context.

The charged nature of the *sarkha*, the Houthi leadership insisted, was merely rhetorical as no imminent threats were ever directed against the US presence in the country. In a response to a question whether the United States considered Houthis as an enemy, US ambassador Gerald Feierstein himself affirmed that they only want to "appear as … being hostile to the United States" and that United States was "never against" them; "we never agreed that they support terrorism," he added.[34] The Houthi slogan, for instance, was spotted nowhere around the US embassy on September 17, 2008, when militants disguised as soldiers detonated two car bombs during the Holy month of Ramadan, leading to the death of sixteen and injury of six Yemenis; an unknown Islamic Jihad group claimed responsibility.[35] Signs of the Houthi *sarkha* were not also traced on September 11, 2012, when hundreds of protestors clashed with US embassy security forces, smashed windows, burned cars, and broke through the main gate. The political instability in Sana'a formed a critical factor in producing a less-friendly environment for local law enforcement forces to intervene at the time. The attacks transcended grievances against the *Innocence of Muslims* film and offered the opportunity for extreme reaction based on growing grievances against the US "war on terror" conduct.[36] The attacks marked not only the eleventh anniversary of the tragic attacks of September 11, 2001, but also served as a manifestation of the US "war on terror" tactics in the Arab and Muslim worlds. They constituted a post–Arab Spring critical moment that called for a serious interrogation of the politics surrounding Arabs' and Muslims' anti-US grievances.

Despite the *sarkha*'s semantic calls for violence as a means to realize the movement's message, Houthis opted to utilize its sentimental value to rally the public around their social, political, and even religious directives. During the three-month negotiations in Kuwait between the Yemeni parties of the conflict in 2016, according to an *Al-Quds al-Arabi* report, Houthi representatives issued "a sincere apology" for the slogan during a meeting with the US Under Secretary of State for Political Affairs Thomas Shannon. The apology justified that the *sarkha* was for "domestic consumption as a means to attract support in the streets and create a common cause between their supporters to keep them united."[37] Critiquing the United States has its own mobilizing currency that Houthis have managed to utilize effectively. In his critique of the US role in promoting democracy in Yemen, al-Emad delivered a message that carried a sense of skepticism and anger that reverberated across the Yemeni society and offered domestic sense to the slogan's circulation:

> Each one has to obtain an attitude toward any colonial country that doesn't want stability in his country. We know that the US pays lip service to democracy, but they are against it and against stability in the country. It is known that the US brought great problems to all countries it set foot in. Explosions and violence in any country coincides with the presence of Americans. Therefore, what is said is only the opposite of what is done.[38]

The chief editor of the Houthi newspaper *Nabth al-Masar*, Osama Sari, published a series of reports that capitalized on this sentiment and questioned the role of US marines in Yemen. In a report titled "al-Marines al-Amreeki and al-laiyali al-hamra'a" (American Marines and Romantic Nights), he published photos and names of US marines dancing with Yemeni women and state officials in one of the halls of Sheraton hotel—the primary residence of US embassy personnel in Sana'a at the time. Sari contextualized the photos in a cultural framework that contrasted American and Yemeni social, cultural, and moral codes and values. He explained:

> The danger of American military presence in Yemen lies in its degenerate and imperial nature that does not offer compassion and mercy in treating women, men, children, and elderly. Its violations target Yemeni family honor. They are people without values, morals, or principles. The Americans came to Yemen to implement one project filled with hatred towards every Arab and Muslim. They cannot be friends, and they do not wish us goodness and prosperity. The information we have about how the marines rape our women and disrespect our families is but a microcosm of a future of more rape and assault on our honor. This will continue unless all Yemenis wake up and angrily scream in the face of everyone who allowed for our land, honor, and dignity to be desecrated.[39]

Sari later accused the US embassy of threatening his life as a result of his reporting, but there was no substantial evidence. The coverage was sensational and polarizing in its depiction of the US embassy as a sponsor of both Yemeni moral degeneration and the AQAP. This propagandist antagonism to the US presence in Yemen may not necessarily have reflected a Houthi institutionalized interest in driving Americans out of the country, but it certainly touched on one of Yemenis' primary demands, that is, integrity and self-control.

Albeit to a limited degree, Houthis capitalized on Yemenis' rising outrage against the US paradoxical policy in Yemen, that is, promoting peaceful transition of power while conducting targeted killings. Perhaps, the most outstanding example of the public outrage that showcased the Houthis' politicization efforts could be traced in the massive rally organized on May 24, 2013, less than four months before the Houthis' armed control of the capital (Figure 11.3). The rally was a reaction to a reported increase in Marines presence in Yemen at the time. Organized under the slogan "No for Government that Grants Entry to American Marines," the rally crossed many streets in the Yemeni capital raising banners that codified their rejection of US hard power: "No for violating sovereignty," "Yemeni military cannot remain silent," "American marines are danger to Yemen and its people," "Down with a regime granting entry to American marines," "May eyes turn blind that witness Marines invasion of Yemeni homes and do nothing," and "A government granting entry to American Marines does not represent the people and their will." The marchers chanted slogans like "you arrogant American, my country is not for imperialists," "Oh! American, get out," and "You invader, get out." The rally echoed the Houthis' political investment in rallying the public through rhetorical appeals for sovereignty and critiques of US hegemony.

Figure 11.3 "No to a Government that Grants Entry to American Marines" Rally, May 24, 2013.

Conclusion

The *sarkha* has been described as a "nihilistic slogan" because of its message of violence, division, disorder, and chaos.[40] In pursuit of empowerment in the immediate aftermath of the 2011 Yemeni revolution, Houthis advanced a twofold policy. They engaged in the political process by contributing to national reconciliation efforts while nurturing power on the ground that resulted in their initial control of their stronghold governorate Sa'ada along with parts of neighboring governorates, for example, Haja (access to the Red Sea), al-Jawf (promising oil reserve), and 'Amran (bordering the capital), before launching their nation-wide mission that laid the foundations for the contemporary turmoil. The solidification of their power eventually sidelined political reconciliation attempts in favor of claiming total control of the country in an increasingly sectarian-based polarizing environment. This process transformed the movement from a weak entity embattling the state into an organized force with well-structured public relations outlets addressing cultural and political issues at the local, regional, and global scales.

At the core of Houthis' rise to power has been their ability to present an interplaying critique of the US hegemony in the region (supporting Israel, invasion of Iraq, drone warfare, etc.) and of the complicity of its allied regimes (e.g., Saudi Arabia, United Arab Emirates, Hadi government). Alongside this process, the *sarkha* preserved the group's autonomy but did not gain Yemenis' full support for two main reasons. First, its message is both polarizing and sectarian. Second, Houthis have developed a pattern of declaring the *sarkha* in the immediate aftermath of winning local wars or destroying houses, leading fellow Yemenis to associate it with the Houthis' organized violence in the country. The *sarkha*, even though it helped Houthis with their immediate recruiting objectives, has eventually lost its desired effects as it now remains an identity marker of a particular sociopolitical and religious community in northern Yemen vying for power at the cost of the country's own instability, and ironically, sovereignty. The civil war conditions have certainly prescribed the failure of the *sarkha* in rallying Yemeni social and cultural politics behind its resistance implications.

Notes

1. Interview with Mohammed Nasser al-Jarraah, Silat al-Jarraah village (May 31, 2013); as quoted in Singh, "Death by Drone," 75.
2. Blumi, *Destroying Yemen*, 2.
3. The coalition comprises the Gulf Cooperation Council countries (GCC) except Oman. Other Arab countries were Egypt, Morocco, Jordan, and Sudan. In 2017, Qatar left the coalition. In 2019, Morocco suspended its participation.
4. The Qutbian conception of religious struggle is spelled out in Qutb's multivolume interpretation of the Qur'an in *Fi Zilal al-Qur'an*. Also see Qutb's critique of the United States in "The America I Have Seen" (1951).
5. See Berman, "The Philosopher of Islamic Terror;" also, Wright, *The Looming Tower*.
6. LeVine and Reynolds, "Theater of Immediacy," 62.
7. Chamayou, *A Theory of the Drone*, 54.
8. "CIA 'killed al-Qaeda suspects' in Yemen," *BBC*.
9. Entous, "US Acknowledges Its Drone Strikes."
10. Office of the Press Secretary, "Fact Sheet."
11. See Benjamin, *Drone Warfare*; Scahill, *Dirty Wars*; Varisco, "Drone Strikes in the War on Terror"; and Singh, "Death by Drone."
12. Scherr, "US Counterterrorism Strikes."
13. Shane's "Drone Strikes Statistics Answer Few Questions, and Raise Many."
14. Watson, "Trump Nixes Public Report on Civilians Killed by Drone Strikes."
15. Al-Muslimi, "Testimony at Drone Wars Senate Committee Hearing."
16. Benson's "US Role in Yemen Covered Up by Its President, WikiLeaks File Reveals."
17. "Obama's Speech on Drone Policy," *New York Times*.

18 Ibid.
19 Shane, "Yemen's Leader, President Hadi, Praises US Drone Strikes."
20 "Yemeni Parliament in Non-Binding Vote against Drone Attacks," *Reuters*.
21 As reported by the Yemeni state news agency SABA; see "Yemeni Parliament in Non-Binding Vote against Drone Attacks," *Reuters*.
22 Interview with Moqbel Abdullah Ali al-Jarraah, Silat al-Jarraah village (May 31, 2013); as quoted in Singh, "Death by Drone," 96.
23 "A Wedding that Became a Funeral" *Human Rights Watch*.
24 Al-Muslimi, "Testimony at Drone Wars Senate Committee Hearing."
25 Mwatana Organization for Human Rights: http://mwatana.org.
26 To learn about Murad Subay's graffiti campaigns, visit https://muradsubay.com/campaigns/12-hours.
27 Al-Houthi, "As-sarkha fi wajh al-mustakbreen."
28 Six wars: (June–September 2004), (March–May 2005), (November 2005–early 2006), (January–June 2007), (March–July 2008), and (August 2009–February 2010).
29 Brandt, *Tribes and Politics in Yemen*, 2.
30 "An Interview with Abdul-Malik Bedreddin al-Houthi," *Manar TV*.
31 Al-Samei, "Houthi Leader Ali Al-Emad to the Yemen Times."
32 The Benghazi attacks in Libya were the most notorious, claiming the lives of American ambassador J. Christopher Stevens and Foreign Service officer Sean Smith, and sparking the Benghazi controversy in Washington, DC.
33 The film was written and produced by Nakoula Basseley Nakoula. Short trailers were released in YouTube two months prior to the embassy attacks.
34 "Asharq al-Awsat Interview: US Envoy to Yemen Gerald M. Feierstein," *Asharq Al-Awsat*.
35 Worth, "10 Are Killed in Bombings at Embassy in Yemen."
36 Ghobari, Mohammed. "Yemeni Protesters Storm US Embassy Compound in Sanaa."
37 El-Bar, "Houthis Apologise to US over Use of 'Death to America' Slogan."
38 Al-Samei, "Houthi Leader Ali Al-Emad to the Yemen Times."
39 Sari, "Al-Marines Yahtafil bi Ihtilal al-Yemen."
40 Al-Daghshi, *Al-Huthyoun wa mustaqbalhum al-askari wa al-siyasi wa al-tarbawi*, 163–71.

References

"A Wedding That Became a Funeral: US Drone Attack on Marriage Procession in Yemen." Human Rights Watch, February 19, 2014, https://www.hrw.org/report/2014/02/19/wedding-became-funeral/us-drone-attack-marriage-procession-yemen.

"An Interview with Abdul-Malik Bedreddin al-Houthi." *Manar TV*, November 29, 2013, https://www.youtube.com/watch?v=TxSNNZzVLs4.

Al-Daghshi, Ahmed Mohammed. *Al-Huthyoun wa mustaqbalhum al-askari wa al-siyasi wa al-tarbawi*. Doha: The Forum for Arab and International Relations, 2013.

Al-Houthi, Hussein Badreddin. "As-sarkha fi wajh al-mustakbreen." Thagafaqurania, January 20, 2014 (original lecture on January 19, 2002), https://www.youtube.com/watch?v=U-SgKYLcEYs.

Al-Muslimi, Farea. "Testimony at Drone Wars Senate Committee Hearing." *C-Span*, April 23, 2013, https://www.c-span.org/video/?c4444260/farea-al-muslimi-testimony-dronewars-senate-committee-hearing.

Al-Samei, Mohammed. "Houthi Leader Ali Al-Emad to the Yemen Times," *Yemen Times*, October 11, 2012.

"Asharq al-Awsat Interview: US Envoy to Yemen Gerald M. Feierstein." *Asharq Al-Awsat*, July 8, 2012, http://english.aawsat.com/2012/07/article55241431/asharq-al-awsat-interview-us-envoy-to-yemen-gerald-m-feierstein.

Benjamin, Medea. *Drone Warfare: Killing by Remote Control*. London: Verso, 2013.

Benson, Pam. "US Role in Yemen Covered Up by Its President, WikiLeaks File Reveals." *CNN*, November 29, 2010, http://www.cnn.com/2010/US/11/28/wikileaks.yemen.

Berman, Paul. "The Philosopher of Islamic Terror." *New York Times Magazine*, March 23, 2003, https://www.nytimes.com/2003/03/23/magazine/the-philosopher-of-islamic-terror.html.

Blumi, Isa. *Destroying Yemen: What Chaos in Arabia Tells Us about the World*. Oakland: University of California Press, 2018.

Brandt, Marieke. *Tribes and Politics in Yemen: A History of the Houthi Conflict*. Oxford: Oxford University Press, 2017.

"CIA 'Killed al-Qaeda Suspects' in Yemen." *BBC News*, November 5, 2002, http://news.bbc.co.uk/2/hi/2402479.stm.

Chamayou, Grégoire. *A Theory of the Drone*. Translated by Janet Lloyd. New York: The New Press, 2015.

El-Bar, Karim. "Houthis Apologise to US over Use of 'Death to America' slogan." *Middle East Eye*, June 29, 2016, http://www.middleeasteye.net/news/death-america-no-more-houthis-apologise-us-controversial-slogan-1908461332.

Entous, Adam. "US Acknowledges Its Drone Strikes." *Wall Street Journal*, June 15, 2012, http://www.wsj.com/articles/SB10001424052702303410404577468981916011456.

Ghobari, Mohammed. "Yemeni Protesters Storm US Embassy Compound in Sanaa." *Reuters*, September 13, 2012, http://www.reuters.com/article/us-yemen-usa-embassy-idUSBRE88C0AM20120913. https://www.hsdl.org/c/u-s-counterterrorism-strikes-combatants-and-civilians-by-the-numbers.

LeVine, Mark and Bryan Reynolds. "Theater of Immediacy: Performance Activism and Art in the Arab Spring." In *Islam and Popular Culture*, edited by Karin Van Nieuwkerk, Mark LeVine, and Martin Stokes, 58–767. Austin: University of Texas Press, 2016.

"Obama's Speech on Drone Policy." *New York Times*, May 23, 2013, http://www.nytimes.com/2013/05/24/us/politics/transcript-of-obamas-speech-on-drone-policy.html.

Office of the Press Secretary. "Fact Sheet: US Policy Standards and Procedures for the Use of Force in Counterterrorism Operations Outside the United States and Areas of Active Hostilities." The White House, May 23, 2013, https://obamawhitehouse.archives.gov/the-press-office/2013/05/23/fact-sheet-us-policy-standards-and-procedures-use-force-counterterrorism.

Qutb, Sayyid. "'The America I Have Seen': In the Scale of Human Values." In *America in an Arab Mirror: Images of America in Arabic Travel Literature, 1668 to 9/11 and Beyond*, edited by Kamal Abdel-Malek and Mouna el-Kahla, 9–27. New York: Palgrave Macmillan, 2000.

Qutb, Sayyid. *Fi Zilal al-Qur'an* (In the Shade of the Qur'an). UK: Islamic Foundation, 2009. Originally published in 1951–65.

Sari, Osama. "Al-Marines Yahtafil bi Ihtilal al-Yemen." *Saada Press*, October 11, 2013, http://www.saadahpress.net/news/news-16154.htm.
Scahill, Jeremy. *Dirty Wars: The World Is a Battlefield*. New York: Nation Books, 2013.
Scherr, Kendall. "US Counterterrorism Strikes: Combatants and Civilians by the Numbers." Office of the Director of National Intelligence, Homeland Security Digital Library, July 12, 2016.
Shane, Scott. "Drone Strikes Statistics Answer Few Questions, and Raise Many." *New York Times*, July 3, 2016, http://www.nytimes.com/2016/07/04/world/middleeast/drone-strike-statistics-answer-few-questions-and-raise-many.html?_r=0.
Shane, Scott. "Yemen's Leader, President Hadi, Praises US Drone Strikes." *New York Times*, September 29, 2012, https://www.nytimes.com/2012/09/29/world/middleeast/yemens-leader-president-hadi-praises-us-drone-strikes.html.
Singh, Amrit. "Death by Drone: Civilian Harm Caused by US Targeted Killings in Yemen." Open Society Justice Initiative and Mwatana Organization for Human Rights, 2015.
Varisco, Daniel Martin. "Drone Strikes in the War on Terror: The Case of Post-Arab-Spring Yemen." Gulf Studies Center, December 1, 2015.
Watson, Kathryn. "Trump Nixes Public Report on Civilians Killed by Drone Strikes." *CBS News*, March 6, 2019, https://www.cbsnews.com/news/trump-signs-executive-order-canceling-public-reports-on-civilian-drone-strike-deaths.
Worth, Robert F. "10 Are Killed in Bombings at Embassy in Yemen." *New York Times*, September 17, 2008, http://www.nytimes.com/2008/09/18/world/middleeast/18yemen.html.
Wright, Lawrence. *The Looming Tower: Al-Qaeda and the Road to 9/11*. New York: Vintage Books, 2006.
"Yemeni Parliament in Non-Binding Vote against Drone Attacks." *Reuters*, December 15, 2013, https://www.reuters.com/article/us-yemen-drones/yemeni-parliament-in-nonbinding-vote-against-drone-attacks-idUSBRE9BE0EN20131215.

12

Interstitial Space of the Art of Protest

Hamid Dabashi

In May 2015, I was invited to Freie Universität Berlin for a keynote on the art of protest, in which I had been interested since the Green Movement in Iran (2009) and the rise of the Arab Spring (2011).[1] In my initial communications with my hosts regarding this lecture, I proposed the title "From the Sublime to the Ridiculous: The Art of Protest, Protesting the Arts," by which I had intended to speak of protest as an act of political defiance against the banality of evil taking place somewhere between two aesthetic exercises—one *defying* and the other *fortifying* the status quo. To do so, I had intended to dwell on two films, Charlie Chaplin's *The Great Dictator* (1940) and Sacha Cohen's *The Dictator* (2012), thereby exploring the contradictory function of art as political gesture—one that is enabling by being ennobling, the other by being astonishingly racist and jejune. How did we get from Charlie Chaplin to Sacha Cohen, and when people laugh at Cohen, what does that laughter mean today?

But in the time between that initial communication and my going to Berlin, I was increasingly drawn to the question of the *space* between forms and genres of art, less about the work of art itself and more about where (the place, the space) it is installed, staged, screened, exhibited. I was directed toward this space by the magnitude of counterrevolutionary forces now mobilized by Saudi Arabia and its allies to reverse the course of history and abort the open-ended horizons of Arab revolutions. Where do artists and their audiences dwell and reside, stage and show? The shift was from temporal—the distance between Chaplin and Cohen—to spatial: the differential of power where things mean and can mean even more.

Deferred Defiance

I became interested in space because what happened in the course of Arab revolutions, especially during the fateful year of 2010, was something to behold and remember, theoretically to allow to unfold and historically to find ways to sustain for posterity. The successive events in Tunisia, Egypt, Libya, Yemen, Bahrain, and then Syria were crafting a new vision of our world in which the collapse of dictatorships was no longer sufficient—Arabs and Muslims were dreaming impossible dreams. The dynamics of revolutionary and counterrevolutionary forces were measuring each other out, maneuvering in and out of each other. Something serious had happened, and that something was finding its way into the realm of creative imagination, into art, literature, and drama, agitating subversive vistas of new horizons. How were we to measure or even grasp such changes? Where were we to archive them?

A major site of contemporary Arab and Muslim art, for example, is the Mathaf, the Arab Museum of Modern Art in Doha, Qatar. What happens to contemporary art—art of protest in particular, of which there are exquisite samples in the permanent collection at Mathaf—when the very existence of Qatar is drawn into the Saudi counterrevolutionary mobilization in Yemen or the pernicious sectarianism in Syria? Has not the art, including the art of protest, become actively, aggressively, violently museumized, neutralized, made irrelevant to the site of revolutionary mobilization? What happens when Qatar itself, as a sovereign nation, becomes the target of an all-out embargo by its own Arab neighbors. In what particular ways can we continue to talk about the "Arab World" or an "Arab Museum?" If Mathaf, as one particularly poignant space for contemporary and modern art, is to represent the totality of the Arab world in terms of its artistic production, to what degree is that space implicated or allowed to transcend its location in a transnational politics of hostility and envy, of rancor and resentment? Can the "Arab world," as a *world*, be allowed a space for an aesthetic intuition of its own transcendence?

My thinking began to be drawn toward the difference between the sublime and the ridiculous, namely between Charlie Chaplin and Sacha Cohen, but eventually shifted to the spatial dimension of that and all other forms of differential modalities precisely because I thought we are in a transitional period in our current history. My concern was no longer about the Hegelian difference between a thesis (the sublimity of Charlie Chaplin's art) and its antithesis (the ridiculous buffoonery of Sacha Cohen) but about the power differential that enables *a deferred defiance*. It was here that I was drawn to the *interstitial* space on which works of protest art are generated and thereby manage to stage a deferred defiance. We were, and have remained, in a revolutionary mood—but that revolutionary mood was not contingent on a revolutionary success such as the ascendency of a socialist state or nationalist ideology. Let me explain this in some detail.

I have introduced and cultivated the idea of deferred defiance in two previous books—my book on Shi'ism as a religion of protest and my book on the Arab Spring as the end of postcoloniality—by which I have intended a thematic reversal of the Freudian notion of deferred obedience in cultures that have killed their primordial fathers, relocating the nexus of command and obedience on cultural sites that keep killing their primogenital children.[2] The current counterrevolutionary mobilization in the Arab and Muslim world, evident in the murderous gang of ISIS domination of the Syrian and Iraqi scene down to the Saudi invasion of first Bahrain and then Yemen, mark a moment when our reflection on the art of protest must necessarily find that effective space where we can think and theorize an art that opposes this counterrevolutionary violence. But the key question is how and on what premise. In the emerging Arab and

Muslim art of protest dwells a delayed defiance, an act of postponed subversiveness, merely suggested here but delivered elsewhere, and in between the here and there is where the art of protests hangs its contemporary significance.

Location of the Art of Protest

Where are the artist and her or his work of art located? Where is the space in which the art of protest takes place, performs itself—art galleries, biennales, film festivals, museums, university campuses, or refugee camps? A sustained politics and aesthetics of dislocation inform our reading of the art of protest; we do not know where we are or even what we are looking at when we look at a picture of the Chinese artist Ai Weiwei posing as the dead Syrian child Aylan Kurdi.[3] Dislocation of Palestinian, Afghan, Iraqi, and Syrian refugees, their dispossession and displacement, is the space upon which the art of protest is dreamed or performed. Palestinian *keys* with no doors left to open must remain the paramount insignia of the location of the art of protest, a place occupied by an apartheid settler colony, protected by an amorphous empire.

The space of the art of protest perforce yields to the sphere of public art of protest, and thus we move from Hannah Arendt to Jürgen Habermas, from public space as the location of politics of liberation to the structural transformation of the bourgeois public sphere, from Arendt's notion of public space as the location of public happiness, namely as the space of political protest, where liberty from tyranny and freedom to be political are asserted, to the narrative sphere of politics. Arendt proposed the following:

> If the ultimate end of revolution was freedom and the constitution of a public space where freedom could appear, then ... no one could be called happy without his share of public happiness, that no one could be called free without his experience in public freedom, and that no one could be called happy or free without participating, and having a share, in public power.[4]

But this is not entirely applicable to our revolutionary time—revolution as open-ended Bakhtinian novel and not total as in Homeric epic.[5] On the platform of these revolutions, the occupied public space (from Azadi to Tahrir to Taksim to Syntagma to *Zuccotti* to Zócalo) yields to their simulacra of public sphere and thereafter, under severe censorial policies of the threatened state, yields to the parapublic sphere that links underground and cyberspace together. This leads us to reconsider the French Marxist urban sociologist Henri Lefebvre and his idea of the production of space.

This is how Lefebvre proposes the idea of "the third space": first is the physical space, second is the mental space, and third is the social space.[6] From Lefebvre we can move to Edward Soja's notion of "third space," what he calls spatial trialectics. Soja's third space is both real and imagined, what he considers spatial justice.[7] Here I propose that the idea of third space is open-ended, miasmatic. We must think of it as a cumulative or evolving trialectics. While Soja and Homi Bhabha point to hybridity and the duality becoming trialectical—and thus the third space opening up—I propose an interstitial space, which is hidden to both first and second spaces. Lefebvre and Soja seem to be too Christian in their preference for trilogy for the world at large, especially if they might be more inclined toward Manichean-Hegelian dialectic. On this trinity we all become more than just Christians. Far more importantly, we become implicated in a post-national trialectics where art loses its power of subversion.

I borrow the concept of interstitial space from art and architecture. Contemporary art historians have already noted the fact that there are many forms of art that defy the accepted boundaries of genres and media. Here, a work of art or fiction becomes its own interspace rather than succumbing to established boundaries. The idea has its resonances in architecture, where an interstitial space is where a building is made more pliable to multiple and varied uses. The way I use interstitial space is to think of it as a location for the urban guerilla artfare, where we perform a revolutionary confiscation of the work of art from the bourgeois public spaces in which it is staged; without depositing it into any bank or museum or biennale, we cash it in for our own revolutionary purposes before auctioneers sell it off in the art marketplace. Our theorization of the work of art is thus entirely predicated on its fragmentary disposition on this interstitial space at the moment of the theoretical confiscation of the commodified work of art, wherein it is fetishized and thus robbed of its politics of emancipation, a fragmented fact that from Walter Benjamin forward we have learned how to transform into allegories.[8]

Existential Reasoning

Let me explain this a bit further. If we were to dwell on the moment that hermeneuticians like Hans-George Gadamer suggest reason is seen incarnate in existence, and therefore, if in order to understand our worldly whereabouts, we would have to categorically abandon the space presumed outside that existential reasoning, then the space of the protest art is where we dwell, where we exist, where we think the world and see the sublime, all at the same time. That space is a space in between, not tertiary but non-numerical, a hidden space, a safe house, where the urban guerilla artfare hits and runs.

Now the question is, How do we read and understand and interpret from this safe house? The question leads us to the consideration of art, subjectivity, and solidarity—where art, subjection, agency, and solidarity all become one, thereby decentering the knowing subject by becoming its own knowable world announces itself, where apathy yields not to sympathy but to empathy, through a revolutionary postcolonial reading of such seminal texts as Max Sheller's 1923 *Zur Phänomenologie und Theorie der Sympathiegefühle und von Liebe und Hass* (*The Nature of Sympathy*).[9] The move will defiantly overcome Kant's triangulated critic of the knowing subject, which becomes a decidedly European knowing subject, thereby rendering the world at large, from humans to things, as a knowable world. The postcolonial subject has no room in the Kantian critique of reason, for she or he is always already delegated to the fixed status of being integral to a knowable world. As such, the postcolonial person is incapable of the sublime and the beautiful.[10] She has to dodge Immanuel Kant and the entire bourgeois public sphere he and his subsequent European philosophers enabled if she is to cultivate who she is and what is sublime and beautiful in her horizons.

From Max Scheler, we could move to Emanuel Levinas, where "the face of the Other" becomes the site of consciousness. But I have an even more radical idea. I propose the Persian poet Hatef Isfahani's (died circa 1783) famous *tarji'-band* poem, in which the poet becomes what we might call a "*verstehende*" subject—he becomes the always othered Other and defends the Other against the self.[11] From Hatef's *tarji'-band*, we learn how to overcome Levinas's limitation, for in this poem, it is not the absolute face of the Other, thereby transcendentalized, but the constantly changing face of multiple Others that becomes the sublated site of otherness as oneself, where the "I" keeps circulating like a mirror around a face that makes it impossible for the "I" to see itself except in the mirror of multiplying Others. Levinas's dialogical interface between the self and the Other becomes not just a trialectics but effectively circumambulatory. The proposition of the decentered subject ultimately becomes *fana fi al-khalq*—dissolution in multitude—as the simulacrum of *fana fi al-haq*—dissolution in truth.

In Hatef's poem, we follow a Muslim who visits a Christian church, a Jewish synagogue, and a Zoroastrian temple and wonders why the worshippers are not Muslims and praying to the same Muslim God, in each case concluding that there was nothing wrong with what they were doing, rather it was his own perceptions of things that kept being corrected by placing himself in the voice of the Other. The refrain after each segment of the poem sings, "That all is He and nothing but He/He is One and there is no similitude to Him." The key moment in all the varied cycles is when the poet says, "*Man-e sharmandeh az Mosalmani*" (I ashamed of being a Muslim), which is here the epistemic premise of successive and sublimating cognitions. Here the subject is neither dual nor even a triad but circulatory, circumambulatory, always substitutional, substitutionary, not absorbed but in fact intensified in subjection of alterity. It becomes the Other only on its way to something else. The subject in each and every case transcends from factual to the phenomenological, the phenomenology of the sublime, of the poetic art allowing for the self to go through sublimation, having *aufgehoben* through multiple alterities.

In the same vein, I propose that the art of protest works through a mirroring act, as if working in a niche, a *mihrab*, where we see the invisible face of the absolute Other in the face of the moving images of the always self-othering Others, those real people who are alienated from themselves. The interstitial space is the occasion and the simulacrum of that politics which enables this space as it bans it. But in thus othering and altering its means, politics gives birth to its own alterity, its own spatial negation—what I often term the "parapublic sphere," where the art of protest dwells. Art conquers this space and surrenders to it at one and the same time. To preempt their own overthrowing, the first thing triumphant tyrannies do is to ban the aesthetic pregnancy of the political and to seek to substitute it with their own state-sponsored aesthetics of submission and surrender. The art of protest preempts that possibility.

The art of protest therefore self-transcendentalizes its location, so much so that a university lecture hall or a gallery or a museum or a street corner or a refugee camp becomes the site of its incidence, but it does not stay there. It self-transcendentalizes—

from location to location—always moving in interstitial in-betweens. The space of the art of protest is thus ipso facto interstitial, somewhere in between, somewhere between the event that occasions it, the art that remembers it, and the theory that seeks to capture its enduring significance. That "where" is where that somewhere becomes the camp—from Auschwitz to Zaatari to Yarmouk—camps where all our *bios* has become *zoë*; the camp suspends urbanity until it is made the ground zero of our future liberations. If protest—its arts or its politics—does not lead to liberation, it is an exercise in futility, whether academic or artistic. The art of protest, always in the limbo, preempts that futility.

The Space and the Spectacle[12]

Let me now get more specific. Revolutions generate their own slogans, vocabularies, ideas, inner dynamics, external manifestations, institutional endurance, and perhaps most important of all, their own iconography—the visual registers that will move and mobilize their presence and their posterity. "Liberté, Égalité, Fraternité" became the most famous slogan of the French Revolution. "Workers of the world, unite!" remains the most potent slogan of all socialist revolutions. "Peace! Land! Bread!" was perhaps the most celebrated slogan of the Russian Revolution. "Neither East, Nor West, [but] the Islamic Republic" was the battle cry of the militant Islamists who took over and derailed the Iranian revolution of 1979. The Arab revolutions are no exception. "People demand the overthrow of the regime" and "Bread, freedom, and social justice" will perhaps remain the mightiest and most universal cry of the Arab revolutions. But until the iconic photo of activist and poet Shaimaa al-Sabbagh's moment of martyrdom on January 24, 2015, captured by twenty-three-year-old Egyptian photographer Islam Osama for Reuters/*Youm El Sabea* newspaper, the Egyptian, and by extension Arab, revolutions lacked a compelling iconic image. They now had it: a young female revolutionary, a leading member of the Socialist Popular Alliance Party, dying, embraced and held upright by a comrade, Sayyed Abu el-Ela, who is kneeling at her feet.[13] All of these particularities will soon fade and fuse into the emblematic synergy of a revolutionary allegory for generations to come. Where is Shaimaa al-Sabbagh now— where is the moment that this photograph was taken? Is this photograph art, politics, or a mere allegory that transcends all such questions?

Long-shot photos of Tahrir Square with people diminished to minuscule scale were perhaps the most globally recognized visual representation of the Arab revolutions. The self-immolation of Mohamed Bouazizi in Tunisia was the initial trigger of these revolutions. But the rare picture of his final and heroic demise is shrouded in the burning fire of anonymity. All those photos, from the suicidal self-immolation of Bouazizi in Sidi Bouzid in Tunisia to Tahrir Square in Cairo—ranging from fleeting snapshots of burning anonymity to large scale and long shot, and thus both lacking in revolutionary personification and character, now pale in comparison with this photo of Shaimaa al-Sabbagh. At the moment of her death, Shaimaa al-Sabbagh became iconic, allegorical, emblematic of an entire nation, an entire people, of a momentous revolution, and that

Figure 12.1 Shaimaa al-Sabbagh—shot and killed by Egyptian security forces. Photo: Islam Osman—Youm El Sabea (Al Youm Al Saabi/Reuters).

entire picture is nothing but a digital memory, has no place except in the recollections of those who have seen it. There cannot be any museum holding that instance. The memorial is ephemeral, invulnerable precisely because it is immaterial.

For posterity, all the brutish ruling Arab potentates, from Bashar al-Assad in Syria to Abdel Fattah el-Sisi in Egypt and everyone else in between, will be dwarfed in comparison with this picture of the dying Shaimaa al-Sabbagh. Captured at the moment of entering eternity, she is the very embodiment of all those Arab and Muslim women and men demanding and deserving a better life. Arab revolutions unfold apace up and down a winding road: the rise and immediate collapse of parliamentary democracy in Egypt, the destruction of the state apparatus in Libya, the flickering signs of hope in Tunisia, the forceful crackdown in Bahrain, the murderous machinations of the ruling regime in Syria, the counterrevolutionary sectarianism holding tight the rope between Saudi Arabia and Iran with immediate, genocidal ramifications in Yemen, the noxious rise of the murderous Islamic State group (IS, formerly ISIS), and the heroic resistances of the Kurds in Kobane. The past is forever left behind, the present is uncertain, the future blurry—but the force of history is now crystal clear for the whole world to see in the figure of one Arab woman standing up as a testimony, a *shâhid* (witness) and a *shahîd* (martyr), for posterity. The dying figure of Shaimaa al-Sabbagh stands for the valiant militancy of Kurdish women of Kobane fighting the IS, the summation of all counterrevolutionary conspiracies gathered in one murderous gang. Shaimaa al-Sabbagh has thus joined eternity precisely because of the impossibility of museumizing the moment of her entering eternity.

Revolutionary Icons Worldwide

From our perspective today, the icon of the French revolution, Eugène Delacroix's *Liberty Leading the People* (1830) is too allegorical, while Emanuel Gottlieb Leutze's *Washington Crossing the Delaware* (1851), as an emblem of the American revolution, is already too Christian fundamentalist, too allegorically triumphalist, too anticipatory, and shrouded in the future of American imperialism to have a global resonance. The long shot black-and-white picture of Lenin mobilizing a crowd in the course of the Russian revolution is too classical a portrait of a full-time revolutionary who has nothing else to do but to lead a massive uprising, as the famous picture of Castro and Che Guevara during the Cuban revolution is too replete with masculinist heroism to register realistically for mortal human beings. The most famous picture of the Iranian revolution raises a portrait of Ayatollah Khomeini to heaven as it dwarfs his followers to the size of little ants.

All these iconic pictures were crucial for their times, and yet they do not travel well across time and space. None of them, now emblematic symbols of bygone ages, comes anywhere near this picture of Shaimaa al-Sabbagh as a potent revolutionary icon specific to our times: the figure of a young woman, a mother, a citizen with ordinary chores and responsibilities, with a child to raise, a partner, a comrade to have and to hold, and then a determined socialist revolutionary—this is the marked difference between this and all other revolutions, led not by the absolutist convictions of what in my book *Arab Spring* (2012) I call "total revolutions" but by the steady determination of the makers of our "open-ended revolutions." As such, the picture will always remain allegorical, universal in its immaterial particularity.

Ours is a revolutionary *time*, not a revolutionary *moment*: the moment of Shaimaa al-Sabbagh's death, precisely four years after the initial success of the Egyptian Revolution, marks the revolutionary time in which we live and that she gave her life marking. Understanding these revolutions requires the steady patience, the analytical skills, the theoretical trajectory, and the temporal endurance of what in the French Annales school of historiography is rightly called *longue durée*. Just because a military coup in Egypt, the bloody reign of Bashar al-Assad in Syria, and the US imperial adventurism in Iraq have come together to produce the monstrosities of IS and its ilk, and regardless of the persistent, discouraging events in Libya, Yemen, and Bahrain, the Arab Spring has not become a winter. Sometimes a metaphor is just a metaphor. How art corresponds with that metaphor is where this picture of Shaimaa al-Sabbagh marks its interstitial space.

The picture of a dying Shaimaa al-Sabbagh projects a rite of passage for all of us in the Arab and Muslim world, leaving behind and bidding loving farewell to the militant moment captured best in the picture of Leila Khaled, the Palestinian freedom fighter, replete with the cognitive dissonance of a girlish innocence and her averted gaze competing with her gun. The photo of Shaimaa al-Sabbagh is far less romantic, far more palpable, real, and tactile in its emotional power; it lacks both that averted girlish gaze of Leila Khaled and that protruding weapon she carries. What it does have is a steady and steely gaze of a determined woman looking into the future of a revolutionary cause from the certainty of her moment of death, its present and public stand. This is the moment when an accidental work of art becomes its own allegory.

Another comparative point of reference is, of course, the video of a dying Neda Agha-Soltan in the course of the Green Movement in Iran—yet another iconic picture to which Shaimaa al-Sabbagh's might allude. But contrary to Sabbagh, who was a revolutionary activist having just led a concerted defiance against the military junta ruling her country, Neda Agha-Soltan was a bystander whose murder by the security forces of the Islamic Republic to instill fear in others is made even more tragic by the random helplessness with which her death was broadcast around the globe. Between the two accidental videos and pictures of Neda Agha-Sultan and Shaimaa al-Sabbagh, the interstitial space of the art of protest becomes emblematic of an age that is building subterranean solidarity among movements and entirely unbeknownst to themselves.

Shaimaa al-Sabbagh's death, however, is different from Neda Agha-Sultan's in a pronounced way: Sabbagh's is decidedly the death of an active revolutionary, a leading voice of dissent, who moments before her death was shouting for "bread, freedom, social justice." She is then chased and shot at close range by masked security forces, just before she is picked up to be carried away by a friend. The photo captures her moment of death, when she is held upright, not just by her comrade's embrace but by her own defiant will against the banality of Sisi's murderous charade. The snapshot now becomes a testimonial not just for the Rabaa massacre of August 2013 but also for all defiant revolutionary acts against tyranny in Egypt, against tyranny everywhere. The interstitial is visually mobile, aesthetically transformative. It universalizes the Egyptian Revolution in terms domestic to its historicity and native to its significance.

The significance of this photo is above all in its utter innocence—and in marking that innocence, it is instantly reminiscent of Michelangelo's *Pietà* in St. Peter's Basilica, with the critical twist that here, the martyr is a woman held by a man (her comrade) rather than a man (the Christ) held by a woman (his mother). The iconic Christian allusion here in the death of a Muslim socialist revolutionary marks the self-transcendence of a moment that points far beyond its immediate historical vicinities. Such cross-referentialities bring the world to the Egyptian moment rather than assimilate the Egyptian into the vacuous West.

Looking at the picture closely, every gesture of Shaimaa al-Sabbagh resonates and saturates the transcending moment. Her manicured red fingernails marking her left hand sitting gently on her comrade's shoulder, gesturing to balance the fist of the right hand clenching as if holding something as it sits on his right shoulder. Her gray sweater marks the splashing of her blood on her left shoulder, while her black scarf links her hair to her chest to her comrade's head. And then her face and her look: gazing, marveling, sad, sedentary, stolid—there is a determined sadness about that face, marking a moment that her death is both descending and ascending on her consciousness. Is it there yet—yes, no, maybe?—is she defiant, incredulous, resigned, accepting? The fearful embrace of her comrade is at once protective and yielding, fearful and in reverence. Every moment, every sign, every gesture in the picture assumes iconic significance only after it has entered the revolutionary consciousness of its location and time.

This picture will be the nightmare of the counterrevolutionaries as its replicas, drawings, paintings, statues, and living memories will compete to capture the allegorical potency of this purgatorial moment of a young woman declaring a history. The death of Shaimaa al-Sabbagh is the birth of the new Arab and Muslim revolutionary woman: a citizen, a mother, a comrade, a defiant hope, and a determined soul refusing to take no for an answer. To capture all of that at a moment of death is in and of itself a work of art no museum will ever have the privilege of exhibiting.

La Vita Nuda: Baring Bodies, Bearing Witness[14]

Let me now give a slightly different twist to the interstitial space of the art of protest and take you to the moment when the body in and of itself gets to stage itself. Here I would like to reflect on the public gestures of two women: the Egyptian blogger Aliaa Magda Elmahdy, who in late 2011 posted naked pictures of herself on her blog by way of a protest "against a society of violence, racism, sexism, sexual harassment and hypocrisy"; and Golshifteh Farahani, a young Iranian actress now living in France who created a sensation in and outside her homeland, especially in the social networking cyber society, by posing half naked for *Madame Le Figaro* and appearing topless in a short black-and-white video clip called *Corps et Âmes* (Bodies and Souls), produced by the prominent French fashion photographer and music video director Jean-Baptiste Mondino. Put together, the two cases of Elmahdy and Farahani stage the body of two young women as the body politic of a revolt where the *corpus anarchicum* aims at and dismantles the self-assuredness of the ruling state.[15]

As with the case of Elmahdy and her compatriots, the nude picture and video clip of Farahani sharply divided Iranians around the world—some celebrating her act as courageous and pathbreaking, dismantling ancient and sacrosanct taboos and thus revolutionary, others condemning her as opportunistic, obscene, immoral, and damaging to the cause of liberty in Iran. The Islamic Republic reportedly banned her from returning to her homeland. Whence the outrage? In its widest sense, clothing is the civilizing posture of humanity. No society, no community, no human gathering is devoid of one form of clothing or another as the formal decorum of becoming a full and public human being; it might be as little as a mere bamboo sheath around the groin or it might extend to fully covered veiling, without even the eyes visible to any intruding gaze. But clothing is definitive of all forms of civility. So the question is, What happens when within any society, not just in Egypt or Iran, a body exposes itself from beneath that veneer of civility?

Our manner of dressing ourselves is the most immediate habitat of our humanity— violently disrupted at times by tyrants who seek to give a different look to that humanity. When Reza Shah Pahlavi (who reigned in Iran from 1925 to 1941) banned the mode of veiling in Iran, which he deemed unseemly to his vision of "modernity," there were women who remained home and never appeared in public until their dying day—because for them to appear in public without their habitual clothing was like forcing New Yorkers to go to work in their bikinis. When Khomeini reimposed that almost-forgotten manner of veiling decades later, generations of women had grown up entirely alien to that manner of veiling. Reza Shah and Khomeini—two tyrants interrupted by one weakling potentate—had fought their fateful battles over the site of our mothers' and daughters' bodies. "Veiling" or "unveiling" thus branded became a matter of state policies, of ideological convictions.

"Offensive" Content

Posing a body beneath or beyond its habitual habitat is disruptive in varied cultures—not just in Iran, Egypt, or the Muslim world. Even in the heart of Europe, when a website publishes an article about Golshifteh Farahani's photos, it does so with the alert, "WARNING: contains nudity," and that warning is not for its Iranian audiences, who mostly read Persian, not any European language. These warnings are not intended for any cleric in Qom or Najaf either but for people in Western Europe or North America who might find these pictures offensive. To enter St. Peter's Basilica in Vatican City in the heart of Rome, women are required to wear "proper attire," as they would when entering any mosque in Qom or Isfahan or Cairo. When Janet Jackson's breast was accidentally exposed during a duet with Justin Timberlake at the Superbowl in 2004, it caused as much uproar in the United States as it might have in Saudi Arabia. The body is the site of all cultural inhibitions.

In varied cultures around the globe, bodies and faces are painted, covered with cloth or leaves, hair is dyed, noses, lips, and cheeks are surgically altered, and colorful contact lenses are placed over dark irises, all as the mannered rituals of societal acceptance and formality. Dressing is the ceremonial ritual of presenting the body in public. From "Sunday best" to "dressed to the nines" to "dressed to a tee" to "three-piece suits," all the way down to "Friday dressing down," from academic regalia to "heroin chic," from the metrosexual to Calvin Klein androgynies, from Muslim veiling to Gap and Benetton advertisements, people clothe themselves by way of walking into the formal gathering of their public persona. No one is ever completely naked—not even in many naturist nudist colonies. Those who dismiss or ridicule the formal dressing of varied cultures are entirely oblivious to how fanatically committed to their own "casual" look they are. All one has to do is force them to wear a tie to a meeting and they cry out loud for their Gap T-shirt and blue jeans.

Revolutionary undressing, in Egypt and elsewhere, exposes the body as the corporeal exhibition of the most naked site of state violence. Whether it is done by Aliaa Magda Elmahdy in her blog or by Golshifteh Farahani in a fashion magazine in Paris but mostly visible on the internet, the social networking that enables such exhibition/ism is the interstitial space of their art of protest. There is no museum or gallery the authorities in Egypt of Iran can send their security forces to shut down. The cat is out of the bag and no censorial politics can catch it. The fact that it is a female body that transforms itself into the art of protest catches the censorial politics of the ruling state (and perforce its patriarchal prejudices) off-guard and exposes its naked violence without any legitimacy clothing.

"Nor Customary Suits of Solemn Black"

This is all to say that no culture, Muslim or otherwise, is totally naked, that all cultures clothe—sacred or secular, Eastern or Western, traditional or modern. But (and here's the rub) the deliberate stripping of clothing that a culture has habitually called "decent"—in gestures ranging from running naked in a soccer stadium with joy, or in protest, or in highly stylized photographic or video installations—is an act of staged formal destruction that disrupts the normality of socializing norms for a deliberate pause. It is the staging of the body for a momentary reflection—where and when it is ordinarily taken for granted and ignored. The vast and varied tradition of nude statues, paintings, and photographs, from the Greeks to the postmodern, are aesthetic pauses for such moments of reflection and do not mean that the Greeks and Romans, or contemporary Europeans or Americans, ordinarily walk around their towns looking like those statues or pictures. Nudity by definition is an act of exhibition—anywhere and anytime. It is the moment that the body stages itself in an impromptu or rehearsed act of protest against any normative complacency.

Art as such is a remissive occasion that, in effect, sustains a culture's inhibitions—not discrediting or dismantling them (if we were to follow Phillip Rieff's theory of culture to its logical conclusions).[16] Golshifteh Farahani is not the first young Iranian woman in recent memory to have taken a naked photo of herself and publicized it, nor was Aliaa Magda Elmahdy the first Muslim to do so. Long before them both, another young Iranian woman, Minou Arjomand, joined an HIV/AIDS advocacy group (ACT UP) for a top-to-toe naked demonstration outside Madison Square Garden in New York City, where the Republican National Convention was taking place in August 2004, protesting against President Bush's AIDS policies. She and her friends later posed for a group portrait that was published in the *New Yorker* magazine.[17]

Minou Arjomand's gesture in New York was far more daring, imaginative, and politically purposeful than Golshifteh Farahani's and Aliaa Magda Elmahdy's in Paris and Cairo put together. But scarcely anyone in the Iranian or Muslim communities noted that picture in August 2004—or even knows about it now—taken, as it was, before online social networking had turned the world inside out. Minou Arjomand joined that group portrait in protest of President Bush's HIV/AIDS policies without any pomp or ceremony and without the slightest publicity drawn to that photo beyond the limited HIV/AIDS epidemic activist circles. But it is precisely by opening the frame of reference back at least to that picture (politically purposeful but far from the madding crowd of internet publicity) that the recent actions of Golshifteh Farahani and Aliaa Magda Elmahdy will make more sense (albeit in rather different political contexts). Breaking the taboo of HIV/AIDS by baring bodies and bearing witness in the United States was no less iconoclastic or courageous than baring bodies and bearing witness against tyranny and repression in Egypt or Iran. The body was the same, the protest different, the occasion instantaneous.

There are other, similarly dramatic but far more fatal gestures perpetrated on one's own body that also need to be included in this frame. Public protest can assume fatal acts of self-immolation, as in the case of Mohamed Bouazizi in Tunisia that set the Arab

Spring aflame or when young unemployed men set themselves on fire in Morocco. The bodily gesture can also assume less fatal turns while being equally shocking to the reigning taboos, as in the cases of Elmahdy, Farahani, and Arjomand. Put together, these are transgressive moments that expose and shatter the ruling inhibitions—from the stigma of the HIV/AIDS epidemic to the indignity of mandatory veiling to the horrors of unemployment to unbearable political tyranny. But in the age of the "society of spectacle" (Guy Debord's idea) having gone amok, one must by all means resist fetishizing a single act of nudity going viral on the internet. For exposing one's body by way of protesting against political tyranny does not mean that if other Egyptians, Iranians, or Muslim women opt to wear their habitual veiling, they are in agreement with the ruling tyranny. What is crucial in all such cases is the spectacle of staging the body as an act of protest.

The Eurocentric neoliberalism now rampant among certain vocal segments of expatriate Egyptians and Iranians equates "liberation" with such acts of anti-veiling defiance, which the Islamophobic Europe and United States then pick up and trumpet *apace*. That equation of extreme unveiling with liberation or even defiance is a patently false equation. There are courageous Muslim women fighting valiantly for their liberties or suffering in the dungeons of Egypt and the Islamic Republic who voluntarily and happily opt to veil. Farahani's or Elmahdy's naked bodies are as dignified acts of defiance as are those of their sisters' veiled bodies in the dungeons of their respective countries. Beyond its Eurocentric, white-identified, and neoliberal appropriation in "the society of spectacle," *la vita nuda*, public gestures such as those of Elmahdy and Farahani expose the amorphous site of contestation between the violence that states perpetrate (whether forced veiling in the Islamic Republic or forced unveiling in France) and resistances that bodies pose. No defense of Farahani's courageous gesture in France is thus complete without *ipso facto* defending the right of immigrant Muslim women to veil in public in Europe if they so choose. Both their bodies, exposed or veiled, are sites of resistance to tyranny.

In the age of globalized capital and aterritorial empires, bodies have emerged as the singular site of resistance to power—from suicidal violence around the globe to young women exposing their bodies to shock and awe of a different sort. In a world that commenced with former US secretary of state Donald Rumsfeld's "campaign of shock and awe" in Iraq and continued with the raping of human dignity on an everyday scale in detention camps from Guantanamo Bay to Bagram Airbase, from Israeli dungeons to Kahrizak and Evin in the Islamic Republic of Iran, these exposed bodies register the always already vulnerable human soul. The systematic reduction of life to biopolitics is done entirely beneath the radar of the instantaneous publicities that accompany such widely publicized acts as those of Elmahdy or Farahani. When the Italian philosopher Georgio Agamben theorized the contours of the *homo sacer*—of the reduction of the civil persona to "bare life" in the society of spectacle and in a "state of exception" that has become the rule—he had already seen through the transformation of civic societies into camps as the *nomos* of the modern. The fact that the Green Movement in Iran or the Arab Spring in the Arab world is recasting the moral map of the region does not mean we have overcome that frightful specter. What these exposed bodies do reveal—whether in self-staging or self-immolation or in the tortured bodies of Iraqi inmates in Abu Ghraib—is the voluntary or involuntary act of subversion inherent in the human body, as the first and final materiality of revolt.

"I Have That Within Which Passed Show"

The photos of Minou Arjomand, Golshifteh Farahani, and Aliaa Magda Elmahdy are the insignia of an age, postmarks from a universal act of defiance. If anything, these pictures are to be compared with the picture of that young Egyptian woman being beaten and dragged by security forces in Tahrir Square, involuntarily exposing her body and underwear[18]—or with the picture of the Yemeni women burning their veils in public protest.[19] The protection of the right to revolt is in anticipation of that liberating moment when these protesters, just like "the Vancouver kissing couple,"[20] will have the choice of a simple and perfectly human act of love overcoming an obscene act of riot police brutality.

These pictures are not acts of obscenity. Quite to the contrary: these are gestures of innocence incarnate—staging of a delayed defiance. Obscenity is the exposure of human body and soul in the torture chambers of Abu Ghraib, Bagram Air Base, Guantanamo Bay, the dungeons of Israeli prison cells, all the way to Kahrizak and other subterranean cells of the Islamic Republic.[21] That is obscenity, not these innocent young women baring their soul in protest. Obscenity is the degeneration of civil society and common civility to detention camps in the United States and barefacedly robbing people of their most basic civil liberties in Egypt or Iran—and as all belligerent states posed to fight each other, they rob their respective citizens even more of their civil liberties. These young men and women are protesting by the only means left to them—the site of their bodies, blowing it up in Palestine, Iraq, or Afghanistan, burning it to ashes in Tunisia or Morocco, exposing its fragile innocence in Egypt or Iran, or in Europe or the United States.

To bear witness, territorial boundaries are no longer the solitary sites of resistance to political violence and tyranny. Our naked bodies, whether we expose or hide them, have become the last remaining corporeality that matters and means. Mohamed Bouazizi opted to burn himself alive, Golshifteh Farahani and Aliaa Magda Elmahdy to stage themselves. But common to their acts is not just the fragile bodies of these young protesters, but the fact that their ruling emperors and corrupt kings and clerics, from one end of the Arab and Muslim world to the other, have long been walking around with their proverbial pants down.

The art of protest can never be museumized, staged in any gallery, curated into normalcy. No museum, biennale, or exhibition can contain them. They are site specific to the moment of their staging: here now, gone tomorrow. By thus being transitory, they occupy an interstitial space that can never be defined, for they have turned the whole world, our very existence, interstitial.

Notes

1. I am grateful to my hosts Sarah Frahm, Anna Maier, and Regine Strätlin, who invited me to Berlin and facilitated my lecture there.
2. Hamid Dabashi, *Shi'ism: A Religion of Protest* (Cambridge, MA: Harvard University Press, 2012); and *The Arab Spring: The End of Postcolonialism* (London: Zed, 2012).
3. For more on this point, see my essay "A Portrait of the Artist as a Dead Boy," *Aljazeera*, February 4, 2016, https://www.aljazeera.com/indepth/opinion/2016/02/portrait-artist-dead-boy-ai-weiwei-aylan-kurdi-refugees-160204095701479.html.
4. Hannah Arendt, *On Revolution* (New York: The Viking Press, 1963), 255.
5. I have detailed this crucial difference in *The Arab Spring: The End of Postcolonialism* (London: Zed, 2012).
6. See Henri Lefebvre, *The Production of Space*, trans. Donald Nicholson-Smith (Oxford: Blackwell, 1991).
7. See in particular Edward W. Soja, *Seeking Spatial Justice* (Minneapolis: University of Minnesota Press, 2010).
8. As outlined in Walter Benjamin, *Ursprung des deutschen Trauerspiels* (1925). For an English translation, see Walter Benjamin, *The Origin of German Tragic Drama*, trans. John Osborne (London: Verso, 2009).
9. See Max Sheller, *The Nature of Sympathy*, trans. Peter Heath (New Brunswick, NJ: Transactions Publishers, 1970/2008).
10. See in particular the notoriously racist passage in Immanuel Kant, *Observations on the Feeling of the Beautiful and Sublime*, trans. John T. Goldthwait (Oakland: University of California Press, 1961/2003).
11. For more on Hatef Isfahani and his legendary poem, see the entry "HĀTEF, SAYYED AḤMAD EṢFAHĀNI" in *Encyclopedia Iranica*, http://www.iranicaonline.org/articles/hatef-sayyed-ahmad-esfahani.
12. The first draft of this part of this chapter was published as "Shimaa al-Sabagh: An Icon of the Arab Revolutions," *Al-Araby al-Jadid*, February 3, 2015, https://www.alaraby.co.uk/english/comment/2015/2/3/shimaa-al-sabagh-an-icon-of-the-arab-revolutions-.
13. For more on the story behind this iconic picture, see Jared Malsin and Olivier Laurent, "The Story behind the Photo of Shaimaa al-Sabbagh's Dying Moments," *Time*, January 30, 2015, http://time.com/3689366/the-story-behind-the-photo-of-shaimaa-al-sabbaghs-dying-moments/.
14. The first draft of this part of the chapter was published as "La Vita Nuda: Baring Bodies, Bearing Witness," *Aljazeera*, January 23, 2012, https://www.aljazeera.com/indepth/opinion/2012/01/201212111238688792.html.
15. I have analyzed in theoretical detail the meaning and significance of this idea in my *Corpus Anarchicum: Political Protest, Suicidal Violence, and the Making of the Posthuman Body* (New York: Palgrave, 2012).
16. For more on Philip Rieff's theory of culture, see his collection of essays *The Feeling Intellect*, ed. Jonathan B. Imber (Chicago: University of Chicago Press, 1990), particularly the essay "The Impossible Culture: Wilde as a Modern Prophet."
17. For more on ACT UP and this photo protest, see http://www.actupny.org/reports/rnc_nyc.html. Accessed June 19, 2018.
18. For more on this incident, see "Woman Beaten by Egyptian Troops in Tahrir Square," *BBC*, December 20, 2011, https://www.bbc.com/news/av/world-middle-east-16267376/woman-beaten-by-egyptian-troops-in-tahrir-square.

19 For details, see "Yemeni Women Burn Veils in Crackdown Protest," *Aljazeera*, October 26, 2011, https://www.aljazeera.com/news/middleeast/2011/10/20111026164441431354.html.
20 For details, see "Vancouver Kiss Couple Were Knocked Down by Riot Police," *Guardian*, June 17, 2011, https://www.theguardian.com/world/2011/jun/17/vancouver-kiss-couple-riot-police.
21 For more on these points, see Hamid Dabashi, "Damnatio Memoriae," in *Speaking about Torture*, eds. Julie A. Carlson and Elisabeth Weber (New York: Fordham University Press, 2012), 140–61.

Index

Abaza, Mona 19–20, 24
Abdul Wahab, Mohamed 74–5
Abidin, Adel 116 n.34
   Abidin Travels: Welcome to Baghdad
      (www.abidintravels.com) 5, 101–2,
      107–14, 116 n.38, 117 n.45
   mainpage to 107–8
   video still 109–10
   on bombing of Al-Jumhuriyya Bridge
      in Baghdad 102–3
   Cold Interrogation 103–5, 111
   early life and education 102–3
acculturation 34, 40, 122
Achar, Gilbert 19
activism. *See* political activism
actors, social. *See* social actors/actions
Adnan, Etel 56, 60 n.2
   affinity/affinitive relations 56–7, 59–60
   creative and imaginative 50
   and geopolitical order 51–5
   transcultural 45–51
   Of Cities and Women: Letters to
      Fawwaz 47, 50
   early life 47
   Paris, When It's Naked 4, 45–8, 52,
      54–5, 58–9, 61 n.10
   Sitt Marie Rose 46–8
   on weather 53
aesthetics 2, 14–15, 38, 40, 46, 70, 72, 77,
      83, 89–91, 93, 223–5, 227, 231, 234
Agamben, Giorgio 235
   on contemporary 69–70
agency 8, 21, 37, 58, 89, 122, 190, 193, 206,
      212, 226
   civil 15
   poetic 83
   political 125
   travel 5, 102, 107, 109, 111
Agha-Soltan, Neda, death of 231
Aikerman, Iain 70–1
al-Assad, Bashar 229–30

al-Emad, Ali 214–15
Algeria 34, 45, 52, 56–7, 74
Algerianism 34, 40
al-Houthi, Abdul-Malik Bedreddin 213
al-Houthi, Hussein Badreddin 212–13
Al Jazeera media 19, 22
Al-Ma'ajalah Massacre, 2009 209
Al-Mawkef Al-Masry (MM) (The Egyptian
      Stance) facebook group 6, 151–3,
      156, 158, 160
al-Muslimi, Farea 209–10
Al-Qaeda in the Arabian Peninsula
      (AQAP) 208–12, 216
al-Qirbi, Abu Bakr 210
al-Sabbagh, Shaimaa, death of 228–32
al-Shabbi, Abu al-Qasim, "The Will to
      Life" 89, 93
al-Shurqubi, Salah, al-Muqata'a (The
      Boycott) 213–14
alterity 121, 125, 139, 194, 198, 227
Anderson, Benedict 21, 198
Anglo-Indian 163
Ankommen app for migrants 53
Appadurai, Arjun 25 n.17, 32, 197
   "Disjuncture and Difference in the
      Global Cultural Economy" 106
Arab-Americans 123, 133
Arab-Canadian *vs.* Canadian-Arab 128–9,
      140 n.3
Arabic music 64–5, 75, 131–2
   maqamat 65
   singers 132
Arab identity 13–14, 24, 121–2, 125, 128,
      130–1, 136–8, 152
Arab-Jewish friendship 63, 76, 78
Arab nationalism 64, 69
Arab Spring 2–4, 8, 13, 15, 17–19, 22–4,
      64, 74, 78, 83–4, 151, 208, 214,
      223–4, 228–30, 234–5. *See also*
      post–Arab Spring
Arab-Western hybridity 121, 125, 136–9

Arab World 2–3, 13–15, 22, 24, 41, 89, 92, 96, 123–4, 151–2, 156–7, 207, 224
  post-revolutionary artistic scene 17–20
Arab youth 6, 121, 126–39. See also Canada, Canadian-Arab youth
Arendt, Hannah 194, 225
Arjomand, Minou 234–6
artistic expression 2, 8, 15, 20–4, 84. See also collective expression and action
artistic production 17–20, 24, 224
art of protest 7, 223–4, 227–8, 231–2. See also graffiti; violence
  location of 225–6
  nudity (nude picture/video) 232–6
Ashcroft, Bill, "Revolution, Transformation and Utopia: The Function of Literature" 89
assimilation 4, 40, 53, 78, 123, 126, 191
Assouline, Albert 73
authentic community/authenticity 18, 68, 70, 72, 76, 92, 197
authoritarianism 22, 72, 77
avant-garde 69, 72
Awad, Luwis 155

Ba'athist Arab nationalism 69
Badiou, Alain 2
  idea of truth 32–3
  procédure de vérité 32
Bahrain 1, 223–4, 229–30
Bains, Jatinder, *Transcultural Research in Mental Health Problems* 30–1
Bakhtin, Mikhail 166
Bakhtin, M. M. 159
Barenboim, Daniel 78
Baubock, Rainer 191–2
Baudelaire, Charles, *Le Spleen de Paris* 49–50
Bayat, Asef 84, 92
Beinin, Joel 69
  on Operation Susannah 68
belonging, transcultural 4, 15, 30, 32–3, 35–6, 40–1, 45–7
Ben Ali, Zine al-Abidine 85–7
Bendjedid, Chadli 57
Benghazi attack in Libya 219 n.32
Benhabib, Seyla 190

Benjamin, Walter 17, 226
Berkani, Derri, *A Forgotten Resistance* 73
Berman, Paul 206
Bhabha, Homi 163, 165, 186, 225
  The Location of Culture 164
  theory of hybridity, criticism 166–7
  third space 191, 194, 225–6
Bilal, Wafaa
  early life 103
  Shoot an Iraqi: Art, Life, and Resistance under the Gun 103
  Virtual Jihadi 102, 104–5, 115 n.15
  opposition and criticism 105
binary cultures, opposition of 122, 139
  British *vs.* Indian 163
  Jordanian *vs.* Syrian 163, 167, 186
  of Self/Other 164–7
Bouazizi, Mohamed 21, 83, 88, 228, 234, 236
Bouraoui, Hédi 3–4, 29
  cyclist perspective study 35
  deterritorialization 39
  early life and education 32–3, 36–7
  from France to United States 33
  Hannibal (fictional character) 39
  Memmi on 33
  nomaditude 40
  on trans/transculture 30, 35–41
  trilogy of 39
  works of 33–5, 38–40
Bourdieu, Pierre, *Language and Symbolic Power* 155
Bourguiba, Habib 83–6
Bramley, Ellie Violet 72
Brandt, Marieke 213
burlesque 4, 70, 72, 77
Bush, George W. 104, 214, 234
Butler, Kim, "Defining Diaspora, Refining a Discourse" 106

cabaret culture 70, 72, 74–5, 77–8
Cairokee, *Sout Al Horeya* 15
Camus, Albert 34
Canada 6, 18, 30–1, 33–4, 40
  attachment formation in (friendship) 129–30
  Canadian-Arab youth 6, 121, 123, 125–33, 136, 139, 139 n.2 (see also Arab youth)

Canadian multiculturalism 4, 30, 37, 137–8
   immigrants 124
   Québec 31, 37, 40
   survey/research (focus groups) 5, 121, 127–8
   transcultural identity 124–5
   transcultural psychiatric studies in 31
Castoriadis, Cornelius 201 n.3
Central European nations 61 n.9
Chamayou, Grégoire 208
Chaplin, Charlie 224
   The Great Dictator 223
Charalambous, Constadina 152
Che Guevara 230
Christian 126, 215, 226, 230–1. *See also* Muslim(s); religion/religious
citizen/citizenship 2, 4, 6, 13, 16, 22–3, 36, 45–6, 52–5, 59, 122–3, 185, 189
   allegiances 4, 7, 51–2, 74, 189, 195
   Benhabib on 190
   cosmopolitan 190
   cultural 126, 197
   digital 21
   dual 124, 190–1
   extension of 53–5, 59
   flexible 126, 194
   global 58
   hierarchal 193
   individual 194–5
   multicultural 190
   multiple 190–1, 193
   ontological 7, 189–90, 192–5, 200
   political 190–5, 197
   poly-citizenship 4, 7, 126, 189
   stakeholder 191
   state-citizen relationship 191
   transferred Indian citizens 192
   transnational 122, 190–1
civil war 46–7, 52, 57, 59, 69, 212–13, 218
Clifford, James, "Diasporas" 106
code-mixing 151, 158
code-switching 6, 151, 153
Cohen, Sacha 224
   The Dictator 223
cohesion 153, 205
collective expression and action 1–2, 151–2. *See also* artistic expression
collective identity/collectivities 1, 159, 190

collectivism 4, 139
colonialism 4, 34, 38, 45, 48, 57, 74, 77, 122. *See also* postcolonial/post-colonialism
colonization 16, 66, 86, 193
communication, methods of (with home countries) 128–9, 143–6
communism 67–9, 76
connectivity 14, 36, 85–6, 103, 106, 127–8, 139, 140 n.3, 145, 196, 198. *See also* cohesion
contemporary art 5, 107, 224, 226
cosmopolitanism 4, 36, 63–6, 68–70, 72, 76–8, 194, 197, 201 n.6
cost-benefit analysis 191, 200
counterrevolutionary 17, 23–4, 223–4, 229, 232. *See also* revolutionary art
counterterrorism 206, 210. *See also* terrorism
creaculture 35–7
critical discourse analysis (CDA) approach 151, 154, 160
cross-culture 37
crossing 37, 151–3, 159–60
Cuban revolution 230
cultural interaction (poiesis) 194
culture 14, 23, 30–1, 39, 105, 123–5, 130–1, 167, 198. *See also* multiculturalism/multiculturality; transculturality/transculturalism/transculture
   American 123–4, 133
   Arabic 8, 105, 121–2, 124–5, 127–8, 130–6, 139, 198
   cultural Darwinism 31
   cultural hybridity 163–6
   cultural identity 6, 24, 41, 122, 136–9
   cultural/multicultural citizenship 126, 190, 197
   cultural production 2, 17–19, 24, 198
   forms of 18
   homogenous 167, 187
   Indian 196–8
   modern 14
   politics and 8, 18, 38
   popular 70, 125–7, 139, 213
   study of 31, 35
   taboos 135
   transnational 16

Darragi, Rafiq 32
darwish/darwich/darwiche 71
Darwishe, Mahmoud 84
Darwish, Sayyid 71
De Angelis, Francesco 156
defiance 23, 88, 223–5, 231, 235–6
Delacroix, Eugène 105
  Liberty Leading the People 230
demands (rights and freedom) 1, 15, 53, 205, 207, 212, 216, 228–9
demarcation 45, 103, 191
Derluguian, Georgi M. 38
determinants/determinism 14, 31, 40, 77
De Unamuno, Miguel 41
diaspora/diasporic 22, 54, 106, 125–6, 128, 130, 191, 193, 195
  digital 5, 106–7
  Indian 192, 195–200
  Iraqi 5
digital citizen 21
digital media 84, 107
diversity 2, 14, 30–2, 38, 40, 54–5, 154, 166, 169
divide-and-rule strategy 68, 75
Dnaz, Thyazyla 18–19
Doss, Madiha 158–9
Dubai 195, 197–8, 201 n.5
DuBois, W. E. B., dual consciousness 164, 198

economic system 23, 35, 52–3, 126, 168, 170, 179, 182–4, 186, 192–4, 196, 199–200
Eco, Umberto 39
Egan, Jennifer 85
Egypt 64–9, 156–7, 223, 229, 232, 234–6
  Cairo 19–20, 23
  Egyptian dialect 155–6
  Egyptian music 71, 132
  revolution in 13, 18–20, 24, 64, 76–7, 230–1
  Tahrir Square 13, 18–20, 22, 228
Egyptian Arabic (EA) 151, 153, 156–60
Elmahdy, Aliaa Magda 232–6
el-Sisi, Abdel Fattah 229
emergent art 7, 14, 165
epistemology 3, 15, 49, 121, 125, 127–30, 133–4
Epstein, Michael 31, 38

essentialism, cultural 14, 35, 166
Eshel, Amir 55–6
ethnic identity/ethnicity 1, 46, 70, 125–6, 192, 197–8
ethno-religious element 24, 34, 36
European Atomic Energy Community 60 n.8
European Coal and Steel Community (ECSC) 52, 60 n.8
European Economic Community 52, 60 n.8
European identity 45, 52–3
European Union (EU) 4, 45–6, 49, 51–5, 58, 190, 192–3
  Eurozone 193
  formation of 4, 48, 52–4, 56, 58–9
  union and exclusion 55–8
exceptionalism 19, 92
exotopy 30
external voting 191

Facebook 5, 83–6, 88, 127, 131, 157. See also Zuckerberg, Mark
  Al-Mawkef Al-Masry (MM) (the Egyptian Stance) group 6, 151–3, 156, 158, 160
  Facebook Revolution 23, 88
  Ouled Ahmed's revolution on 85–6, 88–9, 92–4, 97
  virtual space of 91–3
Fahmy, Ziad 70
Fairclough, Norman 6, 154, 159
faisance approach 38
Fanon, Frantz 74
  Black Skin, White Masks 164
Farahani, Golshifteh 232–6
fascism 70, 74–5, 77
Fattal, Simone 47, 60 n.2
Fayid, Ismail 71–2
Feierstein, Gerald 214–15
Feminist Majority Movement 57
Feroun, Mouloud, *Le fils du pauvre* (The Poor Man's Son) 34
Ferroukhi, Ismaël, *Free Men* 4, 63, 72–3, 75–8
filiation *vs.* affiliation 47–8
Finland 103
folk culture 71
foreign policy 126, 208

Index

Fosse, Bob, *Cabaret* 70, 72
Foucault, Michel 96, 191
France 4, 33, 35–6, 45, 54–7, 235
    Paris 49, 51–5, 57, 59
Franco-Oriental culture 75
Franzen, Jonathan, "What's Wrong with the Modern World?" 85
Fraser 192
French Africans (*pieds noirs*) 34
French Algerian identity 34
French Resistance 74
Freud, Sigmund, *Jokes and Their Relation to the Unconscious* 110
futurity 55–6, 58–9

Gadamer, Hans-George 226
Garrick, Jacqueline, *Trauma Treatment Techniques: Innovative Trends* 110
gender 3, 31, 53, 76, 95, 135, 171, 177–9
Generation of 1898 41
Ghali, Waguih, *Beer in the Snooker Club* 4, 63–70, 72, 76–8
Gilroy, Paul, dual consciousness 164
Global Islamic Media Front 104
globalization 19, 21, 24, 31, 78, 189–90, 192–3, 197
Gomaa, Ehab 20, 24
    "Framing the Egyptian Uprising in Arabic Language Newspapers and Social Media" 18
Goya, Francisco 116 n.41
graffiti 17, 19–20, 23–4. *See also* art of protest
    Subay's campaign 211
The Grand Budapest Hotel (Anderson, Wes) 72
Green Movement in Iran 223, 231, 235
Gregory, Dereck 111
group identity 151, 153
Gulf Cooperation Council (GCC) countries 218 n.3
Gulf Indians 192, 194, 196. *See also* India; United Arab Emirates (UAE)
    cultural acceptance of 198
    education 197
    graduation/employment 196
    second-generation 189, 191, 194, 196, 200
    youth 194–8, 201 n.5

Habermas, Jürgen 201 n.3, 201 n.5, 225
Habiby, Emile, *The Secret Life of Saeed the Pessoptimist* 71
Hadi, Abdrabbuh Mansur 205–6, 210
Halali, Salim 73–6
Hamdi Bey, Osman
    Theologian 115 n.23
    Two Musician Girls 115 n.23
Hamdy, Naila 20, 24
    "Framing the Egyptian Uprising in Arabic Language Newspapers and Social Media" 18
Hanafi, Sari 23
Harrison, Olivia C. 46–8
hegemony 1, 23, 41, 107, 164, 167, 206, 212–13, 216, 218
Heidegger, Martin 194, 200 n.1
Hirschkind, Charles 57
Hishik Bishik Show 70, 76
    Bramley's review of 72
    Fayid's review of 71–2
Hoerder, Dirk 31, 36, 40
Holocaust 73, 77
home country/homeland 51, 93–4, 102–3, 106–7, 121–3, 125–8, 139, 191–2, 197–8, 200, 209
    alternative 175, 185
    methods of communication with 128–9, 143–6
Hometown Baghdad (video series) 102, 112, 114
    "Market Boom" 112–13
    "Symphony of Bullets" 112–13
Honold, Alexander 65
Houthis movement 8, 16, 205–6
    sarkha (scream) slogan 8, 206–8, 212, 217–18
    articulations of 212–16
    theater of immediacy for 208
    vs. Iranian flag 207
Howard, Philip 84
Hughes, Everett C. 31
humanity 33, 35, 40, 66, 69, 71, 76, 232
Hussain, Muzammil 84
Hussein, Saddam 102, 104
Hussein, Taha, *Mostaqbal Al-Thaqafa fi Misr* (The Future of Culture in Egypt) 155

hybridity/hybridization 14, 16, 121–3, 125–7, 129–34, 194
    Arab-Western 136–9
    criticism of Bhabha's theory of 166–8
    cultural 163–6
    of identity 164–6
    Orient 105, 165
    self/Other 20–1, 31–3, 38, 60, 63, 111, 114, 164–7, 178, 182, 185, 227

identity formation, transcultural 5, 7, 121–3, 125, 127, 139, 155
    of Arab transnationals 128–9
identity politics 4, 22, 46, 63, 69, 75, 77, 102
ideology 1, 15, 20, 34, 69, 76, 159–60, 224, 233
    ideology-free revolution 95
    technology vs. 94–6
imaginaries 3, 5, 14, 22–3, 66, 70, 78, 122, 201 n.3
    political 21–3
immigrants/immigration 6, 34, 51, 123–7, 190, 192. See also migrants/migration
imperialism 66, 230. See also neo-imperialism
inclusiveness 5, 15
India 193, 195–9. See also Gulf Indians
    authenticity 197
    development of 196
    Indian diaspora 192, 195–200
Ingres, Jean-Auguste-Dominique 105
inhabitants 37, 56, 196
Innocence of Muslims film 214–15
interaction, forms of 194. See also specific interactions
interculturality 14, 24
internationalism 55
Internet 69, 83–4, 95, 106–7, 132, 213, 233–5
    digital dissent 86
    opposition to 85
    and poetry 90–1
    users in Tunisia 85–6
interstitial space 7–8, 224, 226–7, 230–3, 236. See also space
Iran 8, 207, 212, 229, 232–6
Iraq/Iraqi 102, 112, 230

Baghdad 101, 107, 111–12
    identity 5, 103–5
    Iraqi as Other 111, 114
    Iraq war 102, 105, 109, 111–12
    political environment of 103
Isfahani, Hatef, *tarji'-band* 227
Isherwood, Christopher, *Goodbye to Berlin* 70
Islam 74, 206–7, 212, 214
    Islamic art 224–5
    Sunni tradition 206–7
Islamic Republic of Iran 206, 228, 231–2, 235–6
Islamic State (IS) group 18, 229
Islamophobia 74, 139, 235
Ismail, Salwa 23
Israel 8, 68, 73, 78, 207, 212–13, 218
Israeli-Palestinian conflict 78, 213
Iwamura, Jane 114
    Virtual Orientalism: Asian Religions and American Popular Culture 111

James, William, plural monism 39
Japan 193
Jasmine revolution 13, 21, 92
Jews/Jewish community 75–7, 206–7
    Arabs and 63, 72–4, 76–8
    deportation of 36
Jordon, Middle East
    Jordanian descriptions of Syrians 183
    Jordanian-Syrian marriages 174–80
    nationalization laws 187 n.4
    population based on nationality 171
    survey results analysis 172–3, 185–6
    Syrian culture on Jordanian culture 173–4, 186–7
    Syrian influence in 174
    Syrians in 171–3, 180–3

Kahanoff, Jacqueline, Muslim nationalism 69
Kant, Immanuel 226–7
Kassab, Elizabeth Suzanne 41
    Contemporary Arab Thought: Cultural Critique in Comparative Perspective 40–1
Katz, Ethan B., *The Burdens of Brotherhood: Jews and Muslims from North Africa to France* 75

Khaled, Leila 230
Khaliji-style Islamism 19
Khomeini, Ayatollah 230, 233
kitsch 72, 76
Kraidy, Marwan 165-6
Kuipers, Giselinde 111
Kulthum, Um 71, 74-5
Kundera, Milan 60 n.9
Kuwait 102-3, 215
Kymlicka, Will 190, 193

Laguerre, Michael 106
language 2, 31, 34, 54, 57, 63, 86, 93, 107, 129, 137, 139, 152-6, 159
  Arabic 6, 18, 125, 132-3, 153, 155-6
  democratic 156
  dialect 6, 151-2, 158
    Arabic 155
    Egyptian 155-6
    Tunisian 89-90
  dialogicality of 159
  German 53
  linguistics 151-60
    multilingualism 132-3
    sociolinguistics 6, 152, 154
    variation 154
Lefebvre, Henri 93, 96, 225
Lentin, Jerome 156
Leutze, Emanuel Gottlieb, *Washington Crossing the Delaware* 230
Levantine Arabs 131
Levinas, Emanuel 227
Levine, Mark 17-18, 24
  theater of immediacy 207
Lewis, Jeff 37
liberalism 64, 67, 76-8. *See also* neoliberal/neoliberalism
liberation 31, 74, 76, 111, 225, 228, 235
Libya 223, 229-30
literature 16, 20, 22, 30, 34, 54-5, 64, 123, 126-7, 133, 155-6, 206, 213-14
  Maghrebi 34
  and social networks 85-8
  transcultural 3, 15, 127
locality 32, 34-6
longue durée 230

Maastricht Treaty 60 n.7
Mahmood, Saba 57

Maira, Sunaima 126-7, 139
marginalization 4, 57, 105-7, 114
Marks, Laura 111
mass gatherings 1
mass movements 1, 3, 186
Mathaf, Arab Museum of Modern Art, Doha, Qatar 224
May, Theresa 58-9
media production 18
Mediterranean 31, 39, 41
Mehta, Brinda 17-18
Memmi, Albert 33-4
Merritt, Giles 59
Middle Arabic 155-6
Middle East 18, 22, 24, 50, 58-9, 83, 123, 125, 131, 139
Middle East and North Africa (MENA) 15, 45, 58, 83, 127, 138-9
  media 128-9, 131-2, 146-50
migrants/migration 4, 6-7, 15, 45-6, 52, 54-6, 58-60, 124, 189, 192-4, 196, 198. *See also* immigrants/immigration
  Ankommen app for 53
mobilization 2, 5, 122-4, 126, 224
Mondino, Jean-Baptiste 232
Mortlock, Grace 116 n.33
Mubarak, Hosni 20, 23
multiculturalism/multiculturality 14, 29, 31, 40, 54, 70, 196. *See also* culture; transculturality/transculturalism/transculture
  boutique 37
  in Canada 4, 30, 37, 137-8
  citizenship 190
Musa, Salama 155
Musharrafa, Mustafa 155
Muslim(s) 73-5, 134, 138, 155, 212-16, 224-5, 227, 229-30, 233-6. *See also* Christian; religion/religious
  Arabs and 124, 215, 224
  Jews and 75-6
  migration of 124, 126
Muslim Brotherhood 23, 72

Nagel, Caroline R. 123, 133
narrate/narration/narratives 7, 16, 18, 22-3, 25, 33, 38, 64-5, 84, 89, 97, 191, 200, 205-6, 210, 214, 225

counternarratives 22
discursive 121, 125
historical 17–18, 20, 55
narrators 6, 45–6, 48–60, 64–5, 101, 107, 109–10
political 20, 23–4
re-narrate 3, 5, 13, 15
rescue 205, 208, 211–12
Nasser 23, 65, 68–9, 72, 74
national identity 7, 52–5, 77, 155, 189, 192, 194, 197
nationalism 4, 21, 63–4, 69–70, 72, 76, 78. *See also* post-national space; transnationalism
National Museum of Iraq 107
nation-state model 29, 36, 192–3, 195
Nazi/Nazism 36, 70, 72, 76–7
neo-imperialism 19. *See also* imperialism
neoliberal/neoliberalism 21, 23, 57, 126, 235. *See also* liberalism
The Netherlands 52, 55
Neustein, David 116 n.33
9/11 attacks 18, 73, 114
Nochlin, Linda 105
nomadism 4, 37, 40, 65
non-Arab community 130, 133, 138, 176
normative/normativity 3, 16, 234
North Africa 4, 15, 45, 56, 58–9, 83, 139
Nowjs, Wdsolrk 19

Obama, Barack 208–9
  on causality of drone program 209–10
Occident 105, 193
Omri, Mohamed Salah 92
  "A Revolution of Dignity and Poetry" 84
online politics 84, 91. *See also* street politics
Ordinary Egyptians: Creating the Modern Nation through Popular Culture (Fahmy) 70
Orientalism 20, 165
  virtual 111–12
Ortiz, Fernando 30
Ouled Ahmed, Sghaier 5, 83–6, 89. *See also* poetics/poetry, politicized
  "A Last Letter to the Women of Tunisia" 96
  Al-Qiyada al-Shi'riyya li al-Thawra al- Tunusiyya: Yawmiyyat (The Poetic Leadership of the Tunisian Revolution: A Diary) 89
  censorship and death 85–7
  "A Free Speech to a Free People," excerpt from 91–2
  "Ideology and Technology" 94–6
  "The Lesson of Tunisia," excerpt from 93
  "Love of Country" 93, 96
  "Maqam al Wuquf" (Shrine for Standing) 87
  "The Mouse" 87
  Muswaddat Watan (Draft of a Homeland) 96
  Nachid al-Ayyam al-Sitta (Song of the Six Days) 87, 92, 96
  poetic leadership 89
  The Poetic Leadership 87, 91
  "Qawsaqab" 96
  and revolution (on Facebook) 85–6, 88–9, 92–4, 97
  "Supplications" 94
  "Tunisian All at Once or Never" 93–4
  "Waiting for the Second Round" 86
  "Women" 95
  "Ya Sidi 'Arfinik" (Sir, We Know You) 89–90
  "Yawmiyyat" 91

Pahlavi, Reza Shah 232–3
Palestine 41, 77, 236
pan-Arabism 74, 122, 155, 187
parapublic sphere 225, 227
Peace of Westphalia of 1648 192
Persian Gulf War 102–3, 105
poetics/poetry, politicized 83–4, 87–8. *See also* Ouled Ahmed, Sghaier
  geo-poetics 97
  and revolution 85, 88–9, 97
  of virtual 89–94
political activism 17, 59, 84, 91, 97, 152
political change 15, 17, 23–4, 102, 180, 205
political climate 19–20, 24
political imagination 20–4
political resistance 77
political subjectivity 23, 35
political theory 1–2

populism 70–1, 139
post–Arab Spring 21–2, 151–2, 208, 215.
    See also Arab Spring
postcolonial/post-colonialism 1, 4, 24,
    34–5, 38, 41, 64, 208, 224, 226. *See
    also* colonialism
post-national space 190, 192, 194–5, 197,
    226
Pratt, Mary Louise, linguistics of contact
    152
Prince, Mona 77
protest art. *See* art of protest

Qatar 224
Quest for Bush video game 104
Quest for Saddam video game 104
Qur'an 206
Qutb, Sayyid 206–7, 218 n.4

Rabaa massacre of August 2013 231
race/racial identity/racism 33, 40, 46, 76,
    106, 164, 192, 232
Radakrishnan, R. 197
Rakha, Youssef, "In Extremis: Literature
    and Revolution in Contemporary
    Cairo" 20
Rampton, Ben 6, 152
rap music 84
reflexive individualism 23
refugees 16, 46, 54, 58, 74, 104, 106,
    126
    Arab 4
    Syrian (*see* Syrian refugee in Jordon)
religion/religious 18, 71, 76–7, 94–6,
    134–6, 176, 224, 227. *See also
    specific religion*
representation 5, 7, 21, 24, 36, 111, 114,
    152–4, 157–9, 164, 167, 186, 228
Republican-nationalism model 36
resistance 3–5, 8, 21–2, 41, 46, 73–4, 107,
    178, 185, 207, 209–10, 212, 229,
    235–6
    cultural 17
    poetics of 84
    political 77
revolutionary art 17–20, 24. *See also*
    counterrevolutionary
revolutionary slogan(s)
    'Helping power to collapse' 91
    of Houthis (*see* Houthis movement,
    sarkha (scream) slogan)
    "Liberté, Égalité, Fraternité" (French
    Revolution) 228
    "Neither East, Nor West, (but)
    the Islamic Republic" (Iranian
    Revolution) 228
    "*Nisau biladi/nisaun wa nisf*", feminist
    95
    "Peace! Land! Bread!" (Russian
    Revolution) 228
    "Revolution of shabab al-Facebook" (the
    youth of Facebook) 83, 96
Reynolds, Bryan, theater of immediacy
    207
Rifai, Raouf, *White Flags* 71
rock music 132
Rowe, John Carlos 19
Rumsfeld, Donald 235
Rushdie, Salman 85
Russia 53, 230

Said, Edward 64–5, 78, 165
    contrapuntal reading 4, 64
    filiation *vs.* affiliation 47–8
    on Nasser 68
    Orientalism 105, 111
    on writers and intellectuals 88
Salafis/Salafist 95, 206
Saleh, Ali Abdullah 205, 209, 212
Sari, Osama 216
Satloff, Robert 74, 77
    Among the Righteous 72–3
Saudi Arabia 196, 205–6, 223, 229
Scheler, Max 227
Schengen Zone borders 49, 55, 58
Second World War 36–7, 48, 56, 74
self-identification 21, 128–9, 139
Selvon, Sam, *The Lonely Londoners* 70
Shafak, Elif, "Storytelling, Fake Worlds,
    and the Internet" 85
Shakespeare, William, *The Tempest* 86
Sharaf, Radwa Othman 18, 20, 24
Sheller, Max, *Zur Phänomenologie und
    Theorie der Sympathiegefühle und
    von Liebe und Hass* (*The Nature of
    Sympathy*) 226
Singapore 193
skepticism 209, 215

slogans. *See* revolutionary slogan(s)
Smith, Zadie 85-6
social actors/actions 6, 154, 156-8
social bonds, family 47-8
social boundary 133-6, 152
social change 15, 17, 23, 102
social cohesion 205
social contract 194, 196
social interaction (praxis) 194
social justice 23, 34
social media 84, 90, 96, 127, 132-3, 151, 213. *See also specific companies*
    usage by Arab youth 128
social networks 25, 83-4, 86, 90, 94, 96-7, 233
    literature and 85-8
social theory 1-2
Soja, Edward 96, 225
solidarity 1, 4, 16, 19, 52-3, 57, 63, 70, 78, 84, 226, 231
Soliman, Laila 17
Sontag, Susan 76
Soueif, Ahdaf 68
South Asia 194, 197
Soviet Union 52, 54, 68-9
space 19, 23, 35, 41, 49-52, 59-60, 91, 96-7, 103, 107, 116 n.33, 125, 138, 164, 190, 228-9
    art 19, 225, 228
    colonial 32
    cultural 89, 122, 130, 134-5, 155, 197
    digital 5, 106, 114
    interstitial 7-8, 224, 226-7, 230-3, 236
    liminal 17, 195, 201 n.5
    online/virtual 5, 83-5, 88, 91, 93, 97, 106, 111
    public 1-2, 9, 17, 92, 117 n.45, 122, 182, 190, 193, 225-6
    revolutionary 20, 214
    second 225-6
    single 190, 195
    space-time 154
    technological 96, 106
    third 7, 164, 191, 194, 225-6
    transnational 7, 16, 93, 124, 189, 192
Spain 41
Staeheli, Lynn A. 123, 133
Standard Arabic (SA) 151, 153, 156-60
street art 9, 17, 19

street politics 84, 92. *See also* online politics
stylization 151-2, 154, 159-60
Subay, Murad, Why did you kill my family? campaign 211
subjectivation 1, 23
subjectivity/subjectivities 21, 23, 35, 123, 226
Sufi/Sufism 71-2
supranational entity 190, 192-5
survey/research
    for Arab youth 127-8
    focus groups 5, 121, 127-8, 136
    Jordanian sample survey results, analysis of 172-3, 185-6
    on reading/watching MENA media 131-2
    on socioculture (Jordanians and Syrians) 168-70
Syria 50, 167, 170-1, 175, 182, 223, 229-30
    Aleppo 51, 60 n.6
Syrian refugee in Jordon 6-7, 46, 55, 59, 124, 163-4, 167, 185, 187 n.2
    income and employment 183-4
    influence in Jordon 174
    Jordanian-Syrian marriages 174-80
    Jordanian description of 183
    marriage customs 177, 183
    sociocultural survey (Jordanians and Syrians) 168-70
    Syrian culture on Jordanian culture 173-4, 186-7
    Syrian presence in Jordan 171-2, 180-3

Tal el-Zaatar, siege of 60 n.5
Taylor, Charles 193
technology 48, 54, 83, 85-6, 192, 210
    technological revolution 90
    vs. ideology 94-6
terrorism 105-6, 214. *See also* counterterrorism
totalitarianism 13
tourism 107-13
transculturality/transculturalism/transculture 14-16, 29-31, 46, 51-2. *See also* culture; multiculturalism/multiculturality

affinity/affinitive relations 45–51
belonging 4, 15, 30, 32–3, 35–6, 40–1, 45–7
  Bouraoui on 30, 35–41
  and creaculture 35–7
  territoriality 38–9
  transcultural identity 1–5, 13–14, 16, 23–4
  of Arab transnationals 128–9
  development 124
  formation 121–2, 125, 139
  methodology 127–8
  metissage 121, 123–31
transculturation 3, 5, 15, 122, 166
transethnicity 36
transnationalism 6–7, 76, 125, 189, 193–4, 198. *See also* nationalism; post-national space
trans-sociality 1
Treaty on European Union 52, 60 n.7
Trump, Donald 22, 59, 209
Tuan, Yi Fu 93
Tunisia 84, 93, 223, 229
  Caliban digerati 86
  internet users of 85–6
  Ouled Ahmed's poetics on 93
  state-policed media in 85
  Tunisian Revolution 5, 83–4, 86–9, 91–3, 96
Turkey 193
Twitter 85, 213

Union citizenship in Article 8 52
United Arab Emirates (UAE) 190–2, 195. *See also* Gulf Indians
  Emiratis 195, 197–8, 206
  foreign children born in 195
  Indians/Indian diaspora in 192, 195–8
  non-citizens in 195
The United Kingdom 55, 58, 205
United Nations High Commissioner for Refugees (UNHCR) 171

The United States 18, 21–2, 33–4, 41, 45, 101, 103, 125, 205, 207, 214, 216, 236
  drone program in Yemen 208–12
  "war on terror" campaign 206, 208, 211–12, 214–15
uprising of Arab. *See* Arab Spring
urban 8, 19, 23, 50, 60, 65, 71, 170, 226, 228

van Leeuwen, Fairclough 6, 152, 154, 157
Versteegh, Kees 155
violence 8, 16, 19, 23, 38, 57, 74, 111, 206, 218, 224. *See also* art of protest
  colonial 33, 36, 56
  and digital games 104–5
  undressing 233
virtual Orientalism 111–12
virtual space of social media 5, 83, 89–94
visual art 5, 17, 105
Vora, Neha 196–7

Wald, Kenneth 125–6
Western culture 122, 133–4, 137, 193
Western music 65, 132
Wright, Lawrence 206

xenophobia 186, 194

Yad Vashem Museum, Israel 77
Yemen/Yemeni 205–8, 213, 215–16, 223–4, 230
  counterrevolutionary mobilization in 224
  "No for Government that Grants Entry to American Marines" rally 216–17
  sovereignty 206, 208–10, 212, 214
  US drone strikes in 208–12
YouTube 18, 131–2

Zahnd, Elizabeth A. 18–19
Zuckerberg, Mark 85–6. *See also* Facebook

www.ingramcontent.com/pod-product-compliance
Lightning Source LLC
Chambersburg PA
CBHW062133300426
44115CB00012BA/1905